# Leaders in the Sociology of Education

LEADERS IN EDUCATIONAL STUDIES

Volume 9

*Series Editor:* Leonard J. Waks, *Temple University, Philadelphia, USA*

*Scope:*
The aim of the *Leaders in Educational Studies* Series is to document the rise of scholarship and university teaching in educational studies in the years after 1960. This half-century has been a period of astonishing growth and accomplishment. The volumes in the series document this development of educational studies as seen through the eyes of its leading practitioners.

A few words about the build up to this period are in order. Before the mid-twentieth century school teaching, especially at the primary level, was as much a trade as a profession. Schoolteachers were trained primarily in normal schools or teachers colleges, only rarely in universities. But in the 1940s American normal schools were converted into teachers colleges, and in the 1960s these were converted into state universities. At the same time school teaching was being transformed into an all-graduate profession in both the United Kingdom and Canada. For the first time, school teachers required a proper university education.

Something had to be done, then, about what was widely regarded as the deplorable state of educational scholarship. James Conant, in his final years as president at Harvard in the early 1950s, envisioned a new kind of university-based school of education, drawing scholars from mainstream academic disciplines such as history, sociology psychology and philosophy, to teach prospective teachers, conduct educational research, and train future educational scholars. One of the first two professors hired to fulfil this vision was Israel Scheffler, a young philosopher of science and language who had earned a Ph.D. in philosophy at the University of Pennsylvania. Scheffler joined Harvard's education faculty in 1952. The other was Bernard Bailyn, who joined the Harvard faculty in 1953 after earning his Ph.D. there, and who re-energized the study of American educational history with the publication of *Education in the Forming of American Society: Needs and Opportunities for Study* (University of North Carolina Press, 1960). The series has been exceptionally fortunate that Scheffler provided a foreword to the volume on philosophy of education, and that Bernard Bailyn provided one a foreword for the volume on the history of American education. It is equally fortunate that subsequent volumes have also contained forewords by similarly eminent scholars, including James Banks of the University of Washington, who has been a creative force in social education for decades and the prime mover in the field of multi-cultural education.

The *Leaders in Educational Studies* Series continues to document the growing and changing literature in educational studies. Studies conducted within the established academic disciplines of history, philosophy, and sociology comprised the dominant trend throughout the 1960s and 1970s. By the 1980s educational studies diversified considerably, in terms of both new sub-disciplines within these established disciplines and new interdisciplinary and trans-disciplinary fields.

Curriculum studies, both in general and in the particular school subject matter fields, drew extensively from work in philosophy, history and sociology of education. Work in these disciplines, and also in anthropology and cultural studies among others, also stimulated new perspectives on race, class and gender.

This volume, like previous volumes in the series, brings together personal essays by established leaders in a major field of educational studies. Subsequent volumes in the series will continue to document other established and emerging disciplines, sub-disciplines and inter-disciplines in educational scholarship.

# Leaders in the Sociology of Education

*Intellectual Self-Portraits*

*Edited by*

**Alan R. Sadovnik**
*Rutgers University-Newark, USA*

and

**Ryan W. Coughlan**
*Guttman Community College, City University of New York, USA*

SENSE PUBLISHERS
ROTTERDAM/BOSTON/TAIPEI

A C.I.P. record for this book is available from the Library of Congress.

ISBN: 978-94-6300-715-3 (paperback)
ISBN: 978-94-6300-716-0 (hardback)
ISBN: 978-94-6300-717-7 (e-book)

Published by: Sense Publishers,
P.O. Box 21858,
3001 AW Rotterdam,
The Netherlands
https://www.sensepublishers.com/

All chapters in this book have undergone peer review.

Chapter 9 was originally published in *Anthropology & Education Quarterly*, Volume 39, Issue 1, Pages 77–91, March 2008. All rights reserved. American Anthropological Association. Reprinted here with permission.

*Printed on acid-free paper*

All Rights Reserved © 2016 Sense Publishers

No part of this work may be reproduced, stored in a retrieval system, or transmitted in any form or by any means, electronic, mechanical, photocopying, microfilming, recording or otherwise, without written permission from the Publisher, with the exception of any material supplied specifically for the purpose of being entered and executed on a computer system, for exclusive use by the purchaser of the work.

# TABLE OF CONTENTS

| | | |
|---|---|---|
| Preface | | vii |
| 1. | Leaders in the Sociology of Education: Lessons Learned<br>*Alan R. Sadovnik and Ryan W. Coughlan* | 1 |
| 2. | Continuity and Change: The Making of a Neoliberal Academic Subject<br>*Stephen J. Ball* | 13 |
| 3. | Intellectual Self-Portrait<br>*Jomills Henry Braddock II* | 29 |
| 4. | Thinking about Schools and Universities as Social Institutions: An Intellectual Self-Portrait<br>*Steven Brint* | 37 |
| 5. | Com Muito Axé: Or "Can a Woman Be an Intellectual?"<br>*Sara Delamont* | 57 |
| 6. | Searching for Equity in Education: Finding School, Family, and Community Partnerships<br>*Joyce L. Epstein* | 69 |
| 7. | Striving Towards the Big Questions<br>*Adam Gamoran* | 87 |
| 8. | The Sociology of a Life<br>*A. H. Halsey* | 101 |
| 9. | Engaging the Sociological Imagination: My Journey into Design Research and Public Sociology<br>*Hugh Mehan* | 115 |
| 10. | The Accidental Sociologist of Education: How My Life in Schools Became My Research<br>*Roslyn Arlin Mickelson* | 131 |
| 11. | Power, Purpose and the Rise of the Rest<br>*Gerard A. Postiglione* | 153 |
| 12. | Education, Gender, and Development<br>*Francisco O. Ramirez* | 171 |

TABLE OF CONTENTS

13. Discovering Unseen Social Contexts and Potential Levers for Social Change    185
   *James E. Rosenbaum*

14. Holocaust Memories: Honoring My Mother through Applied Scholarship and Building Academic Programs    201
   *Alan R. Sadovnik*

15. Beginning a Journey and Choosing a Path    217
   *Barbara Schneider*

16. The Making of a Political Sociologist of Education    231
   *Carlos Alberto Torres*

17. Reading and Producing Research across Boundaries That so Often Divide    253
   *Lois Weis*

18. Critical Theory and Education    275
   *Philip Wexler*

19. My Life with the Sociology of Education    287
   *Geoff Whitty*

# PREFACE

When Leonard Waks asked me to edit the Sociology of Education volume in the Sense Publishers series on Leaders in Educational Studies I first looked at two of the volumes already published, one in the Philosophy of Education and one in the History of Education. After reading the chapters in these books, it was easy to follow most of their organization to outline the plan for this volume. We decided not to include a Foreword and Afterword written by two sociologists of education. Rather, we have used our introduction to outline some of the major themes in the chapters and then let the contributors speak for themselves.

I decided that I wanted to include a diverse range of individuals with respect to race and gender, as well as theoretical and methodological orientations. I also wanted an international representation with scholars from not only the United States, but Europe and Asia as well. I wanted these individuals to be of significant stature in the field, thus limiting the list to senior scholars.

After compiling a list of 30 possible contributors, I received 12 no's leaving me with the 18 authors (including me) in the book. The reasons for those who said no were varied, but the most common reason was they were too busy on ongoing research projects. The 18 contributors comprise a sample of the most important scholars in the sociology of education writing since the 1970s and in one case before.

The original list was more diverse with respect to race and ethnicity and gender. This volume has 13 males and 5 females; one African American and one Latino; four scholars from the U.K. and one from Hong Kong. Although this does not adequately represent the diversity of the field, these sociologists of education certainly capture the richness of work over the past five decades and the diversity of theoretical and methodological orientations.

Midway through the submission period I asked my graduate assistant Ryan Coughlan to co-edit the book. He had been an important contributor as co-editor of *Sociology of Education: A Critical Reader* (2015) so I asked him to work on this volume as well. Having him as co-editor provided a second pair of eyes to the editing process; but more importantly he offered the views of an up and coming scholar on the contributions in each chapter.

Editing this book provided both of us with the pleasure of reading about the lives and works of a distinguished group of scholars. The chapters provided a sociology of knowledge with respect to how and why each contributor chose to do their research and in many cases how their lives and families affected their work. Taken as a whole the chapters provide an important history of the sociology of education and display the important themes in the field.

*Alan R. Sadovnik*
*Rutgers University, Newark*

ALAN R. SADOVNIK AND RYAN W. COUGHLAN

# 1. LEADERS IN THE SOCIOLOGY OF EDUCATION

*Lessons Learned*

The Sociology of Education is no different in form than other fields of scholarship in that it depends wholly on the creativity, passion, assiduousness, and luck of the women and men who commit themselves to the advancement of the discipline. Surely world events and the political economy of a given time and place bear tremendous responsibility for shaping research agendas and directing intellectual thought, but it is the humanity and individuality of the scholars who interact with all that surrounds them that defines an academic field. As such, an intimate look into the careers of a selection of leaders in the sociology of education has much to offer those seeking a better understanding of the present state of this field of study.

History and lineage are keys to understanding the present and looking towards the future. It is not coincidental that each of the authors of the intellectual self-portraits in this volume discuss the scholars who inspired them and shaped their own academic journeys. After a brief look at the origins of the sociology of education and the people who inspired the current leaders in the field, it seems logical to consider some commonalities in the lives of the scholars who have shared their stories in this book. A number of themes cut across the lives of these scholars and offer some compelling insight into how the sociology of education has taken its current form. The experiences that turned the people profiled in this book into leaders in the sociology of education have left them with lessons for future scholars in the field. Before concluding this chapter and turning to the individual self-portraits, it will be well worth the time to take a moment and highlight some of the invaluable advice that these leaders in the sociology of education have proffered.

INSPIRATION – THE ORIGINS OF THE SOCIOLOGY OF EDUCATION

Given the contents of this book, it is safe to assume that those of you reading this introduction have a strong foundational knowledge of the sociology of education. Rehashing the origins of the sociology of education in a manner common to textbooks and college lectures would guarantee that we lose your attention to other tasks. Those interested in a more in-depth discussion of the origins of the field should read our introduction to *Sociology of Education: A Critical Reader* (2015). While we will refrain from providing our take on the origins of the sociology of education, we must pause to acknowledge the manner in which the founders of sociology, in general, and the sociology of education, in particular, inspired the current leaders in the field.

Émile Durkheim (1858–1917), who is often credited as the father of sociology, has undoubtedly shaped the minds of all scholars who consider themselves sociologists. Whether one ascribes to Durkheim's functionalist perspective of society, vociferously critiques this work, or chooses to set the work aside altogether, it has an undeniable presence in all of our lives. Several of the intellectual self-portraits that follow specifically discuss the way that Durkheim's work has shaped their intellectual journeys, and a number of the authors even list one of Durkheim's pieces of writing as one of the most influential works they have read.

Gerard Postiglione devotes a good deal of attention to a discussion of how he brought the canonical work of western thinkers, including Durkheim, to his Chinese audience. When discussing the act of bringing Durkheim to Chinese audiences, Postiglione writes,

> The aim for most Chinese scholars at the time was to construct the field with Chinese distinctiveness while keeping abreast of the international mainstream of the field. The field had to be established under "Marxism and Chinese realities." There were also critiques of Durkheim, which were interesting to me since Durkheim resonated in some ways with Confucian discourse and contemporary party dictum on social harmony.

While likely unsurprising to this audience, many of the current leaders in the sociology of education, similar to the audience that Postiglione encountered in China, have offered deep criticisms of Durkheim's functionalism. Many of these critiques are rooted in the work of two other thinkers credited with providing a foundation for the sociology of education: Karl Marx (1818–1883) and Max Weber (1864–1920).

A portion of Hugh Mehan's intellectual self-portrait looks to identify the roots of the sociology of education. In seeking an understanding of the inspiration for this academic field, Mehan writes,

> Marx, Weber, and Durkheim (the "founding fathers" or "holy trinity" of sociology), each in their own way, was driven by an appraisal of and attempt to remedy the malaise engendered by modernity: alienation, inequality, hyperrationality, domination, anomie.

The two phrases—"founding fathers" and "holy trinity"—that Wexler uses to describe Durkheim, Marx, and Weber clearly resonate with many of the other current leaders in the sociology of education. Although Durkheim's omnipresent position in the sociology of education is hard to deny, the current leaders in the sociology of education place a far greater emphasis on the inspiration they have found in Marx and Weber. Steven Brint writes, "Reading Max Weber was the decisive intellectual experience of my life." Philip Wexler notes that his reading of Marx became unmeshed with his day-to-day living at an early age. He writes,

I read a lot, from an early age, and by high school, I was moving around intellectually, between Marx and Nietzsche. But, it was not just books. Rebellion, in daily life and in art, was already displacing indifference and what we learned to call "conformity" ... To have a reflexive critical stance toward whatever was going on, whatever was being taken for granted as natural and better, was something I seemed to have imbibed early on, and which I brought to the intellectual work that has drawn my attention for so long.

The inspiration for many of the current leaders in the sociology of education did not always come directly from Marx and Weber, but rather it came from Marxist and Weberian traditions. Many of the current leaders in the sociology of education came of age in a period of time when the works of Bowles and Gintis and Coleman were gaining prominence. All three of these scholars brought a heightened attention to conflict theory and the inequalities defining the modern education system. Lois Weis writes,

Putting forth their well-known "correspondence principle," Bowles and Gintis argue that schools directly reproduce social and economic inequalities embedded in the capitalist economy... [Their] neo-Marxist sensibilities critique the capitalist economy as the driving force behind the "need" for profit and domination as in conflict with the political economy that promotes democracy and equality. This conflict plays out in classrooms where students are marked by a larger and highly stratified economic structure, and this notion of stratified social structures and the relationship between such structures and educational institutions became the centerpiece of my own thinking on this subject for many years hence.

Weis shares this source of inspiration with a number of the other current leaders in the sociology of education. Whether or not the current leaders in the sociology of education found Bowles and Gintis' arguments to be compelling, they all undeniably came to operate in a field guided by these ideas. As Brint notes, "The weight of sociological work at this time was on the reproduction of class, racial-ethnic and gender privileges through schooling."

These themes of social reproduction and inequality were given particular emphasis through the work of James Coleman. Not only did Coleman inspire many of the current leaders in the sociology of education to ask questions about inequality and education, but his work also led to a heightened focus on empiricism in the field. In Barbara Schneider's intellectual self-portrait, she writes,

Reading the work of James Coleman... about how to determine which interventions were actually creating a "true" effect, my thoughts of becoming a teacher educator were soon replaced by a strong desire to learn more about how relationships, power, authority, roles, responsibilities, and moral imperatives affect human behavior and shape the institutional systems they inhabit.

Schneider goes on discuss the ways in which this work inspired a career of searching for empirical evidence to support theoretical constructs in the sociology of education.

> It was the possibility that high quality evidence could be used to explain social phenomena that motivated my interest and research studies in exploring new ideas for data collection and analytic methods that measured a true effect and others that approximated causal inference.

Many of the sociologists of education in this volume came of age during the battle between the old and new sociologists of education in Britain and France. With the publication of Michael F.D. Young's *Knowledge and Control* (1977), Basil Bernstein and Pierre Bourdieu became the intellectual leaders of the new sociology aimed at analyzing social class inequalities in education. Geoff Whitty writes of Bernstein,

> The sociologist whose work, in my view, remains most helpful in thinking through the relationship between social class and school knowledge is Bernstein, who remained the dominant presence within the sociology of education in the UK until his death in 2000 and indeed beyond. He died just three weeks into my Directorship of the Institute and both the Institute and the field knew they had lost their greatest contemporary scholar. (Power et al., 2001)

Bernstein was the Karl Manheim Professor in the Sociology of Education at the Institute of Education at the University of London, and was succeeded in the chair by two of the contributors to this book Whitty and then Stephen Ball.

Of course, inspiration for the current leaders in the sociology of education was not limited to the "holy trinity" of Durkheim, Weber, and Marx or the handful of other scholars noted above. As you explore the intellectual self-portraits in the chapters that follow, you will find that the current leaders in the field have found inspiration in countless places, both expected and unexpected, from within the field and outside of the field, and from scholarship as well as life experience. The next section offers a brief discussion of a number of themes that arise from these life experiences of the current leaders in the sociology of education. Undoubtedly, the lives of the current leaders and some of the common themes that emerge from their stories help illuminate how the field has come to take its current form.

## EXPERIENCE – THE LIVES THAT SHAPED THE LEADERS IN THE SOCIOLOGY OF EDUCATION

The scholars who contributed to this volume were given tremendous freedom in constructing their intellectual self-portraits, which has led to a collection of autobiographies that approach this challenging form of writing in varied ways. Stephen Ball eloquently captures the difficulty of the task as well as offers insight into the care that those profiled in this book have given to their writing.

Here I must account for myself, make myself coherent, write my biography and thus write myself into existence—at least some parts of myself. And I will do that, I will submit myself to the genre of biography and its rules and tropes. Nonetheless, as I write I am also made aware of the limits of my coherence, and of the fictional quality of some of what follows. As a life and as an intellectual journey my personal trajectory is only sensible, to me, as a set of ruptures and tensions and inconsistencies, which remain unresolved and are difficult to explain.

Ball brings attention to the reality that intellectual journeys are non-linear, that the experiences that shape scholars are often hard to identify and that fact, folklore, and fiction often meld together when attempting to produce a coherent self-portrait. Despite the challenges of writing such an autobiographical piece, the book's selection of current leaders in the sociology of education succeed in offering clear narratives of their intellectual journeys. While there is no single storyline that dominates the chapters that follow, there are some themes worth highlighting in this introduction.

Many of the scholars profiled in this book trace their intellectual journeys back to their families and their childhood; a number of them consider how their social, economic, religious, cultural, and educational roots primed them for careers in the sociology of education. A significant portion of these family histories involve struggles that range from overcoming structural racism and classism to surviving the Holocaust. Jomills Braddock attended an all-Black segregated elementary and secondary school and lived with the grief of having his sister-in-law murdered in the Birmingham church bombing. Following this event, Braddock committed himself to the pursuit of ending racism, and his lifetime of work on desegregation is a testimony to this commitment. Alan Sadovnik directly connects his family history to his work as a sociologist. He writes,

> Both of my parents were Holocaust survivors and the Holocaust became a major theme of my childhood. As I grew into adulthood, I learned a sense of social justice from my parents, which would come to shape much of my work as a sociologist.

Another group of the current leaders in the sociology of education found their passion for this area of study not from their own family history of struggle, but rather through a family that emphasized a need to work towards a more just world. James Rosenbaum writes about the inspiration he found in his father's charitable and social justice-oriented pursuits.

> Like many people, I entered sociology out of a concern for social justice and equity. This decision was largely inspired by my father, a pediatrician who had many low income patients, from whom he learned about the dynamics of poverty and its pervasive effects. His experiences working with low income populations led him to work in progressive causes which he considered to be preventive medicine. He started the first poison control hotline in the state of

Indiana, advised the first Headstart program in Indiana, worked with Planned Parenthood, and spoke publicly about the need for increased supports for disadvantaged populations. My awareness of poverty and my commitment to social justice came out of my admiration for my father and his work.

While most of the scholars profiled in this book pinpoint a spark that flamed their passion for the sociology of education, some do not. Roslyn Mickelson goes so far as to title her chapter "The Accidental Sociologist of Education." Regardless of how they arrived in this field of study, each of the current leaders in the sociology of education share the experience of doctoral education. The commonalities in the experience of doctoral schooling end at the fact that each of these scholars did it. Several have intensely fond memories of building lifelong friendships and immeasurable bonds with their mentors. A. H. Halsey speaks warmly of his close relationship with mentor and co-author Jean Floud. Similarly, Alan Sadovnik places great emphasis on the inspiration he found under the mentorship of Basil Bernstein. And Lois Weis discusses how her time conducting research in Ghana and the people she met on her travels dramatically reshaped her perspectives about power, privilege, and oppression.

Weis is not alone in finding inspiration in international and comparative studies. Carlos Alberto Torres' chapter focuses attention on how living and learning across multiple countries has shaped his thinking and his scholarly work. Adam Gamoran goes a step further, credits some of his success to gaining an international perspective, and implores others to seek solutions beyond the boundaries of what is known to them. He writes,

> From my research on Scotland and Israel, I learned that insights about education in the U.S. are greatly aided by international comparisons. When we focus on our own system alone, we are often blind to possibilities that are rare in our system (such as school-leaving examinations) but common elsewhere.

Whereas the issues of social class and race inequalities dominated research in the field, some scholars, especially Sara Delamont ensured that gender inequalities in education were placed squarely on the table, She writes:

> There is a serious problem in educational research around the erosion of women as authors and as subjects. Work by women is cited less than work by men, because while women cite male and female scholars, most men overwhelmingly cite only work by men. Over time that means research by women does not get included in the literature. Because most of the research on women has been done by women, that means that studies of women also slide below the horizon of the discipline. This claim is documented for many social sciences and the evidence is reported in Delamont. (2003)

The scholars in this book have examined their various research questions through a variety of theoretical lenses and methodological approaches. For example, some of them do a good deal of theoretical work (Ball, Ramirez, Sadovnik, Torres, Weis, Wexler, Whitty); some do mostly quantitative work (Braddock, Gamoran, Halsey, Rosenbaum, Schneider); some do mostly qualitative research (Delamont, Mehan, Sadovnik, Weis, Wexler) and some do mixed methods research combining quantitative and qualitative on one project or using one or the other on different projects (Brint, Epstein, Mickelson, Postiglione, Whitty). Whichever methodology they each have used, as a whole they have demonstrated the power of theory and method in the sociology of education.

Perhaps the single life experience that bifurcates the scholars in this collection more than anything else is whether or not they spent time teaching in the education systems they later wrote about and taught courses on at the university. The experience of working in elementary and secondary schools inspired a good deal of the scholarship conducted by those with such a teaching background. Joyce Epstein made the deliberate choice to gain experience as an elementary school teacher before pursuing her doctoral work. She writes,

> I wanted to know about the "real world" of teaching and delayed entering a doctoral program… I learned about classroom teaching, school leadership, and the wondrous diversity of children's skills, talents, and challenges. I learned about the persistent press on teachers' time; strong and weak principals; how school innovations come and go; and problems that arise when teachers accept slow learners or naughty students as if they were predetermined. Teaching was valuable and, to this day, influences my ideas about what teachers should and should not be asked to do as professional educators.

One experience common to all of the current leaders in the sociology of education is working within the structures of the university. The scholars discuss topics ranging from the pursuit of tenure, to the unending task of securing research funding, to taking on administrative responsibilities. While each of the leaders in the sociology of education profiled in this book has had unique experiences in academia, they all share in the fact that they have tirelessly pursued new knowledge in an effort to better understand how our education systems operate and what they could do to improve.

Some scholars—such as Francisco Ramirez, who has developed a world society perspective and applied it to education, gender and development—have devoted themselves almost entirely to a focused topic of study. Other scholars—such as James Rosenbaum, who has studied topics ranging from tracking to the effect of place on educational outcomes, to college-preparedness—have pursued a diverse set of research interests. Regardless of the depth and breadth of their work, each of the current leaders in the sociology of education profiled in this book has made significant contributions to the field.

The experience that these scholars have amassed is invaluable for future generations of sociologists of education, and the following section attempts to summarize some of the key lessons that can be drawn from the chapters that follow.

## ADVICE – LESSONS FOR FUTURE SCHOLARS IN THE FIELD

Each of the intellectual self-portraits that follows offers a distinct set of lessons for readers that results from the unique journey that each scholar has traveled. One common lesson that results from these stories is that life in academia is unpredictable, requires flexibility, and involves taking on a wide range of roles. The scholars who tell their stories have all worn multiple hats and jumped between jobs ranging from researcher, to teacher, to mentor, to practitioner, and to administrator. At times these current leaders in the sociology of education have felt well-prepared to take on each of these roles, and at other times they have had to learn on the job. Several of the scholars profiled in this book highlight the importance of embracing change throughout their careers and welcoming unexpected opportunities for taking on new research agendas, collaborating with colleagues, and building relationships across sectors.

In Gerard Postiglione's intellectual self-portrait, he recounts the story of traveling and teaching in Europe following the completion of his doctoral work. While traveling through the Middle East, he received a telegram offering him an interview for a faculty position in Hong Kong. When he accepted the job, Postiglione imagined "another brief sojourn of international teaching and research experience." Instead, it led to an entire career working in China, where he remains to this day. Several of the other authors in this book discuss following unexpected pathways that led to rich experiences and opened them to teaching and researching opportunities which shaped their careers. While none of the authors suggest diving into jobs and taking on research projects without careful thought, their lives highlight the benefits of maintaining an openness to unexpected opportunities.

Along with remaining open to new opportunities, the intellectual self-portraits that follow also highlight the importance of remaining open to new collaborations and to building strong relationships. Barbara Schneider recounts stepping away from a position as associate dean at the age of thirty-five to conduct research with James Coleman. While some may wonder why she would have given up this post, Schneider discusses the importance of remaining true to her passions. She writes,

> An associate dean for research, at thirty-five, it became apparent that this career path was leading me astray from what I truly enjoyed most. I was passionate about studying problems, especially those related to educational inequities, challenging conventional assumptions about perceived opportunities, analyzing data, and rethinking how results could and should influence education practice and policy. I regrouped, cut my losses, and took an unusual career path, beginning an eight-year collaboration with James S. Coleman, at the University of Chicago, whose gracious tutelage shaped my intellectual interests and analytic approach into a bona fide sociologist.

Schneider's self-reflection reminds readers that they must not lose sight of why they chose to enter academia and be lured away from accomplishing the goals they set out to achieve. While the lessons from the stories that follow certainly suggest maintaining an openness to unexpected pathways, they also indicate that one should remain grounded and true to their interests.

Many of the scholars in the book were high level administrators for part of their careers—Brint, Gamoran, Postiglione, Ramirez, Sadovnik, Schneider, Weis, Wexler, Whitty. Whitty summarizes the conflict between the administrative and research roles that they all have faced:

> Soon after I was appointed as Director of the Institute of Education, University of London in 2000, someone referred to me as 'Geoff Whitty, who used to be a sociologist of education'. As the post of Director at IOE is roughly equivalent to President and Provost combined in a US higher education institution such as Teachers College Columbia, I have to admit that there were times during my ten year tenure as Director when I was distracted from sociology of education by administrative and financial preoccupations. However, I have always seen my primary academic and professional identity as a sociologist and continue to do so…

Perhaps the most enduring theme and lesson that permeates the chapters that follow is the importance of building relationships. The current leaders in the sociology of education speak of cultivating a wide range of bonds with different kinds of people. Roslyn Mickelson tells the story of a relationship she built with a staff member in the Charlotte Mecklenburg Schools who proved essential in aiding Mickelson's efforts to obtain student-level data. More commonly, the scholars in this book discuss the growth and joy that resulted from building life-long bonds with mentors and mentees. Alan Sadovnik recounts the story of his final visit with Basil Bernstein before his death and the honor of speaking at Basil's memorial service at the Institute of Education. Knowing the fulfillment Sadovnik found in his relationship with Bernstein, it is not surprising to see Sadovnik discuss the strong bonds he has built with his own mentees. He writes,

> I am very proud of the mentoring I did with my students who completed their dissertations, most of whom have gone on to academic careers, either in teaching or administration, with one remaining in an executive position in a non-profit. I believe I had a profound impact on their academic development and careers.

The clear lesson from the intellectual self-portraits by Mickelson, Sadovnik, and others in this book is that the people encountered through working in this field not only enrich our work but also bring unimaginable joy to our lives.

Life in academia can be challenging. At times the work can be overwhelming and isolating. Rejection of all kinds is common—journal articles are turned away, jobs are offered to other candidates, access to data is denied, and applications for funding are set aside. The scholars in this book are successful not because they avoided rejection, rather they are successful because they persevered through rejection.

In an easily relatable story, Roslyn Mickelson discusses the need for perseverance through rejection, particularly early in one's career.

> I submitted the first version of what would become "The Attitude/Achievement Paradox Among Black Adolescents," to the *American Sociological Review*. The reviewers were swift and brutal in their rejection of the manuscript as not ready for primetime. I was not prepared for the rejection. It figuratively knocked the wind out of me and left me intellectually paralyzed for almost two years. Eventually, I garnered the capacity to return to the piece. I sent the revised manuscript to *Sociology of Education*, which published it in 1990 after multiple revisions.

Those working to establish their careers today would do well to remember this story. Mickelson struggled with rejection, but she did not let it overtake her. Instead, she persevered, revised her work, and ended up publishing an article that has had a tremendous impact on the field.

One final lesson from the intellectual self-portraits that is worth drawing attention to comes again from Barbara Schneider. She discusses "the struggle of being willing to stick one's neck out" and proceeds to note that "research, if it is to be meaningful, will not please everyone." Being willing to expose oneself, stand by your research, and face a public and chorus of policymakers who may prefer to ignore scholarly findings takes courage and a deep commitment to the field. Central to this commitment has been the analysis of educational inequality and the application of research to ameliorate such inequality. All of these contributors have made the analysis of educational inequality central to their work, with some playing an active role in trying to solve problems of educational inequality. It is this courage and commitment to the sociology of education that distinguishes the selection of scholars profiled in the pages that follow.

## CONCLUSION

Shortly after submitting his intellectual self-portrait for this volume, A. H. Halsey passed away. His contributions to the sociology of education were undeniable and his impact on the lives of those lucky enough to encounter him were immense. A. H. Halsey is the contributor to this book with the greatest longevity in the field, and as a tribute to his life we wish to conclude this introduction by bringing attention to the words that Halsey uses to commence his chapter. Halsey reminds all of us that our individuality is both a source of inspiration and an obstacle to high-quality sociological work and that we must be both passionate and ruthlessly skeptical if we wish to continue advancing this great discipline. In Halsey's words,

> Experience of life prejudices each and every one of us. I, now in my nineties, declare myself a committed ethical socialist and have done so for over fifty years; but also I have become a disciplined sociologist. The commitment

leads me to passionate advocacy of a particular form of society—the active democracy of an informed citizenry. The discipline compels me to seek truth through empirical evidence, with ruthless scepticism as to sources and methods and with disrespect towards arbitrary authority. But Reader beware! Greet my scepticism with your own scepticism and always remember that words can and do change their meaning as they move through time and space. You are confronted here by an elderly Englishman who has lived and learnt through over ninety years of economic, political, social and cultural change.

## REFERENCES

Delamont, S. (2003). *Feminist sociology*. London: Sage.
Power, S., Brannen, J., Brown, A., & Chisholm, L. (2001). *A tribute to Basil Bernstein, 1924–2000*. London: Institute of Education.
Sadovnik, A. R., & Coughlan, R. W. (2015). *Sociology of education: A critical reader*. New York, NY: Routledge.
Young, M. F. D. (1971). *Knowledge and control: New directions in the sociology of education*. London: Collier-Macmillan.

*Alan R. Sadovnik*
*Rutgers University*
*Newark*

*Ryan W. Coughlan*
*Guttman Community College*
*The City University of New York*

STEPHEN J. BALL

# 2. CONTINUITY AND CHANGE[1]

*The Making of a Neoliberal Academic Subject*

My career in education – moral and occupational – has been marked by dramatic changes and dramatic continuities in what it means to be educated. As a sociological life and as an intellectual journey my biography seems to consist of a set of ruptures and tensions and inconsistencies. These remain unresolved and are difficult to explain but form the backbone of the story I will tell here. Thinking back, the tensions that have made up my personal experience of education have perhaps made necessary a constant need to challenge and unsettle myself, to reconsider, move on, or perhaps move away – to be something else. Here I will attempt to give an account of some of these tensions and of myself in relation to them. In doing so I will write myself as much more coherent that I ever was. I will submit myself to the genre of biography and some of its rules and tropes but avoid some others.

Convention incites me to envisage myself here as a singularity, an individual scholar who writes and thinks as an isolated mind within a network of abstract intellectual influences. However, I am not that singular, I have benefited from and been formed and changed by a whole set of intellectual collaborations and friendships of different kinds. I have been very lucky to have worked within series of exciting and dynamic and demanding research teams with people like Richard Bowe, Diane Reay, Meg Maguire, Carol Vincent, Carolina Junemann, David Gillborn, Nicola Rollock and Antonio Olmedo who have both required and enabled me to think differently, to think outside of the limits of my own intellect and think better. I have also been supported and challenged by people I have written with like Michael Apple and Maria Tamboukou, and I have benefitted from working with several generations of research students who have made it necessary me to explain myself better or have picked up and run with my ill-formed provocations in exciting ways. When I think and write, I am a composite of these experiences and exchanges. The biography I construct in this narrative is very much a collective effort.

## A CHILD OF WELFARE

I was a child of the British welfare state, of the National Health Service, of free milk and orange juice, although my school career beyond primary school was set within a longer, pre-welfare history of class divisions and social privileges. I am now a neoliberal academic working for a global brand, ranked in international comparison sites, for performance related pay in an HE system organised around class divisions and social privileges. The virtues and values of the welfare state, which were the common sense of my childhood, are now reviled and blamed for the state we find ourselves in. In relation to these different regimes of policy the meaning of education and what it means to be educated have been profoundly transformed over the course of my experience of education. Sometimes in relation to this transformation, as Judith Butler puts it "I am other to myself precisely at the place where I expect to be myself" (Butler, 2004). I am going to try to construct a narrative of myself in relation to the move from the welfare state to the neoliberal state, and the related, messy, reiterative interplay between my experiences of education and my evolving intellectual preoccupations as a sociologist of education.

My schooling began at Oak Farm Primary School in the London Borough of Hillingdon, and continued at Charville Lane Primary in Hayes. These were in all senses 'ordinary' schools, full of other ordinary children just like me. The schools still exist. My primary schooling was mainly uneventful and relatively successful. Jennifer Appleyard, whose parents owned the local toyshop, was top of the class in most subjects. I was one of her closest rivals. On the whole, I was good with words but not with numbers. I dreaded Mr. Robinson's mental arithmetic classes and the mustard coloured exercise books – I can still remember the humiliations of calculations in the head that were done too slowly or too hastily. Class positions were allocated by end of year exams and a system of stars given for 'good work' displayed around the classroom wall. Charville Lane served a skilled White working class community, the pupils came from a new build council housing estate to the west and owner-occupied houses to the east. The distinctions in terms of income and life style seemed minimal. I was from the latter. I was confident and comfortable at school, I was in my place, a 'fish in water', as Bourdieu put it. I did not feel the weight of water and took the world about myself for granted (Bourdieu, 1989, p. 43). Like John Burnside (2014, p. 58): 'The older I get, the happier my childhood becomes.'

We were prepared with some care for the 11+[2] examination, although I was blithely unaware of its purpose and significance. I passed with a score that enabled my parents to choose from a second tier of London grammar schools – Hayes Grammar was the local grammar school, but I went to Bishopshalt, a boys grammar school two bus rides away back in Hillingdon. I was the only child from my school to go there. My best friend Colin Campbell and many of my other classmates 'failed' the 11+ and went to the local Secondary Modern school, Mellow Lane. Our friendship did not long survive the division. Colin's attempts to 'call for me' to 'go out' were met with my mother's repeated refrain "he's doing his homework". He stopped coming. As Alan Johnson (2013, p. 124) says in his memoir of a west London childhood, thinking about his friends who passed and failed the 11+ 'our performances on that day would largely determine our futures'.

My move to Bishopshalt signaled the end of my childhood. It was a disaster, my cosy world of class friendships and supportive and kind teachers was a thing of the past. I now found myself in a Bourdeurian nightmare. My habitus encountered a social world of which it was certainly not the product. Just like Alan Johnson, who attended Sloane Grammar, I was adrift in an alien world of gowns, masters, Latin, rugby and cross-country running. Michael Cornes and I were the only working class boys in our year; his father – a pilot – drove a plane. The other boys, most of whom barely even acknowledged my existence, were almost without exception it seemed, the sons of lawyers, doctors or stockbrokers – so much for social mobility. The teaching was dull, didactic and repetitive, lots of talk, board writing and snap questions. The teachers were aloof and disdainful. I was now a 'fish out of water', frightened, isolated, and very ill at ease. My social and cultural capitals and my logic of practice, which had served me fairly well at primary school, were ill-attuned to the institutional habitus of the grammar school. Class distinctions were everywhere and my established dispositions were rendered null and void (Bourdieu, 1986). As Owen Sheers says of his time at Oxford, there seemed to be a secret rulebook that everyone else had access to but me (The Guardian, 13th June 2015, p. 13). I assumed the mantle of school failure by the end of the first week. In the exams at the end of the first year I came 30th out of 33. Much of my time at home was spent struggling with gnomic homework tasks, which made little sense to me and for which my parents were unable to give much practical help. Even my facility with words, which had stood me in good stead at Charville Lane, now seemed inadequate. I lacked the right turn of phrase, the correct grammatical construction, the proper tone and style. My practical sense had no purchase on this world of middle class taste, entitlement and easy accomplishment. I was lonely, unhappy and increasingly alienated. My sense of myself as a learner was changing – I still resent the casual but damaging symbolic violence done to me by the school and the 'masters'.

Because of a change in my father's work, I moved after one year to Havant Grammar School, which had a very different social class mix to Bishopshalt. Even so, my relation to and interest in schooling remained strained, to say the least, for several years to come. Sport and English literature were my only real interests. For some reason Mr. Halford, my French teacher, saw 'something in me' worth working on and in collusion with my mother sought to show me the error of my ways. I began to recover some enthusiasm for schoolwork and was allowed into the 6th form (16–18 years) 'on probation' and for the first time I encountered teachers who could interest and inspire – thank you Mr. Rigby. Most of my grammar school teachers could not teach their way out of a wet paper bag! I find the continuing romantic attachment to the grammar school in English education policy circles laughable, except it is also damaging. The good experiences of a lucky and usually privileged few are used to stand for a whole system that was best at producing failure.

## NEW UNIVERSITIES!!!

At age 18 I got a place at Sheffield University to do History and Social Studies but decided not to go. As a result I lost touch with almost all of my school friends. After seven years in the dull backwaters of grammar schooling I wanted to be in the 'real' world earning a living. I spent 18 months exploring various career options before University re-emerged as a more preferable option than banking or librarianship. I got a place, through the clearing scheme, at the University of Essex, a 'new' university. Indeed, the most politically radical and socially diverse of the post-Robbins[3] 'new' universities. In size and social make up and architecture it was rather like a large comprehensive school – it could not have been more different from Oxbridge and the 'redbricks'. I received a student grant which was about the same as I was being paid by the Portsmouth Library Service. Being slightly older than most 1st years and chastened by the world of work I reveled in the opportunity to read and attend lectures. I began as a politics major – or Government as it was called – but found the subject boring and quickly switched to sociology and chose the sociology of education as my specialist area. I hoped that this would help me make sense of my own experience of education. My tutor for this was Denis Marsden and his book *Education and the Working Class*, written with Brian Jackson (Jackson & Marsden, 1962), was of course on the reading list. Denis and the book played a key role in making sociology something that I wanted to do. The book offered a practice of sociology that made absolute sense to me. It dealt with inequality in a nuanced but visceral way. Inequality as grounded in mundane struggles and compromises, and in the aspirations, failures, complexities and pain of real lives. It is a book I return to often and refer my students to often. It is a timeless classic and its insights are constantly being re-invented by sociologists and educational researchers who think they are saying something new. Reading the book was an extraordinary experience. It was about me, about my life, my experience, my successes and failures, my struggles. The book remains as potent now as it was then, and it anticipated a great deal of Bourdieu's conceptualization of class processes and the textures of class life.[4] It tries to explain 'success' as a way of understanding failure, but it is also about the costs of such 'success'. I first read *Education and the Working Class* at more or less the same time as I read Charles Wright-Mills' *The Sociological Imagination* (Wright-Mills, 1970) and it seemed like a paradigm example of Wright-Mills' version of sociological practice as the linking of 'personal troubles of milieu' to 'public issues of social structure' and historical social forces. It was sociology with a human face. As Wright-Mills put it: 'The sociological imagination enables us to grasp history and biography and the relations between the two within society' (1970, 12). In this case, the relations were between education policy, selective schooling and social class inequalities. Alan Bennett has acknowledged that the book provided the basis for his play *The History Boys*, which is set in Cutlers' Grammar School, Sheffield, a fictional boys' grammar school. The play follows a group of history pupils preparing for the Oxbridge entrance examinations under the guidance of three teachers with contrasting teaching styles. *Education and the Working Class* is about class mobility, class inequality and waste, and about what Denis describes as a 'blockage' – selective education. In stark contrast to the sometimes pathologising focus on working class failure in much of the contemporary sociology of education, *Education and the*

*Working Class* worked with a sample of 90 'successfully' working class children. That is, children who passed the 11+ and went to Huddersfield grammar school, like Jackson and Marsden and many of whom went on to higher education. In postmodern fashion, the two writers are in the text, they are two of the 90. The book is also about them.

In my second year at Essex Colin Lacey's *Hightown Grammar* (1970) was published, based on an ethnographic style study of Salford Grammar school. While *Education and the Working Class* focused mainly on the home end of the class relations of schooling, *Hightown* looked primarily inside the black box of schooling at the processes of distinction, division and exclusion. Again this was a book that captured the processes of schooling to which I had been subject, I was enthralled and outraged. This kind of research was a channel, a productive one it seemed, for the resentments arising from my secondary school career, that shaped what I was and what I might become. Here was a way of confronting and analyzing the 'hidden injuries of class' that are deeply embedded in the English education system. Denis Marsden and Colin Lacey were significant influences in my career as a sociologist – both in terms of substance and method. Colin as my PhD supervisor at the University of Sussex, a model of support and provocation, and Denis as a sympathetic tutor and later one of the examiners of my PhD thesis – published as *Beachside Comprehensive* (1981). The Beachside study sought to trace Denis and Colin's concerns with social class successes and failures into the era of comprehensive education. Denis' pamphlet on comprehensive education policy *Politicians, Equity and Comprehensives* (Marsden, 1971) also played a key role in my emerging interest in the relationship between policy and practice in education. At the time and for sometime to come policy research and research in and on schools existed separately attended to by political scientists and sociologists respectively. I became increasingly interested in understanding the complex ways in which the two were connected.

Another encounter with policy and in retrospect a symbolic moment in the bigger story I am trying to tell here also occurred in my time at Essex. Despite my protests with many others on the streets of Colchester in 1970, a protest I helped organize, Margaret Thatcher then Secretary of State for Education 'snatched' away my free school milk. She also raised the cost of school meals. In a sense the welfare state and the school as a site of welfare were thenceforth under question. A new post-welfare political logic was being adumbrated. Much later Bob Jessop's book *The Future of the Capitalist State* (2002) was important in helping my make sense of Schumpeter's displacement of Keynes as the architect of policy and the concomitant reworking of the form and modalities of the capitalist state – the emergence of the *competition state*.

From Essex I moved to Sussex, another but very different 'new' university, to do postgraduate work in Sociological Studies. Again the generosity of the state supported and made possible my continuing education in the form of an ESRC studentship, which funded my MA and then my PhD work. At the end of the studentship I was lucky enough to get a job as a Lecturer in Education, at Sussex. I had already been doing some teaching in the department. As Heads of Department both Tony Bailey and Tony Becher were incredibly supportive and I had come a long way from Charville Lane. Nonetheless, the class gap between my primary school and university occasionally made itself felt and still does sometimes. There are still moments at which my 'distinction' becomes apparent and the structuring and reproductive work of the 'corporeal hexis' come into view – when my voice or embodiment or tastes are out of place.

My PhD and subsequent research at Sussex, focused on the relations between social class, schooling and education policy, were undertaken within the sensibilities and epistemology of ethnography. I became part of a community of British ethnographers, inspired by the Chicago School of Sociology, and through the late 1970s and 1980s regularly attended the St Hilda's college seminars initially set up and run by Peter Woods and Martyn Hammersley. I edited some St Hilda's books and a book series of school ethnographies with Ivor Goodson.[5] My research methods drew inspiration both from Colin Lacey's work, which was based in the Manchester school of anthropology, and the Chicago school of sociology – I read George Herbert Mead and Herbert Blumer, and thence Howard Becker and Anselm Strauss – both of whom I was later lucky enough to meet.

Ethnography as a research sensibility and a research practice mirrored the tensions of my institutional experiences. It rests on being neither insider nor outsider, but both *Stranger and Friend* as Hortense Powdermaker (1966) puts it in her intellectual autobiography. Even so I retained a sense of dissatisfaction with the direction and possibilities of my work partly in relation to the theoretical and critical limitations of symbolic interactionism and partly in relation to the parochialism of Sussex. My burgeoning interest in policy made me realize the extent to which the real action was going on elsewhere, back in London.

I was also exercised by the problem of who or what I was. Within the disciplinary norms of the sociology of the time it was assumed that we were all a 'something' – a Marxist of a specific variety (Althusserian or Polantzian or Gramscian), a feminist of some kind, a critical realist or whatever. We were supposed to be enfolded gently in the affirmations and 'transcendental teleologies' (Foucault, 1972, p. 172) of one theory or another. This was more than a matter of perspective; it was an allegiance, a sense of identity and ontological security, a basis of mutual recognition and distinction and sometimes therefore a source of public disputation and conflict. Knowing who you were, where you stood, being a something, being a 'wise fool', seemed to have many attractions.

I read widely and tried out various ontological positions for size but none seemed quite to fit. As 'cognitive and motivating structures', as 'already realized ends – procedures to follow, paths to take...' (Bourdieu, 1990, p. 53) they did not seem to work for me, they did not fit me, or perhaps I did not fit them. My moral career at secondary school and as a university sociologist seemed to be mirrored in my theoretical career – both were couched in a sense of unease, a kind of nomadism.

Even so, Bourdieu, who has made his appearance above, was to become increasingly significant in my practice of sociology, his 'experiments' with habitus, capitals and field provided the *method* for a series of ESRC funded research projects stretching across 20 years, interrogating the subtle and persistent ravages of class inequality, increasingly played out in new ways across the fuzzy terrain of various education marketplaces. I was comfortable with Bourdieu's refusal to articulate a joined up social theory and his emphasis on the generative interface between theory and data. *Distinction* (1986) remains for me his outstanding book and underpinned my later preoccupation with class advantage and the class strategies of the middle classes (Ball, 2003b; Vincent & Ball, 2001).

However, in the mid-1980s another French theorist, another Professor of the College de France, who died in 1984, was about to intrude into my modernist anxieties and re-write them. In 1985 with relief and excitement I returned to London to become Tutor for the MA in Urban Education at King's College, following in the footsteps of the admirable Gerald Grace and Geoff Whitty, both now colleagues at the Institute of Education. Aesthetically and demographically King's had much in common with Bishopshalt Grammar – "how nice to hear a demotic accent" remarked a Professor of French at a reception for new staff – but intellectually the challenges and opportunities were invigorating. The MA attracted teachers from across London and beyond who wanted to explore critical perspectives that they might bring to bear on their understanding of the relations between schooling and the urban – Meg Maguire was one of my early students. The course syllabus I inherited required me to read widely in the then dynamic fields of urban theory and state theory. However, the most significant and challenging and compelling reading was Foucault's *Discipline and Punish* (Foucault, 1979). In some ways this was like reading Denis Marsden – a version of what is sometimes called 'the Foucault effect' (Gordon et al., 1991) – again it was about me and my experience of schooling, but now I read myself as a subject in the 'eye of power' (Foucault, 1980). Like Marsden and Lacey, Foucault's attention was focused on mundane processes and quotidian practices, on minute institutional divisions and categorisations, on 'the little tactics of habit' (1979, p. 149) but as part of 'an apparatus of total and circulating mistrust' (ibid., p. 158), and as modalities of power – discipline and regulation. I began the MA course each year by taking students out for a walk around the area of Waterloo station, to look at the Victorian schools, the Peabody housing estates, and the local laying-in hospital. I wanted them to see the urban landscape as a grid of power, and as literally and in effect the architecture of the modern state, as a 'disposition of space for economico-political ends' (ibid, p. 148). Concomitantly, inside these institutions, 'Technical social science began to take form within the context of administration' (Dreyfus & Rabinow, 1983, p. 134), that is, as professional expertise – teachers, social workers, sanitary engineers, doctors emerged as state actors and enactors of the state. *Government* in the 19th century, as the 'political technology of the body' (Foucault, 1979, p. 26), was increasingly concerned with the minds and bodies of its *population* – and their wellbeing and thus the 'health' of the nation and its security.

As Foucault put it in the title of one of his College de France lecture series, *Society must be defended* (2004). In visiting the buildings we were beginning a genealogy of ourselves as the effects and subjects of power and as managers of the population. In 1990 I edited a collection of papers drawn from a conference held at King's (Ball, 1990a), which brought together a set of papers which deployed Foucauldian concepts and methods to explore schooling.

The relationships between policy and practice also made sense to me in Foucauldian terms. Disciplinary power was still very evident in the organisational and pedagogical practices of schools. Regulation – biopolitics – was evident in the left-over eugenics which underpinned the 11+ examination I sat, and the claims made in the Norwood Report (Norwood Report, 1943), the dangerous an unsafe basis for tripartite education, that it was possible to identify three types of child with three types of mind by testing for 'intelligence'. The welfare state came back into view, in a very different way, through a very different lens. William Beveridge, architect of the British welfare state was a president of the Eugenics Society. The struggle between eugenicists and environmentalists at the LSE – hotbed of eugenics in the 1930s – was the starting point of the sociology of education in Britain (Ball, 2008).

Foucauldian analytics and concepts were becoming increasingly important to the objects of my research concerns – I was making increasing use of discourse, power and subjectivity as tools in my work on education policy. Equally important to me was the style and stance of Foucault's work, the kind of scholar and intellectual he was, and his own struggles not to be 'a something' and to avoid and erase disciplinary boundaries. I was attracted to what Dreyfus and Rabinow (1983, p. 121) call his 'ethical and intellectual integrity' and his efforts to 'produce a new ethical form of life which foregrounds imagination, lucidity, humour, disciplined thought and practical wisdom' – his *pessimistic activism*. In many respects Foucault only really makes sense when his substantive works are read and understood in relation to his refusal to accept the inscriptions and limits and structures of 'normal' social science and the rejection of all possible foundations of belief and thus the constant challenge of 'not knowing what and how to think' (Burchell, 1996, p. 30). As Johanna Oksala (2007, p. 1) suggests: 'To get closer to Foucault's intent, it helps if one is willing to question the ingrained social order, give up all truths firmly fixed in stone, whilst holding on to a fragile commitment to freedom'. There is a dual ambivalence here, one aspect in relation to scholarship and one in relation to the practices of government within which we are enmeshed and the relationship between to two – power/knowledge. Confronting this ambivalence involves finding ways to work in the tensions between technologies of competence and technologies of the self. Finding ways to create our own lives through action and thought 'within a space of uncertainty' (Taylor, 2011, p. 80). We are always freer than we think. I will come back to that.

The essential point about reading Foucault is that he requires us to confront not simply the ways in which we are produced and made up as modernist and neoliberal researchers but also the ways in which we might be revocable – how we might be different. He makes me appropriately uneasy, or rather speaks to my unease, in a productive and generative way. This is a productive unease that is different from the nomadic dissatisfactions of my earlier career. It requires a constant struggle against the governmentalities of scientism to find a proper rigour, a thoughtful reflexive and practical rigour—a rigour that goes beyond the niceties and safety of technique to find a form of epistemological practice that is not simply self-regarding. Similarly, Bourdieu was critical of what he called the 'intellectualist bias' which always arises when researchers are insufficiently critical of the 'presuppositions inscribed in the act of thinking about the world' (Bourdieu & Wacquant, 2001, p. 39) and the failure to grasp 'the logic of practice' which is embedded in this.

As Foucault put it: 'Do not ask who I am and do not ask me to remain the same: leave it to our bureaucrats and our police to see that our papers are in order. At least spare us their morality when we write' (Foucault, 1972). In not remaining the same he is also it has to be said decidedly inconsistent. The search of an essential Foucault is a fool's errand. Nonetheless, this inconsistency, the constant revision of thought, creates spaces for the readers and users of his work to be creative and to be adventurous. All of this is demanding and liberating in equal measure.

With the wisdom of hindsight and in contemporary sociological parlance I can think about this now as an attempt to escape from the powerful binaries that demarcate the sociological field and a renunciation of the grand theoretical divides that make up the history of sociology. That seems about right – but while in the midst of my discomforts and dilemmas what it was that discomforted me did not seem so clear cut and my responses certainly did not seem intellectually coherent.

## LIVING THE NEOLIBERAL UNIVERSITY

Higher Education is now a very different place from the one I entered as an undergraduate and later as a lecturer. I began working in a 'new' welfare university and now find myself living the life of a neoliberal academic, a neoliberal subject. In this sense, in some respects, as I did at the beginning, I am again writing and researching about myself, about my performance and reformulation – now within the incitements of neoliberal productivity. The practices and technologies that make up and re-make HE have changed inexorably as a result of a ratchet effect of many small moves, initiatives and reforms over 40 years. These have worked upon the funding and accountability of and access to HE, in different ways, to change what it means to teach and research in HE. Universities are now sites of calculation, investment and productivity, thoroughly integrated into the discourses of the economy. The practices and technologies to which I refer produce a 'dense network of vigilant and multidirectional gazes' (Foucault, 1979, p. 176) and 'lateral effects' which run through the basic 'message systems' of HE – curriculum, pedagogy, assessment and management. At their most visceral and intimate these practices and technologies effect the transformation of our social relations and practices into calculabilities and exchanges, that is into the market form – with the effect of commodifying of our educational practice. This is a 'remoralisation' of our relation to the state and to ourselves (Peters, 2001, pp. 59–60).

Needless to say both Bourdieu and Foucault are more than a little helpful in thinking about neoliberalism. Foucault's 1978–79 College de France lectures *The Birth of Biopolitics* (Foucault, 2010) offer a remarkable genealogy of liberalisms and concomitantly of the state and the diabolical interplay between globalization and neoliberalism – *New liberalspeak: a new planetary vulgate* as Bourdieu and Wacquant (2001) call it. In different ways Aiwah Ong, Jamie Peck, Wendy Larner and the wonderful John Clarke, also help me think about and research neoliberalism, have all worked with and used Foucault to interrogate the mobile technologies of neoliberalism. That is, both the big-N, the neoliberal political economy 'out there' and the little-n, the neoliberal 'in here', in our daily life and in our heads, in our appetites and instincts. The latter, the little-n, is in HE realised through a set of local practices which articulate the mundane rhythms of our email traffic, our form-filling, or peer reviewing, and re-modulate the ways in which we relate to one another as neoliberal subjects – individual, responsible, striving, competitive, enterprising. The former, the big N, the constantly expanding realm of exchange relations and competition within education and education services, has generated a new iteration of my policy community ethnographies, worked on with Carolina Junemann (Ball, 2007; Ball, 2012a; Ball & Junemann, 2011) and Diego Santori (Santori, Ball, & Junemann, 2016) which had begun in 1980s (Ball, 1990b). These 'network ethnographies' are informed by a range of political sciences literatures which attend to the shift from *government* to *governance*, especially the writing Bob Jessop, Mark Bevir and Chris Skelcher. This parallels and in part draws upon Foucault's account of the shift of emphasis within processes of government from *discipline* (welfare) to *governmentality* (neoliberalism). Perhaps if I am creative enough I can establish a kind of coherence here after all?

The latter, the little n, has generated a series of papers on performativity (e.g. Ball, 2003a, 2012b, 2015b), with an appreciative nod to Judith Butler and J-F Lyotard. Performativity is a key mechanism of neoliberal management, a form of hands-off management that uses comparisons and judgements in place of interventions and direction. It is a moral system that subverts and re-orients us to its truths and ends. It makes us responsible for our performance and for the performance of others. The technologies of performance (the REF, H-Index, impact narratives etc.) constantly generate new and excruciating visibilities within which we as academics relate to one another, and in relation to which we must seek our place and our worth and to fulfill our needs and desires. We are constantly expected to draw on the skills of presentation and of inflation to write ourselves and fabricate ourselves in ever lengthier and more sophisticated CVs, annual self-reviews and target setting and performance management audits, which give an account of our 'contributions' to research and teaching and administration and the community. Typically now applications for posts and for promotion run to 40/50 pages and are littered with scores, indexes and ratings intended to demonstrate our productivity. We are constantly incited to make spectacles of ourselves and the danger is that we become transparent but empty, unrecognisable to ourselves in a life enabled by and lived against measurement. Our days are numbered – literally. These techniques do not simply report our practice; they inform, construct and drive our practice. The force and brute logic of performance are hard to avoid. To do so, in one sense at least, means letting ourselves down, in terms of the logic of performance, and letting down our colleagues and our institution. These are also 'dividing practices', which work to identify, valorize and reward the successful and productive – the 'affiliated' (Miller & Rose, 2008, p. 98), and to target for exile or for reform those who fail to re-make themselves in 'the image of the market' (Gillies, 2011, p. 215). As a result there is for many of us in education a growing sense of ontological insecurity; both a loss of a sense of meaning in what we do and of what is important in what we do. There is a sense of constant change and concomitant anxiety and insecurity and increasing precarity – what Lazarrato calls the 'micro-politics of little fears' (Lazzarato, 2009, p. 120) – neoliberal affects. Performativity works to render teaching and learning into calculabilities, it also generates market information for choosers, enables the state to 'pick off' poor performers, and makes it possible to translate educational work, of all kinds, into contracts articulated as forms of performance delivery, which can then be opened to 'tender' and competition from private providers by means of 'contracting out'.

In the nexus of all of this, I again find myself out of place and uncomfortable. My habitus is ill-adjusted to market sensibilities. This is not a version of HE that seems to have much to do with intellectual curiosity, creativity or critique. I am as I said before 'other to myself' (Collini, 2012).

My intellectual responses to these 'problems' are constructed through a method of research and analysis which is, clearly, deeply paradoxical. This is made up of a commitment to ethnography on the one hand, and the adoption of Foucauldian analytic sensibilities on the other – an unstable but productive aporia. That is, a particular and confrontation between theory and data. This is evident in the relationships and affinities which connect up policy network analysis (Ball, 2012a) and microphysical flows of power, and the dualistic analysis of policy as text and discourse, as topology and dispositif, as agency and subjectivity (Ball, 2015b). This draws on the need, as Michael Apple (1995) puts it, to think post and neo together, at the same time. So somewhere in this elision between hermeneutics and post-structuralism I remain concerned about very modernist problems of inequality and social injustice in relation to social class and race in particular. My work on choice, that essential neoliberal practice of envy, rivalry and striving, and means of exercising and reproducing privilege, has been one focus of this in various sectors of the education market (Vincent & Ball, 2001; Rollock et al., 2014). Welfarism and neoliberalism have produced very different political economies of education but very much the same structural inequalities. The more things change... .

## WHAT AM I?

In relation to all of this I have begun to try to attend to the possibilities of refusal and contestation and in particular to think about subjectivity as a site of struggle – a modern form of politics for a modern form of government. That is, to think beyond or alongside resistance about the possibilities of refusal. With Antonio Olmedo (Ball & Olmedo, 2013), I have tried to think about some of the most intimate aspects of our experience of ourselves and the possibilities of certain 'arts of existence' in relation to contemporary neoliberal education and the confrontation of *governmentality* on its own grounds. This rests on Foucault's conceptualisations of neoliberal government as a particular configuration of the relationship between *truth and power and the self* (and thus ethics) or what Dean terms 'the rapport between reflexivity and government' (Dean, 2007, p. 211) and draws in particular on some of Foucault's later work on 'the care of the self', *parrhesia* – truth-telling – and ethics (Ball, 2015b). In his later lectures, Foucault identified two avenues of the care of the self as the two primary concerns of western philosophy: 'On the one hand, a philosophy whose dominant theme is knowledge of the soul and which from this knowledge produces an ontology of the self'. And on the other hand, a philosophy as test of life, of bios, which is the ethical material and object of an art of oneself' (Foucault, 2011). It is the latter with which I am concerned in this biography – on paper and in practice. That is, who or what I am and how could I be different?

Within all of this as an academic subject I am made uncomfortable again, out of place once more, my home in the ivory tower is being flattened by neoliberal bulldozers to make way for a fast-fact HE franchise in which all knowledge has is price. I began with both fond memories of and a critique of welfare education and end with a critique of neoliberal education, and have inhabited and struggled with the discomforts of both. I am left with a sense of process rather than destination, unease and refusal rather than affirmation, in a space in which I am (im)possible and in which sociology as a vocation as something I do, is being re-inscribed as a resource for the management of the population, which is how it began. This is a space nonetheless in which I continue and struggle.

In the end I wonder who and what it is that I have written here. What kind of fiction is this Stephen Ball who comes into view in the pages of this article? Is it someone I might be or might become, or is it a character who never was and who otherwise does not really exist? There were fleeting moments in the text when I seemed to glimpse someone I recognise, but at other times there is really nothing but smoke and mirrors, an aspiration, a fabulation, a re-writing of the self or to paraphrase Foucault – a deliberate, self-conscious attempt to explain and express myself to an audience within which I exist and from whom I seek confirmation.

## NOTES

1. This chapter draws upon another version of what I have become. That is, S. J. Ball 'Accounting for a sociological life: influences and experiences on the road from welfarism to neoliberalism'. doi:10.1080/01425692.2015.1050087: Published online: 30 Jun 2015, British Journal of Sociology of Education.
2. A test of intelligence used for allocation to different types of secondary schooling.
3. The Robbins Report (the report of the Committee on Higher Education) was commissioned by the British government and published in 1963. The report recommended immediate expansion of universities, and the number of full-time university students rose from 197,000 in the 1967–68 academic year to 217,000 in the academic year of 1973–74 with "further big expansion" thereafter.
4. See Ball (2011).
5. These were published by Anna Clarkson's father Malcolm in his Falmer Press imprint – Anna has been my book editor at Routledge for many years.

## MY FAVOURITE TEXTS BY OTHERS

Basil Bernstein (1971) "On the classification and framing of educational knowledge", in: M. Young (Ed.) *Knowledge and control: new directions for the sociology of education*, London: Collier-Macmillan.

Pierre Bourdieu, (1986) *Distinction: A Social Critique of the Judgement of Taste*, London: Routledge.

Michel Foucault (1970) *The Order of Things*, New York: Pantheon.

Brian Jackson and Dennis Marsden, (1962/1966) *Education and the working class*, Pelican, Harmondsworth.

Colin Lacey (1970) *Hightown Grammar: the school as a social system*. Manchester: Manchester University Press.

## MY FAVORITE PERSONAL TEXTS

Ball, S. J. (1987) *The Micro-Politics of the School: Towards a theory of school organization*. London: Methuen.

Ball S. J. (1993) "What is Policy? Texts, Trajectories and Toolboxes." *Discourse*, 13 (2), pp. 10-17.

Ball, S. J. (2003) "The teacher's soul and the terrors of performativity" *Journal of Education Policy*, 18 (2), pp. 215-228.

Ball, S. J. (2012) *Global Education Inc.: new policy networks and the neoliberal imaginary*. London: Routledge.

Ball, S. J. (2013) *Foucault, Power and Education*. New York: Routledge.

## REFERENCES

Apple, M. (1995). *Education and power*. New York, NY: Routledge.

Ball, S. J. (1981). *Beachside comprehensive*. Cambridge: Cambridge University Press.

Ball, S. J. (Ed.). (1990a). *Foucault and education: Disciplines and knowledge*. London: Routledge.

Ball, S. J. (1990b). *Politics and policymaking in education*. London: Routledge.

Ball, S. J. (2003a). The teacher's soul and the terrors of performativity. *Journal of Education Policy*, *18*(2), 215–228.

Ball, S. J. (2003b). *Class strategies and the education market: The middle class and social advantage*. London: Routledge Falmer.

Ball, S. J. (2007). *Education Plc: Private sector participation in public sector education*. London: Routledge.

Ball, S. J. (2008). Some sociologies of education: A history of problems and places, and segments and gazes. *The Sociological Review*, *56*(4), 650–669.

Ball, S. J. (2011). Social class, families and the politics of educational advantage: The work of Dennis Marsden. *British Journal of Sociology of Education*, *32*(6), 957–965.

Ball, S. J. (2012a). *Global Ed. Inc.: New policy networks and the neoliberal imaginary*. London: Routledge.
Ball, S. J. (2012b). Performativity, commodification and commitment: An I-spy guide to the Neoliberal university. *British Journal of Educational Studies, 60*(1), 17–28.
Ball, S. J. (2015). Subjectivity as a site of struggle: Refusing neoliberalism? *British Journal of Sociology of Education*. doi:10.1080/01425692.2015.1044072. Accessed June 16, 2015.
Ball, S. J., & Junemann, C. (2011). Education policy and philanthropy—The changing landscape of English educational governance. *International Journal of Public Administration, 34*(10), 646–661.
Ball, S. J., & Olmedo, A. (2013). Care of the self, resistance and subjectivity under neoliberal governmentalities. *Critical Studies in Education, 54*(1), 85–96. Reprinted in Tracking the neoliberal juggernaut: http://explore.tandfonline.com/page/ed/rcse-vsi-neoliberalism.
Bourdieu, P. (1986). Forms of capital. In J. Richardson (Ed.), *Handbook of theory and research for the sociology of education*. New York, NY: Greenwood Press.
Bourdieu, P. (1986). *Distinction*. London: Routledge.
Bourdieu, P. (1989). Towards a reflexive sociology: A workshop with Pierre Bourdieu. *Sociological Theory, 7*(1), 26–63.
Bourdieu, P. (1990). *The logic of practice*. Cambridge: Polity Press.
Bourdieu, P., & Wacquant, L. (2001). Neo-Liberal neospeak: Notes on the new planetary vulgate. *Radical Philosophy, 105*(Jan/Feb), 2–4.
Burchell, G. (1996). Liberal government and techniques of the self. In A. Barry, T. Osborne, & N. Rose (Eds.), *Foucault and political reason*. London: UCL Press.
Burnside, J. (2014). *I put a spell on you*. London: Jonathan Cape.
Butler, J. (2004). *Undoing gender*. New York, NY & London: Routledge.
Collini, S. (2012). *What are universities for?* London: Penguin.
Dean, M. (2007). *Governing societies: Political perspectives on domestic and international rule*. Maidenhead: Open University Press.
Dreyfus, H. L., & Rabinow, P. (1983). *Michel Foucault: Beyond structuralism and hermeneutics*. Chicago, IL: University of Chicago Press.
Foucault, M. (1972). *The archeology of knowledge*. New York, NY: Vintage.
Foucault, M. (1979). *Discipline and punish*. Harmondsworth: Peregrine.
Foucault, M. (1980). *Power/Knowledge: Selected interviews and other writings*. New York, NY: Pantheon.
Foucault, M. (2004). *Society must be defended: Lectures at the collège de France, 1975–76*. London: Penguin.
Foucault, M. (2010). *The birth of biopolitics: Lectures at the college de France 1978–1979*. Basingstoke: Palgrave Macmillan.
Foucault, M. (2011). *The courage of truth: Lectures at the college de France 1983–43*. London: Palgrave Macmillan.
Gillies, D. (2011). Agile bodies: A new imperative in neoliberal governance. *Journal of Education Policy, 26*(2), 207–223.
Gordon, C., & Miller, P. (Eds.). (1991). *The Foucault effect: Studies in governmentality*. Brighton: Harvester/Wheatsheaf.
Jackson, B., & Marsden, D. (1962). *Education and the working class*. Harmondsworth: Penguin.
Jessop, B. (2000). *The future of the capitalist state*. Cambridge: Polity Press.
Johnson, A. (2013). *This boy*. London: Batam Press.
Lacey, C. (1970). *Hightown grammar*. Manchester: Manchester University Press.
Lazzarato, M. (2009). Neoliberalism in action: Inequality, insecurity and the reconstitution of the social. *Theory, Culture and Society, 26*(6), 109–133.
Marsden, D. (1971). *Politicians, equity and comprehensives*. London: Fabian Society.
Miller, P., & Rose, N. (2008). *Governing the present: Administering economic, social and personal life*. Cambridge: Polity Press.
Norwood Report, T. (1943). *Curriculum and examinations in secondary schools*. London: HM Stationery Office.
Oksala, J. (2007). *How to read Foucault*. London: Granta Books.

Peters, M. (2001). Education, enterprise culture and the entrepreneurial self: A Foucauldian perspective. *Journal of Educational Enquiry, 2*(2), 58–71.

Powdermaker, H. (1966). *Stranger and friend: The way of an anthro-pologist*. New York, NY: W. W. Norton & Company, Inc.

Rollock, N., Gillborn, D., Vincent, C., & Ball, S. J. (2014). *The colour of class: The educational strategies of the Black middle class*. London: Routledge.

Santori, D., Ball, S. J., & Junemann, C. (2016). Financial markets and investment in education. In A. Verger, C. Lubienski, & G. Steiner-Khamsi (Eds.), *World yearbook of education 2016: The global education industry*. New York, NY: Routledge.

Taylor, D. (2011). Practices of the self. In D. Taylor (Ed.), *Michel Foucault: Key concepts*. Durham, NC: Acumen.

Vincent, C., & Ball, S. J. (2001). A market in love? Choosing pre-school child care. *British Educational Research Journal, 27*(5), 633–651.

Wright-Mills, C. (1970). *The sociological imagination*. Harmondsworth: Penguin.

*Stephen J. Ball*
*Institute of Education*
*University of London*

JOMILLS HENRY BRADDOCK II

# 3. INTELLECTUAL SELF-PORTRAIT

BACKGROUND

Even though I grew up in a family of educators (my mother and father were both principals and an older sister was an elementary school teacher) I had no early interest in entering the education profession. Nevertheless, growing up in this family environment and attending segregated schools in the South made me keenly aware of educational issues and inequities at an early age. Further, having been assigned outdated textbooks with no remaining spaces for entering my name, taking science classes with less lab equipment than I had in my Gilbert's home chemistry sets, taking PE classes and playing varsity basketball on outdoor courts, and generally being educated in inferior facilities provided me with an experiential awareness of educational inequality under de jure segregation that left me feeling cheated. Like many other black students, I felt robbed of opportunities to compete both academically and athletically with putatively superior white students. Ironically, despite the limitations imposed on my education by the dual and unequal system of segregation, my consistently high standardized test scores raised suspicions of cheating from school district officials, creating myriad problems for my father (principal) including, among other things, a cross burning on our front lawn.

In hindsight, I can understand my father's apparent apprehension when the Supreme Court ruled in Brown to desegregate public schools on May 17, 1954. I was a sixth grader at the time, and I vividly recall that my father did not share my excitement when he and I heard the news announced on the radio while sitting outside together talking (likely discussing hunting, fishing, or sports). My father was not a very expressive person so he didn't say very much, yet it was clear the Supreme Court ruling left him more anxious than elated. Looking back at the way in which desegregation was implemented in many southern communities where many all-black schools were closed and black teachers and administrators fired, his anxiety was not unfounded (even though he personally, never experienced school closings or dismissal).

At the same time, my personal excitement and anticipation about the prospect of attending integrated public schools never materialized. Five years after *Brown* I left my all-black high school when I earned an early admission scholarship to Morehouse College in Atlanta. Even though I was a sixth grader at the time of the *Brown* decision, my first integrated class was many years later as a part-time student at Queens College in New York in 1965. My extensive exposure to the realities of segregated secondary and postsecondary schooling shaped my awareness of and concern with educational inequity. Additionally, coming of age in the Civil Rights era—my college freshman year was at the beginning of the student sit-in movement in Atlanta, and my graduate school years at Florida State University coincided with the height of the Black Student Protest Movement—nurtured my sense of collective responsibility and commitment to activism. The Morehouse years were especially influential in this regard as Atlanta became an epicenter of civil rights demonstrations, and Morehouse (along with Spelman, Clark, Morris Brown, and Atlanta University) became an incubator for student activists.

My commitment to becoming an agent of change was heightened in 1963 when Carole Robertson, my 14 year-old sister-in-law, was killed in the Birmingham church bombing. At the time of the church bombing, I was living in New York and this "critical incident" led to a life-long search for a path to combat racism and inequality. During this time period, I worked as a community organizer for the New York City Commission on Human Rights, the South Jamaica Community Organization, and later as Program and Personnel Director for the Archdiocese Head Start Program in Detroit. I left the Head Start position to attend graduate school with the intent of returning to pursue change through community organizing and activism. However, early in my graduate training, I had an epiphany in realizing that pursuing an academic career offered an alternative path for promoting social change. At Florida State University, I was keenly aware of the underrepresentation of African American faculty and the significance of that underrepresentation for the type of scholarship produced. So I began to see academic research and teaching as potential mechanisms of change. In my quest to become an agent of change, I was inspired by a number of African American scholars, both junior (Harry Edwards, Joyce Ladner, Robert Staples) and senior (Edgar Epps, James Blackwell, Charles Willie) whose work influenced the field in a variety of ways. I was also inspired by White academics like Robert Blauner whose scholarship challenged racial inequity and promoted social justice. However, perhaps my most significant role model for academic activism was Kenneth Clark—a prominent African American social psychologist. In addition to his widely recognized scholarship and leadership role as a social scientist in *Brown*, Clark played a leadership role in advancing community-based research through HARYOU (Harlem Youth Opportunities Unlimited) and MARC (Metropolitan Applied Research Center). His life and career inspired my interest in academic activism. As a result, I have devoted much of my academic career to using scientific scholarship in advancing public understanding and social policy around issues pertaining to equity and equality in education.

## MY ENTRY INTO DESEGREGATION RESEARCH

Although my doctoral dissertation compared black students' experiences and activism at historically black and historically white colleges, my entry into desegregation research began in earnest when I joined the Center for Social Organization of schools (CSOS) at Johns Hopkins University. As a post-doctoral fellow in 1978, my training in social psychology and race relations neatly meshed with James McPartland and Robert Crain's' well-established structural expertise in school effects research and their interest in the long-term effects of school desegregation. Being a part of CSOS shaped my research in many different ways. One of the most significant influences led me to a greater focus on social context. CSOS was the National Institute of Education's R & D Center responsible for conducting basic research to understand contextual effects on educational outcomes. Because my graduate training was largely in social psychology, my experience working with colleagues at CSOC provided a deeper appreciation of the influence of social contexts and social processes.

When I joined CSOS, the school desegregation literature and research agenda was dominated by studies focused on short-term, individual, outcomes (attitudes and achievement test scores) associated with school racial composition. Myer Weinberg's comprehensive reviews of desegregation research (as well as the influential reviews of St. John, NIE, and others) clearly illustrate this short-term focus. Our CSOS desegregation research team (McPartland, Crain and Braddock) sought to expand the focus of social science research to include greater attention to the long-term effects of desegregation by examining educational, career, and social outcomes for graduates of segregated and desegregated schools. Rather than focusing solely on what individuals think or feel as a result of attending segregated or desegregated schools (as most researchers guided by contact theory would likely suggest), the CSOS desegregation project examined what individuals do as a result of attending segregated or desegregated schools. This behavioral perspective, influenced by Crain & McPartland's prior work, was evident in my first CSOS study, "The Perpetuation of Segregation across Levels of Education: A Behavioral Assessment of the Contact-Hypothesis," which was based on my dissertation data. This study found that—net of qualifications, geography, and college inducements—black graduates of segregated high schools were more likely to enroll in historically black colleges (HBCU's) than historically white colleges (HWCU's). This study was followed by numerous collaborative studies with Jim McPartland using large-scale national longitudinal data. The consistent and cumulative evidence from these studies led to the development of "perpetuation theory" (the idea that segregation is perpetuated across school levels and across institutional settings). These studies produced a body of research which informed educational policy and court decisions in a variety of ways, and across a range of contexts. It also established a broader rationale for school desegregation policies. Instead of focusing only on how desegregation may benefit individuals by increasing student test scores or changing attitudes, this research examined how desegregation contributes to the structure of opportunities in adult life. Indeed, this body of research and expert testimony based on it played a significant role nationally in a number of important court cases, including Kansas City, Yonkers, Milwaukee, and Hartford. This long-term effects research has also been a centerpiece in many amicus briefs in recent school desegregation cases, including several filed before the Supreme Court, e.g., *Parents Involved in Community. Schools v. Seattle School District No. 1* (551 U.S. 701). The long-term effects studies also provided a basis and research model for both the *Bollinger* and *Grutter* higher education cases.

In addition to studies examining macro-contextual like school racial composition, I was also influenced at CSOS by Robert Slavin who stimulated my interest in studying micro-contexts within-schools—such as academic program tracks and ability groups—which differentially distribute learning opportunities. Here too, my research interests were aimed at informing educational policy and practice, and deepening public understanding regarding the academic and social consequences of academic sorting. My research on tracking also entered the policy domain in a variety of ways through congressional briefings, the national media, and through diverse organizational channels including the National Education Association, American Federation of Teacher's, National Governor's Association, National School Boards Association, among others. My research on equality of educational opportunity also includes school sports. More recently, my research agenda has expanded to include Title IX and gender equity issues, including examining gender and race equity trends in access to and participation in interscholastic athletics. Among the interesting findings in this area of research is the emerging evidence the African American females are not benefitting from Title IX, in the same way as White females. This White/African American female sport participation disparity is, indirectly, a consequence of school racial isolation—high schools attended by African American females are less likely to offer sports (volleyball, soccer, crew, etc.) which have been broadly adopted to provide more equitable participation opportunities for girls to comply with Title IX.

## THE EVOLUTION OF DESEGREGATION RESEARCH

One key idea emerging from my reflection on desegregation scholarship is that, on balance, the collective impact of the voluminous body of post-*Brown* desegregation studies may have been more harmful than helpful to African Americans. I believe that desegregation researchers (including myself), have asked the wrong questions with respect to *Brown* and equality of educational opportunity. This applies to both the short-term effects studies and the long-term effects research. It even applies to the new focus on compelling state interest studies. Each of these approaches is misguided, to varying degrees, in their lack of attention to access to equal educational opportunities. While social scientists have unquestionably made substantial contributions to equity and social justice in American society through their studies of school desegregation, one has to wonder to what extent *current* debates over the achievement gap and the effectiveness of *Brown* in producing equality of educational opportunity may be a consequence of researchers having *earlier* asked the wrong questions. If *Brown* represented, as many people believe, a judicial ruling about a moral, ethical, and fundamental right of citizenship, it is appropriate to question whether studies of school desegregation should have ever been framed as "evaluations" of desegregation policy. After all, we don't evaluate women's suffrage, the voting rights act, or other civil liberties in the same fashion as we have assessed African American children's right to attend any publically supported school. Historically, constitutional rights are more often examined, and fine-tuned where necessary, in order to make them work well, not "evaluated" to determine if they should exist.

I have come to believe firmly that following *Brown*, school desegregation research should have been quite similar to the gender equity research following *Title IX*. In a conversation nearly forty years ago with Sue Klein, a NIE staff official, I recall her pointing out that gender equity advocates did not support research aimed at "evaluating" *Title IX*. This was especially so having witnessed the damage done by years of research purporting to assess the efficacy of *Brown* and school desegregation from a school effects perspective. Reliance on a school effects perspective led to judgments about whether school desegregation was succeeding or failing based on changes in student's test scores or intergroup attitudes. Inexcusably, these judgments were made usually within a short period of time following implementation of a desegregation court order. Unlike a new curriculum, pedagogical approach, or incentive system, school desegregation was not an educational intervention that one could reasonably expect to have a direct effect on student test scores. Even true educational interventions are typically allowed more time to "work" before being deemed ineffective than was generally the case with school desegregation evaluations. Assessing the efficacy of the *Brown* decision largely on the basis of *ach*ievement test gaps is akin to assessing *Title IX's* effectiveness on the basis of math or science performance disparities between males and females. Fair and reasonable assessments of *Title IX* monitored the extent and quality of female's access to math and science courses to assess whether *Title IX* is "working." Likewise, fair and reasonable assessments of *Brown* should have monitored the extent and quality of Black student's access to equitable learning opportunities. As a consequence of girls increased access to math and science participation opportunities, over-time the male-female performance gaps have narrowed. Although most Americans would find that a laudable outcome, I do not believe women, or advocates of gender equity, would want the nation's commitment to *Title IX* and gender equity in education to be tied to questions about science and mathematics performance gaps. It seems to me, for *Brown*, as was the case for *Title IX*, the important research questions should have examined access to opportunities, with a focus on implementation and fidelity of implementation of desegregation policies and plans to promote equitable opportunities to learn. Had that approach been taken, perhaps today, the race achievement gap might mirror the closing gender science/math gap.

From the outset, civil rights advocates, including the NAACP, believed that school segregation was related to African Americans access to the American opportunity structure. These early advocates expected that school integration would bring about equitable access for African American students to the resources, experiences, and connections that facilitate full and equal participation in mainstream American society. Although evaluation research experts always point out the importance of asking the right questions (i.e., questions regarding outcomes clearly rooted in the expressed objectives of programs), it is clear that research on school desegregation subsequent to *Brown* was not grounded in the same set of understandings that guided the plaintiffs, and the Court. For example, during oral argument before the U.S. Supreme Court, Thurgood Marshall contended that, "Equal means getting the same thing, at the same time and in the same place." One might expect, given the plaintiff's focus and the legal ruling, that desegregation researchers would have focused on parity in representation of African American and white students in schools, classrooms, and courses as educational equity outcomes rather than the cognitive and affective outcomes that came to dominate the desegregation research agenda. Instead of focusing on the learning opportunities and educational climates provided to African American and Latino students in desegregated schools, most social science studies chose instead to examine academic achievement outcomes, which are at best, indirectly linked to desegregation policy. For advocates, school desegregation was not pursued as an educational program or treatment, but rather, a vehicle to provide equitable access to learning contexts.

## THE FUTURE OF DESEGREGATION RESEARCH

As the United States rapidly becomes both more racially and ethnically diverse, and increasingly segregated across race-ethnic boundaries, there are compelling reasons for educational researchers and policy makers to be concerned about the future of school desegregation. Both singly, and in combination, growing diversity and increased segregation may pose threats to the nation's stability and well-being by undermining the social cohesion needed to bind American citizens to one another and to society at large. A significant body of research has documented the critical role of school desegregation in preparing the nation's youth for living in an increasingly diverse society. Unfortunately, the current policy relevance of that body of short- and long-term desegregation research has diminished for the Supreme Court. In several recent rulings, the Court has focused increasingly on state rather than individual harms and benefits in determining the acceptability of school district efforts to promote educational diversity. However, the Court's ruling in *Grutter* and other recent cases emphasizing compelling state interest requirements offer a challenge for researchers to make a paradigm shift in order to provide relevant new evidence in support of diversity initiatives. Most research examining the merits of educational diversity has virtually ignored consequences for society at-large. Demonstrating that a race-conscious education policy represents a compelling state interest requires aggregate level evidence that K-12 diversity offers collective benefits that extend beyond individuals. In this regard, a dissertation recently completed by Ashley Mikulyuk, my graduate student, provides compelling evidence of the potentially positive impact of both school and neighborhood diversity on community level social cohesion and economic productivity and well-being. Using data based on 29 metropolitan communities in the Social Capital Community Benchmark Survey, she found that communities with more diverse schools and neighborhoods experienced greater economic productivity and well-being (higher per capita GDP, lower skill segregation, and lower education gaps) and were more cohesive across a wide range of indicators (general social trust, interracial trust, trust in government, interracial friendship networks, and social distance). More studies along these lines should allow social scientists to continue to play an important role in providing the courts with solid evidence upon which to inform their decisions concerning educational diversity.

Unfortunately, however, new compelling interest studies focused on collective benefits, like the earlier short- and long-term studies focused on individual benefits, also do not address equitable learning opportunities. As I have argued, most short-term studies of school desegregation were misguided in focusing largely on learning outcomes rather than learning opportunities. Even though the long-term studies focus on educational returns in adulthood have generally been more useful, the long-term outcome research also failed to consider learning opportunities. Ironically, the courts were later confronted with equitable learning opportunities issues such as tracking and ability grouping, which in effect, re-segregated students within the same school building, as so-called second generation school desegregation problems. In retrospect, however, it is abundantly clear that equitable learning opportunities should have been addressed as first, not second, generation desegregation problems. It is not unreasonable to suggest that had strong research on access to learning opportunities—like that of Mickelson, 2001; Oakes, 1995; Epstein, 1985, and others—become the dominant paradigm for assessing the efficacy of school desegregation interventions early on, the nation might be in a very different place today with regard to race and equality of educational opportunity. Regrettably, however, twenty-three years after *Brown*, a major review of the research on desegregation expressed surprise at how few studies had actually examined the influence of tracking and grouping on achievement in the context of desegregated schools (Weinberg, 1977, p. 85). In essence, researchers had done extensive examination of differences in achievement test performance without examining variations in associated student learning opportunities. Put differently, researchers (and the courts) should have more appropriately evaluated school desegregation as the dependent variable—evidence of equitable access to learning opportunities. Had this occurred, the voluminous body of research on school desegregation as an independent variable—including both its short- and long- term effects on achievement and other related outcomes—could be viewed as important value-added basic research evidence of its efficacy as educational policy instead of evidence of its failure.

## MOST INFLUENTIAL TEXTS

Clark, Kenneth B. *Dark ghetto: Dilemmas of social power*. Wesleyan University Press, 1989.
Crain, R. L. (1970). School integration and occupational achievement of Negroes. *American Journal of Sociology* (75), 593-606.

Durkheim, Émile. *Rules of sociological method*. Simon and Schuster, 1982.
Gordon, M. M. 1964. *Assimilation in American Life: The Role of Race, Religion, and National Origins*. New York: Oxford University Press.
Oakes, J. (1985). *Keeping track: How schools structure inequality*. New Haven: Yale University Press.
Rist, R. (1978). *The invisible children*. Cambridge, MA: Harvard University Press.

## MY FAVORITE TEXTS BY OTHERS

Bowen, W. G., & Bok, D. (1998). The Shape of the River: Long-term Consequences of Considering Race in College and University *Admissions*. Princeton, N.J.: Princeton University Press.
Epstein, J. (1985). After the bus arrives: Resegregation in desegregated schools. *Journal of Social Issues, 41*, 23-43.
McPartland, J. M., & Crain, R. L. (1980). Racial discrimination, segregation, and processes of social mobility. In V. T. Covello (Ed.), *Poverty and Public Policy*. Boston: Hall.
Wells, A. S. (2002). The "consequences" of school desegregation: The mismatch between the research and the rationale. *Hastings Constitutional Law Quarterly, 28*(4), 771-797.
Weinberg, M. (1978). *Minority Students: A Research Appraisal*. Washington, D.C.: National Institute of Education.

## REFERENCES

Epstein, J. (1985). After the bus arrives: Resegregation in desegregated schools. *Journal of Social Issues, 41*, 23–43.
Mickelson, R. A. (2001). Subverting Swann: Tracking and second generation segregation in Charlotte-Meckingburg schools. *American Educational Research Journal, 38*(2), 215–252.
Oakes, J. (1995). Two cities: Tracking and within-school segregation. In L. Miller (Ed.), *Brown plus forty: The promise*. New York, NY: Teachers College Press.
Weinberg, M. (1978). *Minority students: A research appraisal*. Washington, DC: National Institute of Education.

*Jomills Henry Braddock II*
*University of Miami*

STEVEN BRINT

# 4. THINKING ABOUT SCHOOLS AND UNIVERSITIES AS SOCIAL INSTITUTIONS

*An Intellectual Self-Portrait*

EARLY LIFE

I was born in Albuquerque, NM in 1951. My father, one of the first computer systems analysts, worked in the defense industry at Sandia Laboratories. My mother raised three boys and acted in local theater. Both of my parents were Jewish, but secular by orientation. Though neither held advanced degrees, they were politically liberal and intellectually oriented. When I told my parents at age 9 that I had no intention to continue with Sunday school, my mother agreed as long as I promised to read an illustrated treatise on the world's major religions. My paternal grandfather was a self- employed plumber who had migrated to the United States as a young man and had a fourth grade education. My maternal grandfather, also an immigrant, owned four western wear stores in New Mexico. My mother's sister had married into a wealthy family in New York. I consequently developed a heightened sense of status and class differences from an early age, and an appreciation for the working class greatly influenced by my creative and free-thinking paternal grandfather.

I played football and wrestled as an adolescent, and I continued to be an avid reader. Vance Packard and J. D. Salinger were particular favorites. After my parents' divorce, my mother remarried, and we moved to suburban Kansas City. I was one of the few of my classmates who left Kansas for college. At UC Berkeley, I was an editor and columnist on the *Daily Cal* newspaper and played intramural sports. I had the experience of studying with Troy Duster, Kenneth Jowitt, Philippe Nonet, Philip Selznick, and Neil Smelser. At Troy's home, jazz was on and his painting easel was always up. Speaking hardly a word, he let the undergraduates in the senior seminar struggle over the works of theorists like Norman O. Brown and Herbert Marcuse. Unlike most of my fellow undergraduates, I had a dim view of most normative theorizing, and I wrote a senior essay entitled, "A Critique of the Frankfurt School's Critical Theory."

I attended graduate school at Harvard, where I studied with Ann Swidler, James A. Davis, and Daniel Bell. I became engaged with educational studies in 1977 as a research assistant for Jerome Karabel, who had obtained a large grant from the National Institute of Education to study "power and ideology in higher education." Karabel also ran a weekly evening seminar in which we discussed books of theoretical significance that bore on educational studies. Here I encountered and debated works by Bourdieu, Bowles and Gintis, Collins, Konrad and Szelenyi, Jencks, Meyer and Rowan, Sarfatti Larson, and many others. Those who attended the seminar included Paul DiMaggio, Kevin Dougherty, David Karen, Katherine McClelland, David Stark, David Swartz, and Michael Useem. My dissertation, "Stirrings of an Oppositional Elite," written under the supervision of Daniel Bell, used survey data to analyze the plausibility of the various "new-class" theories that were circulating at the time. These theories foresaw the development of a new intellectually oriented professional class with distinct interests from business elites. I was the first to examine "new-class" theories systematically with empirical data (see Brint, 1984).

## INTELLECTUAL ORIENTATION

I have worked at the intersection of the sociology of education, the sociology of the professions, and the study of middle-class politics. In my work on schooling, I have taken the explicit purposes (or functions) of schooling (cultural transmission, socialization, and social selection) more seriously than most sociologists, but I have historicized them, subjected them to critical analysis, and rooted them in political contestation. I have identified the key features of schools and universities as social structures, while simultaneously examining them as objects of contestation influenced by powerful external actors who attempt to use them to advance new forms of organization that reflect their major constituencies' interests and ideals. I have "frozen" schools and universities as crystallized social structures, and I have watched them "flow" over time under the influence of contending forces. My approach reflects the characteristic Weberian interests in the causes of transformations in social organization and the characterization of the crystallized structures that emerge from these transformations. Like Weber, I have emphasized the ideal and material interests of organizational managers as much as those of powerful external actors. Much of my work has been motivated by skepticism toward the dominant but dubious views of intellectuals and policy makers. Some has been motivated by a search for better data with which to answer questions in which I became interested.

## U.S. TWO-YEAR COLLEGES

In *The Diverted Dream* (1989), Karabel and I examined a new type of educational organization, the two-year junior (later community) college, founded for the first time in 1900. We emphasized that the junior colleges were justified on the basis of the progressive American ideology of opportunity, but in fact their founding was sponsored by leading university presidents and deans who saw the new colleges as a way to create a bulwark between their own institutions and the large numbers of under-prepared students they feared would seek admission. We also focused on the interests of the small band of junior college specialists who sought to escape the sense of subordinate status they experienced by adopting a new identity as the leading provider of occupationally-relevant post-secondary education. We emphasized the subsequent assembly of a powerful coalition of supporters for the new colleges' mission, led by the Kellogg Foundation, the Carnegie Corporation, and the Nixon Administration. We developed a framework in which the interests of powerful social actors in the colleges' environment is refracted through the lens of managerial interests in developing a distinctive status and identity.

Community colleges are the greatest success story of U.S. higher education in the 20th century, judging by the share of post-secondary students they enrolled. We accounted for this success by emphasizing their organizational assets: geographical closeness to most students, low cost, dual tracks (transfer and occupational), and the development of community support through offering adult education and avocational courses. We also emphasized that the institutional success of the community colleges was built on a massive failure: most students failed to complete any degree. We attributed these failures to the students' lack of preparation for college work, the colleges' low levels of student support services, and the confusing proliferation of pathways through the colleges.

In subsequent work on the origins and transformation of community colleges (Brint & Karabel, 1991), we criticized neo-institutional theories of schooling for failing to appreciate the role of powerful influences in the environment on the founding and transformations of educational institutions. We also criticized the neo-institutionalists' failure to take managerial interests into account. We used the community college case to offer generalizations about the environmental opportunities and organizational asset bases that allowed for the successful entry of new forms into established educational systems. In a later work of self-reflection (Brint, 2003), I regretted the tendency in *The Diverted Dream* to equate transfer to four-year colleges with better labor market opportunities, acknowledging that some occupational programs, such as nursing and electronics technology, showed generally strong labor market outcomes. I also emphasized, more than we had originally, the role of political progressivism as an element in the founding of the first junior colleges. At the same time, I observed that conditions for young people entering community colleges had deteriorated in several respects following the publication of *The Diverted Dream*, given the evidence that remedial courses were growing but with only limited success and the large number of students who were unable to find the classes they needed to make timely progress to their degrees.

## U.S. FOUR-YEAR COLLEGES AND UNIVERSITIES

In *The Ends of Knowledge*, now nearing completion, I examine organizational and cultural change in U.S. four-year colleges and universities between 1980 and 2015. Theoretically, the book focuses on the structural consequences of expansion and demographic change. In human systems, I argue that growth is misconceived as simply a flow, a magnification, or a flowering. It typically brings benefits, to be sure, but these benefits are unequally distributed. To understand the consequences of growth fully it is important to see that it occurs within systems of interaction. That means that it is *channelled*. Growth follows along previously structured paths and it occurs in contexts that give it shape. That means also that it creates *new openings*. It permits the possibility of new organizational forms built by educational entrepreneurs who find that they can compete successfully with existing organizations. It causes *pooling* of common sentiment. It creates new interest groups and it motivates other groups to oppose their assertions. Under conditions of scarcity and preference, it creates *fissuring* of structures. It expands fissures within systems and creates divergent trajectories. Growth stimulates many of those who are newly incorporated to great effort, while at the same time risking lower levels of performance on average. It causes the development of *outlets*. It creates and legitimates safe zones for those who cannot succeed on the educational terms of the system, bringing the margins closer to the center and even, at times, giving the margins precedence over the center. It encourages the construction of *barriers*. It promotes the development of new forms of academic differentiation and higher levels of credentialing as protection against the dilution of performance norms. And it creates competition among potential *regulators*. It commands the attention of the powerful, and it creates interests among some with vision and resources to direct its power toward ends they identify as in the public interest.

Under the urging of a growth coalition led by the major philanthropies and the White House, I argue that the higher education industry in the United States is moving toward complete market penetration. Unlike many consumer product industries in which adaptive upgrading of products is required for firms to stay in business over the long run, higher education can pursue market penetration without adaptive upgrading simply by setting up incomparable quality levels through selective admissions and granting baccalaureates to those whose performance would not pass muster in the better secondary schools. In the context of selective admissions and no industrywide standards for baccalaureate level performance, the paradox of market penetration is that it provides real opportunity for many who would otherwise be excluded, while at the same time ensuring that the average college degree counts for less and less with respect to the cognitive side of human capital development.

I emphasize the identification of first-generation students as a key status group in the press for complete market penetration. Where financial aid is available, upwardly mobile first-generation college students, most of them from low-income backgrounds, are the human power source driving market penetration. They have the pride of coming from families that overcame obstacles to achieve the American dream and the motivation to prove their worth against those who doubt it. They are the natural audience for the rhetoric of opportunity and the natural repository for resentment against social exclusions. Social incorporation is essential to the teleology of market penetration. It therefore should come as no surprise that a harmony of interests exists between college and foundation presidents who take up the values of inclusion and diversity and the students whose persistence will be required to realize the college completion agenda. Although built on the rhetoric of opportunity, the higher education system continues to yield disproportionate benefits to those who are well prepared by family and prior school background to succeed at the levels that count. The paradox of the first-generation is that students misrecognize the endpoint of the system as opportunity and degree attainment, rather than market penetration, and consequently run the risk of a bitter awakening when the futures that seem to beckon materialize in a disproportionate way for the already advantaged.

I also emphasize the development of a mass intellectual and professional stratum. A larger undergraduate population produces a larger graduate population, both because more graduate students are needed to staff undergraduate sections, and because undergraduates who want to stand out in labor markets in which the baccalaureate has become normative without standing for have little choice but to pursue higher level degrees. These higher level degrees, particularly the first professional degrees and the doctorate create something that is truly new human society, a mass of people with advanced degrees. These people are trained to read the literatures in their fields, to consider empirical evidence, and to reason systematically through problems and are absorbed not just in universities, but also in a wide range of institutions in society. Some of these people become idea and knowledge generators in their own right. Universities consequently are no longer the "service stations" for society, as Kerr (1963) viewed them. Instead the conventions of research permeate and universities become one center of ideas and knowledge generation among others. This becomes increasingly true as tenure track positions in colleges and universities fail to keep pace with the growth of undergraduate enrollments, and more doctoral degree recipients seek employment outside the university. Universities continue to generate many ideas and inventions, but they also become more a partner than a source. Many ideas and inventions are jointly produced by research workers inside and outside the university. Equally, ideas that are generated outside of the university enter universities for refining and testing. In this respect the university becomes more often a reviser and adjudicator of ideas and less often a source.

I emphasize the phenomenon of dynamic creativity at the top of the system and mass processing at the bottom. The resources available to the top 40 or so U.S. research universities have allowed them to extend the distance between themselves and the remaining 6,000 colleges and universities in the country. Drawing on large endowments, extraordinary grant funding, and high tuition charges, the top of the system is remarkably productive, both in its research accomplishments and in the educational opportunities it provides. One measure of leadership dynamics can be found in the production of influential articles, which have become more concentrated over time. A new model of the "creative" type of man is developing at these institutions, in business and engineering as much as in design and the arts. For example, students have the opportunity at MIT to install workshops in their dormitory rooms, so that they can build and tinker all night, if they wish, and students at Stanford can work on projects with professors whose innovations launched the digital revolution. If they have good ideas to bring to market, they will have access to venture capital funds to pursue them. By contrast, in some public institutions, students choose from among dozens of fully online degree and certificate programs and hundreds of individual online classes. Even those that are taught face-to-face often feature assessments based on machine-graded examinations. I argue that changes in the stratification structure of U.S. higher education in these ways mirror changes in the opportunity structure of American society, where the top tenth of one percent of households, by recent estimates, own twenty-two percent of the country's wealth (Saez & Zucman, 2014).

I also discuss disciplinary divergence. When college going was rare, the prestige of the disciplines mattered little. Science and engineering were prestigious because of their association with industrial and technological progress, but the humanities were also prestigious because of their association with wealth and cultivation. The arrival of mass higher education challenged and finally eroded that rough equality. Academic status became associated with perceptions of rigor and capacities for abstraction. Mathematics and physics stood atop of this hierarchy, with only economics and philosophy from the social sciences and humanities ranking high. A parallel hierarchy of labor market opportunities undoubtedly impressed students and their parents more—with engineering and business students having the best chance at good salaries, followed by those in physical and life sciences, the social sciences, the humanities and the arts, and, finally, education and human services. These hierarchies are the result not only of the relative demand for educated labor, but also the elimination of many prospective majors from the more advantaged quantitative fields. While providing a relatively stable prestige order, useful to university administrators in the allocation of resources, the hierarchy and the elimination process also created awkward imbalances in university life, including the reliance of universities on non-quantitative fields to provide "soft landing" spots more than rigorous training requirements and to subsidize the sciences and engineering. Faculty members in non-quantitative fields taught on average more for lower pay, confronted less motivated students, and, perhaps for these reasons, also required less from their students. The humanities are particularly challenging. Nevertheless, given their distinctive role within the university, their still-healthy enrollments, and the continuing support they receive from cultural institutions, it would be a mistake to see the humanities as facing extinction.

However, humanities fields with few majors are endangered. The disciplinary hierarchy has been reinforced by the educational improvement efforts of professional accreditors and the identifications of those who teach interpretive fields. Engineering and business accreditors are now requiring that students develop social as well as technical skills, reducing long-standing advantages of the humanities and social sciences. By contrast, large numbers of students and faculty in the humanities and interpretive social sciences fields identify with the dispossessed whose condition mirrors their own.

I chart the drift upward of policy making authority. The federal government has of course been an important actor in U.S. higher education since the time of the Morrill

Act. Research universities could not perform their work without federal funding for research, and neither colleges nor universities would survive without the billions of dollars provided by the federal government in Pell grants, guaranteed student loans and indirectly through tax benefits for parents whose students attend college. Prior to the 1990s, the system was marked by decentralization, with peer review important in the distribution of grants and financial aid awarded to students to use as they saw fit. Since the 1990s, a new more activist regulatory and policy environment has begun to emerge. The major philanthropies have been the leaders of the movement toward prescriptive centralization guided by the college completion agenda. The Obama Administration has signaled its intention to play a more directive role as well. The Administration's plan centered on a ratings system that would compare colleges to one another on the measures the Administration identified as important to American families, including average tuition costs, graduation rates, and average amount of debt at graduation. Prescriptive centralization can create greater focus on meeting important national goals, but it risks the vitality that comes from a decentralized system upholding a wide variety of values. The State is understandably concerned with efficiency, but high quality education is often not particularly efficient.

## THE COLLEGES & UNIVERSITIES 2000 PROJECT

The *Ends of Knowledge* was influenced by papers my research group and I produced in the years 2000–2014 with the support of foundation and National Science Foundation funding. During this time, the *Colleges & Universities 2000 Project* team, which I directed, constructed two large databases: the Institutional Data Archive on American Higher Education (IDA) and the College Catalog Study Database (CCS). We also constructed a database on the consequences of the Great Recession for U.S. higher education based on coding of reports found in LexisNexis for a sample of more than 300 colleges and universities. These databases became important sources for our work on U.S. higher education.

We found a technique for identifying the latent structure of the higher education field through cluster analysis of institutional characteristics, with findings that departed from the accepted view promulgated by the Carnegie Classification. We found the key structural characteristics to be selectivity, control, and highest degree awarded. We identified seven primary organizational locations in the system and showed that college and university presidents chose as reference institutions those in the same structural location. We also showed that aspirations to move up the hierarchy were common among the higher enrollment and financially stronger institutions in each segment. Upwardly mobile public institutions tended to want to offer higher level degrees and upwardly mobile private institutions tended to want to become more selective (Brint, Riddle, & Hanneman, 2006).

We studied curricula extensively. We found that the center of gravity in U.S. higher education since the 1930s has been occupational-professional education, with a brief reversion to emphasis on arts and sciences in the 1960s (Brint et al., 2005).

Our studies led us to develop many reasons to criticize neo-institutional theories of the convergence of organizational structures to mimic dominant models. We found that multiple models of general education have been supported by legislative fiat, informal networks, or long-standing conventions (Brint et al., 2011). Similarly, we found that interdisciplinary programs have been much more popular at liberal arts oriented institutions, larger institutions, and high-status institutions than elsewhere in the system (Brint et al., 2009). Large and high-status organizations have been much more likely than others to add newly emerging academic fields, such as neuroscience and international business (Brint et al., 2011), and they have been much more likely to protect declining liberal arts fields such as romance languages (Brint et al., 2012). The capacity for adaptation that comes from high enrollments and robust finances allow some institutions to innovate without withdrawing from traditional fields. The opposite is true for low capacity institutions. Mission also matters: liberal arts oriented institutions tend to stay that way; they are reluctant to add occupational fields or to withdraw from traditional arts and sciences fields (Brint et al., 2005; Brint et al., 2012). Public institutions also show distinctive missions; unlike privates they are more interested in developing specialists in a broad range of fields than in cutting edge creative work in a smaller number of fields (Brint, 2005). They have inherited a strong interest in applied fields that serve society, and they have much greater interest in making social contributions through providing opportunities to low-income populations (Brint, 2007). Nor have we seen convergence in decision-making structures; large public universities tend to involve more actors in decision making, while private institutions are more likely to include members of their boards in all levels of decision making (Apkarian et al., 2014).

We also explored the influence of market forces in U.S. higher education. The term "market forces" has been used to encompass a wide range of external and internal influences. Only some of these market forces have been influential. For example, we found that patterns of donor support and changing student interests do affect the growth and decline of academic fields. However, changes in labor market conditions and government funding priorities did not show effects on the growth and decline of fields. Moreover, the pattern of progressive enclosure of labor market opportunities in professional and managerial occupations, particularly in those occupations in which fewer than 80 percent but more than half of workers had college degrees in 1980, were as important as any of the market forces we studied (Brint et al., 2013).

## STUDENT CULTURE AND TEACHING REFORM

Another strand of work that contributed to *The Ends of Knowledge* grew out of survey analyses of the student experience through my involvement as a faculty associate at the Center for Studies in Higher Education at UC Berkeley. Here I served with my colleagues John Aubrey Douglass and Gregg Thomson as a principal researcher on the UC Undergraduate Experiences Survey (UCUES) and later in the same role on the Student Experience in the Research University (SERU) Survey. The latter included some two dozen major public research universities and nearly a dozen international partners.

Our research using these data initially focused on disciplinary differences. We found important differences in cultures of engagement between science and engineering fields and humanities and social science fields. Net of covariates, the culture of engagement for students in science and engineering grew out of a focus on improving quantitative skills, studying with and helping others, conscientious attendance in class, and it was rooted in a high value placed on prestigious and well-paying jobs. The culture of engagement for students in humanities and social science fields was, by contrast, associated with active participation in class, asking "insightful" questions, interaction with professors, and other measures of overt interest in class materials (Brint, Cantwell, & Hanneman, 2008). A subsequent study explored differences between the disciplines in work effort, conscientiousness, and analytical and critical thinking. Students in science and engineering disciplines scored high on work effort (as measured by hours spent studying and attending class). They also scored higher on measures of conscientiousness. We expected students in the humanities and social sciences to shine on our measures of analytical and critical thinking, but instead, we found few disciplinary differences on these measures (Brint, Cantwell, & Saxena, 2012).

From my experience as an instructor, I had developed concerns about the average level of students' academic engagement and competence. Cantwell and I studied time use in the University of California and found that students were spending more than 40 hours a week on average in social and recreational activities but only 26–27 hours a week on study and attending class. Women, students who had achieved high GPAs, and science and engineering students were more likely to spend longer hours in study (Brint & Cantwell, 2010). In a subsequent study, we developed a theory of student disengagement and studied the composition of disengaged student populations. We found that one-quarter of students said they rarely if ever participated in class or communicated with their professors and one-fifth of students said they worked on their studies 18 hours or less each week and completed 50 percent or less of assigned reading (Brint & Cantwell, 2014). Sadly, the results of this work added to a long list of research, beginning with Derek Bok's *Our Underachieving Colleges* (2006) that question the extent to which U.S. research universities are successful as teaching and learning institutions.

These findings led me to wonder whether students were learning as much or more in student clubs and organizations. Our research failed to confirm this hypothesis, but we found that one-fifth or more of our respondents said they had had three or more experiences planning events, promoting events, facilitating discussions and recruiting new members – all experiences relevant to success in adult life. These findings of course have important implications for the future of physical campuses and the substitutability of online instruction for the physical campus experience.

The obverse side of this interest in student culture has been an interest in the prospects for the reform of teaching. I described the rise of "the new progressivism" in college teaching based on project based learning and ample opportunities for interactive engagement. I questioned whether the new progressivism was typically accompanied by enough rigor and accountability for reading and study to lead to improved subject matte mastery. I discussed the sources of decline in requirements in non-quantitative fields, pointing to deteriorating labor market prospects in interpretive disciplines, the interests of higher education senior leaders in maintaining and expanding enrollments, and the concerns of many faculty members not to discourage under-prepared students from low-income backgrounds. I questioned whether the accountability movement would accomplish much to change these dynamics. I emphasized that most faculty members treated accountability requirements as compliance make-work and failed to see their relevance to student achievement. In addition, some faculty members resented the intrusion of external agencies into the classroom (Brint, 2011). At the same time, I emphasized that a good empirical record has emerged on practices associated with effective teaching in large lecture courses, and that the evidence from this work has the potential to improve undergraduate teaching and learning dramatically (see Brint & Clotfelter, 2016).

## SCHOOLING IN COMPARATIVE-HISTORICAL PERSPECTIVE

A final major interest has been in the understanding of schooling in a comparative-historical perspective. The centerpiece of this work is *Schools and Societies* (2016), now in its third edition. The book combines an organizational analysis of the structures of schooling; an emphasis on affinities between social and educational change; and a Weberian approach to the multi-sided struggles for control of curricula, educational opportunities, and educational policy.

The book emphasizes that social institutions are intended to raise standards and to reduce the variability among children that would otherwise exist. They owe their success to the implementation of authority structures, rules, comparatively small classes, grading as a means to create status hierarchies among children related to school goals, the alternation between work and recreational time, and the creation of classroom environments in which work tasks are of pre-eminent significance. Schools can organize in a variety of ways to increase learning, notably by spending more time on task, by providing adequate learning materials, and by grouping children effectively. However, learning is only one way to raise standards and to reduce variability. The book endorses the insights of John Meyer and Brian Rowan (1977) about the importance of "ritual categories," such as "credentialed teacher" and "college graduate," as legitimating forces and mechanisms for hiding variability. It also emphasizes socialization messages both within and outside the classroom.

My intuition was that socialization was more important than any of the other ostensible purposes of schooling. By socialization, I mean the effort to inculcate and reinforce authority-approved attitudes and behaviors. The book differentiates three dimensions of conformity: behavioral, moral, and cultural. It also distinguishes four socio-historical forms of school-based socialization: the village/communal pattern, the industrializing pattern, the bureau-corporate pattern, and the elite pattern. The first transformation is from the relatively free-flowing village/communal pattern to an industrial pattern characterized by very stringent demands for behavioral control and moral conformity. The bureau-corporate/mass consumption pattern, which comes into play in middle-class neighborhoods in wealthy countries is based on impersonal control through rules and routines, relatively lower levels of moral discussion and training, and many more choices in classroom and extracurricular life. Through such mechanisms, students are acculturated to a world of bureaucratic organization and mass consumption.

I emphasize that schools are also a staging ground for developing skills in informal socialization. Just as the classroom is well designed to produce orderly and industrious employees, the playground and other informal spaces are well designed to produce adults with at least minimal levels of interpersonal skills. This production is connected to structural features of the playground. These spaces are loosely supervised by adult monitors, but not directed by them. Many children mix freely on the playground and therefore relations with a wide variety of types of children are possible. Children are similar in age, bringing a rough equality, but are usually not close neighbors or family members, encouraging repeated encounters with "strangers." On the playground, children must learn to build core groups of supporters and deal with bullies, 'tagalongs,' tattletales, false friends, snobs, and other familiar childhood types. Through confronting many types of children and diverse issues related to trust, confidence and conflict, children can become skillful navigators of relationships.

I was skeptical of the idea, associated with the work of Melvin Kohn (1972) and Samuel Bowles and Herbert Gintis (1979), that the schools propagate class-based patterns of socialization. In work with Michael T. Matthews and Mary C. Contreras (2001), studying working-class and middle-class primary schools in Southern California (and including one elite private school), I found that the main socialization messages were quite similar across schools. These messages focused on order and effort: sitting still, not bothering other children, and working hard. These are not properly construed as capitalist forms of socialization; one would not have found any different basic pattern in Bolshevik Russia or Maoist China. Instead, they express features of life in highly-organized, economically advancing societies. Anthropologists have shown that tolerance for disorder, wandering attention, and irregular effort are more common in remote regions of agrarian societies with low or moderate development trajectories. In this study, we were surprised by how few messages in any of the classrooms concerned intellectual virtues (curiosity, creativity, independent thinking). We also discovered that schools use concepts drawn from the broader culture, such as citizenship and self-esteem, and redefine them in ways that support the authority structure of the school. In the schools we studied, citizenship, for example, had nothing to do with exercise one's rights, including the right to protest. Instead, a good citizen was one who consistently followed rules.

With respect to cultural transmission, the book focused on historicizing the rise and fall of subject matter and linking these curricular changes to developments in the economy, the state, and society. I identified a number of patterns of correspondence, some related to economic relations, others to social incorporation, and still others to national political priorities. I emphasized that agrarian subjects give way as the rural economy gives way to commercial and industrial life. I emphasized that subject matter associated with highly cultivated elites tend to give way to subject matter that reflect aspirations for social incorporation. (For example, Latin and art history fall, while literature and history representative of minority group experiences gain). Both immigration patterns and national geopolitical interests affect language teaching. (For example, European languages and Russian fall, while Asian languages and Arabic gain). Coalitions are often important in transformations of curriculum. Mathematics and science entered the curriculum not only because of the advocacy of scientists, but because calculation became a more important social capacity with the rise of commercial civilization and business people favored more widespread facility with calculation. More generally, I emphasized the interplay of the State, the liberal professions, and social movements in the formation of the curriculum. One can say that the curriculum is primarily the product of the overlapping interests of the State and the liberal professions.

National language and history teaching, for example, encourage identification with the nation-state. But the messages of literature and history are the province of textbook writers who are themselves professors or who have worked closely with professors. Progressive educators, a fraction of the liberal professional stratum, fought to bring the arts and physical education into the curriculum. The State has little interest in these fields, but it conceded space. Educators have been persuasive that a focus solely on "serious" subjects is too taxing for children. However, "back to basics" movements are very popular with State officials, as well as conservatives, and cuts to the arts and physical education are tolerated if it appears that children are not succeeding in core fields. The State's interest in social incorporation has been an important influence since the Civil Rights movement and, goaded by social movement activists, has led to many changes in the literature, history, and social science curricula.

With respect to social selection, the weight of sociological work at this time was on the reproduction of class, racial-ethnic, and gender privileges through schooling. Although I acknowledged the many advantages that students from the dominant groups held in converting economic and social privileges into scholastic attainments, I also resisted what I regarded to be a one-sided emphasis on inequality. I emphasized that educational attainment itself, rather than class background or measured intelligence, is the most important influence on later life chances. Hundreds of thousands of students from the bottom half of the income distribution are identified as academically promising by school systems and thereby provided with the encouragement and tools to advance through the educational system. This capacity of the system is greatly enhanced by the existence of neighborhood schools whose students are drawn from relatively homogeneous and class differentiated populations. Because every school produces hierarchies, some students in poor neighborhoods will, by definition, achieve high rank within their schools. By contrast, if students from highly educated families were distributed more evenly across schools the opportunity to re-sort students based on school achievement would be markedly lower.

Within this context, I emphasized that social class is a constant divider across the world. Students from well-educated families come to school with a wide set of advantages. Their parents tend to use larger vocabularies, read to them at night, encourage their literacy, set aside study spaces, insist on completion of homework, provide them tutoring, get involved in the schools, travel abroad, and expose them to cultural institutions. Not all of these practices exist in every society, but these are characteristic of the types of family practices that can lead to scholastic advantages. I characterized race and ethnicity as a variable divider, because some racial-ethnic minorities do very well in school systems, while others do not. I noted the importance of timing of arrival in the host country (better to arrive at a time of rapid industrialization), the distribution of rural versus urban backgrounds, and the influence of oral versus written traditions. I also emphasized the study cultures characteristic of members of different ethnic groups once they have arrived in a host country. I characterized gender as a declining divider and, somewhat against the grain at the time, speculated on the advantages that girls held over boys in academic achievement. I also emphasized the continuing disadvantages women faced in the labor market and, within higher education, in the most highly marketable science and engineering disciplines.

I distinguished the main forms of variation in the structure of schooling systems in the advanced societies and identified consequences of these variations. I focused on distinct starting points: elite preparation and democratic uplift. These starting points influenced the trajectory of mass schooling, with the former typically leading to greater ability-based tracking and slower rates of expansion. These differences are also linked to the size of the population studying vocational subjects in secondary school. Following the work of James Rosenbaum, I emphasized differences between systems, such as the German and Japanese systems, that create close connections between occupationally oriented secondary school students and employers and those that do not create these connections (see, e.g., Rosenbaum & Binder, 1997; Rosenbaum & Kariya, 1989). Finally, I emphasized differences between systems that link admission to higher levels in the educational system to examination scores and those that use a wider range of criteria. The former tend to create a more highly concentrated focus on academics during secondary school years. These structural features were historically related to life chances, with highly tracked systems with large vocational systems and heavy emphasis on test-based mobility associated with weaker chances for success in the educational system for students from lower SES backgrounds. Students' sense of status boundaries, their commitment to discipline in study, and their levels of opportunity consciousness as compared to class consciousness are also, I argued, related to these structural characteristics of school systems. At the same time, educational expansion and the "watering down" of entrance tests have been worldwide phenomena since the 1970s and have consequently led to much greater similarity across systems in the industrialized world. Levels of inequality in society have become a much more important influence on life chances and structural differences between systems a less important influence.

I also analyzed the structures of schooling in the developing world. I emphasized the effects of colonial legacies on the structure of schooling, with most postcolonial societies erecting systems modeled in large part on those of their colonial rulers. These countries have faced the problems of poverty, traditionalism, and physical insecurity as limits on educational achievement. Nevertheless, one can see differences in the first post-colonial generation between mass mobilizing and status quo oriented (often authoritarian) leaders in these countries, with the former being more interested in and more successful in developing mass literacy and educational opportunities for the poor. The World Bank and other major international donors created a blueprint for educational development that was widely influential in the second post-colonial generation. The World Bank argued that most educational policymaking in the developing world had been a disaster with too much funding of higher education relative to primary schooling, too much funding of vocational education relative to general education, and too little private investment in schooling relative to public investment. The policies it advocated can be characterized as "back to basics" at the primary level and "let the market decide" at the post-primary level. As economic circumstances have diverged in the developing countries so too have schooling conditions. High- income countries such as Argentina, Taiwan, and Kuwait, show educational attainment profiles similar to those of industrialized societies, while educational attainments have improved only very slowly, if at all, in low-income countries and regions.

I expressed skepticism about the singularly important role of schooling in promoting economic development without discounting its relevance to this objective. When a commitment to human capital development through schooling is combined with political stability, declining population growth, effective policies for the advancement of trade and industry, and macroeconomic stability to prevent over-borrowing low-income developing countries begin to experience strong rates of growth and development. But investing in schooling without these other "success ingredients" does not typically lead to the achievement of development aims.

## TOWARD A BROADER FRAME FOR THE SOCIOLOGY OF EDUCATION

In recent years I have been involved in efforts to expand the frame of the sociology of education. I remarked on the limited scope of the sociology of education in the first edition of Schools and Societies (1998), noting that "in adult life, the knowledge taught in school does not necessarily count for more than other forms of knowledge, such as common sense, popular culture, merchandising, folklore, and religious belief" (p. 98), and implying that a broader sociology of education would be less school focused and would instead contrast schooling with competing culture- producing and knowledge-creating institutions. I broadened this nascent critique in an essay "The Collective Mind at Work" (2009 [2013]) in which I conducted a content analysis of a decade of articles in the journal Sociology of Education. I concluded that the "collective mind," as represented in the journal, was heavily quantitative, focused on K-12 schooling in the United States, and had as its major theme the effects of inequalities on academic achievement and educational attainment. In the essay I called for a sociology of education that was more international in scope, more open to qualitative work, more connected to non-school based educational influences and institutions, and focused as much on "school-to- society" links (i.e. school inputs to the shaping of society and culture) as on as "society-to-school" links (i.e. the influence of inequality on schooling). I embraced the field's achievements in the study of inequality, but argued that a more rounded perspective would lead to a better appreciation of schooling's role in the construction of society and culture.

This essay helped to launch an intellectual movement to broaden the scope of our sub-discipline, though it was certainly not the only source for that movement. The first culmination of the movement will come with the publication of Jal Mehta and Scott Davies's edited volume, *Education in a New Society*. My contribution to the volume examines the institutional geography of "knowledge trade" between universities and other social institutions. Today it is evident that knowledge originates in many institutions—universities in the United States account for only about half of basic research and much less than that of applied research. I develop a view of the university in this complex institutional ecology that partially dethrones the university as knowledge generator while at the same time showing its essential role in the adjudication of knowledge claims. I argue that the metaphor of economic trade provides a potentially illuminating lens for understanding academic knowledge and its intercourse with knowledge originating in other institutional domains. I develop a vocabulary for understanding the primary forms of interaction between academic knowledge and knowledge originating in other spheres of society. A *knowledge-producing institution* is any institution that creates a body of knowledge that shapes practice and is based on more than assertion, convention, or opinion. Examples include: formulas for successful popular culture genres, influential management tools such as "the balanced scorecard," yogic philosophy and practice, charettes in architecture, and scenario planning in the military. I develop a vocabulary for discussing universities and the institutional geography of knowledge trade. *Knowledge exports and imports* are bodies of knowledge that pass into new institutional arenas and are either appropriated wholesale, or are subjected to processes of testing, refinement, and revision consistent with the practices and purposes of the adopting institutional arena. *Trade routes* describe the direction and heaviness of the traffic from one institutional domain to another. *Barriers to cross-institutional trade* in order of severity consist of corrupted knowledge goods (i.e. those influenced by the interests of the importing institution), failed exchanges, and, in rare instances, boycotts and blockades. *Meta-cognitive metropoles* are the centers of adjudication of truth claims. When one broadens the scope of knowledge creation beyond academe, it seems clear that knowledge generation is not a monopoly of academe, but that the adjudicatory function remains a near-monopoly (Brint forthcoming).

## CONCLUSION

An intellectual self-portrait ought to be a recounting not only of how one thought about the subjects of one's work, but the personal and intellectual influences on that thinking. My own experiences of ambivalence about schooling no doubt played an important role in the development of my thinking. I found reading to be a magic carpet that brought me wherever I wanted to travel and into deep encounters with people I wanted to know more about. Family relations in our household were sometimes rocky, and I consequently valued the predictable structures and practices of school. Yet I was often terrifically bored by classroom life—to the extent that I refused to attend school for nearly an entire year at age eight. I experienced tensions throughout my early life reconciling my intellectual interests with the business orientation of my maternal family. I was emotionally moved by the attempts of the first professors I met to heal the wounds of the Kansas City riots of 1968 by bringing together adolescents from the suburbs and the inner-city for "rap sessions" about race. This experience led me to see the possibilities of teaching in a different light. I was greatly influenced by my teachers at Berkeley, particularly by the clarity and structure of Neil Smelser's lectures (and his good humor in the face of student-radical critics) and the freedom of thought and creativity fostered by Troy Duster. Close intellectual friendships with Jerome Karabel, Eliot Freidson, and Robert Hanneman were pivotal influences on my thinking and my work. I was fortunate to find a kindred spirit and constantly stimulating interlocutor in my wife, the historian Michele Renee Salzman. Reading Max Weber was the decisive intellectual experience of my life. I have done my best to carry Weber's sensibilities and lessons into the study of schooling.

## MY FAVORITE TEXTS BY OTHERS

Max Weber, *The Sociology of Religion*
Willard Waller, *The Sociology of Teaching*
Reinhard Bendix, *Nation-building and Citizenship*
Philip Selznick, *Leadership in Administration*
Seymour Martin Lipset, *Political Man*
Richard Hofstadter, *Anti-Intellectualism in American Thought*

Clark Kerr, *The Uses of the University*
Gianfranco Poggi, *The Development of the Modern State*
Daniel Bell, *The Coming of Post-Industrial Society*
Randall Collins, *Conflict Sociology*
John W. Meyer and Brian Rowan, "Education as an Institution"
Randall Collins, "Some Comparative Principles of Educational Stratification"
Magali Sarfatti Larson, *The Rise of Professionalism*
Randall Collins, *The Credential Society*
Jerome Karabel and A.H. Halsey, "Introduction" In Karabel and Halsey, *Power and Ideology in Education*
Eliot Freidson, *Professional Powers*
W. Richard Scott, *Organizations: Rational, Natural, and Open Systems*
W. Richard Scott, *Organizations and Institutions*
Eliot Freidson, *Professionalism: The Third Logic*
John W. Meyer, "Reflections on Institutional Theories of Organization." In Royston Greenwood et al. *Institutional Theories of Organization*

## MY FAVORITE PERSONAL TEXTS

"'New-Class' and Cumulative Trend Explanations of the Liberal Political Attitudes of Professionals" *American Journal of Sociology*, 1984.
*The Diverted Dream (with Jerome Karabel)* New York: Oxford University Press, 1989.
"Institutional Origins and Transformations" In Walter W. Powell and Paul J. DiMaggio (eds.) *The New Institutionalism in Organizational Studies*. Chicago: University of Chicago Press, 1991.
*In An Age of Experts*. Princeton: Princeton University Press, 1994.
"Professionals and the Knowledge Society" *Current Sociology*, 2001.
"Gemeinschaft Revisited" *Sociological Theory*, 2001.
"Socialization Messages in Primary Schools: An Organizational Analysis" *Sociology of Education*, 2001.
"Creating the Future: The 'New Directions' in American Research Universities" *Minerva*, 2005.
*Schools and Societies*, 2nd ed. Stanford: Stanford University Press, 2006.
"Reference Sets, Identities, and Aspirations in a Complex Organizational Field: The Case of American Four-Year Colleges and Universities" (with Mark Riddle and Robert A. Hanneman) *Sociology of Education*, 2006.
"The Market Model and the Rise and Fall of Academic Disciplines" (with Kristopher Proctor, Scott Patrick Murphy and Robert A. Hannenan) *Sociological Forum*, 2011.
"The Collective Mind at Work" *Sociology of Education*, 2013.

## REFERENCES

Apkarian, J., Mulligan, K., Rotondi, M. B., & Brint, S. (2014). Who governs? Academic decision-making in U.S. Four-year colleges and universities, 2000–2012. *Tertiary Education and Management, 20*(2), 1–14.
Bok, D. (2006). *Our under-achieving colleges*. Princeton, NJ: Princeton University Press.
Bowles, S., & Gintis, H. J. (1979). *Schooling in capitalist America*. New York, NY: Basic Books.
Brint, S. (2003). Few remaining dreams: Community colleges since 1985. *Annals of the American Academy of Political and Social Science, 586*(March), 16–37.
Brint, S. (2005). Creating the future: 'New Directions' in American Research Universities. *Minerva, 43*, 23–50.
Brint, S. (2006). *Schools and societies* (2nd ed.). Stanford, CA: Stanford University Press.
Brint, S. (2007). Can public research universities compete? In R. L. Geiger, C. L. Colbeck, C. K. Anderson, & R. L. Williams (Eds.), *The future of American public research universities* (pp. 91–118). Rotterdam: Sense Publishers.

Brint, S. (2011). Focus on the classroom: Movements to reform teaching and learning in U.S. colleges and universities, 1980–2005. In J. C. Hermanowicz (Ed.), *The American academic profession* (pp. 44–91). Baltimore, MA: Johns Hopkins Press.

Brint, S. (2013). The collective mind at work: A decade in the life of U.S. sociology of education. *Sociology of Education, 86*, 273–279.

Brint, S. (Forthcoming). *The ends of knowledge: Organizational and cultural change in U.S. Four-Year Colleges and Universities, 1980–2015*.

Brint, S., & Cantwell, A. M. (2010). Undergraduate time use and academic outcomes. *Teachers College Record, 112*, 2441–2470.

Brint, S., & Cantwel, A. M. (2014). Conceptualizing, measuring and analyzing the characteristics of disengaged student populations: Results from UCUES 2010. *Journal of College Student Development, 55*(8), 808–823.

Brint, S., & Clotfelter, C. T. (2016). Higher education effectiveness: An introduction. In S. Brint & C. T. Clotfelter (Eds.), *Higher education effectiveness* (pp. 2–37). New York, NY: Russell Sage Foundation Press.

Brint, S., & Karabel, J. (1989). *The diverted dream: Community colleges and the promise of educational opportunity in America, 1900–1985*. New York, NY: Oxford University Press.

Brint, S., & Karabel, J. (1991). Institutional origins and transformations: The case of American Community Colleges. In W. W. Powell & P. J. DiMaggio (Eds.), *The new institutionalism in organizational analysis* (pp. 337–360). Chicago, IL: University of Chicago Press.

Brint, S., Contreras, M. C., & Matthews, M. T. (2001). Socialization messages in primary schools: An organizational analysis. *Sociology of Education, 74*, 157–180.

Brint, S., Riddle, M., Turk-Bicakci, L., & Levy, C. S. (2005). From the liberal to the practical arts in American colleges and universities: Organizational analysis and curricular change. *The Journal of Higher Education, 76*, 151–180.

Brint, S., Riddle, M., & Hanneman, R. A. (2006). Reference sets, identities, and aspirations in a complex organizational field: The case of American four-year colleges and universities. *Sociology of Education, 79*, 126–140.

Brint, S., Cantwell, A. M., & Hanneman, R. A. (2008). The two cultures of undergraduate academic engagement. *Research in Higher Education, 49*, 383–402.

Brint, S., Turk-Bicakci, L., Proctor, K., & Murphy, S. P. (2009). Expanding the social frame: The growth and distribution of interdisciplinary degree-granting programs in American colleges and universities, 1975–2000. *Review of Higher Education, 32*, 155–183.

Brint, S., Proctor, K., Murphy, S. P., Mulligan, K., Rotondi, M. B., & Hanneman, R. A. (2011). Who are the early adopters? The institutionalization of academic growth fields in U.S. four-year colleges and universities, 1975–2005. *Higher Education, 61*, 563–585.

Brint, S., Cantwell, A. M., & Saxena, P. (2012). Disciplinary categories, majors, and undergraduate academic experiences: Rethinking Bok's 'Under-achieving Colleges' Thesis. *Research in Higher Education, 53*, 1–25.

Brint, S., Proctor, K., Mulligan, K., Rotondi, M. B., & Hanneman, R. A. (2012). Declining academic fields in U.S. four-year colleges and universities, 1970–2006. *The Journal of Higher Education, 83*, 583–613.

Brint, S., Proctor, K., Murphy, S. P., & Hanneman, R. A. (2012). The market model and the growth and decline of academic fields in U.S. four-year colleges and universities, 1980–2000. *Sociological Forum, 27*, 275–299.

Brint, S., Proctor, K., Murphy, S. P., Turk-Bicakci, L., & Hanneman, R. A. (2009). General education models: The changing meanings of liberal education in American colleges and universities, 1975–2000. *The Journal of Higher Education, 80*, 605–642.

Kerr, C. (1963). *The uses of the university*. Cambridge, MA: Harvard University Press.

Mehta, J., & Davies, S. (Forthcoming). *Education in a new society*. Chicago, IL: University of Chicago Press.

Meyer, J., & Rowan, B. (1977). Institutionalized organizations: Formal structure as myth and ceremony. *American Journal of Sociology, 83*, 340–363.

Rosenbaum, J. E., & Binder, A. (1997). Do employers really need more educated youth? *Sociology of Education, 70*, 68–85.

Rosenbaum, J. E., & Kariya, K. (1989). From high school to work: Market and institutional mechanisms in Japan. *American Journal of Sociology, 94*, 1334–1365.

Saez, E., & Zucman, G. (2014). *The distribution of U.S. wealth, capital income, and returns since 1913* (Unpublished paper). University of California, Department of Economics, Berkeley, CA.

*Steven Brint*
*University of California*
*Riverside*

SARA DELAMONT

# 5. COM MUITO AXÉ

*Or "Can a Woman Be an Intellectual?"*

The phrase of the title, which is in Brazilian Portuguese, means 'with maximum energy' or 'with all the force you can muster'. The subtitle is one I used when speaking at a conference in Finland to celebrate the 400th anniversary of the University of Helsinki. I asked rhetorically 'Can an Intellectual be a Woman? Can a Woman be an Intellectual?' and focused on the women of the First (1890–1920) Chicago School of Sociology. If the first phrase is my aim, the second is my 'meaning of life' question. The first phrase needs further explanation. *Axé* is a word of Yoruba (West African) origin, used in the African-Brazilian religion *Candomblé* and, as *Ache* in African-Cuban Santería, to mean the power of the gods and goddesses (*Orixas* in Portuguese, *Orichas* in Spanish). It is used in the African-Brazilian dance and martial art, *capoeira*, to mean positive energy, or a positive charge a bit like The Force in *Star Wars*. The phrase is the title of a *capoeira* song composed by *Mestre* (Master) Kenura called 'Woman, oh Woman'. The song urges, or exhorts, women to play *capoeira* with maximal emotional and physical engagement. *Capoeira* is the only martial art that is always done to music: five instruments are played including drums, songs in a call and response pattern are sung, and everyone claps the rhythm. The music raises the *axé*, so the players have more energy and the games are better.

I have chosen the first phrase for two related reasons. It summarises my academic life because I have always tried to engage in educational research with *muito axé*. For the past fourteen years I have been doing educational research on *capoeira* classes in the UK, focusing on the learning environment and on how it is taught and learnt far away from Brazil: that is diasporic *capoeira* (Assuncao, 2005). This is the first autobiographical piece I have written for an educational research audience in the USA, so I have sketched in the other autobiographical fragments that have been published which are probably unknown to readers of this volume, because they are located in books or periodicals issued outside the USA or not in educational journals. This piece does not recapitulate those earlier reflections. There are three items (Delamont, 2012a, 2003, 2008) in sociological or feminist publications, and one educational paper in a journal based in New Zealand (Delamont, 2006). Delamont (2012a) is an autobiographical paper in a collection of symbolic interactionist writing, that contrasts my life with that of my mother who was a bohemian neopagan witch. It adds to the brief 'personal note' in my book *Feminist Sociology* (Delamont, 2003, xiii) and Delamont (2008) includes a reflexive autobiographical element in a paper on feminist methods. Most relevant to what follows here is Delamont (2006) which locates my educational research in the context of some biographical episodes. In this essay I have given a very brief outline of my life and career, contextualised in the context of the UK education system, and then focused on the key ideas that have driven my educational research since 1968, when I began my doctoral research, in sections on the growth of ethnography, a weakness I freely confess to, and my three key principles.

## BRIEF LIFE HISTORY

I was born in 1947 in Southampton, a port on the south coast of England. I went to a single sex selective secondary (grammar) school near Southampton, and then to Cambridge to Girton College (then all female) to read Archaeology and Anthropology, specialising in Social (in American terms, cultural) anthropology. From the age of seven I had planned to be a barrister (a trial lawyer) but by the time I was 17 I had discovered that all the men I knew reading law were finding it very dull *and* that to be a barrister I would need a parental subsidy for about five years after graduation. Deciding that there would not be any such subsidy I chose to be an anthropologist instead.

England had the 11+ exam for my generation, which I passed in 1956 to get to grammar school, and I was the first pupil from the new school (it had opened in 1954) to get into Oxford or Cambridge. Girton, founded in 1869 by feminists (see Delamont, 1989), was the first college for women at either Oxford or Cambridge, and its feminist tradition was still strong in the 1960s. I got a first class degree in 1968 and went to Edinburgh to do a PhD in educational research, committed to ethnographic fieldwork as the method of choice. The UK does not have education as a subfield of anthropology so I was *de facto* migrating to sociology. The UK PhD does not have any courses or examinations: it is entirely earned by researching a thesis. My thesis was classroom observation in an elite Scottish girls' school (I call by the pseudonym St Luke's) and I defended it in 1973. By then I had been appointed to a lectureship in England, at Leicester. It was there that I became involved in the ORACLE (Observational Research and Classroom Learning Environment) Project, which ran from 1975–1981. That project is published in Delamont and Galton (1986).

In 1976 I moved to a lectureship in the sociology department at Cardiff (the capital of Wales) where I have been ever since. So since I turned 21 I have lived in Scotland (for five years) and in Wales, spending only three years in England. The four nations of the UK have different education systems at school and university level, and only England's is run from London, a fact most English and nearly all non-British educational researchers are unaware of. I have never married, or had any children: Paul Atkinson and I have lived together since 1970. I love detective stories (mysteries), cricket, *capoeira*, Brazilian music and visiting Italy and Greece.

The highlights of my research of the past 45 years have been projects located where anthropology, sociology and history intersect to focus on education, broadly defined. I have also written and taught about the anthropology of the Mediterranean and of Brazil, and published on qualitative methods. My doctoral research and my time at Girton led me to investigate the modern (since 1848) history of education for clever elite women in the UK and in other English speaking countries. That work is presented in Delamont (1989) and a series of papers. The ethnography of 'St Luke's' led on to other ethnographic research in educational settings, such as English and Welsh comprehensive secondary schools. An interest in how social classes and other social entities such as professions, science, and academic disciplines are reproduced in western societies, can be seen in all my work, usually with gender as a core theme, and often focused on elites. Those ideas are all apparent in work on how academic social science and science disciplines reproduce themselves: a funded project that was sadly based only on interviews not observation, with doctoral students and their supervisors (see Delamont, Atkinson, & Parry, 2000). In 2002 I began the investigation which I am still doing on *capoeira* and in 2009 I added a subsidiary ethnography of *savate* (French kick boxing), for reasons explained below.

I have been lucky enough to hold office and get awards. BERA (The British Educational Research Association) was founded in 1974 with 100 invited inaugural members of which I was one. I served as the first ever woman President in 1984, and was given the John Nisbet Award for lifetime service in 2015. I was involved in the founding of ALSIS, the forerunner of the UK Academy of Social Sciences, in the 1980s, and was elected an academician (a fellow) in 2000. I was awarded a DScEcon in 2007, and accepted as a Fellow of the Learned Society of Wales in 2014. In 2013 the BSA (British Sociological Association) gave me its Lifetime Award. Ironically I still think of myself as primarily an anthropologist. Generally, I describe myself as an ethnographer, a feminist, and a symbolic interactionist, rather than by discipline.

## ETHNOGRAPHY GROWS

The whole of my career has coincided with the growth of research in classrooms and schools. In 1968 it was still rare to find educational research (in any sector, formal or informal, for any age group, or any purpose) that focused on the processes of teaching and learning as they happen. There are four main ways in which research in education settings has grown and developed. There is a tradition of coding the teaching and learning using a pre-specified schedule to produce statistical generalisations. Flanders (1970) is a famous pioneer, and the ORACLE projects were a landmark UK project in that tradition. (See Croll, 1986 for an overview.) Linguists have worked on the talk in educational settings, usually making live recordings for subsequent transcription and analysis (Mehan, 1979; Sinclair & Coulthard, 1974). Researchers have experimented with audio visual recording, the technicalities changing as the technologies have evolved, from time lapse photography, through to full filming, with both amateur and professional 'crews' (Walker & Adelman, 1976).

My own preference has always been for ethnography, the fourth approach. By ethnography I mean, as I have explained elsewhere, (Delamont, 2012b): the use of traditional fieldnotes and ethnographic interviewing to gain access to the participants' world view(s). Fine (2003) calls this 'peopled ethnography' and has used it in the American high school (Fine, 2001) as well as many other settings. In the USA that approach spread from the anthropologists of education out to other disciplines, in the UK the approach was pioneered by people who were sociologists with intellectual sympathies for anthropological methods and for American symbolic interaction. Throughout my career the use of ethnography in educational settings: schools, colleges and informal ones: has grown steadily. In the USA the use of ethnography was pioneered by anthropologists (see Spindler, 2000), such as George and Louise Spindler and Murray and Rosalie Wax. The journal *Anthropology and Education Quarterly* and the big Handbooks (Anderson-Levitt, 2012; Levinson & Pollock, 2011) are the showcases of that approach today. In the UK there is no tradition of anthropological ethnography of education but the method has grown in popularity consistently since the pioneering work of Hargreaves (1967), Lacey (1970) and Lambart (1982).

The use of ethnography in the UK was more sociologically informed, drawing on the symbolic interactionism of the Chicago School. Its early years are described in Hammersley (1982) and its variety in Atkinson, Delamont and Hammersley (1988). The differences between the American and British 'traditions' are discussed in Delamont and Atkinson (1995) and Delamont (2012b, 2014). During the 1990s the mainstream educational research journals became more receptive to ethnographic work, and two specialist journals *Qualitative Studies in Education* (QSE) and *Ethnography and Education* were established. My academic career has been paralleled by, and a contribution to, the movement to make ethnographic research on education more acceptable and better recognised. My doctoral research on pupils' classroom styles and strategies in a Scottish elite girls' school, subsequent projects on the first weeks of new pupils in six English secondary schools (Delamont & Galton, 1986), and on mainstreaming pupils with learning difficulties in Welsh secondary schools were part of a trend. Since 2003 I have been doing ethnography on how two martial arts are taught and learnt, and there is no problem about placing that fieldwork in educational journals (Delamont, 2005; Stephens & Delamont, 2010).

## A WEAKNESS CONFESSED

I love embedding educational research in literature from beyond social science research, such as travel writing, poetry and crime fiction, and framing my findings or arguments with metaphors from other fields. All my writing starts with 'catchy' titles and quotes from some non-educational source. Delamont (2014) uses Zora Neale Hurston's (1935) *Of Mules and Men* to provide chapter subtitles ('Heading my toenails', p. 183) and opening themes 'ah come to collect some old stories'. In the advisory text on how to be a great doctoral advisor the chapters all open with quotes from Dorothy L. Sayers's (1972) *Gaudy Night*; a mystery set in an Oxford women's college in the 1930s. My textbook on fieldwork (Delamont, 1992, 2002, 2016) has an extended metaphor: the golden journey to Samarkand drawn from a poem by Flecker (1947) all about 'the last blue mountain' and trade goods of 'spikenard, mastic and terebinth'. The plenary address to the joint conference of the New Zealand and Australian Educational Research Association in 2003 used another bit of Flecker – about the four great gates of Damascus – to exemplify four possible journeys an educational research project can take, including, metaphorically, one into the terrifying and deadly desert. The only exception, which uses a conventional social science text to provide the quotes at the heads of the chapters, is the book on doctoral study, draws on Bourdieu (1988).

These flights of fancy annoy some people, but they are the way I get every project started: when writing up my part of the ORACLE project I played with writing on Greek myths about oracles at Delphi and elsewhere to begin. I have learnt that whatever strategy 'works' to get the writing going should be *used*: therefore when I am starting to write anything I find the catchy title, the opening quote, the extended metaphor(s) and if a book, set up the folders for the chapters so I can then *write*.

## KEY PRINCIPLES

There are three key principles which drive my research.

### *A Firm Commitment to Traditional or "Peopled" Ethnography (Not to Qualitative Research More Broadly)*

The term 'peopled ethnography' which comes from Fine (2003) and Brown-Saracino, Thurk and Fine (2008) captures my chosen method perfectly. I mean by this ethnographic research where the data are gathered by the researcher being physically present in the setting and regarding any formal or informal conversations as subsidiary to, and intellectually less important than, the fieldnotes. The popularity of qualitative research by interview, and the loose terminology of describing something as ethnographic when it is only an interview study dismay me. My beliefs here are spelled out in Delamont (2014, 2016).

Interview data of all types, whether oral history, narrative, or responses to questions, and gathered from individuals or groups, in real locations or cyberspace, are, for me, less valuable and interesting than observational data. What people, whether school pupils, college lecturers, driving instructors or Japanese master potters, *do*, watched closely over a long period, is far more important to me than anything anyone says. *Sharing* the boredom or the danger, the heat or the cold, the noise or the silence, at six a.m. or ten p.m. with the learners and teachers is, for me, what educational research is meant to be about. In contrast the interview is like eating in a drive in burger bar, while ethnography is slow food, regional ingredients lovingly combined by an expert (Walford, 2009).

S. DELAMONT

*A Perpetual Struggle to Do Educational Research Which Fights Familiarity (Not Staying in Any Comfort Zone)*

The need to make the familiar strange was articulated by Blanche Geer (1964) and Howard Becker (1971), and then reiterated by Wolcott (1981) and Young (1981). Subsequently Lave and Wenger (1991), Singleton (1998, 1999) and Varenne (2007) have also called for educational researchers to look beyond mainstream schools in their own culture in order to make education anthropologically strange which will, coupled with tough reflexivity, lead to higher quality educational research. I have published a good deal on fighting familiarity, alone (Delamont, 2005), with Paul Atkinson (*e.g.* Delamont & Atkinson, 1995) and others (*e.g.* Atkinson, Coffey, & Delamont, 2003; Delamont, Atkinson, & Pugsley, 2010). The biggest difficulty I have in explaining the history of the familiarity problem is that I have done so very frequently since Delamont (1981) and there seem to be no novel ways to relate the sad story.

Geer (1964) set out the familiarity problem when describing her initial fieldwork for the study of liberal arts undergraduates at Kansas published as *Making the Grade* (Becker, Geer, & Hughes, 1968). She noted that inexperienced ethnographers often find fieldwork and all its precursor and successor stages baffling. Such people 'can spend a day in a hospital and come back with one page of notes and no hypotheses' (1964: 384) complaining that 'everyone knows what hospitals are like'. Geer showed how she had to re-configure her own preconceptions about the lives of American liberal arts undergraduates to develop decent foreshadowed problems, and made a plea for all ethnographers to do likeways.

Becker, her co-investigator on two ethnographies of higher education, made the same point in 1971 in a footnote added to a paper by Wax and Wax (1971). He stressed that doing fieldwork in American school classrooms was hard, because they were 'so familiar that it becomes impossible to single out events that occur in classrooms as things that have occurred' (1971: 10). Getting such observers to 'stop seeing only the things that are conventionally "there" to be seen' *is*, Becker continues 'like pulling teeth' (1971: 10). Wax and Wax (1971) was a clarion call for 'a solid body of data on the ethnography of schools', and Becker was highlighting the difficulties posed by familiarity that faced those trying to gather that mass of data. In the UK at the same time, but intellectually independently Young (1971) argued that too much educational research 'took' its agenda from educational insiders (educators) rather than 'making' its own research questions.

Ten years later Wolcott (1981) elaborated those points in a self-critical reflection on his research. Coming from anthropology, Wolcott wrote that 'central features of education are so taken for granted that they are invisible' (1981: 253). He added that the graduate schools of education in the USA should systematically send their doctoral students to observe teaching and learning in an unfamiliar setting while admitting he had only once done that: when he sent a nurse educator into a school of nursing. For me that chapter is the most powerful of all Wolcott's many important writings.

When Lave and Wenger (1991) argued that American educational research was far too obsessed with American schools rather than studying learning in other contexts, they failed to mention that Geer, Becker and Wolcott had already proposed a widened, non-school focus. Singleton (1998, 1999) writing when the journal *AEQ* celebrated its thirtieth birthday, once again argued that insights into learning and teaching should be gained by contrastive investigation. Varenne (2007) produced a similar argument in *Teachers College Record* a decade later. Sadly, from my perspective, none of the attempts I had made between 1981 and 2006 to propose strategies for fighting familiarity had been noticed by Lave, Wenger, Singleton or Varenne. Some of the scholars who have diagnosed the familiarity problem have not made practical proposals to help researchers diagnose and tackle it. In contrast I have concentrated on advocating six strategies to fight familiarity, which are set out below.

a. Revisiting the insightful educational ethnographies of the past.
b. Studying formal educational settings in other cultures.
c. Taking the standpoint of "the other."
d. Studying unusual schools, or other actors in the usual schools.
e. Studying education outside "education."
f. Using a non sexist lens (good research has to challenge gender) in reading, citing
g. and research design.

These are all based on the need for reading much more widely outside educational research than many scholars do. My list of favourites shows that principle as I practice it.

My strategies are based on reading more widely than is customary to develop better foreshadowed problems (the ethnographic equivalent of the hypothesis), and on deliberately gathering data in 'uncomfortable' ways. Strategies a, b, d and e can be based on reading to search out contrastive educational settings that can then be used to develop ideas. The ethnographies of the past are important because educational research tends to be very 'shallow': studies are quickly discarded as 'old' because, in England, for example, they were done before State schools were given control of their own finances (in 1988) or when clever state school pupils all learnt Latin (between 1944–1970). In fact careful reading of an old ethnography can force the researcher to confront their own, and the actors' assumption about school. Similarly reading about schooling in, for example France (Reed-Danahay, 1996; Anderson-Levitt, 1987) can lead to recognising that taken for granted features of education in one's own culture are actually radically different from those 'normal' elsewhere, and those worth studying.

During fieldwork it is possible to devise ways to see the familiar as strange. Forcing oneself to take the standpoint of a person different from oneself (*i.e.* if a man, imagine being female) and do the research that way. If clever, work hard to experience things as a failure and to see the school from the perspective of a failure (A failing teacher, a failing coach, a failing counsellor, or a failing pupil).

There are many studies of anti-school boys, of course, but very few on those utterly miserable loners, who cannot do the work, for whom every instant is a baffling misery. If 'white', explore the school as it is experienced a Chinese or Hispanic person. Choosing to study an unusual school is a good way to get culture shock – as Peshkin (1986) a Jew did in a fundamentalist Christian school, or Bullivant (1978) a Christian Australian in an Orthodox Jewish school. A period of research not in a school, in some other context where learning and teaching take place such as a kickboxing gym or an Irish dance class can re-focus the research in schools.

There are two other strategies which I have not used myself. One is to use the sociological perspective of ethnomethodology, the other, advocated by Mannay (2011) is to use visual methods to enforce the researcher to focus on alternate angles on the field setting.

*The Duty to Combat the Erosion of Women as Author and Subject*

There is a serious problem in educational research around the erosion of women as authors and as subjects. Work by women is cited less than work by men, because while women cite male and female scholars, most men overwhelmingly cite only work by men. Over time that means research by women does not get included in the literature. Because most of the research on women has been done by women, that means that studies of women also slide below the horizon of the discipline. This claim is documented for many social sciences and the evidence is reported in Delamont (2003). It is not clear how this feature of the educational research culture can be changed. First, it is necessary to gather the data and confront male authors with their citation practices, but it may be that only a radical change in the customary procedures of journals and even regulation will actually 'work'.

Currently it is not unusual to referee a paper submitted to a journal or a chapter for an edited collection, and discover that *no* publications on the topic by women are cited. However, pointing out that key studies by women are not cited does not necessarily get them incorporated. On one occasion, when a draft handbook chapter came in to me as editor that included no work on women, or by women, the male author was told that about twenty studies on or by women, specified with the full references, should be added, only to get the response paraphrased here as: 'I have never heard of any of those works, and so have never read them, and I do not have time to do so'. As editor it is hard to insist either to get the recalcitrant author to conform or worse to decide the chapter must be recommissioned when the whole project may be seriously delayed.

About thirty years ago most social science journals re-wrote their instructions to authors to forbid sexist and racist language. It is time for a parallel change to require all authors submitting papers to ensure that in their citations at least a third of the items are authored by women, and to require referees to check that and make suggestions for publication by women to be included if the target is not met. That would address the citation imbalance but not the erasure of women from the canon.

Behar and Gordon (1995) edited a collection of papers that focused on women who had been erased from the history of American anthropology, partly because they lived bohemian or transgressive lives and partly because they wrote in non-traditional ways. Educational research in the UK has routinely ignored its women scholars, and there is no parallel collection re-visiting and re-evaluating their contributions to the canon.

In my own sub field of school ethnography many of the women published papers and book chapters but not monographs (Delamont, 1989) and the standard overviews of that subfield, all by men, are ruthlessly sexist (Delamont, 2000, 2002, 2003). More worrying, when such an erasure is carefully documented, as Deegan (1988) has done for the women of the first Chicago School, many men continue to write as if that work had not been done. Moore (2013) for example, published a book about Basil Bernstein which systematically ignored all the women who worked with Bernstein, all his thinking on gender, and all the women scholars who had used his work to explore educational issues. In that one book the publications of about twenty women scholars were erased from the record of the structuralist tradition in educational sociology. No graduate student starting out from that book, published by a leading house, would know that Bernstein's originality lay precisely in the importance he placed on gender when no other sociologists of education in the UK thought beyond male class inequalities.

Fighting on this issue is my main retirement project.

## MY FAVOURITE TEXTS BY OTHERS

1. J. Lowell Lewis (1992) *Ring of Liberation.* Princeton: Princeton University Press.—A wonderful ethnography of *capoeira* in Brazil
2. Hugh Bicheno (2003) *Crescent and Cross: The Battle of Lepanto 1571.* London: Phoenix
3. Ruth Landes (1947) *City of Women.* — Sally Coles's (1995) work on Ruth Landes shows her as a classic example of a woman deliberately marginalised and erased from social science. The book is an ethnography of the African Brazilian religion *Candomblé* in Salvador de Bahia in 1938, rubbished at the time, but subsequently regarded as the 'best' account once the clouds of racial prejudice had cleared.
4. Carolyn Morrow Long (2001) *Spiritual Merchants.* — This explores the market in folk remedies and in objects and potions to hold lovers and keep away evil (such as John the Conqueror Root) central to North American Hoodoo or Voudou.
5. James Lee Burke (1995) *In the Electric Mist with the Confederate Dead.* — My favourite of the Lee Burke books about the tormented Dave Robicheaux, set in the country round New Orleans.
6. Amanda Cross (1981) *Death in a Tenured Position.* — A reminder of the deeply engrained hostility to women academics found in apparently liberal, tolerant universities.

## MY FAVOURITE PERSONAL TEXTS

There are four books I feel particularly fond of:

1. *Interaction in the Classroom* (1973) — which was my first monograph
2. *Knowledgeable Women* (1989) — because it uses a structuralist anthropological framework to analyse the history of elite women's education

3. *Feminist Sociology* (2003) — which pulls together my feminism
4. *Key Themes in the Ethnography of Education* (2014) — which sets out my manifesto for educational research.

I hope that the monograph on the capoeira research, in press, will join those four.

The 'best' papers again in the sense of those I am proudest of are:

1. 1974: 'Classroom research: A cautionary tale' (with David Hamilton) — because it was the first peer reviewed journal article we had accepted, and Nate Gage requested an offprint of it.
2. 1980: 'The two traditions' (with Paul Atkinson).
3. 1981: All too familiar? — This was my first formulation of the familiarity problem.
4. 1984: 'A woman's place in education'. — This was my presidential address to BERA.
5. 2005: 'Four Great Gates'. — This was my keynote plenary to the joint conference of the New Zealand and Australian educational research association in Auckland in 2003.
6. 2007: 'The only honest thing'. — This is an attack on autoethnography.
7. 2008: 'Up on the roof' (with N. Stephens) *Cultural Sociology*. — This paper presents the best of the capoeira project and was shortlisted for the Sage prize for 2008.
8. 2012: 'Performing research or researching performance?' — This was a plenary at the big Urbana Champaign qualitative research conference, and argues for peopled ethnography rather than autoethnography.

## REFERENCES

Anderson-Levitt, K. (1987). Cultural knowledge for teaching first grade. In G. Spindler & L. Spindler (Eds.), *Interpretive ethnography of education at home and abroad* (pp. 171–194). Hillsdale, NJ: Laurence Erlbaum.
Anderson-Levitt, K. (Ed.). (2012). *Anthropologies of education*. New York, NY: Berghahn.
Assuncao, M. R. (2005). *Capoeira*. London: Routledge.
Atkinson, P. A., Delamont, S., & Hammersley, M. (1988). Qualitative research traditions. *Review of Educational Research, 58*(2), 231–250.
Atkinson, P. A., Coffey, A., & Delamont, S. (2003). *Key themes in qualitative research*. Walnut Creek, CA: Alta Mira Press.
Becker, H. (1971). Footnote. Added to the paper by M. Wax and R. Wax (1971) Great tradition, little tradition and formal education. In M. Wax, S. Diamond, & F. Gearing (Eds.), *Anthropological perspectives on education* (pp. 3–27). New York, NY: Basic Books.
Becker, H., Geer, S., & Hughes, E. (1968). *Making the grade: The academic side of college life*. New York, NY: Wiley.
Bourdieu, P. (1988). *Homo academicus*. Cambridge, MA: Polity Press.
Bullivant, R. M. (1978). *The way of tradition*. Melbourne: ACER.
Brown-Saracino, J., Thurk, J., & Fine, G. A. (2008). Beyond groups. *Qualitative Research, 8*(5), 547–567.
Croll, P. (1986). *Systematic classroom observation*. London: Falmer Press.
Delamont, S. (1981). All too familiar? *Educational Analysis, 3*(1), 69–84. (Reprinted in S. Delamont (ed) *Ethnographic Methods in Education*. London: Sage, Four Volumes. Volume 1 pp. 279–294)
Delamont, S. (2005). Four great gates. *Research Papers in Education, 20*(1), 85–100.
Delamont, S. (2006). Where the boys are. *Waikato Journal of Education, 11*(1), 7–26.
Delamont, S. (2008). Confessions of a rag-picker. In S. Delamont & P. Atkinson (Eds.), *Gender and education. Volume 3: Feminist methods* (pp. 317–329). London: Sage.
Delamont, S. (2012). Milkshakes and convertibles. In N. Denzin (Ed.), *Studies in symbolic interaction* (Vol. 39, pp. 51–70). Bingley: Emerald.
Delamont, S. (2014). *Key themes in the ethnography of education*. London: Sage.
Delamont, S., & Atkinson, P. (1995). *Fighting familiarity*. Cresskill, NJ: Hampton Press.
Delamont, S., Atkinson, P., & Parry, O. (2000). *The doctoral experience*. London: Falmer.

Delamont, S., Atkinson, P., & Pugsley, L. (2010). The concept smacks of magic. *Teaching and Teacher Education, 26*(1), 3–10.
Fine, G. A. (2003). Towards a peopled ethnography. *Ethnography, 4*(1), 41–60.
Flanders, N. (1970). *Analysing teaching behaviour*. New York, NY: Addison-Wesley.
Flecker, J. E. (1923). *Hassan: The story of Hassan of Baghdad and how he came to make the golden journey to Samarkand*. London: Heineman.
Flecker, J. E. (1947). *Collected poems*. London: Secker and Warburg.
Geer, B. (1964). First days in the field. In P. Hammond (Ed.), *Sociologists at work* (pp. 372–398). New York, NY: Basic Books.
Hurston, Z. N. (1935). *Mules and men*. New York, NY: Lippincort. (1990 edition, New York: Harper Perennial)
Lave, J., & Wenger, E. (1991). *Situated learning*. Cambridge: Cambridge University Press.
Mehan, H. (1979). *Learning lessons*. Cambridge, MA: Harvard University Press.
Peshkin, A. (1986). *God's choice*. Chicago, IL: The University of Chicago Press.
Reed-Danahay, D. (1996). *Education and identity in rural France*. Cambridge: Cambridge University Press.
Sayers, D. L. (1972). *Gaudy night*. London: Gollanz.
Sinclair, J., & Coulthard, M. (1974). *Towards an analysis of discourse*. Oxford: Oxford University Press.
Singleton, J. (Ed.). (1998). *Learning in likely places*. Cambridge: Cambridge University Press.
Singleton, J. (1999). Reflecting on the reflections. *Anthropology and Education Quarterly, 30*(4), 455–459.
Spindler, G. (Ed.). (2000). *Fifty years of anthropology and education*. Mahwah, NJ: Erlbaum.
Stephens, N., & Delamont, S. (2010). Roda boa! *Teaching and Teacher Education, 26*(1), 110–113.
Varenne, H. (2007). Alternative anthropological perspectives on education. *Teachers College Record, 109*(7), 1539–1544.
Walford, G. (2009). The practice of writing ethnographic fieldnotes. *Ethnography and Education, 4*(2), 117–130.
Walker, R., & Adelman, C. (1976). Strawberries. In M. Stubbs & S. Delamont (Eds.), *Explorations in classroom observation*. Chichester: Wiley.
Wolcott, H. F. (1981). Confessions of a 'trained' observer. In T. S. Popkewitz & B. R. Tabachnik (Eds.), *The study of schooling* (pp. 247–263). New York, NY: Praeger.
Young, M. F. D. (1981). Introduction. In M. F. D. Young (Ed.), *Knowledge and control* (pp. 1–17). London: Collier-Macmillan.

*Sara Delamont*
*Cardiff University*

JOYCE L. EPSTEIN

# 6. SEARCHING FOR EQUITY IN EDUCATION

*Finding School, Family, and Community Partnerships*

STARTING OUT

Growing up in Queens in New York City, I attended P.S. 23, P.S. 20, and Flushing High School where, year after year, I found that school was the best place to be. There was much to learn from mostly excellent teachers from kindergarten through high school. In a high school of about four-thousand students with multiple school shifts, there was always something interesting going on. There also were some inherent contradictions. "Keep learning and be creative," were messages at school. Society told girls: "Become a teacher, nurse, or secretary." I planned to become a good teacher, as directed.

Perhaps, my road to research in the sociology of education started in elementary school in Flushing. This town has an interesting history. The name derived from Vlissingen, a Dutch town, when the Dutch ruled New Netherlands (later New York) in the 1600s. A museum—the Bowne House, built around 1661—introduced students to local history and John Bowne's commitment to religious freedom. His decision to allow Quakers to meet in his home influenced later attention to religious freedom in the Bill of Rights. A friend lived in the Bowne House where her parents were caretakers. For us, the museum was just someone's house to visit for play. Yet, John Bowne's themes of equality, tolerance, and respect for diversity resonated over the years to reinforce the importance of equity in education and to shape my deepest interests.

Following the conventional path, I prepared to become a teacher at Lesley College (now University). I was excited about the clarity, creativity, and humor required to teach early adolescents. Also, I was curious about research in education. Before starting to teach, I attended the unique Palfrey House Program at the Harvard Graduate School of Education for a Master's Degree in Human Development. The program combined attention to anthropology with John Whiting, social psychology with Roger Brown, and sociology with Gordon Allport and Thomas Pettigrew. The latter two professors team-taught a course on research on desegregation of schools. It was the Civil Rights Era and the year of Freedom Schools, with one in Roxbury, Massachusetts, where we volunteered as a course activity. My paper for that course set me thinking about the persistent gap in the quality of schools for children in segregated schools and in affluent and poverty-stricken communities. It was clear, then and now, that issues of equity and opportunities for social mobility are at the heart of school improvement, student learning, and life's options. The Palfrey House Program required that I compare disciplines and helped me identify sociology as the one to address issues of equity in education.

## TEACHING TO LEARN

I wanted to know about the "real world" of teaching and delayed entering a doctoral program. I taught school for six years in Newton, Massachusetts; Los Altos, California; and Montgomery County, Maryland—mostly grades 4 and 6. Even in good systems, there were blatant differences among the schools, with some in pockets of poverty. There also were differences within schools and classrooms in the experiences of students whose parents had many or few years of formal education and for students who were tracked by ability and doing poorly in class.

I began to meet with my students' families because preteens needed multiple sources of support. Parent-teacher conferences were conducted once a year, but most teachers contacted parents only when their students had academic or behavioral problems. This seemed to me to be too late for preventing trouble and failures. I did not know it then, but my views about tapping parents' knowledge and support to increase students' success would return as a major research agenda on school and family partnerships.

I learned about classroom teaching, school leadership, and the wondrous diversity of children's skills, talents, and challenges. I learned about the persistent press on teachers' time; strong and weak principals; how school innovations come and go; and problems that arise when teachers accept slow learners or naughty students as if they were predetermined. Teaching was valuable and, to this day, influences my ideas about what teachers should and should not be asked to do as professional educators.

Teaching children to write was my favorite subject. The best short-term results of this work were classroom books of children's poetry that were created every year—still in storage because they were too precious to throw away. The best long-term result of this work was meeting the mother of one student years later who told me that my classes influenced her daughter to become a writer. Elementary and middle grades teachers rarely learn what happens to their students. The mother's recall of my emphasis on writing with sixth graders was like an apple for the teacher.

Keeping research in mind, I took an Independent Studies class in social psychology at Stanford University, which led to my first co-authored publication in *Sociometry* (Alexander & Epstein, 1969). While teaching in Maryland, I worked part-time for a research firm that studied many social and educational topics (e.g., education in prisons, libraries in mental hospitals) that expanded my understanding of program evaluations beyond school walls.

## FINDING DISCIPLINE: STUDYING AND IMPROVING SCHOOLS

After my then-husband completed his doctorate and we settled in Maryland, it was my turn to return to graduate school in the 1970s. My interest in the sociology of education had an exciting home at Johns Hopkins University, where Professors James Coleman, Peter Rossi, James McPartland, Edward McDill, John Holland, Doris Entwisle, and others offered a solid education in the theory, methods, and goals of sociology.

The Department and faculty were closely tied to the Center for Social Organization of Schools (CSOS), which opened opportunities for quantitative research in the sociology of education. CSOS was a place for cutting edge research, great discussions, ambitious field-based applications, and good humor. As a "soft-money" Center, researchers were fully supported by grants, which is a challenging and risky way of life, but important for having time to conduct large field studies in collaboration with educators. From 1966 on under directors Coleman, McDill, Holland, and McPartland—the last served in leadership positions for over forty years—CSOS researchers produced thousands of reports and publications and developed major intervention programs. Success for All (1987, now on its own campus), Talent Development Middle and High Schools (1995, now Talent Development Secondary-TDS), and the National Network of Partnership Schools (NNPS, 1996) were designed, studied, and scaled up over the years to improve school organization, curriculum and instruction, leadership and management, and family engagement—all with the goal of improving students' learning and success in school. These and other programs (Baltimore Education Research Consortium-BERC, Early Learning, Diplomas Now, and Everyone Graduates Center) continue to combine basic and applied research to improve policy and practice. I still feel lucky to be part of this remarkable place.

In the mid-1970s, sociology of education was still an emerging field. Our computers ran limited regression analyses with up to fifteen variables. At CSOS, the main computer, card reader, tape spinners, and printer took up an entire carriage house. As a graduate student, I could enter a set of regression or subgroup analyses on what was called the "night ghost" starting at 5 p.m. If the program cards were correct, a pile of printed output would be ready the next morning. If I made an error, I had to wait my turn for the next overnight run. These were exciting advances in quantitative analyses that consumed doctoral students and experienced researchers, alike.

When I started my doctoral studies at Johns Hopkins University, scholars were arguing the question: Which is more important—the school or the family? The highly influential Coleman Report (Coleman et al., 1966) was still making waves and the argument raged through the 1970s. The report concluded that the family was most important for student success in school. Okay, but the argument—families OR schools—seemed specious to me. Why should this be a contest where one context wins over the other? Part of the problem was a lack of adequate measures of school climate, curriculum and instruction, and students' opportunities to learn. Because these measures were missing, the influence of the school was artificially low and the influence of the family was inevitably exaggerated. In my dissertation, I was able to examine new questions about school and family connections with better data on school and classroom variables and that addressed issues of equity in the quality of schooling and students' opportunities to learn.

*Dissertation Study*

Despite every graduate student's dream, there is no perfect study, but I was part of a pretty wonderful natural experiment. A local district was in the process of building new schools for an expanding student population. Some new buildings were open-space schools, whereas earlier schools were traditionally built with walled classrooms. The district leaders wanted to know whether to continue building schools with pods and rooms without walls or return to more typical buildings. School programs differed, too, with more open, project-based curricula in open-space environments, compared to more teacher-directed lessons in traditional schools.

One main question, then, asked: Did one group of students benefit in achievement, attitudes, and other outcomes in one type of building or with one type of teaching approach or another? My advisor, Dr. James McPartland, and I developed original surveys for students, parents, and teachers about school organization, climate, teaching styles, family decision-making styles, student behaviors, friendships, and attitudes. The district provided student background and achievement data for over 6000 students in 39 elementary and secondary schools. The two-year study was filled with challenges—even intrigue. It was an incredible learning experience for this young scholar.

After completing my dissertation, I was invited to join the CSOS Research Faculty to continue the longitudinal study of open and traditional schools and to complete reports and publications. We focused on the effects on students of contrasting authority structures in school (i.e., more or less shared decision-making by teachers and students) and at home (more or less shared family decision-making by parents and children). In the early 1980s, interaction research or person-environment and trait-treatment studies were emerging. We extended these models to pose person-environment-environment questions of whether students with particular traits and from different family environments responded significantly better in open or traditional schools.

A major finding was that, over time, there were no consistent achievement effects on students in the differently organized schools (McPartland & Epstein, 1977). That is, open and traditional schools posted similar achievement results for students, but there were differences in contrasting school organizations on other outcomes. For example, using longitudinal data, I explored whether highly independent students and those with high locus of control did better in high-participatory schools, where students controlled more aspects of the academic environment. Controlling on grade eight measures, I found that students moving from grade eight in ten middle schools to grade nine in six high schools gained in independence, positive attitudes about school, and report card grades in high-participatory family and school environments (Epstein, 1983).

The study reported simple ordinal interactions. Some students benefitted more than others in high-participatory schools, but, on average, other students were helped—not harmed—in these settings. Challenging school environments (e.g., high-participatory teaching in any building) had compensatory effects that helped students strengthen important character traits (i.e., independent thinking; positive attitudes about school; better report card grades) (Epstein, 1984). The results indicated that schools can alter their authority structures to encourage more participation by students in decision making activities to improve students' actions and abilities through high school and beyond.

Another important finding was that specific actions taken by families and schools were more important than ascribed characteristics for influencing positive student outcomes. The study confirmed that it was no longer enough to use easily-collected or "mechanical" survey items (e.g., size of school, size of family, parents' education, SES) to understand the effects on student learning and development. On the decade-long question of "families or schools," our study, with better data than in the past, showed that both contexts—families and schools—were important at all school levels for student achievement, behavior, and attitudes.

*Quality of School Life*

Several of my early major publications were on the Quality of School Life (QSL)—connections of student satisfaction with school and student achievement in open and traditional elementary, middle, and high schools. The QSL is a twenty-seven-item scale for use with students in grades four through twelve. It has three subscales on student satisfaction with school, attitudes toward teachers, and commitment to classwork (Epstein & McPartland, 1976). Jim McPartland and I considered the potential of the QSL. There was an over-emphasis in schools on student test scores—much like today. We believed that educators would benefit if QSL were part of a standard achievement test battery that provided information on student attitudes along with achievement test scores. That never happened, although it still sounds like a good idea. The QSL was published for about ten years, translated in several languages, but then went out of print. Now, still used and useful, it is distributed by CSOS at no cost to researchers and graduate students.

Some findings about student attitudes were particularly interesting. Satisfaction with school was unrelated to IQ; had a small, significant, positive association with report card grades; and had strong, significant, positive connections with teachers' reports of students' participation in class (Epstein, 1981). Data showed that student satisfaction with school decreased across the grades, unless something intervened to make school interesting and important to students. Even today, too many students are sad, mad, or bad in school. The early findings suggest that schools can alter the school climate with more active and participatory learning to improve student attitudes and improve students' chances of completing high school.

*Friends in School*

Other unique data were collected in open and traditional schools on students' selection and influence of friends (Epstein & Karweit, 1983). On patterns of selection, I found that more students selected a friend, were named as a friend, and reciprocated friendship choices in high-participatory classrooms. Fewer students were neglected or isolated. Expected patterns of selecting friends based only on similarities of social class, sex, race, and achievement were tempered by schools that created new conditions for peer interactions, such as working in groups on shared projects.

On patterns of influence, longitudinal data indicated that friends influenced each other, mainly in a positive direction. For example, on average, students with no plans for college changed their intensions over one year if they made friends with a student with college plans, particularly if the friendship choice was reciprocated. Another interesting finding was that in open space or high-participatory schools that valued independent behavior, students became more self-reliant over one year if they had friends who were strongly self-reliant. The results reinforced the fact that school environments may be designed to improve social processes to boost students' success in school.

*Middle School Studies*

Starting in the Center for Research on Elementary and Middle Schools (CREMS, 1985–90) and continuing for several years, colleagues and I studied the design and effects of schools for early adolescents. Middle schools were recognized as a separate level of schooling, supported by research on early adolescent development and by changing demographics. When the number of students exceeded space in elementary schools, some students were moved to middle schools. Was this a good idea or was it better to keep students in smaller, familiar K-8 buildings?

Jim McPartland and I developed a survey administered to a probability sample of 2400 schools that contained Grade 7. Doug MacIver and I analyzed these data (Epstein, 1990; Epstein & MacIver, 1990) and reported the first national statistics on the prevalence and purposes of key middle school components, including grade span, school size, ability grouping, advisory periods, guidance counselors, teacher teams, curriculum, instruction, transitions, sports and clubs, remedial instruction, and teacher certification.

We learned, for example, that across the U.S. there were thirty grade spans that included grade seven, from the familiar (6–8, 7–9) to the unique (7 only, 2–7).

Most importantly, grade span was not the determinant of student achievement. Rather, the quality of the school program and learning opportunities affected reports of student success. At the time, some parents were opposed to middle schools, which were larger and further from home than elementary schools. Others viewed middle schools as important stepping stones to high school with services (e.g., counselors who were specialists in early adolescent development) and courses (e.g., foreign language, advanced math) that were not available in most elementary schools. Both sides used the same findings to support their arguments. That was a lesson in the politics of education research.

## CHANGING THE QUESTION: THE PATH TO PARTNERSHIPS

Starting in 1981, colleagues and I considered new ways to study school and family influences on student learning and development. I wanted to change the question to delve deeper into this research agenda. The old questions were: Are families important? Are families more important than schools? It was clear—a social fact—that families are important in every child's life. This result was confirmed across studies because there always are variations in parents' behaviors—some are involved and others not. This variation is essential for showing that children do better in school if their families are engaged in their education and comfortable in their connections with teachers. But variation in a general population of parents and children is just another word for *inequality*—necessary for finding significant research results but counter-productive for increasing the number of families involved and the number of students benefitting from positive family engagement. My new question was: *IF families are so important, HOW can schools engage all families in ways that contribute to more students' success in school?* With this change, I hoped to make an original contribution to research on school organization. Historically, family engagement was treated as external to schools and about the parents. The new question asked whether and how teachers and administrators could work with parents and community partners from the earliest years on to help more children be ready for school, do their best learning every year, and graduate from high school with plans for the future. This made connections of educators, families, and students part of school organization—central for school improvement—and about the students.

Henry Jay Becker and I began basic research with a study of six-hundred elementary schools in urban, rural, and suburban districts in Maryland (Becker & Epstein, 1982). This was one of the first large-scale studies with data from about 3,700 teachers, administrators, parents, and students on attitudes and practices of parental involvement. As might be expected, some teachers and principals were doing more than others to engage families in children's education at school and at home. We also studied the results of schools' practices of partnerships on the actions and behaviors of parents, and the attitudes and achievements of students (see readings in Epstein, 2011).

Prior studies asked parents if and how they were involved at school and at home, but omitted important variables such as what teachers and administrators did to organize and encourage parental involvement. Without accounting for schools' outreach patterns, prior studies reinforced the stereotype that only some parents with years of formal education would or could be involved in their children's education at school or at home.

One consistent result of our early studies was that teachers had different views of parents than parents had of themselves. Many teachers thought that most parents did not want to be involved or were unconcerned about their children's education. They were unaware of parents' hopes and dreams for their children. Most parents reported that they conducted many activities at home, but needed more information to guide their children's success at each grade level. Neither teachers nor parents understood that students wanted their families to be knowledgeable partners in their education in age-appropriate ways.

The study of elementary schools was followed by explorations with several colleagues of middle and high schools. Field studies were conducted with a good partner at the Fund for Educational Excellence in Baltimore. Baltimore City Public Schools was "our teachers" from 1987 through 1995. The district's area superintendents and school-based teams helped us learn what worked in a large and economically-distressed community to engage all families. We started with eight pilot schools, then fifteen, and scaled up to over one-hundred ninety schools.

We learned that if school teams reached out to all families, large numbers of previously uninvolved parents responded eagerly and well at all school levels. These findings contradicted long-held stereotypes that families with low income, racial minorities, single parents, employed moms, and those with less formal education would not or could not be partners with teachers in their children's education.

Among many interesting results, we learned the critical importance of the word "unless." That is, partnerships declined across grade levels, in poor communities, with fathers, single parents, employed parents, and those living far from school *unless* schools established a welcoming climate and implemented goal-linked practices of partnership to increase student success at each grade level. The surveys developed for these studies for teachers, parents, and students are now available for researchers, graduate students, and educators. (see Publications and Products at www.partnershipschools.org.)

The early studies prompted a change in terminology from *parent involvement*, which focused on the parent's actions, to *school, family, and community partnerships*, which recognized that key people in all three contexts shared responsibility and had roles to play to increase students' success in school at all grade levels.

*A Center on Partnerships*

With interest growing in the connections of schools and families, Don Davis at Boston University and I were awarded the Center on Families, Communities,

Schools, and Children's Learning, 1990–1996. The Center included about twenty researchers in psychology, sociology, social work, and policy studies from several universities who studied topics of family and community engagement from birth through high school. The highly productive research team produced over two-hundred reports, handbooks, classroom materials, videos, surveys, and other publications and products (http://eric.ed.gov/?id=ED402058).

In 1991, Don and I also started the International Network (INET) of Scholars on School, Family, and Community Partnerships—a forum for researchers across countries to report their work. Now, INET and its sister organization, European Research Network about Parents in Education (ERNAPE), meet in alternating years to strengthen international connections in research, policy, and practice. With the Center's research and development and the international network, the field of school, family, and community partnerships was maturing in important ways.

*A Permanent Home Base*

In the past, the research centers at Johns Hopkins changed names with each new federally-funded grant. In 1996, to ensure a permanent home for research and development on family and community engagement, I established the Center on School, Family, and Community Partnerships within CSOS. A six-year implementation grant from NICHD from 2003 to 2009 supported my work and studies by colleagues Mavis Sanders, Steven Sheldon, and Frances Van Voorhis. We were able to learn more about leadership on partnerships at the school and district levels, new designs for family engagement in homework, and effective scaling-up strategies in many locations.

Translating research for use in practice requires researchers to be "multilingual" by speaking the languages of research and practice. This means turning beta coefficients into useful workshops, tools, and materials that fit educators' needs; publishing articles in peer-reviewed research journals and in practitioners' publications, and presenting work at professional conferences and at practitioners' meetings (Epstein, 1996). It also means learning from practitioners about challenges that pose questions for new and better research studies. These translations and collaborations cannot be easily accomplished by professors whose departments reward only traditional research and teaching. At CSOS, however, the funded centers were required to show that research would be useful in practice.

NATIONAL NETWORK OF PARTNERSHIP SCHOOLS (NNPS)

By 1995, my colleagues and I learned many lessons from scores of studies on family and community engagement. To share this knowledge, I established a network to guide schools, districts, states, and organizations to use the research-based tools and training that we developed to improve their policies and practices of partnerships (Epstein, 1995). Thinking this might be a three-year project, we named the network

*Partnership 2000*. About two-hundred schools, thirty districts, and eight state departments of education accepted the opportunity to work with us. As the year 2000 approached, more districts and schools wanted this kind of guidance, and we changed the name of the project to National Network of Partnership Schools (NNPS). At this writing, NNPS is in its nineteenth year with over six-hundred collaborating schools, districts, organizations, and states. Over five-thousand schools, districts, organizations, and states have partnered with NNPS over the years, obtained our *Handbook for Action* (Epstein et al., 2009 and see www.partnershipschools.org), and began some work to strengthen their partnership programs. With our practitioner-partners, NNPS made major contributions to improve research, policy, and practices of partnerships, including the following.

*Theory*

All research must be based on strong theory. In the late 1980s, I developed the *theory of overlapping spheres of influence*, which posits that, in education, more students will achieve and succeed in school if their families, schools, and communities work together and share responsibilities for student learning and development (Epstein, 1987, 2011). The theory redesigned, redirected, integrated, and extended sociological theories of organizations, Lightfoot's (1978) view of spheres of influence, and Bronfenbrenner's model of multiple contexts for student development (1979) to reflect the simultaneous and dynamic connections and influences of home, school, and community.

In my theory of overlapping spheres of influence, an external model shows that the degree of overlap of home, school, and community changes with different age levels and social forces. An internal model recognizes that the student is the main actor in learning and the reason for the complex relationships of parents, teachers, and community partners. The theory now is used across disciplines to study the results of contextual conditions and interpersonal relationships on student learning, behavior, and other school outcomes.

*Framework*

Based on many studies, I defined a framework of six types of involvement. First, we conducted studies to confirm that the types were separable with characteristic practices, unique challenges, and different results—hence a typology. Then, we explored how each type of involvement contributed to particular school goals (e.g., improve reading, math, attendance) (Epstein et al., 2009).

The six types of involvement, in brief, are: (1) parenting—help all families understand child and adolescent development and help all schools understand their children's families; (2) communicating—establish two-way exchanges about school programs and children's progress; (3) volunteering—recruit and organize parents' assistance at school, home, or in other locations; (4) learning at home—provide information and ideas to families about how to help students with homework and other curriculum-related activities; (5) decision making—have parents from all backgrounds serve as representatives and leaders on school committees and advocates for their own children; and (6) collaborating with the community—identify and integrate resources and services from the community to strengthen school programs and students' experiences, and enabling students and families to contribute to their communities.

Schools choose among hundreds of practices or design new activities for each type of involvement and solve inevitable challenges (e.g., different technologies or languages to communicate with families). Each type of involvement requires two-way connections for educators and families to exchange information as they share responsibilities for children's education.

*Nested Leadership*

A major contribution of our research on partnerships is the concept of nested leaders across policy levels. At the school level, leadership takes the form of an Action Team for Partnerships (ATP) consisting of teachers, administrators, parents, and other family or community partners, and students at the high school level. The ATP writes an annual action plan to engage all families in activities linked to specific goals in its own School Improvement Plan for a positive school climate and for student attendance, behaviors, and achievements in specific subjects.

At the district level, studies show that a designated leader is needed to guide schools on partnerships. One study—the first with quantitative analyses of "nested data" of schools within districts used Hierarchical Linear Modeling (HLM) to study the simultaneous work of district leaders and school teams in developing their partnership programs. Results indicated that schools guided by district leaders for partnerships had higher quality programs and greater outreach to all families than did schools that worked on their own, without district guidance and support (Epstein, Galindo, & Sheldon, 2011). Another study of nested leadership confirmed that schools with active district facilitators established partnership programs with higher percentages of engaged parents and higher rates of student attendance than did schools without this guidance and support (Epstein & Sheldon, in press).

*At the Home Base*

NNPS provides handbooks, newsletters, e-briefs, planning and evaluation tools, and on-going professional development in conferences, workshops, webinars, and on a website. NNPS requires every member to evaluate progress every year, analyzes the data, and reports the results, with customized reports to districts of their own schools' data. Researchers use these data to identify essential elements that improve program quality from one year to the next. To date, eight essential elements were identified that guide the work of districts and schools in NNPS: leadership, teamwork, written plans, implementation of planned activities, evaluations, collegial support, funding, and networking (Epstein et al., 2009; Epstein & Sheldon, 2006). NNPS's mission is to "grow" expert leaders who develop and strengthen these essential elements as they continually improve their partnership programs.

*TIPS Interactive Homework*

Colleagues and I continue to conduct studies on the engagement of parents with students on homework. Teachers tell parents that they should help their children with homework, but what does *help* mean? Parents cannot and should not be asked to *teach* every subject at every grade level to students of every ability level. To address this problem and to strengthen Type 4-Learning at Home activities, I designed a new approach to homework, *Teachers Involve Parents in Schoolwork (TIPS)*. With *TIPS*, teachers design interactive homework that requires children to demonstrate and discuss skills that they are learning in school with a parent or family partner, and discuss how the adult uses the skill in the real world (Epstein, Salinas, Jackson, & Van Voorhis, 1992, rev. 1995, 2001). Studies show that in TIPS classes, on average, more parents at all grade levels are involved with their children on homework in positive ways, and more students complete more homework and improve their skills, grades, and scores (Epstein & Van Voorhis, 2001, 2012; Van Voorhis, 2011).

*Preparing Future Educators for Partnership Program Development*

For decades, many research publications on partnerships concluded with a statement on the need for preservice and advanced education to prepare future teachers and administrators to work better with parents. Most colleges, however, give little or limited attention to helping educators understand that partnerships are part of their professional work in every school (Epstein & Sanders, 2006).

In 2001, I published a textbook (2nd edition, Epstein, 2011) to increase the number of professors of education and the social sciences who are comfortable discussing the theory, research, and practical applications of school, family, and community partnerships in their courses for future teachers, administrators, and social researchers. The text includes readings of basic research with guidelines for professors and students, questions to discuss, activities, and field projects. The number of courses covering partnership topics have increased, but not enough to ensure that all teachers are up to date in knowledge and skills on partnerships. This remains an important agenda.

*Lessons Learned*

It is gratifying that many schools, districts, states, and organizations refer to my and colleagues' research and publications in their policy statements, recommendations, and missions for school improvement, and recognize the need for equitable programs that engage all families in ways that contribute to student achievement and other goals for student success in school. At the federal level, too, my and others' studies and applications influenced the recommendations for parent involvement in the Elementary and Secondary Education Act starting in 1988. By 2001, the ESEA (then called *No Child Left Behind* and updated to the *Every Student Succeeds Act-ESSA*) specified requirements for nested leadership of states, districts, and schools to organize programs to engage all parents in activities to improve students' achievement and behavior. (See examples of district and state policies that are consistent with the research base in chapter 4, Epstein, 2011.)

Among many lessons learned, perhaps the most important is the need to combine research-based essentials with opportunities for creative, local designs. Educators do not like fixed or one-size-fits-all programs that omit attention to "place." In NNPS, we found that a purposeful mix of formal theory, required research-based structures and processes, and flexible options for local creative work corrects some of the rigidity in other intervention models. For strong and productive partnerships, customized programs are essential to accommodate differences by grade level, school improvement goals, and the needs and interests of diverse populations of students and families. Creative activities implemented by members of NNPS are shared each year in annual books of *Promising Partnership Practices* and in a *Partnership Awards,* resulting in a library of over 1,200 goal-linked activities that others may adopt or adapt (see Success Stories at www.partnershipschools.org).

Looking across years of studies, my colleague Steve Sheldon and I summarized seven cross-cutting principles that should guide educators to improve partnership practices and help researchers plan new studies. The overarching lessons learned state the need to (1) broaden terminology from *parental involvement* to *school, family, and community partnerships* to recognize the shared responsibilities of educators, parents, and others for children's learning and development; (2) understand the multidimensional nature of involvement; (3) view the structure of partnerships as a component of school and classroom organization; (4) recognize multilevel leadership for involvement at the school, district, and state levels; (5) focus involvement on student outcomes; (6) acknowledge the importance of increasing the equity of involvement of parents to promote more successful students; and to (7) advance knowledge and improve practice with more rigorous studies (Epstein & Sheldon, 2006).

People ask me, with some disbelief, *"Are you still studying the same thing?"* It is unusual to conduct programmatic research to build a knowledge base and follow new questions over thirty years. But, each step in research and development is new and different—never the same. And, research on partnerships is on-going—never completed. One of the hardest questions that has been answered only in part is: How do students process their parents' involvement activities for more success in school? Studies are needed of alternative interventions with longitudinal data on achievement and other student outcomes that also measure mediating factors that affect students' acceptance of parents' guidance and ultimate results on student attitudes, behavior, and learning.

How much progress has been made to improve school, family, and community partnerships in practice? Some days it seems that a great deal of progress has been made. In NNPS, many districts have Leaders for Partnerships who are expertly guiding schools to strengthen and sustain their programs of family and community engagement. Other days, we consider that there are over 14,000 districts and nearly 100,000 schools in the U.S. Far too many remain unaware of the effective new approaches to partnership program development. They continue to conduct "parent involvement" in old and inequitable ways. There is still much to do to "scale up" goal-linked partnership programs at the state, district, and school levels.

## REFLECTION

When I started my studies, families and schools were studied separately. Now, there are hundreds of researchers exploring all aspects of partnerships. The American Sociological Association (ASA) section on Sociology of Education, along with most divisions and a dedicated Special Interest Group (SIG) in the American Educational Research Association (AERA) now regularly feature research on family and community engagement. It was very meaningful to me to have received the Elizabeth Cohen Distinguished Career in Applied Sociology of Education Award from the Sociology of Education SIG of AERA. It is, indeed, an honor to be recognized by one's peers for both research and its application in policy and practice.

This is, now, an important field of study—not a contest between contexts, as once was the case. The connections and effects of home, school, and community are understood as complex and overlapping contexts for student success in school and in life. By changing the question about parental involvement, my colleagues and I redirected studies of family and community engagement. By linking research with policy and practice, we have demonstrated that it is not enough for researchers to identify inequalities in family engagement. It also is necessary to design and test approaches to increase the equality of involvement among families who were previously not engaged in their children's education. In practice, by creating research-based tools and training, we are identifying the "how to," which should help all districts and schools develop sustainable programs of school, family, and community partnerships.

There are parallels of this work with challenges in medicine. In medical research, it is unethical to withhold treatment from patients when one intervention is shown to be consistently more effective than another or than placebo—business as usual. In education, hundreds of studies and decades of field tests confirm that when families and the community are engaged in children's education, students do better in school, have better attendance, graduate from high school, and make plans for education or training after high school. The accumulated evidence suggests that it may be unethical for districts and schools to withhold this treatment—i.e., well-planned, goal-linked programs of school, family, and community partnerships—from students from preschool through high school. The steps are clear, structures and processes are feasible, and costs are low for organizing effective and equitable practices to engage all families and benefit students.

Thinking over my professional life, it is necessary to return home. My parents loved their three daughters. They expected us to go to college—an emerging opportunity for girls at the time. We followed traditional paths for women in teaching and nursing. As society changed, we changed too. The art teacher became a well-known artist; the oncology nurse moved to Switzerland, practiced nursing, and is an author and lecturer in multi-languages. The middle grades teacher became a sociologist who designs and studies programs to improve school, family, and community partnerships in this and other countries. The three sisters are proud of each other's accomplishments and have wonderful and successful children.

My son was an important influence on my research during his school years. I knew that if I had questions about his school and his progress, other parents had the same need-to-know to guide their children across the grades. My son brought family engagement to life, and with my daughter-in-law, now shows how parental involvement remains important for the quality of life.

Was my upward mobility unique to the time or can today's striving students do the same? At a time when schools aim to prepare students to compete for jobs in the global economy, it is necessary to ensure that upward mobility is alive and well for students across the country. Good schools, good teachers, caring and engaged parents, and healthy communities will continue to determine whether students move on and move up. It is imperative, then, to conduct research and apply confirmed results in practice to improve schools, engage all families in their children's education, and ensure that all students reach their full potential.

## MY FAVORITE TEXTS BY OTHERS

### *(and many more along the way)*

Bronfenbrenner, U. (1979). *The ecology of human development.* Cambridge, MA: Harvard University Press.

Coleman, J. S., Campbell, E. Q., Hobson, C. J., McPartland, J. M., et al. (1966). Equality of educational opportunity. Washington, DC: Government Printing Office.

Lightfoot, S. L. (1978). *Worlds apart: Relationships between families and schools.* New York: Basic Books.

Litwak, E., and H. J. Meyer. (1974). *School, family, and neighborhood: The theory and practice of school-community relations.* New York: Columbia University Press.

Valentine, J., and E. Stark. (1979). *The social context of parent involvement* in Head Start. In E. Zigler and J. Valentine (Eds.), *Project Head Start: A legacy of the war on poverty* (pp. 291–314). New York: Free Press.

Waller, W. (1932). *The sociology of teaching.* New York: Wiley.

J. L. EPSTEIN

## MY FAVORITE PERSONAL TEXTS

### Books

*The quality of school life* (1981).
*Friends in school: Patterns of selection and influence in secondary schools* (1983), with N. L. Karweit.
*Education in the middle grades: National practices and trends* (1990), with D. Mac Iver.
*School, family, and community partnerships: Your handbook for action, third edition* (2009) (1997, first edition; 2002, second edition), with colleagues.
*School, family, and community partnerships: Preparing educators and improving schools* (2011) (2001, first edition).

### Articles/Chapters

"The concept and measurement of the quality of school life," *American Educational Research Journal*, 1976 (with J. M. McPartland).
"Longitudinal effects of person-family-school interactions on student outcomes," in *Research in Sociology of Education and Socialization*, Kerckhoff (ed.), 1983.
"School/family/community partnerships: Caring for the children we share," *Phi Delta Kappan*, 1995.
"New connections for sociology and education: Contributing to school reform," *Sociology of Education*, 1996.
"Moving forward: Ideas for research on school, family, and engage all families in their children's education and community partnerships," in *SAGE Handbook for research in education: Engaging ideas and enriching inquiry*, C. F. Conrad and R. Serlin (eds.), 2006, with S. B. Sheldon.
"Levels of leadership: Effects of district and school leaders on the quality of school programs of family and community involvement," *Educational Administration Quarterly*, 2011, with C. Galindo and S.B. Sheldon.

## REFERENCES

Alexander, C. N., & Epstein, J. L. (1969). Problems of dispositional inference in person perception research. *Sociometry, 32*, 381–395.
Becker, H. J., & Epstein, J. L. (1982). Parent involvement: A survey of teacher practices. *Elementary School Journal, 83*, 85–102.
Bronfenbrenner, U. (1979). *The ecology of human development.* Cambridge, MA: Harvard University Press.
Coleman, J. S., Campbell, E. Q., Hobson, C. J., McPartland, J. M., Mood, A., Weinfeld, F. D, & York, R. L. (1966). *Equality of educational opportunity.* Washington, DC: Government Printing Office.
Epstein, J. L. (Ed.). (1981). *The quality of school life.* Lexington, MA: D.C. Heath/Lexington Books.
Epstein, J. L. (1983). Longitudinal effects of person-family-school interactions on student outcomes. In A. Kerckhoff (Ed.), *Research in sociology of education and socialization* (Vol. 4, pp. 101–128). Greenwich, CT: JAI Press.
Epstein, J. L. (1984). A longitudinal study of school and family effects on student development. In S. A. Mednick, M. Harway, & K. Finello (Eds.), *Handbook of longitudinal research* (Vol. 1, pp. 381–397). New York, NY: Praeger.
Epstein, J. L. (1987). Toward a theory of family-school connections: Teacher practices and parent involvement. In K. Hurrelman, F. Kaufmann, & F. Losel (Eds.), *Social intervention: Potential and constraints* (pp. 121–136). New York, NY: DeGruyter.
Epstein, J. L. (1990). What matters in the middle grades – grade span or practices? *Phi Delta Kappan, 71*, 438–444.
Epstein, J. L. (1995). School/family/community partnerships: Caring for the children we share. *Phi Delta Kappan, 76*, 701–712.

Epstein, J. L. (1996). New connections for sociology and education: Contributing to school reform. *Sociology of Education, 69*(May), 6–23.

Epstein, J. L. (2011). S*chool, family, and community partnerships: Preparing educators and improving schools* (2nd ed.). Boulder, CO: Westview Press. (2001, first edition)

Epstein, J. L., & Karweit, N. (Eds.). (1983). *Friends in school: Patterns of selection and influence in secondary schools*. New York, NY: Academic Press.

Epstein, J. L., & Mac Iver, D. J. (1990). *Education in the middle grades: National practices and trends*. Columbus, OH: National Middle School Association.

Epstein, J. L., & McPartland, J. M. (1976). The concept and measurement of the quality of school life. *American Educational Research Journal, 13*, 15–30.

Epstein, J. L., & Sanders, M. G. (2006). Prospects for change: Preparing educators for school, family, and community partnerships. *Peabody Journal of Education, 81*, 81–120.

Epstein, J. L., & Sheldon, S. B. (2006). Moving forward: Ideas for research on school, family, and engage all families in their children's education and community partnerships. In C. F. Conrad & R. Serlin (Eds.), *Sage handbook for research in education: Engaging ideas and enriching inquiry* (pp. 117–137). Thousand Oaks, CA: Sage.

Epstein, J. L., & Van Voorhis, F. L. (2001). More than minutes: Teachers' roles in designing homework. *Educational Psychologist, 36*, 181–193.

Epstein, J. L., & Van Voorhis, F. L. (2012). The changing debate: From assigning homework to designing homework. In E. Reese & S. Suggate (Eds.), *Contemporary debates in childhood education* (pp. 263–273). London: Routledge.

Epstein, J. L., Salinas, K. C., Jackson, V. E., & Van Voorhis, F. L. (1992, revised 1995, 2001). *Manuals for teachers and prototype activities: Teachers Involve Parents in Schoolwork (TIPS)* (in math, language arts, science/health, and math interactive homework in the elementary and middle grades). Baltimore, MD: Johns Hopkins University, Center on School, Family, and Community Partnerships. Retrieved from www.partnershipschools.org

Epstein, J. L., Sanders, M. G., Sheldon, S., Simon, B. S., Salinas, K. C., Janson, N. R., Van Voorhis, F. L., Martin, C. S., Thomas, B. G., Greenfield, M. D., Hutchins, D. J., & Williams, K. J. (2009). *School, family, and community partnerships: Your handbook for action* (3rd ed.). Thousand Oaks CA: Corwin Press. (1997, first edition; 2002, second edition)

Epstein, J. L., Galindo, C., & Sheldon, S. B. (2011). Levels of leadership: Effects of district and school leaders on the quality of school programs of family and community involvement. *Educational Administration Quarterly* (EAQ), *47*, 462–495.

Lightfoot, S. L. (1978). *Worlds apart: Relationships between families and schools*. New York, NY: Basic Books.

McPartland, J. M., & Epstein, J. L. (1977). Open schools and achievement: Extended tests of a finding of no relationship. *Sociology of Education, 42*, 133–144.

Van Voorhis, F. L. (2011). Costs and benefits of family involvement in homework. *Journal of Advanced Academics, 22*, 220–249.

*Joyce L. Epstein*
*Johns Hopkins University*

ADAM GAMORAN

# 7. STRIVING TOWARDS THE BIG QUESTIONS

When I was a young academic, my maternal grandfather, a seasoned scholar, used to ask me to describe my research. After listening patiently to my recitation, he would puff on his pipe and ask, "But when are you going to tackle the Big Questions?" His own scholarship was very much focused on Big Questions, such as whether socialism was a more humane economic system than capitalism, and whether competing governments were likely to blow up the world in the next few years.

My intellectual journey has traversed a few Big Questions, but mostly I have been concerned with smaller matters, such as why some students learn more than others, even in the same schools, and whether and why a particular program, implemented at a particular time and place, helps improve children's development. I don't think there's any other way to address the Big Questions—such as why are some people rich and others poor, and how can we best advance equal opportunity—other than to answer the smaller questions in ways that add up, over time, to answer the larger issues.

## WHERE DO RESEARCH QUESTIONS COME FROM?

Curiosity is a major motivator for scientific endeavors. Why do things work as they do? In my experience, a researcher who is not motivated to *figure it out* soon loses energy and focus. The landscape of lost studies is littered with unfinished projects of researchers who lacked the intrinsic interest to pursue their problems to resolution.

Yet curiosity is insufficient, and another key ingredient of research questions is importance. If curiosity provides the drive to pursue research questions, importance makes the pursuit worthwhile. What makes a question important is specific to the context in which it is asked. When I was a graduate student in the early 1980s, the major work that provided a context for the sociology of education was the 1966 study *Equality of Educational Opportunity*, known as the Coleman Report after its lead author, sociologist James S. Coleman. The Coleman Report was requested by the U.S. Congress to demonstrate what was then the prevailing wisdom, that poor children exhibited low levels of academic performance because they attended poor schools. Unexpectedly, Coleman and his colleagues found that schools were a lot more alike than they were different, and most of the variation in student achievement occurred within schools rather than between schools. Differences in student achievement, the Report showed, were more closely tied to variation in students' family background, which varied within as well as between schools, than to school resources such as per pupil expenditures. Not only were the assumptions that led to the Report incorrect, but the interpretation of findings was often wrong: many writers simplified the findings to, "Schools don't make a difference; families make the difference" (Hodgson, 1975, p. 22). In fact, the Coleman Report did not reveal that schools were inconsequential, but it did show that variation among schools mattered less for variation in school performance compared to differences that students brought with them to school. Hence, the prevailing interpretation among researchers at the time was that differences among students were primarily driven by their family backgrounds rather than by their experiences in school.

From my first day as a graduate student in the University of Chicago's sociology of education doctorate program, I had the good fortune of working on a study of "how schools work" led by the renowned sociologist, Robert Dreeben, and the esteemed scholar of reading, Rebecca Barr. This husband-and-wife team was just about to go to press with *How Schools Work* (Barr & Dreeben, 1983) (I prepared the index for that classic work), which would result in a major reorientation of thinking about how variation in student learning occurred. *How Schools Work* focused on the "technology" of teaching and learning in classrooms, demonstrating that learning occurs when teachers apply the resources at their disposal—time, curriculum, and their own abilities as well as those of their students—to the task of learning, in this case, reading in first grade.

The study I worked on as a graduate student was a follow-up to *How Schools Work*. Among its central aims was to provide a closer look at a device that teachers used to organize instruction: the arrangement of students into instructional groups within the classroom. My dissertation, a study of the effects of ability grouping on reading in first grade, grew out of a sociological puzzle—why does achievement vary within schools? Do features of schooling have anything to do with it, or is it all a matter of variation in family background? Could it be that students from different origins have varied experiences of schooling, and those experiences, rather than family background *per se*, account for within-school variation in learning? If so, what is it about varied student experiences that induces variation in learning? What made the question important, rather than merely a puzzle to be solved, was the centrality of understanding unequal educational outcomes, a core concern of both sociology and social policy.

Yet another sociological concern provided further background for my early research. Stanford sociologist John Meyer had recently published a series of studies, some with his student Brian Rowan, focusing on the symbolic power of schooling to confer status on those who obtain formal qualifications (Meyer, 1977; Meyer & Rowan, 1977, 1978). Among Meyer's most prominent studies was his 1977 article in the *American Journal of Sociology* on "the effects of education as an institution." One of Meyer's propositions was, "In modern societies, adult status is assigned to persons on the basis of duration and type of education, holding constant what they may have learned in school (p. 59)." I viewed this perspective as a direct contrast to the standpoint of my mentors, Barr and Dreeben, whose work might have been taken to say, "In modern societies, adult status is assigned to persons on the basis of what they may have learned in school, holding constant duration and type of education." I aimed to use my study of teaching and learning in first grade reading to test the symbolic and technical perspectives against one another. I took ability group assignment as a sort of "charter," a formal status conferred on students, and tested whether the charter alone, or students' experiences of schooling within their groups, yielded variation in achievement. I found that while ability group assignment seemed to have an independent effect early in the school year, by the end of first grade, the effects of grouping were entirely attributable to the instruction provided by teachers to students in the groups. I took this as evidence that the technical work of schooling was an important trigger for student learning (Gamoran, 1986).

## LEARNING OPPORTUNITIES AND STUDENT ACHIEVEMENT

Building on my studies of first grade reading, I set out to test for similar patterns at the secondary school level. I collaborated with an English professor, Marty Nystrand, to examine whether variation in teaching across ability groups accounted for learning differences. The Wisconsin Center for Education Research (WCER) provided a conducive environment for our work, and in fact it was the director of WCER, Marshall S. "Mike" Smith, who brought us together in what would otherwise have been an unlikely collaboration. (Little did I know that two decades hence, I would come to serve as director of WCER for nine years.) Nystrand devised an approach for measuring instruction based on the way teachers and students talked to one another (see Nystrand, 1997). In contrast to the usual lecture-recitation format of most classes, some teachers gave students greater voice in the classroom by asking questions without predetermined answers ("authentic" questions), by incorporating students' words into subsequent questions ("uptake"), and by fostering genuine discussion. Instruction of this nature, we reasoned, would be more engaging for students and thus produce more learning. Based on data we collected from twenty-five middle and high schools, we found this to be the case, and part of the reason that students in high-track classes learned more than students in low-track classes was that they experienced more engaging instruction (Gamoran et al., 1995; Nystrand, 1997).

Throughout my career I have moved back and forth between relatively small-scale data sets that I have collected myself, and large-scale national surveys collected by the U.S. Department of Education and other federal agencies. The former were invariably more detailed on points I wished to address, but the latter have the advantage of being nationally representative. I thought the national data would provide the leverage I needed to expose what I regarded as the underlying limitations of the Coleman Report. Using a new national survey called High School and Beyond, I sought to show that variation among schools *did* make a difference for variation in learning if one measured the "right" aspects of schools: those that set the conditions for learning. I thought some schools would have larger academic tracks, leading to more academic coursetaking on average, resulting in higher achievement in the school as a whole. For the most part, I was wrong—one of many times in my career that my results have defied my expectations. In "The stratification of high school learning opportunities" (1987), I showed that differences *within* schools in students' tracking and coursetaking experiences made a big difference for learning. In fact, achievement differences between tracks were larger than differences between students in school and those who had dropped out. By contrast, differences among schools were of modest consequence for variation in student achievement. Despite my intentions to the contrary, my findings largely reaffirmed rather than contradicted the Coleman Report.

My research on tracking, learning opportunities, and achievement was afflicted with two main shortcomings. First, my earliest work (e.g., Gamoran, 1986, 1987) had failed to account for the nested structure of schools as organizations. Because instruction was delivered in clusters, such as schools, classes, and instructional groups, measures of achievement of students in those clusters were not independent of one another, and statistical methods that ignored non-independence were likely to underestimate the degree of variability among the measures, possibly erroneously regarding a non-significant effect as statistically significant. Second, questions could be raised about whether models like mine, which relied on statistical controls to make fair comparisons among students, had taken into account unobserved sources of variation among students that could be associated with both the key independent variables and the outcomes under scrutiny. If not, I could have mistakenly accepted a spurious association as causal. For example, if students in high and low tracks differed in unobserved ways not accounted for by the statistical controls, then those unobserved differences (for example, in motivation) could account for achievement differences, rather than tracking itself. Both of these issues emerged as salient in the research literature during the early years of my career, and my colleagues in the sociology department at Wisconsin did not hesitate to point out that my work was vulnerable to both concerns. I spent much of the rest of my career attempting to answer these challenges (see Gamoran & Mare, 1989, and Gamoran, 1992, for my initial responses to these vulnerabilities reflected in Gamoran, 1987).

## FROM SOCIOLOGICAL PUZZLES TO EDUCATION POLICY CHALLENGES

Without my realizing it, the primary motivation for my research had shifted from solving sociological puzzles (for example, "why do some students learn more than others?") to educational policy concerns (for example, "how can we reduce inequality in student learning?"). Of course, the two are closely related, and both had always been present in my research, but over time the balance shifted. Initially, I made this shift in the context of research on tracking. Having learned how tracking tended to magnify inequality, I asked, can tracking be reduced, and if so, would that lessen inequality? I had the chance to address this question in a study of Scottish secondary education, thanks to a Fulbright fellowship to the University of Edinburgh in 1992–1993. Like the rest of the U.K. and much of Europe, Scottish schools have an examination system that largely determines students' prospects for future schooling. Formerly, the Ordinary grade examinations given at age sixteen were limited to the academically elite students. Beginning in the late 1980s, the O-grade system gave way to Standard grade, which allowed access to all students regardless of prior academic performance. I found that the implementation of Standard grade—a shift from more tracking to less tracking—resulted in more equitable opportunities for learning and more equitable outcomes by social background for Scottish young people (Gamoran, 1996). However, even under this reform, students from disadvantaged origins tended not to achieve the highest levels of academic success, indicating that when inequality is suppressed at one level it may still emerge elsewhere (Gamoran, 1997). My year in Edinburgh resulted in long-term collaboration with Scottish scholars that continues to this day (e.g., Iannelli, Gamoran, & Paterson, 2011).

Another international collaboration allowed a different sort of test of how tracking systems in varied contexts may have different results. Hanna Ayalon and I compared differentiation within academic programs in Israel and the United States. In Israel, students at all levels of the academic program have an incentive to perform at their best, because they take examinations that serve as a gateway to higher education and, in some cases, employment. In the U.S., by contrast, students outside the highest academic level have little incentive to perform at their best: because the vast majority of post-secondary institutions are minimally selective, even students who have mediocre high school records can attend college. Our findings indicated that whereas more differentiated schools in the U.S. produced the familiar pattern of inequality by social background, more differentiation in Israeli schools was linked to *less* inequality, apparently because a greater array of levels gave more students the chance to succeed on the high-stakes exams (Ayalon & Gamoran, 2000). The broader lesson we drew was that context matters: even for something as common as tracking, the context in which it is implemented makes a difference for how it affects student outcomes.

From my research on Scotland and Israel, I learned that insights about education in the U.S. are greatly aided by international comparisons. When we focus on our own system alone, we are often blind to possibilities that are rare in our system (such as school-leaving examinations) but common elsewhere. In addition to my own research, I have had the opportunity to advance international comparative research by leading collaborative comparative studies. As a member of the National Research Council's Board on International Studies of Education (BICSE), I co-edited with Andrew C. Porter (my Wisconsin colleague, mentor, and predecessor as director of WCER) a book on methodological advances in cross-national surveys of educational achievement (Porter & Gamoran, 2002). (Following my experience on BICSE, I have served on many National Research Council panels, and I now chair the Board on Science Education).

Next, I had the chance to co-edit, with long-time colleagues Yossi Shavit and Richard Arum, an international comparative study of stratification in higher education (Shavit, Arum, & Gamoran, 2007). Shavit had pioneered the mode of collaborative comparative studies of social stratification with Hans-Peter Blossfeld in their famous (1993) book, *Persisting Inequality*. The mode of collaboration involved recruiting participants from several different countries, each of whom would author a chapter specific to their country using comparable statistical models. The editors would then synthesize the findings in an introductory chapter. *Persistent Inequality* showed that contrary to expectations of some that modernization would lead to more equitable educational outcomes, inequality of educational attainment by social origins persisted in eleven of thirteen countries throughout the twentieth century (the exceptions were Sweden and the Netherlands). In our 2007 book, *Stratification in Higher Education*, we followed the same mode of collaboration but both the findings and our interpretation shifted. Overall, we found "more inclusion than diversion," by which we meant that the expansion of higher education served to draw in students who would formerly have been left out, more so than to divert them to lower-status institutions that would keep them from socioeconomic success in the long run. Even when inequality persisted, we argued, this could be regarded as "inclusive" because as secondary education became nearly universal, the population eligible for higher education became more heterogeneous, so that a similar level of inequality with a more heterogeneous population was a victory of sorts for inclusiveness. Such insights could be gleaned only from international comparisons, not from studying one country at a time.

From my comparative work, it should be evidence that sociological concerns had not disappeared from my interests, though they commanded less of my attention than my policy focus. Perhaps the strongest example of how my research interests shifted from sociological to policy concerns appears in my 2007 edited book on *Standards-Based Reform and the Poverty Gap: Lessons for No Child Left Behind*. This book compiled papers presented at a conference I organized at the Institute for Research on Poverty, another long-time supporter of my work at the University of Wisconsin-Madison. The book emerged just as the federal accountability in education law, known as No Child Left Behind, was set to be reauthorized. (No Child Left Behind was the 2002 incarnation of the Elementary and Secondary Education Act, originally passed in 1965. Though scheduled for reauthorization in 2007, that did not actually occur until 2015 under a new name, the Every Student Succeeds Act). In an introduction that synthesized the findings of the chapter authors, I argued that No Child Left Behind had two main accomplishments. First, it highlighted inequalities by poverty status as well as by race/ethnicity, language minority status, and disability status—gaps that had often been obscured in the past, especially in schools with high test scores overall but lower scores for disadvantaged groups. Second, it focused the attention of educators on seeking new approaches to teaching that would enhance student learning, particularly in contexts of inequality. Moreover, No Child Left Behind offered some good ideas for how to raise achievement and reduce gaps, such as providing free tutoring for low-income students who struggled to keep up, placing highly qualified teachers in every classroom, and choosing instructional strategies backed up by evidence from research. Unfortunately, these ideas were implemented so weakly and inconsistently that they did not do much for performance or inequality, and as a result the law fell far, far short of its ideals.

## A FOCUS ON CONTEXT AND MECHANISMS

Questions about context had always been salient in my research, and their centrality increased as I sharpened my focus on education reform. With my Wisconsin colleagues Walter Secada and Cora Marrett, I laid out my agenda in a chapter in the *Handbook of Sociology of Education* (2000). Having been convinced by earlier work (e.g., Newmann & Associates, 1996; Elmore, Peterson, & McCarthey, 1996) that professional development for teachers could drive instructional change, we argued that effects of professional development were contingent on context: specifically, on the presence of resources that would enable teachers to enact what they had learned. By resources, we meant conditions such as material resources (e.g., money), human resources (e.g., skills and commitments), and social resources (e.g., relationships among teachers). With Secada and others, I developed these ideas in a book (Gamoran et al., 2003), and proceeded to undertake new studies of school programs and school context.

For example with another Wisconsin colleague, Geoffrey Borman, I led a study of an effort in the Los Angeles Unified School District (LAUSD) to provide professional development for teachers to improve teaching and learning in elementary school science. The National Science Foundation provided funding for this project. LAUSD was planning to roll out a new "immersion" approach to teaching science (called "immersion" because students and teachers would be "immersed" in the practice of science) and associated professional development. The reform had to be phased in due to resource constraints and, at our urging, district officials agreed to randomize schools for earlier and later implementation. This allowed us to test the causal effects of the reform. Coming along just when the U.S. Department of Education agreed to fund my proposal to establish at Wisconsin a predoctoral training program in education sciences focused on causal inference (which continues today under the leadership of Borman and others), the study also provided a fertile training ground for our students, one of many large-scale, collaborative studies that my colleagues and I initiated over the next several years to provide training in research that allowed judgments of cause and effect (other examples included Gamoran et al., 2012; Witte et al., 2014; Harackiewicz et al., 2014; Goldrick-Rab et al., 2016; Borman et al., 2016).

In another case of results that defied my expectations, the immersion program failed to elevate student achievement. On the contrary, after the first year of implementation, achievement was *lower* in schools whose teachers were randomly selected for the immersion curriculum and professional development, compared to the control schools (Borman, Gamoran, & Bowdon, 2008). Subsequent analyses demonstrated why this occurred: whereas teachers exposed to the immersion program implemented the first two steps in the cycle of science inquiry, asking questions and gathering data with students, their instruction failed to follow through to formulating explanations based on the data, connecting the explanations to scientific knowledge, and justifying the explanations (Grigg et al., 2013). In other words, teachers and students pursued part of the scientific *process* apparently at the expense of scientific *content*. This pair of studies provides a good example of how tracing the mechanisms through which a reform process occurs can shed important light on why it works—or breaks down.

As a successor to our first collaboration, Geoffrey Borman obtained a grant from the Institute of Education Sciences (IES) at the U.S. Department of Education to implement an intervention to mitigate the effects of stereotype threat across all eleven middle schools in Madison, WI. Stereotype threat occurs when members of a marginalized group internalize a stereotype that others hold and, under conditions of such threat, perform worse than their capabilities would otherwise allow on high-stakes tasks (Steele, 2010). After extensive testing in laboratories, several small-scale studies in real schools had shown that helping students to think differently about themselves, for example by affirming their values as multifaceted individuals or by strengthening their sense of belonging, could mitigate the effects of stereotype threat and improve performance. Focusing on the minority student achievement gap, our study found positive effects of interventions designed to reduce stereotype threat (Borman et al., 2016), particularly in schools in which the degree of threat was likely to be greatest: where the proportion of black and Hispanic students was relatively small and the achievement gap was relatively large (Hanselman et al., 2014). This study provides another instance of how the effects of an educational program may depend on its context.

One more case reveals how the two sides of my interests—solving sociological puzzles and addressing policy concerns—may operate together. Lynn McDonald, the founder of a family-school engagement program called FAST (Families and Schools Together) came to me with an idea. FAST operates by bringing families to a structured program of interaction of parents with their children, parents with other parents, and families with school staff for eight weekly sessions, followed by two years of monthly follow-up meetings led by parents. She proposed that FAST enhances "social capital," that is, relations of trust and shared expectations among persons in a social network, and that her program offered a chance to test the effects of social capital on children's academic and social development. I saw it as an opportunity to test the effects of a key education reform (family engagement), and to test a prominent sociological theory (social capital), at the same time. With our colleagues Ruth López Turley and Carmen Valdez, we obtained support from the National Institute of Child Health and Human Development to study FAST and social capital in fifty-two schools in San Antonio and Phoenix. Half the schools were randomly selected for FAST, and half served as controls. The study represents an intervention-based approach to test sociological theory (Fiel, Shoji, & Gamoran, 2015). Social capital theory is difficult to test because the causal direction is ambiguous: if child outcomes are better in the context of social capital, is that because social capital promotes positive outcomes, or because social capital emerges where children are thriving? Yet one cannot randomize families to social capital, so how can we identify the causal pattern? Our solution was to randomly assign schools to the FAST intervention, which provides an exogenous stimulus to social capital, and use that exogenous variation to test for causal effects. We found strong evidence that FAST elevates social capital (Gamoran et al., 2012; McCarty, 2014; Rangel, 2016) and that this effect is sustained over time (Rangel, Shoji, & Gamoran, 2014). Moreover, FAST participation yielded lower levels of children's behavioral problems, which we interpreted as social capital effects (Turley et al., in press). However, our analyses of achievement in third grade, two years after FAST, have not yielded social capital effects on academic outcomes (Gamoran et al., 2016).

For all of these large, collaborative studies, the Interdisciplinary Training Program (ITP) in Education Sciences at WCER was an essential resource, as it provided waves of bright, energetic doctoral students to contribute their labor and their considerable intellectual talents to the research. At the same time, the studies served as essential resources for the students, because they provided both training that the students needed to prepare for their future scholarship, and the raw materials for conference presentations, journal articles, and dissertations that helped launch their careers. The IES predoctoral interdisciplinary training programs were intended to prepare a new generation of researchers capable of conducting research on "what works" in education, and the ITP met that aim. Yet I always spoke to our students of two "subversive" aspects of our own program. First, in contrast to goals prevalent at IES in the early 2000s, we were not interested solely in "what works" but *how*, that is, in the mechanisms through which programs might have their effects. Second, and also in contrast to IES whose mission was oriented to policy and practice, ITP projects emphasized their disciplinary foundations in two ways. First, discipline-based theories motivated the studies (as in the social capital and stereotype threat projects described above). Second, social science disciplines were essential for identifying the purported mechanisms through which the programs had their expected effects, as in the elementary science study mentioned earlier.

## THE FUTURE OF EDUCATIONAL INEQUALITY

By the turn of the twenty-first century, I finally felt ready to tackle the Big Questions that my grandfather had urged upon me two decades earlier. In 2001, I published what I regarded as an audacious attempt to predict the future of racial and economic inequality in U.S. education. The baseball player and erstwhile philosopher Yogi Berra is credited with saying, "prediction is difficult, especially about the future," which sounds amusing but in social science research, has the ring of truth: we are constantly developing prediction models based on data from the past; when we try to apply those models to the future, our efforts are even more perilous.

Such was the case with my effort to forecast the future of educational inequality (Gamoran, 2001). Based on trends in the twentieth century, I offered two predictions for the twenty-first. First, I predicted that racial inequality would decline substantially. This prediction was based on a "virtuous cycle" in which good things happen and, when compounded, lead to further positive results. In this case I aregued, a twentieth century drop in the black-white test score gap and a convergence in rates of high school completion would pay off in the next generation with further improvements for African American students and narrowing gaps in achievement and attainment. Second, I predicted that socioeconomic inequality in education would not diminish. This prediction, too, was based on past trends in which inequality by socioeconomic circumstances persisted largely unabated throughout the twentieth century. I suggested that by 2010, we would know whether my predictions were correct.

Unfortunately it is now apparent that my predictions have failed. Racial inequality has declined far more slowly than I anticipated and socioeconomic inequality, by some measures, has intensified (Gamoran, 2015). What happened to the virtuous cycle? First, as some of my critics anticipated early on (Gosa & Alexander, 2007), increased education pays off less for blacks than for whites (Long, Kelly, & Gamoran, 2013). This pattern reflects a variety of conditions including a longer time to degree for blacks, greater use of equivalency degrees rather than diplomas, lower quality schooling, and lower levels of family wealth which may hamper postsecondary completion and career launches. Second, I failed to anticipate the importance of the rise in mass incarceration for racial educational inequality. The last quarter of the twentieth century witnessed a staggering increase in incarceration rates, with African American males dramatically overrepresented. Incarceration not only limits the education of those imprisoned, but harms the educational outcomes of their offspring, particularly boys (Haskins, 2014). Mass incarceration has shattered the virtuous cycle. Meanwhile, socioeconomic inequality in education has gotten worse because of increasing economic inequality overall (Reardon, 2011), as well as because of increasing segregation by income and an increasing concentration of poverty in U.S. cities (Sharkey, 2013), and increasing differences across levels of parents' education in the time that parents spend engaging in developmental activities with their children (Putnam, 2015).

Despite the failure of my predictions, I have not despaired for the future. On the contrary, my new position as president of the William T. Grant Foundation has given me the chance to support (though not undertake myself) new research that may point the direction towards a more prosperous and equitable future. The Foundation's mission is to support research to improve the lives of young people. I arrived at the Foundation in September 2013, and working with our Board and staff, we launched a new initiative in spring 2014 to support research on programs, policies, and practices that reduce youth inequality. Meanwhile, for several years prior to my arrival, the Foundation supported studies of the use of research evidence in decisions that affect young people. In 2015, we launched a new phase of this work, calling on researchers to study how to create the conditions in which research evidence will be used, and to test the common assumption that when decisions are informed by research evidence, the targets of decisions—in our case, children and youth—are the beneficiaries.

Why hold out confidence in the power of research to light the way, when the past is darkened by unsuccessful efforts? First, knowledge has accumulated about ways to reduce inequality. From early child care to class size reduction to social-psychological interventions, we have learned much about ways to reduce inequality, although they have not yet been implemented in coherent, sustained, and comprehensive ways (Gamoran, 2014). Second, inequality as a social issue has captured the attention of leaders across the nation and the world, on all sides of the political spectrum, so there may be greater collective will to address inequality than at any time since economic inequality began to rise in the 1980s (Gamoran, 2015). For these reasons, addressing inequality need not be a futile task, and research may have an important role to play.

## MY FAVORITE TEXTS BY OTHERS

Barr, R., & Dreeben, R. (1983). *How schools work.* Chicago: University of Chicago Press.

Coleman, J. S., Campbell, E. Q., Hobson, C. J., McPartland, F., Mood, A. M., Weinfeld, F. D., & York, R. L. (1966). *Equality of educational opportunity.* Washington, DC: U.S. Government Printing Office.

Jencks, C., & Phillips, M. (1998). *The black-white test score gap.* Washington, DC: Brookings Institution Press.

Meyer, J. (1977). The effects of education as an institution. *American Journal of Sociology, 83,* 55-77.

Olneck, M. R. (1993). Terms of inclusion: Has multiculturalism redefined equality in American education? *American Journal of Education, 101,* 234–260.

Rosenbaum, J. S. (1976). *Making inequality: The hidden curriculum of high school tracking.* New York: John Wiley & Sons.

Rowan, B. (1990). Commitment and control: Alternative strategies for the organizational design of schools. *Review of Research in Education, 16,* 353-389.

Sewell, W. H., Hauser, R. M., & Featherman, D. L. (1976). *Schooling and achievement in American society.* New York: Academic Press.

Shavit, Y., & Blossfeld. H-P. (1993). *Persisting inequality: Changing educational attainment in thirteen countries.* Boulder, CO: Westview Press.

## MY FAVORITE PERSONAL TEXTS

Gamoran, A. (1987). The stratification of high school learning opportunities. *Sociology of Education, 60,* 135 155.

Gamoran, A., & Mare, R. D. (1989). Secondary school tracking and educational inequality: Compensation, reinforcement, or neutrality? *American Journal of Sociology, 94,* 1146-1183.

Gamoran, A. (1992). The variable effects of high school tracking. *American Sociological Review, 57,* 812-828.

Gamoran, A., Nystrand, M., Berends, M., & LePore, P. C. (1995). An organizational analysis of the effects of ability grouping. *American Educational Research Journal, 32,* 687-715.

Gamoran, A. (1996). Curriculum standardization and equality of opportunity in Scottish secondary education, 1984-1990. *Sociology of Education, 29,* 1-21.

Gamoran, A., Secada, W. G., & and Marrett, C. B. (2000). The organizational context of teaching and learning: Changing theoretical perspectives. Pp. 37-63 in M. T. Hallinan (Ed.), *Handbook of the sociology of education*. New York: Kluwer Academic/Plenum Publishers.

Gamoran, A., Editor. (2007). *Standards-based reform and the poverty gap: Lessons for No Child Left Behind*. Washington, DC: Brookings Institution Press.

Grigg, J., Kelly, K. A., Gamoran, A., & Borman, G. D. (2013). Effects of two scientific inquiry professional development interventions on teaching practice. *Educational Evaluation and Policy Analysis, 35*, 38-56.

Hanselman, P., Bruch, S. K., Gamoran, A., & Borman, G. D. (2014). Threat in context: School moderation of the impact of social identity threat on racial/ethnic achievement gaps. *Sociology of Education, 87*, 106-124.

Gamoran, A. (2015). *The future of educational inequality: What went wrong, and how can we fix it?* New York: William T. Grant Foundation. Available at: http://blog.wtgrantfoundation.org/post/124249227732/presidents-comment-the-future-of-educational

## REFERENCES

Ayalon, H., & Gamoran, A. (2000). Stratification in academic secondary programs and educational inequality: Comparison of Israel and the United States. *Comparative Education Review, 44*, 54–80.

Barr, R., & Dreeben, R. (1983). *How schools work*. Chicago, IL: University of Chicago Press.

Borman, G. D., Gamoran, A., & Bowdon, J. (2008). A randomized trial of teacher development in elementary science: First-year effects. *Journal of Research on Educational Effectiveness, 1*, 237–264.

Borman, G. D., Grigg, J., & Hanselman, P. (2016). An effort to close achievement gaps at scale through self-affirmation. *Educational Evaluation and Policy Analysis, 38*, 21–42.

Coleman, J. S., Campbell, E. Q., Hobson, C. J., McPartland, F., Mood, A. M., Weinfeld, F. D., & York, R. L. (1966). *Equality of educational opportunity*. Washington, DC: U.S. Government Printing Office.

Elmore, R. F., Peterson, P. L., & McCarthey, S. J. (1996). *Restructuring in the classroom*. San Francisco, CA: Jossey-Bass.

Fiel, J., Shoji, M., & Gamoran, A. (2015). An intervention approach to building social capital: Effects on grade retention. In Y. Li (Ed.), *Handbook of research methods and applications in social capital* (pp. 262–291). Cheltenham, England: Edward Elgar Publishing.

Gamoran, A. (1986). Instructional and institutional effects of ability grouping. *Sociology of Education, 59*, 185–198.

Gamoran, A. (1987). The stratification of high school learning opportunities. *Sociology of Education, 60*, 135–155.

Gamoran, A. (1992). The variable effects of high school tracking. *American Sociological Review, 57*, 812–828.

Gamoran, A. (1996). Curriculum standardization and equality of opportunity in Scottish secondary education, 1984–1990. *Sociology of Education, 29*, 1–21.

Gamoran, A. (2001). American schooling and educational inequality: A forecast for the 21st century. *Sociology of Education, Extra Issue*, 135–153.

Gamoran, A. (Ed.). (2007). *Standards-based reform and the poverty gap: Lessons for No Child Left Behind*. Washington, DC: Brookings Institution Press.

Gamoran, A. (2014). *Inequality is the problem: Prioritizing research on reducing inequality*. New York, NY: William T. Grant Foundation.

Gamoran, A. (2015). *The future of educational inequality: What went wrong, and how can we fix it?* New York, NY: William T. Grant Foundation.

Gamoran, A., & Mare, R. D. (1989). Secondary school tracking and educational inequality: Compensation, reinforcement, or neutrality? *American Journal of Sociology, 94*, 1146–1183.

Gamoran, A., Nystrand, M., Berends, M., & LePore, P. C. (1995). An organizational analysis of the effects of ability grouping. *American Educational Research Journal, 32*, 687–715.

Gamoran, A., Secada, W. G., & Marrett, C. B. (2000). The organizational context of teaching and learning. In M. T. Hallinan (Ed.), *Handbook of the sociology of education* (pp. 37–63). New York, NY: Kluwer Academic/Plenum.

Gamoran, A., Anderson, C. W., Quiroz, P. A., Secada, W. G., Williams, T., & Ashmann, S. (2003). *Transforming teaching in math and science: How schools and districts can support change*. New York, NY: Teachers College Press.

Gamoran, A., Turley, R. N. L., Turner, A., & Fish, R. (2012). Differences between Hispanic and non-Hispanic families in social capital and child development: First-year findings from an experimental study. *Research in Social Stratification and Mobility, 30*, 97–112.

Gamoran, A., Miller, H. K., Fiel, J., & Valentine, J. L. (2016). *Family engagement effects on student achievement: A challenge to social capital theory*. Paper to be presented at the annual meeting of the American Educational Research Association, Washington, DC.

Goldrick-Rab, S., Kelchen, R., Harris, D. N., & Benson, J. (2016). Reducing income inequality in educational attainment: Experimental evidence on the impact of financial aid on college completion. *American Journal of Sociology, 121*, 1762–1817.

Gosa, T. L., & Alexander, K. L. (2007). Family (dis)advantage and the educational prospects of better off African American youth: How race still matters. *Teachers College Record, 109*, 285–321.

Grigg, J., Kelly, K. A., Gamoran, A., & Borman, G. D. (2013). Effects of two scientific inquiry professional development interventions on teaching practice. *Educational Evaluation and Policy Analysis, 35*, 38–56.

Hanselman, P., Bruch, S. K., Gamoran, A., & Borman, G. D. (2014). Threat in context: School moderation of the impact of social identity threat on racial/ethnic achievement gaps. *Sociology of Education, 87*, 106–124.

Harackiewicz, J. M., Rozek, C. R., Hulleman, C. S., & Hyde, J. S. (2012). Helping parents to motivate adolescents in mathematics and science: An experimental test of a utility-value intervention. *Psychological Science, 40*, 899–906.

Haskins, A. R. (2014). Unintended consequences: Effects of paternal incarceration on child school readiness and later special education placement. *Sociological Science, 1*, 141–158.

Hodgson, G. (1975). Do schools make a difference? In D. M. Levine & M. J. Bane (Eds.), *The inequality controversy: Schooling and distributive justice* (pp. 22–44). New York, NY: Basic Books.

Iannelli, C., Gamoran, A., & Paterson, L. (2011). Scottish higher education, 1987–2001: Expansion through diversion. *Oxford Review of Education, 37*, 717–741.

Long, D. A., Kelly, S., & Gamoran, A. (2011). Whither the virtuous cycle? Past and future trends in Black-White inequality in educational attainment. *Social Science Research, 41*, 16–32.

McCarty, A. T. (2014). *The role of parent social resources in high poverty schools and the promise of family engagement programs for reducing income-related inequality in children's mental health and academic skills* (Unpublished doctoral dissertation). Department of Sociology, University of Wisconsin-Madison, Madison, WI.

Meyer, J. W. (1977). The effects of education as an institution. *American Journal of Sociology, 83*, 55–77.

Meyer, J. W., & Rowan, B. (1977). Institutionalized organizations: Formal structure as myth and ceremony. *American Journal of Sociology, 83*, 340–363.

Meyer, J. W., & Rowan, B. (1978). The structure of educational organizations. In M. Meyer (Ed.), *Environments and organizations* (pp. 78–109). San Francisco, CA: Jossey-Bass.

Newmann, F. M., & Associates. (1996). *Authentic achievement: Restructuring schools for intellectual quality*. San Francisco, CA: Jossey-Bass.

Nystrand, M. (1997). *Opening dialogue: Understanding the dynamics of language and learning in the English classroom*. New York, NY: Teachers College Press.

Porter, A. C., & Gamoran, A. (Eds.). (2002). *Methodological advances in cross-national surveys of educational achievement*. Washington, DC: National Academies Press.

Putnam, R. D. (2015). *Our kids: The American dream in crisis*. New York, NY: Simon & Schuster.

Rangel, D. E. (2016). *Parental relationships and social capital in the school-community context: A multiple method study with low-income Mexican-origin families* (Unpublished doctoral dissertation). Department of Sociology, University of Wisconsin-Madison, Madison, WI.

Rangel, D. E., Shoji, M. N., & Gamoran, A. (2014). *Family engagement and social capital: An empirical test with families in low-income Latino communities*. Paper presented at the annual meeting of the American Sociological Association, San Francisco, CA.

Reardon, S. F. (2011). The widening academic achievement gap between the rich and the poor: New evidence and possible explanations. In G. Duncan & R. Murnane (Eds.), *Whither opportunity?* (pp. 91–115). New York, NY: Russell Sage.

Sharkey, P. (2013). *Stuck in place: Urban neighborhoods and the end of progress toward racial equality*. Chicago, IL: University of Chicago Press.

Shavit, Y., & Blossfeld. H.-P. (1993). *Persisting inequality: Changing educational attainment in thirteen countries*. Boulder, CO: Westview Press.

Shavit, Y., Arum, R., Gamoran, A., & Menahem, G. (2007). *Stratification in higher education: A comparative study*. Stanford, CA: Stanford University Press.

Steele, C. M. (2010). *Whistling vivaldi: How stereotypes affect us and what we can do*. New York, NY: W. W. Norton & Co.

Turley, R. N. L., Gamoran, A., Turner, A., & Fish, R. (In press). Reducing children's behavior problems through social capital: A causal assessment. *Social Science Research*.

Witte, J. F., Wolf, P. J., Cowen, J. M., Carlson, D. E., & Fleming, D. J. (2014). High stakes choice: Achievement and accountability in America's oldest school voucher program. *Educational Evaluation and Policy Analysis, 36*, 437–456.

*Adam Gamoran*
*William T. Grant Foundation*
*(Emeritus) University of Wisconsin, Madison*

A. H. HALSEY†[1]

# 8. THE SOCIOLOGY OF A LIFE

Experience of life prejudices each and every one of us. I, now in my nineties, declare myself a committed ethical socialist and have done so for over fifty years; but also I have become a disciplined sociologist. The commitment leads me to passionate advocacy of a particular form of society—the active democracy of an informed citizenry. The discipline compels me to seek truth through empirical evidence, with ruthless scepticism as to sources and methods and with disrespect towards arbitrary authority. But Reader beware! Greet my scepticism with your own scepticism and always remember that words can and do change their meaning as they move through time and space. You are confronted here by an elderly Englishman who has lived and learnt through over ninety years of economic, political, social and cultural change.

Consider, for prominent example, my assertion, detailed below, of the desirability of a society of democratic ethical socialists. My personal experience has led me to link this ideology strongly to the British Labour Party and the respectable working class in the first half of the twentieth century. But my friend Frank Field, the Labour MP for Birkenhead, argues cogently that the ethical ideology has wider and deeper roots in British society beyond the confines of working-class Labour supporters.[2] No-one, he claims, is as famous a legislative ethical social reformer as the Victorian aristocrat, Lord Shaftsbury, and he was a life-long Tory! My account is biased by personal experience. No party or class can claim a monopoly of the ethical socialist outlook. It must stand on its own as an invitation for loyalty from all human beings whatever their class or creed, their religion or gender, their age or nationality.

Education is precious: it is the necessary possession of citizens in a democratic society, necessary to both a productive economy and to wise government, to both livelihood and living, to both wealth and culture. The future of any rich and contented democratic country will depend on universal participation in the enlightenment of its people 'from the cradle to the grave.' The past has generated stratification, exclusion and inequality in schooling. Education has always been positional, cursed by hereditary kinship, gender, ethnicity and caste. Evolution from traditional societies with a hierarchy of educated minorities and illiterate masses has recently accelerated with modern expansions of opportunities for learning, locally and internationally, through traditional tuition and distance communication. The rise of the sociology of education echoes the broad movement of countries as organisations of teaching and research from the restrictive past towards a bounteous future. But there remain problems and resistances from vested interests, from residual ignorance, inadequate resources, and lack of political will which still prevent the efficient use of social science as a powerful tool in the creation of a fully developed civilisation.

Professor Sadovnik and his colleagues are among the progressives in promoting educational expansion. They do not hesitate to include advertising the importance of the sociology of education in furthering the expansionist cause and my vanity is flattered by their invitation to me to write an account of my experiences as a leader in the development of this specialism. Yet I hesitate. The word 'icon' in our time has escaped from the dictionary of religion into the mainstream of secular culture. Searching for celebrities, though never absent from the history of warfare, politics, literature and the arts, is now rampant on television and is dubiously employed in attributing discoveries to individuals in the natural or social sciences. It is even more doubtful as a stimulus to education where it may distort reality and mislead the reader or listener. So in what follows I compromise between vanity and modesty and leave judgement of my own work to colleagues. Conveniently saving my embarrassment, in 2006 the *Oxford Review of Education* included me in a short list of Oxford dons, beginning with the philosopher T.H. Green, who had led modern educational thought in Britain, with an article by George and Teresa Smith extolling my career: and other colleagues, in the same issue, made laudatory references to my work. For my own part I prefer to hope that some future historian of sociology will refer to me in a footnote as a chronicler of the first generation of professional sociologists in Britain in the twentieth century and as a contributor to historical and survey work in the sociology of education.

My first formal introduction to the sociology of education came with my graduation at the London School of Economics. That was in 1950 and I will come back to it shortly but first I must describe the aspiring cohort of graduate students at LSE in the early 1950s. I did so initially and at greater length in an article in the *European Journal of Sociology* and subsequently in my *History of Sociology in Britain*. As an undergraduate at LSE from 1947 I found myself among a remarkable group of mainly ex-service men who were interested in becoming professional sociologists and especially keen to understand both their own education and the social possibility of expanding, even universalising, a widely informed citizenry. Basil Bernstein was one of them. He later became famous as the foremost European contributor to a rapidly developing sociological theory of educational learning and selection. There was also Ronnie Dore, the leading expert on Japanese education and Ralf Dahrendorf who joined us later in 1952 and was so knowledgeable about German schools and universities. The only woman in the student group was Olive Banks who began her graduate work in the sociology of education but later transferred her attention to feminism. And there was Asher Tropp who wrote an early study of school teaching as a profession. They were altogether a lively, enthusiastic and ambitious set of young sociologists who together formed the British Sociological Association and aspired successfully to fill the leading posts in the sixties in the multiplying university departments of sociology in the UK and abroad.

It had been different before the war when isolated individuals such as T. H. Marshall, David Glass or Jean Floud came into sociology. Jean was born in provincial England in 1915, the daughter of a shop assistant and therefore marginal to the great bulk of the industrial urban and rural manual working class. Her country, though a leading imperial and colonising power, was internally exhausted by War and still rigidly stratified by classes and status groups forming a hierarchy of wealth, power, prestige and influence. The whole economic, political and social structure was beginning to change in her generation but was still culturally dominated by a ruling class of landed aristocrats and a rising professional upper middle class of highly educated civil servants—the British equivalent of the German Bildungsbürgertum, which set such high store by the encouragement of advanced educational standards among its children.

Meanwhile some eighty-five per cent of Britons were manual workers, typically leaving school at fourteen. Only two per cent of the population attended the universities and these were disproportionately drawn from the upper and middle classes. Women in Jean's youth were even more discriminated against, educationally, politically and occupationally. The fruity and patrician voices she may have heard occasionally in the early days of wireless were the messengers of a distant realm of educated and high-minded civility, dominantly male, with only the faintest chance of access through publically funded eleven plus places in a state grammar school. Nevertheless she was blessed with a superior mental capacity and also with an ardent desire to climb the steep educational ladder and to join the elevated metropolitan upper-middle class in a cultivated style of life and language very different from that of her own childhood milieu.

When I first met her at LSE just before I graduated she had completed this improbable journey of self-reconstruction. I was one of the dozen or so LSE sociology students who, in the early 1950s, aspired to become professional teachers of that subject. My personal loyalties were to people like Eric Liddell—the flying Scotsman,[3] who said after his victories at the 1924 Olympic games in Paris that 'God made me fast. And, when I run, I feel His pleasure,'—Arthur Lewis, the Nobel prizewinning West Indian economist, Barbara Wootton, the Cambridge social reformer and above all, R.H Tawney, the brave egalitarian. He looked and spoke like an untidy angel who had learnt English only from the Authorised Version.[4] Here is what I wrote in an article for the *European Journal of Sociology (1981).*

> It had been different before the War, when the handful of British recruits to sociology was made up of isolated individuals… The possibility of academic expansion and cultural openness was virtually inconceivable. If, like David Glass or Jean Floud, they came from the working or lower-middle classes, they were under strong pressure to assimilate in dress and speech to the culture of the higher metropolitan professionals and so to be heard by the post-war students as people who used words like 'telephone' or 'motor' as

verbs rather than nouns. For us, service in the army, navy or air force had engendered a patriotic Attleean ethical socialism which would also transform T. H. Marshall's world – the Cambridge voice, the shy self-assurance, the faint air of *ennui*. Moreover the newcomers were more impressed by David Glass's suave erudition and Jean Floud's vivacious intelligence than by their socially elevated appearance. They were assimilators, perforce or by choice. Our intended journey was an intellectual and professional one; the vehicle and travelling clothes were secondary.

I was glad to accept when Jean chose me as her research assistant in 1950 and we set out to establish the sociology of education as a central branch of the social sciences. There followed a frantic decade of research and publication. Our *Social Class and Educational Opportunity* was published by Heinemann in 1956, a trend report and annotated bibliography of the specialism in *Current Sociology* (Vol. VII, No. 1) in 1958, and a first reader, *Education, Economy and Society* by the Free Press in 1961.

Though a pre-war product, Jean was young for her years. She had a glittering femininity, a twinkling eye and a smile which lit up the whole of her attentive face. She had graduated in 1936, met, fell in love with, and married the handsome and cultivated Peter Floud in 1938, spent the war in educational administration and returned to a lectureship at LSE in 1946 to live in Well Walk, Hampstead in a perpendicular Victorian house with heavy white internal doors, high ceilings, a grand piano and William Morris curtains. She was devoted to her upper-class communist husband, a rising curator at the Victoria and Albert Museum, and to her three children. All the signs in the 1950s pointed towards a prosperous future of academic success and familial happiness.

But it was not to be. The crushing blow came in 1960 with Peter's sudden death. She was abruptly left as a single mum with three eager and lively children. Time for both mothering and for social research became agonisingly scarce. Successful academics have to learn by the time they are forty that early promise has to be reinforced by sustained daily devotion to their chosen subject with all the grinding labour of keeping abreast of a mounting body of literature, the boring repetitiveness of survey and investigation, and the ceaseless flow of official statistics. Jean had learnt from the Floud family that the Floud's were not only naturally bright but also nurtured in a comfortable home and highly educated in expensive private boarding schools and the colleges of Oxford and Cambridge. Thus Peter and his younger brother Bernard had been sent to Gresham's School to live and learn alongside such luminaries as W. H. Auden, Benjamin Britten and Boris Ford. Accordingly and privately she thought of herself as inadequately educated and she lacked the confidence to acquire the statistical skills of multiple analysis which were being developed by international contributors to the sociology of education, including Raymond Boudon in France or James Coleman or Otis Dudley Duncan in America.

Such skills require time and application, and added to all this there was for her the temptation of administration.

No-one in the 1950s had read as widely as Jean in the sociology of education. She knew the German, French and American literature and it's varied and unsatisfactory history in the form of 'educational sociology' as may be confirmed by perusal of our annotated bibliography of which I can affirm that she wrote three quarters. She had, for example, read and appreciated Émile Durkheim's *Evolution Pedagogique en France,* years before it was translated into English. Indeed, I think it is fair to say that by 1961, after T. W. Schultz and his colleagues at Chicago had calculated high returns to investment in education and when the OECD staged its conference at Kungalv in Sweden to review the relation between education and economic growth, Jean had reached the zenith of her critical powers in the sociology of education and was insisting that education needed to be analysed like any other major and modern social institution. Formal schooling was of importance but only in relation to other educational institutions such as the family, the peer group, the churches and chapels, the media etc. Measured intelligence had to be distinguished from innate capacity and a whole range of abilities had to be identified and all had to be seen as interactive in combination and conflict in the process of turning biological organisms into adult social personalities as workers and citizens. It was at this point that Jean faced the upheaval of a move to Oxford and there she gave up empirical research on the problems of the sociology of education, turning instead to philosophy, law and administration. Nevertheless for me she remains a significant pioneer in the branch of sociology to which I and many others have given a lot of subsequent attention.

## SOURCES OF INFLUENCE

I have listed 10 books by which I have been deeply influenced. It is noticeable that most of them are by authors who have not thought of themselves as sociologists of education but have offered a vision of an ideal society, which inspired me to advocate a social policy of ethics as distinct from Marxist socialism. I begin with Thomas More's *Utopia* (1516) that gave expression to a view of society as a whole, which fit completely to my personal childish dreams of a totally transformed country of democratic citizens committed to hard work and just relations with others, to honour and service to the community, and to an indifference to material wealth or social rank. I also include William Morris's *News from Nowhere* as a modern version of the same moralised society and I have added R.H Tawney's classic works of attack on capitalist society published in 1921 and 1931.

Orwell's influence on me was similarly great. I hesitated between *Animal Farm* or *1984* but chose instead his "Politics and the English language" as an exemplary reminder to all newcomers that sociologists of education must themselves be educators in the use of plain English to ensure that truth is sought in promoting the understanding of social intelligence as part and parcel of a cultivated citizenry. These more modern advocators of reformed education in a new society are accessible whereas Thomas More belonged to a pre-industrial era and wrote in Latin and published in Louvain. Perhaps the best beginning text for the newcomer is an elegant essay by George M. Logan and Robert M. Adams as an introduction to More's *Utopia* in the Cambridge texts on the history of political thought (*CUP, 1988*).

My class origins, a rural childhood, the RAF and LSE combined and collided to make me the Attleean socialist and the devoted sociologist that I became. But there were also some powerful people along the way. Edward Shils, I hasten to mention, inspired me not only through his confidence in the dignity of European Social Science, but also his American assumption that global understanding was there to be grasped and used by strenuous application of sociology. The BBC also gave benign opportunities of broadcasting to hitherto unknown exponents of the spoken word of whom I was one. I was noticed and encouraged by Ron Gass and his colleagues at the OECD in Paris and thereby given the chance to survey educational arrangements all over the member countries including America, Europe, Japan and the Antipodes. And I found Oxford to be a stimulus with its talented colleagues at Barnett House and Nuffield College, notably Anthony Heath, John Goldthorpe, Diego Gambetta, John Ridge, George Smith and others too numerous to mention.

Another Oxford don has to be added: G.D.H Cole. He preceded me there. G.D.H. Cole was born in 1889, went to St. Paul's school, and became an outstanding scholar with a mature and passionate heart and a cool, clear brain. He read the earlier William Morris's artistic and romantic novel *News from Nowhere* and decided that he himself could be nothing else but a socialist all his life. He went up to Balliol in 1908, joined the Oxford University Fabian Society, started his life-long career as a socialist educator and journalist in his first term and received a double first in Classical Moderations and Lit. Hum., which resulted in a seven year prize Fellowship at Magdalen on graduation in 1912. Cole's conversion to socialism via *News from Nowhere* was an entry into the Labour movement of an idealistic kind for the son of a successful Tory estate agent. He wrote in November 1910:

> I became a Socialist because as soon as the case for a society of equals, set free from the twin evils of riches and poverty, mastership and subjection, was put to me, I knew that to be the only kind of society that could be consistent with human decency and fellowship and that in no other society could I have the right to be content. The society that William Morris imaged seemed to me to embody the right sort of human relations and to be altogether beautiful and admirable.[5]

Thus Cole, while still a school boy, suddenly saw a new society which was democratic, fraternal and egalitarian. Unlike the Fabian ideal society advocated by Sidney and Beatrice Webb, which he saw as elitist, centralised, and state-controlled by bureaucrats, he thought that workers could do it for themselves, become a self-governing community of working people with power spread beyond the political sphere into diffused local centres of cooperative producers and consumers, educated by their experiences in work, life and leisure into a civilised society of equal and free citizens. These were Cole's ideals and his personal life was devoted to their practical attainment.

## MY PERSONAL CAREER

I was born in Kentish Town in 1923, the second of what became an eight child family. As a family we were temporarily welfare dependents or 'on the parish' as my Cockney mother would have said in those far-off days... Although still perhaps the leading imperial and industrial nation, Britain was also still poverty stricken, rigidly stratified and socially rather than politically organised in its schooling, housing and welfare provision. My father was a railway porter on the London, Midland and Scottish Railway (LMS) but ill from his First War wounds. In 1926 the LMS sent him back to the country to work and regain his health as a porter- signalman at one of its whistle-stops in Rutland. All these personal and familial facts have been elaborated in my autobiography and in a book entitled *Changing Childhood*.[6] I am now (2014) ninety-one years of age and have spent the last fifty years as a fellow of Nuffield College, Oxford and an emeritus professor of the university. My own career[7] is largely explained by four factors. First was the 11+ examination, which made a tiny bottleneck of educational opportunity for working-class children to escape from elementary education into grammar schools and thereby to be released from the manual labour to which the great majority of their peers were fated. Second was the local Rowlett Scholarship, which paid for the required cap and blazer and the travel expenses. But third, and in the circumstances crucial, was the War, in which I unlearned the attitude to university as 'not for the likes of us' by noticing that some of my fellow cadets in pilot training who had come from independent schools were a lot slower than I was in learning the theory of flight and yet were already planning to go on to one Oxford or Cambridge College or another after the War. I therefore resolved to take the entrance examination to the London School of Economics. The London School of Economics experience was the fourth factor. It launched me into a career in academia.

## FUTURE PROBLEMS FOR SOCIAL POLICY

My great grandchildren and their fellow members of that generation will grow up in a world of both ancient and novel problems. The ancient problem of drunkenness now takes new forms in drug abuse; the old order of discipline now takes more sophisticated expression in parental uncertainty and in the substitution of bribes for good behaviour in the shape of a surfeit of commercialised toys. Old selfishness persists: now it is a challenge to citizenship, an obstacle to attaining the common good. For my mother Ada and her son John, debt was a disgrace. Now it is commonplace. Ada and John were children of poverty. My great grandchildren have toys in abundance. They are children of affluence. But whether the flow of human selfishness and concern for others have changed is probably an unanswerable question. Some say that greed has increased. Others point to the enlargement of horizons of aid to Africa and the poorer parts of the world. I prefer to assume that both selfish greed and idealistic willingness to serve wider philanthropic causes are fundamentally constant. The problem is to fashion a social environment for children that maximises opportunities for altruism and minimises temptations to sin. That problem has to be seen as a moving target in public policies towards families, schools, sports, and games, learning and leisure—all the things that form the character, and predispositions of future citizens. It is a colossal challenge to all adults.

My siblings and I grew up in a rural world of poverty and inequality. But despite mass unemployment and the threat of warfare from totalitarian regimes abroad, it was also a world of hope and security. What they shared were two things from a now departed and irretrievable world. These are the proud isolation and internal discipline of a large and lively family and, second, but connected, the community of a council estate and village elementary school dominated by an Anglican Church with its cubs, brownies, scouts, guides, fetes, choir, and mission hall. These conditions, at least in Britain and Scandinavia, encouraged a collective outlook within which both the spirit of what we now call citizenship as well as the development of individual personality and personal dreams could unconsciously prosper. If those personal dreams were thwarted, as was conspicuously the case with my sister Violet, or obstructed, as with Joan's resolve to become a nurse, or delayed, as was Anne's determination to become a teacher, or diverted, as with John's ambition to become a football superstar, there were some substantial compensations. Vi became the best loved of my siblings for her devoted care of the younger children. Sid's presents of vegetables and flowers were gratefully recognised by the neighbours. John, Joan and Anne were successful emigrants, spouses and parents.[8] And, a precious inheritance from village childhood, Christian belief was retained by Joan and passed strongly to my daughters Ruth and Lisa and onto my granddaughter Kate who ignored her manifest academic talents and trained as a midwife. Even as I write she is busy on a church related trip to Tanzania, climbing Kilimanjaro and extending her midwifery training. Looking back over the Halsey history I realise that my atavistic tendency to glorify my kin has to be watched. Moreover, there is a general tendency in sociology to exaggerate the effects of family structure. Nevertheless, I am impressed by the recorded views of the affines and particularly by the opinions of Torsten, the German son of my sister Anne, who deliberately changed his name back to Halsey.

The language used to express either social or personal dreams of future life has changed over the generations. Belief in Christian religion and the importance of the Labour Party as means to the attainment of 'the New Jerusalem' or of 'socialism' were taken as beyond question by my parents. Loyalty to both Church and party has persisted in my children and grandchildren. But both have weakened. My son Robert identifies fairness to others as the common underlying ethic, and Ruth, while remaining devoutly Anglican, married a declared atheist who was even more strongly a supporter of the Labour Party. My great grandchildren may be neither Christian nor socialist but may believe just as fervently in equality for all children and public service for all adults. The language scarcely matters. Only within the context of social policy can the Halsey tale serve as a minor guide from the irretrievable past. The story encourages the belief that childhood can be supported by public policies. Belief in the state, what Tawney always referred to as a 'serviceable drudge,' has declined sharply, especially since the 1980s when Thatcherism came to dominate Westminster and later Whitehall. Like most working-class people of her generation, my mother saw Lloyd George as a champion of ordinary people with a programme of social reform culminating in post-war Attleean socialism. Decency was commonly taught by parents, priests and teachers to millions of children in every generation. But it also depended on stable families, the prime agencies of collective solidarity. Together these families, churches, chapels and schools, combined to rear most children as responsible adult citizens: freedom, humour and respect informed the local streets, shops, pubs and workplaces and extended to national even international government. The ends were settled: only the means were disputed. They have turned out to be much more complicated, more than ever liable to be corrupted.

The respectable working-class family that was exemplified by the past Halseys certainly worked: but at a high cost in imprisoning mothers and daughters in the kitchen, in the taboo on male participation in 'women's work,' and in the systematic denial of educational opportunity to its children. These traditional conflicts and confinements are no longer needed. Positive social opportunities are now open to a richer country. For children, there is more serious investment in comprehensive schooling by well-paid and well-respected teachers, supported by moral mentors drawn from the upper forms of schools, colleges and the burgeoning 'third-age' of grandparents, and backed by generous public services for education and leisure. These are possible and affordable investments in child-rearing in a rich new society. Compared with our Victorian ancestors our grandchildren are importantly more in command of their circumstances. Technological competence has transformed human possibilities. True we have survived the worst economic slump for a century and still face global problems of over population, climate changes and nuclear war. Yet, In any case, nothing must be allowed to dislodge the improvement of childhood from its high place in social policy. It can remain to make both government and the voluntary sector our 'serviceable drudge.' As the oldest survivor of a departing generation, I would challenge the rising generation to complete the making of the reformed world dreamt of, striven for, but never fully realised by their ancestors.

## SOCIOLOGY OF HIGHER EDUCATION

The other main area to which I have contributed is higher education. This is also a consequence of industrialism in its modern history and increasingly an extension of the process of social selection which qualifies individuals for entry into the enlarging occupations at the top of the work force in post-industrial society. I noticed in the 1950s that two publications of the earlier twentieth century might probably be thought of as the foundation addresses to modern sociological discussion of higher education. They both appeared in 1918, they are both still relevant to our twenty-first century future. One was a speech delivered by Max Weber in Munich on science as a vocation (Gerth & Mills, 1947). The other was by the Norwegian- American sociologist, Thorstein Veblen, an ironic protest against 'the conduct of universities by business men' (Veblen, 1918).

Independently, and with distinctive contrast of style, these two sociologists set the stage for the debate which has become a staple of parliaments, common rooms and the media—the adaptation of corporate structures of feudal origin to the economy of modern countries. Weber put his emphasis on the demand set up by modern economies for highly trained specialist manpower, the advance of bureaucracy in all forms of social organisation and the 'proletarianisation' of the university research worker and teacher. He also adumbrated a major theme of interpretation of the European universities, namely the role of America as a portent of the European future. In the Germany of his day the career of the *Privatdozent* was still 'generally based upon plutocratic prerequisites.' Veblen too saw the scholar as a member of a thwarted class. In his analysis of the power structure of higher learning in America he stressed the function of the university as itself a business enterprise in competition with other universities, bureaucratically organised under its president or 'captain of erudition' in pursuit of the aims of 'notoriety, prestige and advertising in all its branches and bearing' at the expense of scholarship and to the accompaniment of a vast competitive waste of resources.

My own contribution to the Weberian/Veblen tradition has been threefold. I have watched the development of American higher education and its growing influence on the expansion of universities and other institutions of higher learning in Europe and elsewhere in the world. Thus I gratefully accepted invitations from OECD to take part in the inspection of the educational systems of various member countries including the USA itself and cumulating in a report on California in 1989 in Paris followed by a further 'conversation' at Berkeley in 1990. The whole process has been admirably summarised by the distinguished historian, Sheldon Rothblatt, and published by the Center for Studies in Higher Education in 1992 under the title *The OECD, the Master Plan and the Californian Dream*. It deserves to be read by all students of the sociology of higher education.

My second contribution has been to take an idea from Max Weber's study of the classical Chinese literati, an elaborate system of recruitment to the mandarin class, and I applied it to the Oxford colleges as an example from the 19th and early 20th centuries of education designed to foster an imperial elite. Weber had distinguished three types of personality, the charismatic leader, the cultivated man and the expert. Charisma may be found in any form of social organisation whether military, religious, political or educational. The cultivated man, and more recently woman, was characteristically formed in Oxford. The expert is increasingly the mark of leadership in the world league of research universities and is recognised as an exemplar of erudition and research in his or her subject, be it Coptic, Metallurgy or Econometrics. The sociology of higher learning is focussed on the struggles for power and prestige between these types of personality. Hence the title of my own favourite book *The Decline of Donnish Dominion* (OUP, 1995).

Third and finally I have raised the questions of how the idea of a college as distinct from University may adapt itself in the future. The college means bonding, a *gemeinschaft*, an assumption almost of kinship. The college is a kind of household. Thomas More made a utopia of early sixteenth-century London, with a population at the time of about 45,000, by granting everyone a college fellowship at birth and surrounding the city with four great hospices against specialized misadventures. Commensality was not only a means of securing cuisinary economies of scale but also a pedagogical method of learning the complex art of civilized conversation, of exchanging news and gossip, of appreciating the music of minstrels—all part of a way of life rooted in a religious *koinonia*, a community of sharing, a daily routine centred on the worship of Jesus Christ.

But the collegiate tradition, past and present, needs further dissection. It would after all explain the high morale and high performance in field sports depicted in the film *Chariots of Fire,* or the thieving efficiency of Fagin's boys portrayed by Charles Dickens in *Oliver Twist*, or the sustained fighting power of the Wehrmacht in World War Two because of its carefully constructed primary groups in fighting units. In the same way the long history of the Oxford colleges exemplifies many forms of collegiate spirit, directed, for example, to religious fervour, or to social exclusiveness, or to rowing prowess.

Our purpose now is to discover how colleges nurture intellectual achievement and particularly the fate of the meritocratic movement originating in the nineteenth century and reaching new heights since the Second World War. Oxford is now committed to maintaining a high place in the so-called 'world league' of leading research centres. Its colleges are not the only institutions dedicated to that end; there are also departments, centres, laboratories, clubs and seminars in which the same precious spirit prevails. So what is to be the distinctive contribution of the college to success in this ambition, the intellectual advance of science and scholarship?

The future graduate college must be centred on a narrow range of expertise, but it has to be tempered by the spirit of the traditionally cultivated person if it is to realise the ambition of contributing to the democratically *justified* leadership of an increasingly specialised and interdependent world of science, scholarship and politics. There have been perhaps three stages in the evolution of Oxford—from the twelfth century to the sixteenth century it was a clerical institution, from the sixteenth century to the nineteenth century it was an Anglican federation of colleges organised as a finishing school for the sons of the clerical and secular establishment, and finally it became, in the twentieth century, an aspiring world university struggling to remain collegiate with expanding science, rising graduate studies, and increasing governmental interference.

A new form of collegiate living developed strongly in the second half of the nineteenth century. It was the product of the movement towards meritocracy in the election of fellows, of democracy in college government, and of reform in the previously corrupt system of examination. Architecturally the college began as a safe haven against vengeful townsmen, a pious retreat from gaming and houses of ill repute: now it is turned into quaint space of study and repose. The lodge, a small entry into a large interior, was easily defended against marauding bows and arrows. Cells on staircases originally designed for individual monastic prayer were later adapted first for tutors *in loco parentis* and now into study bedrooms (some *en suite* for tourists) with convenient access to a dining hall and neglected chapel. The hall itself, once elaborately organized for congenial conversation and libidinal satisfaction in the absence of wives, is now a busy lunch-time cafeteria and a splendid venue for ceremonial dinners. Quads, once a regulated space for quiet perambulation, are now thronged with visitors and, especially in the long summer vacation, given over to the remunerative trade of conferences and summer schools for multitudinous students from abroad. So the collegiate tradition has been reinvented again and again through the centuries and especially in the nineteenth when Anglican faith began to wane and secular meritocracy began to wax. An imperial Civil Service was created and science invaded higher learning. Chapel is now attended by eccentric minorities, scientists predominate in new Middle Common Rooms and women are commonplace at high table as well as among undergraduates. All these have been revolutions accommodated pretty much without bloodshed.

## CONCLUSION

We can summarise the modern history of rich countries as one of expanding education and contracting of what our grandparents would confidently call the working class. The same historical period has also seen a widespread growth of equalising opportunity to acquire both learning and power. Women, ethnic minorities and above all the lower classes have been seen as the victims of traditional inequality. In the past fifty to eighty years progress has been made towards equalising the chances of women and ethnic minorities. But class chances, measured in relative terms, seem to have remained stable. After the acceptance of the Robbins Report in the 1960s the social sciences began to flourish in the expanding British universities. At the same time, the British class system was changing towards more 'room at the top' with the expansion of the salariat and the shrinkage of the working class of manual workers. Consequently there was an absolute rise in upward mobility, although, as our 1972 study showed, no change in relative rates.[9] All over the world there is a search for educational reform towards equality of opportunity. With respect to gender and ethnicity these efforts have succeeded. With respect to class they have failed. Not everything has been done in Europe or America to establish greater equality of condition. I am here repeating the criticism of capitalist society that R. H. Tawney formulated in his classic books of 1921 and 1931, *The Acquisitive Society* and *Equality*.[10]

Could we go further along the Tawney path? A significant number of sociologists, including Phillip Brown at Cardiff University, Hugh Lauder at the University of Bath and Adam Swift at Oxford University, would now seek to reduce the variability of social rewards; for example, by returning to seriously progressive taxation of the rich and raising the level of minimum wages or extending the provision of citizen incomes. Such strategies would help to ease our endemic race towards competitive market success, reduce the widespread search by the middle and upper classes for new and old defensive expenditure on education as a positional good for their children and loosen the pressure on schools and colleges from preparing the next generation for livelihood rather than living. A fair, free and contented society lies in that direction. It is essential that the aim of social policy has to be not only to maximise gross national product but also to protect the well-being of individuals in a secure society. Herein lies the modern challenge: to social science, for a complex research programme aimed at solving the age-old problem of social inequality; and to politics, to discover the means to reach such a noble goal.

## ENDNOTES

[1] A. H. Halsey completed this chapter shortly before his death at the age of ninety-one on October 14, 2014.
[2] See Field, Frank (2007). 'Britain's ethical tradition and the end of the world', Chapter 2, pp. 23–34, in AHH, *Democracy in Crisis*, Politico's.
[3] See Magnusson, Sally (1981). *The Flying Scotsman, A Biography*, NY USA: Quartet Books.
[4] See Shils, *Edward Portraits*, p. 192.
[5] See Carpenter, L.P.; *G.D.H. Cole (1973). An Intellectual Biography*, Cambridge University Press.
[6] See Halsey, A.H. (1995). *No Discouragement*. Basingstoke: Macmillan. and (2009) *Changing Childhood*. Oxford: Nuffield College.
[7] What follows owes much to my 'Reflections on Education and social mobility' *British Journal of Sociology of Education*, 34; 5–6, 2013, whether by summary, paraphrase or repetition.
[8] It seems to me that further research would show that emigration to the colonies was an important causative factor in promoting upward mobility from working class origins among Britons in the nineteenth and twentieth centuries.
[9] I am impressed by an intervention written by E. Bukodi and John Goldthorpe on intergenerational mobility ("Class Origins, Education and Occupational Attainment in Britain: Secular Trends or Cohort Specific Effects?" *European Societies* 13: 345–73. Oxford University Department of Social Policy, 2011). An excellent and illuminating new analysis of birth cohort data that demonstrates the methods now available and which, inter alia, substantively contradicts the basis of current political panic over alleged declining intergenerational mobility. It shows that there is no evidence of change in rates of mobility (relative or absolute) among recent British birth cohorts. See also, Heath, A. and Payne, C. in Halsey, A. H. & Webb, J. (2002) *Twentieth Century British Social Trends*. Basingstoke: Macmillan.
[10] See Tawney, R. H. (1921). *The Acquisitive Society*. London: G. Bell & Sons. And (1931) *Equality*. London: George Allen & Unwin.

## MY FAVOURITE TEXTS BY OTHERS

Thomas More, *Utopia* 1516
William Morris, *News from Nowhere* 1890, London: Penguin Classics

A. H. HALSEY

Max Weber (Gerth & Mills), *From Max Weber, Essays in Sociology*, 1946. London: Routledge & Kegan Paul
R. H Tawney, *The Acquisitive Society* 1921. London: G. Bell & Sono
George Orwell, 'Politics and the English Language' 1946. London: *Horizon* Vol 13, Issue 76, pp. 252-265.
Edward Shils, *Portraits: A Gallery of Intellectuals*, 1997. Chicago: University of Chicago Press.
Raymond Boudon, *Education, Oppurtunity and Social Inequity*, 1974. London.
James Coleman, *Equality and Achievement in Education*, 1990. London: Westview Press.
Michael Young, *The Rise of the Meritocracy*, 1958. London: Thames & Hudson.
Basil Bernstein, *Class Codes and Control*, 1977. Trends in Theory of Educational Transmission.

## MY FAVOURITE PERSONAL TEXTS

A. H. Halsey, *No Discouragement: an autobiography*, 1996. Basingstoke: Macmillan.
A. H. Halsey, *Decline of Donnish Dominion: the British academic professions in the twentieth century*, 2nd edition, 1995. Oxford University Press.
A. H. Halsey, *A History of Sociology in Britain*, 2004. Oxford University Press.
A. H. Halsey, A. Heath & J. Ridge, *Origins and Destinations: family, class and education in modern Britain*, 1980. Oxford University Press.
A. H. Halsey & J. Webb, *Twentieth-century British Social trends*, 2000. Basingstoke: Macmillan.

## REFERENCES

Durkheim, E. M. (1977). *The evolution of educational thought: Lectures on the formation and development of secondary education in France*. London: Routledge & Kegan Paul.
Floud, J. E., & Halsey, A. H. (1958). The sociology of education. *Current Sociology, 7*(3), 165–193.
Floud, J. E., Halsey, A. H., & Martin, F. M. (1973). *Social class and educational opportunity*. Westport, CO: Greenwood Press.
Halsey, A. H. (1961). *Education, economy, and society: A reader in the sociology of education*. New York, NY: Free Press of Glencoe.
Halsey, A. H. (1981). Provincials and professionals: The British post-war sociologists. *European Journal of Sociology, 23*(1), 150–175.
Halsey, A. H. (1992). *Decline of donnish dominion: The British academic professions in the twentieth century*. Oxford, England: Clarendon.
Halsey, A. H. (2004). *A history of sociology in Britain: Science, literature, and society*. Oxford: Oxford University Press.
Hoyles, M. (1979). *Changing childhood* (1st ed.). London: Writers and Readers Publishing Cooperative.
*Oxford review of education*. (2006). Oxford, England: Routledge Journals.
Rothblatt, S. (1992). *The OECD, the master plan and the California dream: A Berkeley conversation*. Berkeley, CA: Center for Studies in Higher Education.
Veblen, T. (1918). *The higher learning in America: A memorandum on the conduct of universities by business men*. New York, NY: B. W. Huebsch.
Weber, M., Gerth, H. H., & Mills, C. W. (1946). *From Max Weber: Essays in sociology*. New York, NY: Oxford university press.

*A. H. Halsey*[†]
*University of Oxford*

HUGH MEHAN

# 9. ENGAGING THE SOCIOLOGICAL IMAGINATION[1]

*My Journey into Design Research and Public Sociology*

> The sociological imagination enables its possessor to understand the larger historical scene in terms of its meaning for the inner life and the external career of a variety of individuals. It enables him to take into account how individuals, in the welter of their daily experience, often become falsely conscious of their social positions. Within that welter, the framework of modern society is sought, and within that framework the psychologies of a variety of men and women are formulated. By such means the personal uneasiness of individuals is focused upon explicit troubles and the indifference of publics is transformed into involvement with public issues.
>
> (C. Wright Mills, 1959:5)

C. Wright Mills (1959) enjoined social scientists of my generation to shun "abstracted empiricism" and "grand theory" to make our research relevant for social justice. In the current historical context, Mills's call for politically engaged research has been reframed as "public sociology" (Buroway, 2005; Buroway et al., 2004). Dell Hymes (1972) and Peggy Sanday (1976) encouraged anthropologists to adopt a similar progressive role. Adding their voices to that conversation, Bradley Levinson et al. (1995), Levinson and Margaret Sutton (2001), and Douglas Foley and Angela Valenzuela (2006) invoke critical ethnography and Luke Lassiter (2005) and Les Field and Richard Fox (2007) promote collaborative ethnography.

Although I have been influenced by Mills since early in my career, it has not been until recently that I have engaged Mills's dictum more fully and conscientiously in my work. In this article I first chronicle the changes in my research, especially those that have moved me closer to Mills's vision for sociology and Hymes's reinvented anthropology. As I spend more time attempting to create and describe equitable educational environments and less time documenting educational inequality, I have adopted a version of "design" or "collaborative" research. After I describe the distinctive features of that approach, I describe the possibilities and limitations of trying to conduct research while participating in the phenomenon under investigation.

This article is written in response to the offer by Foley and Valenzuela (2006), who encourage ethnographers to explore and publish about our collaborative methodological and political practices. A problem plaguing retrospective reflections is the urge to make one's career moves seem more rational than they actually were at the time. I try here not to rewrite biography and history to serve that purpose.

## FROM DESCRIBING EDUCATIONAL INEQUALITY TO ATTEMPTING TO CREATE EDUCATIONAL EQUALITY

My early empirical studies were, for the most part, concerned with the social construction of educational inequality by school sorting practices, including educational testing (Mehan, 1973, 1978:59–65; Mehan & Wood, 1975:37–46), tracking (Cicourel & Mehan, 1985), and special education placements (Mehan et al., 1986). My work—and that of colleagues who influenced me considerably (notably Courtney Cazden, Aaron Cicourel, Michael Cole, Fred Erickson, Susan Florio, Peg Griffin, and Ray McDermott)—documented how low-income students of color were treated differently than their middle-income white contemporaries in face-to-face interactions with teachers, testers, and counselors. At the same time, I directed the University of California, San Diego's (UCSD) teacher education program, which infused information about cultural differences in language use and the deleterious effects of school sorting practices into theory and methods courses.

Increasingly disillusioned with the separation of my policy and research work and my inability to convince people that inequality was produced in moment-to-moment interaction, I turned my attention to documenting attempts by educators to construct social equality. This switch took tangible shape with my study of the Achievement Via Individual Determination (AVID) program, an untracking program that sought to prepare underrepresented minority students for college by placing them in college preparatory classes, accompanied by a system of academic and social supports (Mehan et al., 1996).

## BUILDING AN EDUCATIONAL FIELD STATION

My formulation of the theory of action undergirding AVID contributed to the rationale for building a 6–12 school on the UCSD campus for the education of low income students. The construction of the Preuss School emerged in a very specific historical and political context. The Regents of the University of California eliminated the use of race and gender as factors in University admissions in 1995. A small, albeit fervent, group of UCSD faculty, community members, and students led by Thurgood Marshall College Provost Cecil Lytle proposed that UCSD open a college-preparatory school on campus for low-income students so that they would be well prepared to "walk in the front door" of any University of California (UC) campus or other respectable college.

This initial proposal was rejected, first by the Academic Senate, and then by UCSD's new chancellor after a contentious public debate, in which not only the concept of the charter school but also tacit definitions of community, equality, and the university itself became the object of contest and struggle. Fueled by a public outcry, editorials decrying the university as elitist, and pressure from the UC Regents to embrace a bold initiative to address the lack of diversity on UC campuses, a more comprehensive plan was later approved by the chancellor and the faculty (Rosen & Mehan, 2003). The more comprehensive plan created the Center for Research on Educational Equity, Access, and Teaching Excellence (CREATE) to monitor the progress of the on-campus school, conduct research on educational equity, and use the Preuss School as a model for schools in local school districts to improve the education of underserved minority youth. I became director of CREATE in 1999.

We conceive of CREATE as an "educational field station" (Mehan & Lytle, 2006). Educational field stations, first proposed by the University of California Black Eligibility Task Force (Duster et al., 1990), are analogous to UC agricultural field stations. UC agricultural field stations developed and disseminated research that has made agriculture one of the major industries in California. Based on that logic, other UC research programs, including those in space and ocean exploration, structural engineering, health care, and computer technology, have been developed that contribute to economic development and the public good under the aegis of the university's broader public mission. CREATE seeks to extend that logic to educational equity issues by encouraging the University to face the challenges emerging from the recent cultural and demographic shifts in our society, just as it faced previous economic and industrial shifts.

The question facing us now is: How do we forge a civil society in the face of ethnic, cultural, and socioeconomic diversity? That is a question for public debate to be sure; but, more importantly, we at UCSD think that diversity is a research and policy question that our university, because it is a public university, has the obligation to confront seriously. This is the role we envision for CREATE (Mehan & Lytle, 2006). CREATE researchers provide a wide range of technical, cultural, and structural resources to schools with high proportions of underrepresented minority students (Jones et al., 2002; Yonezawa et al., 2001), conduct basic and design research at the Preuss School and other public schools, and make the lessons we learn about how to build a college-going culture available to researchers, educators, and policy makers in the educational field.

The Preuss School, a single-track, college-preparatory public charter school on the UCSD campus, is at the center of CREATE's educational field station model. The express purpose of the school is to prepare students from low-income backgrounds for college and to serve as a model for public school improvement. The faculty and staff select through a lottery low-income sixth grade students with high potential but underdeveloped skills. In the 2004–05 school year, 59.5 percent of the student population was Latino, 12.8 percent African American, 21.7 percent Asian, and 6 percent white and "other" (McClure et al., 2006).

We derived the principles of the Preuss School from current thinking about cognition and the social organization of schooling. Research on detracking and cognitive development suggests all normally functioning humans have the capacity to complete a rigorous course of study in high school that prepares them for college and the world of work if that course of study is accompanied by a system of social and academic supports (Bruner, 1986; Cicourel & Mehan, 1983; Laboratory of Comparative Human Cognition, 1983; Mehan et al., 1996; Meier, 1995). Following the logic of that research, the Preuss School only offers college-preparatory classes. The school's curriculum fulfills or exceeds the University of California and California State University entry requirements.

Recognizing that the students who enroll at Preuss are differentially prepared, the educators at the school have instituted a variety of academic and social supports or "scaffolds" to assist students meet the challenges of the rigorous curriculum required for entering four-year colleges and universities. Most notably, the school extends its year by eighteen days, which gives students more opportunities to meet the academic demands of the school. UCSD students serve as tutors in class and after school. Students still in need of help are "invited" to participate in. additional tutoring sessions during "Saturday Academies."

## EXTENDING THE MODEL TO NEIGHBORHOOD SCHOOLS MEDIATED BY CREATE

By preparing students from underrepresented minority backgrounds for college, the Preuss School is intended to help increase the diversity on UC campuses, which was reduced by the regent's decision to ban affirmative action. The school is also intended to be a model in that the principles developed at the school are available to be adapted by other schools. While "Cal Prep" at UC Berkeley and "The Wildcat School" at Arizona have been influenced by our work, the most notable example of adaptation of the principles developed at Preuss School is occurring at Gompers Charter Middle School (GCMS) in Southeast San Diego, mediated by CREATE.

The original Gompers Secondary School had been an urban 7–12 school in Southeast San Diego for over 50 years in a community with a high crime rate and a lengthy history of gang-related violence. This school, unable to meet its No Child Left Behind (NCLB) performance targets for six consecutive years, was required to restructure. After months of deliberation, a working group of parents, teachers, administrators, and community leaders (notably from the San Diego Chicano Federation and the San Diego Urban League) recommended to the school board of the San Diego Unified School District (SDUSD) that the school be reconstituted as a charter school in partnership with UCSD CREATE.

UCSD's involvement was provoked by aroused parents who pointed out that seventy families living in Southeast San Diego had at least one child attending Gompers and at least one child attending the Preuss School. Those children, they informed the SDUSD in many raucous meetings, were succeeding academically, so why can't there be a similar school in the neighborhood? Why did their children need to ride a bus to La Jolla (one of the wealthiest neighborhoods in the county) for a quality education? Why can't they just walk across the street? Parents' firsthand knowledge of the difference a school could make in the lives of their children helped to create an empowered and informed community.

Despite the vocal support of neighborhood parents, the formation of GCMS, like the formation of the Preuss School, endured a lengthy and contentious political process. The SDUSD school board, over the objections of the superintendent, vocal teachers, and parents, removed the principal of Gompers, a charismatic young Latino who had vehemently supported the conversion of the "old" Gompers to a charter school in partnership with UCSD. Parents, leaders of community groups, my university colleagues, and I all saw this as a naked attempt to decapitate the leadership of a burgeoning movement to gain local control over education in historically underserved neighborhoods. If that was, in fact, the SDUSD board strategy, it failed. Instead of deflating, the movement expanded. An increasing number of community groups, newspapers, and community members rallied to the cause.

Precipitously firing the school's principal was not the only oppositional board action. The board initially defined the proposal as a call for a new, start-up, charter school, then changed its position. It declared that Gompers was a conversion charter, not a start-up charter, which would require the petitioners to secure the approval of fifty percent of the tenured faculty as well as fifty percent of the school's parents. The board gave the petitioners thirty days to secure the necessary signatures. Despite the fact that the conversion of Gompers from a conventional public school to a charter school would eliminate certain teacher union provisions, and did not guarantee any teachers continued employment, fifty-eight percent of the school's full-time, unionized teachers voted for the proposal to establish Gompers as a partner of UCSD. Indeed, the union representative from Gompers spoke eloquently in favor of the charter petition before the school board. After begrudgingly conceding that the petitioners had met all the conditions they had imposed, on March 1, 2005, the San Diego Unified School District Board of Education unanimously approved the petition to establish GCMS as a UCSD partnership school. The school, which opened its doors to students on September 6, 2005, enrolls 841 students (thirty-five percent of which are African American, ten percent are Asian, fifty-three percent are Latino, and two percent are white) and employs forty-five teachers.[2]

Charter schools are controversial and are not the only way to improve public schools. But there are certain circumstances—such as the deleterious situation in Southeast San Diego—in which the conversion of failing public schools to charter schools does make sense. The district had let Gompers and other schools in Southeast San Diego slide into deplorable conditions—reminiscent of Jonathan Kozol's descriptions in *Savage Inequalities*: the students' toilets did not flush, paint peeled from walls, lights were left broken, and playgrounds were dustbowls. More important than poor material resources was the absence of rich educational resources. For example, when the "old" Gompers started classes in Fall 2004, fourteen faculty positions were vacant. Despite constant appeals to the district office, six math and science positions remained unfilled in January. Subjecting students to a string of substitute teachers in broken-down facilities is not acceptable—a situation that led parents to take matters into their own hands, including asking UCSD to join them in their efforts to improve the quality of education for their children.

## MOVING BEYOND ETHNOGRAPHIC DESCRIPTION AND TOWARD DESIGN RESEARCH

Finding the appropriate relation between practitioners and researchers has continually challenged the field of education. The "research-development-dissemination evaluation" model of the research-practice connection (Brown et al., 1999) currently dominating the field divides the labor between researchers and practitioners. Researchers study important educational questions and transmit their findings to practitioners through publications. Practitioners in districts, schools, and classrooms, in turn, attempt to put research results into practice.

A second dichotomy exists routinely between researchers and practitioners. Practitioners are often the objects of study rather than participants in constructing research and interpreting results. Value orientations, long established in the field, underpin and sustain these dichotomies. The abstract mental work associated with conducting basic research has traditionally been held in higher regard in faculty reward systems than the concrete practical work of applying research to public policy. The conventions and practices of research universities value "discovery research," the separation of subjects from the objects of research, and reports written by members of the academy, not natives (Lagemann, 2000). It is no wonder, then, that seeking alternatives to the current situation needs to be done carefully, preferably by faculty with tenure.

When researchers assume little or no responsibility for making their research useful and practitioners assume little or no responsibility for evaluating useful practice, then "neither research nor practice benefits" (Brown et al., 1999:29). If researchers and practitioners consider sharing responsibility for research and practice, then it is possible to consider alternatives to the current situation. I have found that the design research program that Brown et al. (1999) espouse can be used productively in research on education because it concentrates explicitly on improving practice and simultaneously building theory that advances fundamental understanding.

Design research is committed to improving complex educational systems by having researchers and practitioners work together, often for a long-term engagement, to frame research problems and seek their solutions (Brown et al., 1999:33–34). Design research builds on but goes beyond ethnographic research, traditionally defined. From its earliest formulations (e.g., Malinowski, 1922), the ethnographic task has involved attempting to describe and interpret events, objects, and people from the point of view of the members of society rather than employing the names, categories, scripts, or schemas derived from either "objective science" or the researcher's own culture. In a manner reminiscent of Mills's call for a sociological imagination, "critical ethnographers" argue that we need to shift the focus of our research attention—studying the powerful not the powerless and challenging questionable legal, medical, media, and corporate practices. If we look at any institution, convention, policies, or practices from the standpoint of those who have the least power, then we would be in a better-position to expose the ideas/ practices, and histories of groups that have been silenced (Apple, 2006).

My CREATE colleagues and I incorporate the injunction from critical ethnography to document oppression in its many forms and to make this information accessible to the public. But we feel we cannot only be critics. We try to aid in the reconstruction of educational environments. And we resist dividing the labor between ethnographers and practitioners in which researchers conduct "basic research" and practitioners implement research findings. We attempt to implement a program in which practitioners and researchers co-construct basic knowledge and simultaneously attempt to build progressive policy.

While still remaining faithful to anthropologists' "emic" perspective, some ethnographers have also become somewhat critical of the power dynamics inherent in the relationships between observer and participant. They have recognized, as Geertz notes, "we [researchers] see the lives of others through the lenses of our own grinding and that they look back on ours through ones of their own" (Gonzalez, 2004:17). This critical self-reflection has led to a reformulation of researcher roles, at least in some corners of ethnographically informed educational research. One such role shift involves the move from: "being a so-called participant observer to becoming an especially observant participant. This means paying close attention to not only one's point of view as an observer but also to one's relations with others (who one is studying and working with) and one's relations with oneself" (Erickson, 1996:7).

Worrying about "one's relations with others" and convinced that ethnography—or any scientific investigation for that matter—is not politically neutral, critical ethnographers have made explicit their political, cultural, and ideological assumptions in the analysis. Because researchers cannot avoid using analytic terms and categories that are politically loaded, I agree with critical ethnographers who assert that all analytic statements must be subjected to scrutiny to determine whose interests are being served, and whose are being suppressed.

## SOME CHALLENGES IN CONDUCTING DESIGN RESEARCH AND DOING PUBLIC SOCIOLOGY

It should be clear from the above summary of my current work that I am deeply involved in attempting to construct equitable learning environments while studying that process. Furthermore, I have definite opinions. Statements interpreting a school board's action as "a naked attempt to decapitate the leadership of a burgeoning movement," the school board's vote as a "begrudging concession," and the reassignment of a principal as a "precipitous firing" are not exactly exemplars of the "objective," "neutral," or "disinterested" observations ethnographers are traditionally taught to compose. Against this brief historical chronicle, I will now present some of the many possibilities and limitations entailed in trying to do a public sociology through design research, using my previous research on AVID and my current school reform efforts to simultaneously construct productive learning environments for low income students of color and conduct research on that process as examples.

Because researchers intervene in the activity by participating in its design and the design of the research about that activity, researchers' actions partially constitute them. The special nature of design research makes explicit the ethical issues that are embedded (often implicitly) in the conduct of other styles or forms of research. A carefully documented ethnographic study of any organization, but especially one self-consciously trying to engage in change, will inevitably expose tensions, contradictions, and gaps between intentions and actions.

We have found that participants, naturally enough, want to emphasize the positive aspects of their organization and students' learning, while ethnographically informed researchers are more likely to want to "tell it like it is." This difference engenders tensions over which aspects of events are to be made public. Because of my commitment to designing schools that alter the conventional manner in which education is delivered to poorly performing students, some academic colleagues as well as reporters from newspapers have both questioned my ability and, by extension, the ability of CREATE, to offer "fair" assessments of the development of the schools and the students' performance in them. My response to these detractors is to say that the activity of conducting research is never value neutral. Even the declaration of value neutrality or presuppositionless inquiry is a political position—and probably impossible to achieve in practice. Researchers, especially those engaged in observational studies, shape research by their selection of topics to investigate, materials to analyze, instances of data to interpret (Cicourel, 1964; Levinson & Sutton, 2001; Peshkin, 1991). Researchers do not simply observe and report "brute facts;" they mold materials into interpretations.

The inevitable reflexive relation between researchers and objects of study is made even more complicated in our design research because of the special relationship that we have to the schools. These special relations cut two ways. On the one hand, they facilitate entree because some degree of trust has been established because of our involvement in the political fracas that led to the formation of Preuss and GCMS; on the other hand, reviewers can conclude that our objectivity is clouded by these close relations. Rather than ignore these close relations, we acknowledge and make them visible in our analyses. Therefore, our findings cannot be viewed as some objective representation of the "truth," but, instead, our most thorough and accurate representations of our interpretations of research materials.

Furthermore, this difference in interests reaffirms that status differences between researchers and practitioners need to be negotiated constantly in design research. At a minimum, the reflexive relationship between researchers and participants needs to be made an explicit part of the analysis (Cicourel, 1964; Harding, 1998). This injunction means attending not only to theory, data gathering and analysis, but the relation between researcher and practitioner as well. Research cannot proceed without participants' support, trust, and active engagement.

## TRYING TO RESOLVE THE AMBIGUITY OF MULTIPLE ROLES

While the tenets of our approach can be clearly stated in theory, the new researcher roles that derive from design research are difficult to negotiate in practice. Ongoing, close interaction between practitioners and researchers promises richer and more authentic findings than might emerge from a more traditional study. In practice, the complexities associated with collaboration are daunting. In our work with Preuss and GCMS, we attempt to go beyond writing a description of "what's going on here" (the goal of classical ethnography), and we attempt to go beyond assessing the fidelity of the relationship between policy-as-intended with policy-as-enacted (as occurs in traditional evaluation).

In addition to carrying out our university-mandated annual evaluation of the Preuss School and studies of the adaptation of the principles that the Preuss School developed by other schools, I occupy many other roles simultaneously. These put my CREATE colleagues and myself into many situations that renders the research a complex and conflict-laden process. The circumstances that result from school university collaborations places us in the position of interacting with district leaders, principals, and teachers, especially when CREATE provides technical assistance in the form of after-school programs, tutors, computers, parent education, and teacher professional-development opportunities. The ensuing relationships provide an entree to schools and other educational situations and also help build the rapport necessary for effective ethnography and documentation. But gaining access to people in positions of power generates problems of another sort. Because I want my research results and recommendations heard by policy makers, I must avoid softening controversial conclusions or reducing complex issues to twenty-second sound bites.

My most complex role mixes political advocate with basic researcher. Led by Cecil Lytle, members of the planning committee advocated on behalf of the proposed on-campus charter school before committees of the UCSD Academic Senate, the UC Regents, members of the legislature, and community groups in the city. When it was my turn to speak, I grounded my presentation in research, citing those studies that suggested schools could make a difference in the lives of underserved youth. But there was never any doubt about my position. I did not present a neutral assessment of tracking practices, for example. Critical of the underrepresentation of low-income students of color in high-track classes, I was clearly an advocate for the idea of the campus becoming intimately involved in the education of underserved youth by building a school that prepares students to be prepared to go to college, if they so choose.

My mixed researcher-advocate role was even more intense in the run-up to the establishment of GCMS. After Lytle and I were approached by the outgoing

SDUSD Superintendent, Alan Bersin, and Gompers neighborhood parents, we attended twice-weekly planning meetings at the school. These meetings, which started in September 2004 and lasted until March 2005, when the school board finally approved the charter petition, often went from 5:00 p.m.–8:00 p.m. on Tuesday and Thursday evenings. Follow-up meetings with the deposed principal took place over Sunday breakfasts. Because the parents had family or work responsibilities, they often could not attend the entire meeting every evening. The constantly changing cast of characters necessitated repeating the group's work to gain consensus. I can't remember how many times I had to clarify that UCSD was not going to "take over" Gompers and run it as a UCSD entity in the way that UCSD manages Preuss. Often, seemingly established positions on curriculum, governance, and the like changed when new parents joined the debate.

When Lytle and I returned to the relative quiet of university life, we often wondered what would emerge from the organized chaos of planning meetings. While at UCSD, I often found myself dreading yet another three-hour meeting in a stuffy room without food. But when we returned to the fervor and passion expressed by engaged parents and teachers, we knew it was impossible to abandon this living example of democracy in action, even when more pristine university commitments beckoned.

In discussions about the theory of action to guide GCMS or the design of its academic plan, I also stated my position clearly. I believed that teachers, with university and community support, could create a school with a college-going culture of learning in the Gompers neighborhood. Again, when trying to convince parents—and, later, the school board—that a school with a rigorous curriculum supported by academic and social scaffolds was warranted and possible, I grounded my position in research evidence.

Parents, teachers, the teachers' union, community groups, and the SDUSD were not the only constituents that needed to be convinced that CREATE should extend its partnership work into low-income communities. The UCSD administration needed to be convinced as well. This situation was tenuous because our move to Gompers coincided with the arrival of another new chancellor. Citing concerns over the extra costs associated with running a school (transportation, extra salaries, etc.) in an uncertain budgetary world, the chancellor and her senior staff expressed alarm that CREATE might be promising to grant GCMS the same status as the Preuss School. Even when Lytle and I made it clear that Gompers would establish an independent 301c3 charter, and we would play mostly an advisory role (serving on the school's board of directors, conducting research, advising on curriculum and instruction), the UCSD administration's concerns were not quelled.

Issues raised when we first proposed the on-campus charter school resurfaced: active K-12 involvement is not in the university's mission. We parried that point by reminding our colleagues that extending the Preuss model to urban schools is a vital part of CREATE's mission. New concerns were raised. What if the school failed, we were asked. Lytle and I were taken aback by the fear of failure critique, given that our university engages in many risky and controversial research endeavors: stem cell research, climate change research, cancer research. Could it be that concern masks a deeper one, a widely held belief that "those kids" cannot succeed, even when afforded a powerful system of social and academic supports?

## TRYING TO RESOLVE THE CONUNDRUM OF UNWITTING ACCESS TO INSIDER KNOWLEDGE

My multiple roles produce another complication—this having to do with unwittingly gaining access to insider knowledge. Many parents, community members, and SDUSD educators know me only as a practitioner who shares their desire to enable disadvantaged students to obtain better opportunities to learn, not as a member of a research team studying school improvement, the Preuss School, and GCMS. As a result, I sometimes find myself privy to information that is significant to the research project but that was not explicitly marked as such. The question that arises in such situations is: what to do with the information? Can I "use" it in my descriptions? Or is this information off the record? I often wish I had a two-brimmed hat of the sort Sherlock Holmes is often depicted wearing. On one bill I would write researcher. On the other I'd write educator, to remind the people with whom I interact what my role is on any particular occasion.

During the course of our study of school reform in San Diego (Hubbard et al., 2006), my colleagues and I developed a strategy that helps resolve the ambiguity presented by access to insider knowledge that I continue to use today. Like journalists who distinguish between "on-the-record" and "off-the-record" comments, we treat any information acquired in a situation not formally designated as a research encounter as off the record. Only information that has been acquired through official tape-recorded interviews, public presentations, or published documents is used as grounds for the interpretations and conclusions that appear in print. Or information we initially receive off the record is put on the record by conducting a formal interview. These strategies only partially respond to the challenge, however. We must take seriously the need to develop more systematic and transparent methods to limit others' perception of researchers as spying critics instead of helping practitioners.

## FORGING COLLABORATIVE RELATIONSHIPS

Even as trusting relationships between researchers and practitioners grow, differences between the two remain. Researchers and practitioners come from different backgrounds and, in some respects, privilege different things. Practitioners want to learn about the strategies that will make the most improvement in their local situation. Researchers are more interested in abstracting generalizations from local circumstances. These are not necessarily mutually exclusive priorities. They can be supportive if both are thoughtful. Yet they can impede collaborations because each somewhat differently shapes the way business is conducted. Thus, collaborative arrangements that lead to real improvement in teaching and learning require conscious effort.

In our research, we are committed to constructing opportunities for a conversation with our educational colleagues. One way of doing so is to report preliminary data and analysis around a particular topic. My CREATE colleagues, Makeba Jones and Susan Yonezawa, conduct focus groups with students about their perceptions of schools before and after their conversion from a large comprehensive school to smaller, more personalized schools.

Collaborative conversations are also fostered by joint publications. During the course of our research on AVID, I wrote a piece with its director (Swanson et al., 1994) and papers with the principal of the Preuss School (Alvarez & Mehan, 2004, 2006). Jones and Yonezawa make oral presentations, prepare analytic reports, and produce joint publications for the educators so they can assess the school's development incorporating students' perspective on the conversion of large to smaller schools (Jones & Yonezawa, 2002).

For practitioner colleagues, co-constructing publications based on project findings has meant learning a new language. For my research colleagues and me, this process has meant becoming sensitive to the multiple dimensions and challenges in school improvement. For example, AVID characterizes the success of students in their program as a function of their "individual determination." We proposed, based on our research, that the success of AVID students was influenced considerably by the social capital generated by AVID teachers and counselors who mediated relations between students and their academic teachers and college admissions officers. Many conversations and exchanges of drafts transpired before the AVID educators realized that our interpretation emphasizing social processes did not negate the individual actions of students or undercut the integrity of their theory of action. Eventually, AVID incorporated expressions we used to describe the program, such as "social and academic scaffolds" and "social capital" in their descriptions.

A similar, although much less contentious, process has unfolded with the Preuss School. The school principal quickly saw the connection between social science concepts and the school's innovative practices. She now incorporates research-based terminology such as scaffolding and detracking in her many presentations about Preuss to professional audiences and the constant stream of educators, researchers, and politicians who visit the school. In both cases, a negotiated editing process produced a narrative that was mutually acceptable to researchers and practitioners and helped us guard against producing an account that was self-serving and glossy.

## CONCLUSION

In my recent work, I have attempted to create and describe equitable educational environments, not just document educational inequality. My UCSD colleagues and I envision CREATE as an "educational field station" in which we simultaneously provide technical, cultural, and structural resources to schools with high proportions of underrepresented minority students; conduct basic and design research at our on-campus school and other public schools; and make the lessons we collaboratively learn about how to build a college-going culture available to researchers, educators, and policy makers in the educational field.

These moves have brought me closer to C. Wright Mills's injunction to make empirical research relevant for public policy. Mills's call for applying the sociological imagination has been reframed as "public sociology" and "critical ethnography." Buroway (2005) reminds us that sociology originated with a moral imperative. Marx, Weber, and Durkheim (the "founding fathers" or "holy trinity" of sociology), each in their own way, was driven by an appraisal of and attempt to remedy the malaise engendered by modernity: alienation, inequality, hyperrationality, domination, anomie. As sociology fought for legitimacy among the social sciences, however, it imported positivism, a move that pushed the moral commitment to the margins.

Richard Shweder reminds us: "the knowable world is incomplete if seen from any one point of view, incoherent if seen from all points of view at once, and empty if seen from nowhere in particular" (2006:3). Given the choice between incompleteness, incoherence, and emptiness, Shweder opts for incompleteness, a stance critical ethnographers and I would support. Critical ethnographers have replaced the grand objectivist vision of speaking from a universalist, presumably objective, standpoint with the more valid one of speaking from a historically and culturally situated stand point (Foley & Valenzuela, 2006) and reject the incoherence, intellectual chaos, and nihilism that can arise when one privileges no view at all—the stance of some radical, postmodern skeptics (Shweder, 2006).

Critical ethnographers offer cultural critiques by writing about ruling groups, ruling ideologies, and institutions, often from the underside. Writing a critical ethnography is a political statement (Foley & Valenzuela, 2006). It can give voice to the voiceless and challenge the taken-for-granted assumptions and actions of the privileged. Here, researchers aim "to use their scholarship to assist various decolonizations" (Wood, 1999:3). The egalitarian ideal of cotheorized and cowritten ethnographies takes anthropology in exciting new directions, but it is not easy to "decolonize" research. The pressures from the academy to produce "scientific" research (i.e., individualized, objective discovery) works against letting participants decide research questions and contribute to publications as does the instinct to make the report look good to the academy and pleasing to the natives (Foley, 2007).

Buroway et al. (2004) seek to restore a balance between basic research and a commitment to social justice. It is not enough for sociologists and anthropologists to write op-ed articles for newspapers or appear on television talk shows because these are often thin pieces aimed at passive audiences. Instead, they challenge sociologists and anthropologists to enter the dialogue about issues of social concern based on bodies of theoretical knowledge and peer-reviewed empirical findings. Without a solid theoretical and empirical foundation, sociological and anthropological claims can evaporate into shrill and empty critiques. Without a commitment to social justice, even well-crafted empirical studies will not necessarily further the public interest.

My experience with design research in the service of a public sociology suggests general implications for researcher-practitioner collaborations. The challenge for such collaborations is, however, to respect the local needs of practitioners, while on the other to develop more useable and generative knowledge for the field. Design research demands that investigation and the development of an end product or innovation occur in cycles of design, enactment, analysis, and redesign. The skills, goals, and knowledge of the participants, as well as the relationships that exist between the actors involved in the work, significantly affect the ability to build and transfer theoretical understandings. Design-research projects, followed by the joint authorship of a publication, illustrate the advantages of collaboration around problems of practice. These intimate collaborations illustrate how a researcher can become an actor who is instrumental in changing practice, and practitioners can acquire a new language that guides their work.

## ACKNOWLEDGMENTS

I am pleased to acknowledge the many helpful suggestions made by Gordon Chang, Raquel Jacob-Almeida, Paula Levin, and Margaret Riel. I also appreciate Doug Foley, who encouraged me to write this chapter—and pushed me to reflect deeply on these issues. The limitations remain my own.

## NOTE

[1] For more information on Gompers Charter School, see http://www.gomperscharter.org
[2] This chapter is reproduced by permission of the American Anthropological Association from Anthropology & Education Quarterly, Volume 39, Issue 1, Pages 77–91, March 2008. Not for sale or further reproduction.

## MY FAVORITE TEXTS BY OTHERS

Buroway, Michael. 2005. For Public Sociology. *American Sociological Review* 70 (1): 4-28.
Erickson, Frederick. *Talk and Social Structure*. London: Polity Press.
Lareau, Annette. 1989. *Home Advantage*. London: Falmer.
Lareau, Annette. 2003. *Unequal Childhoods*. Berkeley: UC Press.
Mills, C. Wright. 1959. *The Sociological Imagination*. New York: Oxford University Press.
Oakes, Jeannie. 2005. *Keeping Track*. 2nd Edition. New Haven: Yale University Press.
Varenne, Herve & R. P. McDermott. 1998. *Successful Failure*. Boulder CO: Westview Press.

## MY FAVORITE PERSONAL TEXTS

Hugh Mehan and Houston Wood. 1975. *The Reality of Ethnomethodology*, New York: Wiley.
Hugh Mehan. 1979. *Learning Lessons*. Cambridge: Harvard University Press.
Hugh Mehan. 1993. Beneath the Skin and Between the Ears: A Case History in the Politics of Representation. Seth Chailkin and Jean Lave (eds.), *Understanding Practice: Perspectives on Activity and Context*. Cambridge: Cambridge University Press.
Hugh Mehan. 1995. Resisting the Politics of Despair. *Anthropology and Education Quarterly* 26 (3): 239-250.

Hugh Mehan. 2009. A Sociological Perspective on Opportunity to Learn and Assessment. In *Assessment, Equity, and Opportunity to Learn.* J. P. Gee, et al (eds.), Cambridge: Cambridge University Press.

Hugh Mehan. 2012. *In the Front Door: Constructing a College-going Culture of Learning.* Boulder CO: Paradigm Publishers.

## REFERENCES

Alvarez, D., & Mehan, H. (2004). Providing educational opportunities for underrepresented students. In D. Lapp (Ed.), *Teaching all the children* (pp. 82–89). New York, NY: Guilford Publications.

Alvarez, D., & Mehan, H. (2006). Whole school detracking: A strategy for equity and excellence. *Theory into Practice, 45*(1), 82–89.

Apple, M. (2006). *Educating the "Right" way.* New York, NY: Routledge.

Brown, A., Greeno, J. G., Resnick, L. B., Mehan, H., & Lampert, M. (1999). *Recommendations regarding research priorities: An advisory report to the national educational research policy and priorities board.* New York, NY: National Academy of Education.

Bruner, J. (1986). *Actual minds, possible worlds.* Cambridge, MA: Harvard University Press.

Buroway, M. (2005). For public sociology. *American Sociological Review, 70*(1), 4–28.

Buroway, M., Gamson, W., Ryan, C., Pfohl, S., Vaughan, D., Derber, C., & Schorr, J. (2004). Public sociologies. *Social Problems, 51*(1), 103–130.

Cicourel, A. V. (1964). *Method and measurement in sociology.* New York, NY: Free Press.

Cicourel, A. V., & Mehan, H. (1985). Universal development, stratifying practices and status attainment. *Social Stratification and Mobility, 4,* 3–27.

Duster, T., Cicourel, A. V., Cota Robles, E. H., Doby, W. C., Ellis, R., Frye, H. T., Haywood, J., Justus, J. B., Keller, E. J., Lave, J. C., Mitchell, H., Powell, G. J., Reed, R., Sandoval, J. H., Watson, J. A., & Watson, J. W. (1990). *Making the future different: Report of the task force on Black student eligibility.* Oakland, CA: Office of the President of the University of California.

Erickson, F. (1996). On the evolution of qualitative approaches to educational research: From Adam's task to Eve's. *Australian Educational Researcher, 23*(2), 1–15.

Field, L., & Fox, R. G. (Eds.). (2007). *Putting anthropology to work.* Oxford: Berg.

Foley, D. (2007). Reflections on the symposium. In L. Field & R. G. Fox (Eds.), *Anthropology put to work.* New York, NY: Berg.

Foley, D., & Valenzuela, A. (2006). Critical ethnography: The politics of collaboration. In N. K. Denzin & V. S. Lincoln (Eds.), *Sage handbook of qualitative research* (3rd ed.). New York, NY: Sage.

Gonzalez, N. (2004). Disciplining the discipline: Anthropology and the pursuit of quality education. *Educational Researcher, 33*(5), 17–25.

Harding, S. (1998). *Is science multicultural? Postcolonialisms, feminisms and epistemology.* Bloomington, IN: Indiana University Press.

Hubbard, L., Mehan, H., & Stein, M. K. (2006). *Reform as learning: When school reform collided with school culture and community politics in San Diego.* New York, NY: Routledge Falmer.

Hymes, D. H. (Ed.). (1972). *Reinventing anthropology.* New York, NY: Pantheon.

Jones, M., & Yonezawa, S. (2002). Student voice, cultural change: Using inquiry in school reform. *Equity and Excellence in Reform, 35*(33), 1–10.

Jones, M., Yonezawa, S., Ballesteros, E., & Mehan, H. (2002). Shaping pathways to higher education. *Educational Researcher, 3,* 3–17.

Laboratory of Comparative Human Cognition. (1983). Culture and cognitive development. In W. Kessen (Ed.), *Mussen's handbook of child psychology, Vol. 1: History, theory and method* (4th ed.). New York, NY: Wiley.

Lagemann, E. (2000). *An elusive science: The troubling history of education.* Chicago, IL: University of Chicago Press.

Lassiter, L. E. (2005). *The Chicago guide to collaborative ethnography.* Chicago, IL: University of Chicago Press.

Levinson, B., & Sutton, M. (Eds.). (2001). *Policy as practice: Towards a comparative sociological analysis of educational policy.* Westport, CT: Ablex.

Levinson, B., Foley, D., & Holland, D. (Eds.). (1995). *The cultural production of the educated person: Critical ethnographies of schooling and local practice*. Albany, NY: State University of New York Press.

Malinowski, B. (1922). *Argonauts of the Western Pacific: An account of native enterprise and adventure in the archipelagoes of melanesian New Guinea*. London: Routledge and Sons.

McClure, L., Morales, J. C., Strick, B., & Jacob-Almeida, R. (2006). *The Preuss School at UCSD: School characteristics and students' achievement*. San Diego, CA: University of California, CREATE. Retrieved April 1, 2007, from http://create.ucsd.edu/ evaluation

Mehan, H. (1973). Assessing children's language using abilities. In J. M. Armer & A. S. Grimshaw (Eds.), *Comparative sociological research*. New York, NY: Wiley-Interscience.

Mehan, H. (1978). Structuring school structure. *Harvard Educational Review, 48*(1), 32–64.

Mehan, H., & Lytle, C. (2006). *Creating educational field stations: A remedy and a model for diversity and access in higher education*. Berkeley, CA: Boalt Hall School of Law.

Mehan, H., & Wood, H. (1975). *The reality of ethnomethodology*. New York, NY: Wiley Interscience.

Mehan, H., Meihls, L. J., & Hertweck, A. J. (1986). *Handicapping the handicapped: Decision making in students' educational careers*. Stanford, CA: Stanford University Press.

Mehan, H., Hubbard, L., Villanueva, I., & Lintz, A. (1996). *Constructing school success: The consequences of untracking low achieving students*. Cambridge: Cambridge University Press.

Meier, D. (1995). *The power of their ideas: Lessons for America from a small school in Harlem*. Boston, MA: Beacon.

Mills, C. W. (1959). *The sociological imagination*. New York, NY: Grove.

Peshkin, A. (1991). *The color of strangers, the color of friends*. Chicago, IL: University of Chicago Press.

Rosen, L., & Mehan, H. (2003). Reconstructing equality on new political ground: The politics of representation in the charter school debate at the University of California, San Diego. *American Educational Research Journal, 40*(3), 655–682.

Sanday, P. R. (1976). *Anthropology and the public interest: Fieldwork and theory*. New York, NY: Academic Press.

Shweder, R. A. (2006). *Why do men barbeque? Recipes for cultural psychology*. Cambridge, MA: Harvard University Press.

Swanson, M. K., Mehan, H., & Hubbard, L. (1994). The AVID classroom: A system of academic and social support for low achieving students. In J. Oakes & K. H. Quartz (Eds.), *Creating new educational communities. Ninety-fourth yearbook of the national society for the study of education*. Chicago, IL: University of Chicago Press.

Yonezawa, S., Jones, M., & Mehan, H. (2001). Partners for preparation: Constructing and distributing social and cultural capital to achieve diversity. In W. G. Tierney & L. S. Hagedorn (Eds.), *Extending outreach: Strategies for accessing college*. Albany, NY: State University of New York Press.

Wood, H. (1999). *Displacing natives: The rhetorical production of Hawaii*. Boulder, CO: Rowman and Littlefield.

*Hugh Mehan*
*University of California*
*San Diego*

ROSLYN ARLIN MICKELSON

# 10. THE ACCIDENTAL SOCIOLOGIST OF EDUCATION

*How My Life in Schools Became My Research*

The arc of my intellectual journey as a scholar is captured by the title of the chapter, *The Accidental Sociologist of Education: How My Life in Schools Became My Research*. For much of the journey I essentially stumbled along the pathway of a scholarly career. Until the last decade I rarely deliberately chose a direction. My research has always critically examined how schools' institutional arrangements, policies and practices contribute either to the transformation or reproduction of social and educational inequality associated with race, ethnicity, gender, and social class. Every topic interrogates the ways that these forces shape educational processes and outcomes. I have conducted research on the education of homeless and street children in Brazil, Cuba, and the US; business leaders and school reform; the political economy of educational policy; collaborative teacher professional cultures; tracking; and parental involvement. Currently, I am examining these dynamics with respect to science, technology, engineering, and mathematics degrees in higher education. I cannot talk about the origins and development of every one of these topics so in this essay I focus on two themes that have animated much of my research. The first is the ways that the dynamics of race, class, and gender inequality in the larger social order influence students' educational attitudes, behaviors, and outcomes. The second involves the ways the race and class compositions of schools shape outcomes across students' life course.

## THE BEGINNING

I am a Canadian immigrant of Eastern European Jewish heritage. My mother emigrated from Poland to Canada when she was a small child and my father's parents came from the Ukraine and Romania. She dropped out of high school after falling behind in her studies while recovering from a year-long bout of rheumatic fever. Self-educated, she was highly literate and spoke several languages. My father was born in Canada. After high school he joined the Royal Canadian Air Force during World War II. My parents met in Montreal during the war, married before my father served overseas, and I was born in Ottawa after he returned. When I was six months old my parents and I arrived in Los Angeles to join my paternal extended family that had already set down roots in southern California.

We were rather poor when I was young. New clothes meant a package arrived with clothes from older cousins. During my elementary school years we were also one of only a handful of Jewish families in our neighborhood and I felt marginalized by the combination of poverty, immigrant status, and being a member of a religious minority; that is, we never had a Christmas tree. Elementary school didn't come easily. My mom kept my elementary school report cards and they reveal that I was never a brilliant student—barely above average at best! I never felt smart. To make matters worse, my mother's older sister had two manifestly brilliant sons and I knew I could never compete with them, especially in science and mathematics.[1] I gravitated toward English and social studies.

Once our family arrived in Los Angeles my father began a small business that capitalized on the burgeoning automobile culture in LA. His business sold new and reconditioned batteries to gas stations and car dealers and it eventually prospered. About the time I entered junior high we had become members of the middle class. We moved to La Dera Heights, a Los Angeles County neighborhood sandwiched among the cities of LA, Inglewood, and Culver City. Roughly half of the population of La Dera Heights was middle-class Jews and I no longer felt marginalized by my social background.

## PUBLIC EDUCATION

I am a product of public schools. I began my elementary education in the Los Angeles Unified School District (LAUSD) and completed secondary school in the Inglewood Unified School District (IUSD), even though La Dera Heights was an unincorporated area in Los Angeles County. About ten years before our family moved to the area, residents had arranged for the neighborhood to merge into the overwhelmingly white IUSD so that their children would not have to go to high school with African Americans who were integrating the neighborhoods nearest to LAUSD's Dorsey High School. So throughout middle and high school I was bussed roughly 25 minutes each way to the IUSD for purposes of racial segregation. The bus was a club house on wheels where twice a day I socialized with my friends. Ironically, I later spent much of my scholarly career researching the consequences of busing for desegregation elsewhere.

After high school I attended my local university, the University of California, Los Angeles (UCLA). Actually, I sort of stumbled into UCLA. First, and foremost, it had a reputation for enrolling lots of suitable Jewish men and I knew I wanted to find a husband at college. I realize this is a cringe-worthy reason to select a school but it was genuinely one of the reasons I applied to UCLA. The second reason was UCLA was twenty minutes north of my home on the local freeway, I-405. It never crossed my mind that I'd go to school away from home. My parents and I never had a single conversation about that option.

As the first member of my nuclear family to attend a university, I didn't know much about the application process, and I certainly wasn't strategic about my higher education plans. I applied just for one—UCLA. I didn't take the SAT because it wasn't required for UCLA. My high school grade point average was good but not stellar. I had the requisite courses required for entry into the University of California system in 1965 and to my surprise, I was accepted. Actually, my GPA was much better than I thought. In 1983 while I was conducting my dissertation research at Inglewood High, I riffled through student records and decided to check on my own history at the school. I discovered that I had been in an honors program in social studies and English throughout high school. Thus, my course grades were weighted. Aha! This explained why I got into UCLA with what I thought was a rather pedestrian high school grade point average.

Looking back on my own high school education, I see the issues that animate my career as a sociologist of education foreshadowed in my secondary school experiences. My first inklings of what became my adult awareness and sensitivity to how schooling intersected with race and class emerged during high school. First, I noticed social class. My neighborhood was an unofficial satellite of the city of Inglewood, a white middle class suburb in Los Angeles County. La Dera Heights was known as 'pill hill' because so many physicians' families lived there. With one exception, my friends all lived in La Dera Heights. We hung out together, dated each other and avoided the kids in the working class flatlands of the city of Inglewood proper. I then became aware of race. At that age, I never noticed my whiteness. With the exception of a handful of Asians, my high school classes were all white because of academic tracking. The same two Chinese American students were in my English and social studies classes. I didn't realize when I attended high school that it had a sizeable Chicano population. No Chicanos were in my college preparatory classes. It was only when I perused my high school yearbook with adult eyes sensitized by formal education did I realize that my high school was not all white or middle class—there was a huge working class and Chicano student population—after all, this was southern California. Not a single Black child attended IHS when I was enrolled.

## COLLEGE

I began my college education in the fall of 1965. My first semester at UCLA cost $80.00. My final quarter of graduate school in 1984 cost $400.00. Fall quarter undergraduate fees in 2014 were $5155. My first semester at UCLA was very intellectually challenging. I didn't know how to study, to write, to think critically, and I was primarily focused on getting a husband. I failed the freshman English placement exam and had to enroll in a noncredit course officially called Subject A and unofficially called bonehead English composition. But I learned how to write in that class. My French placement exam was also a humiliation. After four years of high school French I placed into the first semester of college French – so I switched to Italian, which I came to love. Molto bené! I chose anthropology as a major because cultural anthropology fascinated me; physical, archaeology, and linguistics—not so much. But by the time I finished my junior year, I started taking political science and sociology classes and fell in love with the latter.

I came into my own intellectually during the first few years of undergraduate study. One key factor in this transformation was my success in finding a suitable husband within the first four months of my arrival at UCLA. Finding a mate allowed me to check off this goal from my 'to do' list and it freed me to concentrate on my studies unencumbered by the time and emotional demands of searching for a husband. I married Tom in December 1967 and we divorced in November 1970.

The UCLA campus was a fascinating place in the mid to late 1960s. The summer before I entered UCLA the Watts riots brought LA to its knees. UCLA's campus roiled with ethnic tensions, anti-war and civil rights protests, and early feminist movement. I met with members of the Campus Crusade for Christ. I was curious and my mom was needlessly scared I would convert. I protested the Vietnam War on campus and at the Thanksgiving dinner table I argued about it with chicken hawk relatives. I shared the elevator in the student union with Angela Davis. My first husband, once a proud Young Republican to annoy his German-Jewish parents, became an anti-war McCarthy Democrat. A dog-eared copy of the federal selective service (military draft) law was so much in demand, the library left it permanently chained to a counter in the College Library's reading room. We protested the carpet bombing of Cambodia and when four Kent State students were killed by national guard troops, I joined fellow students from across the nation and went on strike.

## BECOMING A TEACHER

Armed with an anthropology degree and minors in political science, sociology, and humanities, I needed to make a decision about the direction I would take after graduation in 1969. It was too soon to have children. And because I anticipated that my roles as mother and wife would be the center of gravity of my adult identity, I wanted a career that would be compatible with these roles. In my circumscribed worldview, I was limited to becoming a teacher, a social worker, or a nurse. Here is how I decided to be a teacher. Nursing was out because it involved math and science, two subjects I feared and loathed. I knew next to nothing about what a social worker did but I reasoned I wouldn't be a good one because I likely would bring other people's problems into my own life.

Teaching, with its ostensible 8am to 3pm schedule, with the promise of weekends and summers free, was perfect for my future as wife and mother. I planned to drop in and out of the labor force based on my reproductive schedule. What I actually experienced as a teacher makes my naïveté appalling! Nonetheless, the summer following my 1969 graduation from college I entered UCLA's secondary teaching credential program and by June 1970 I had earned a lifetime California social studies secondary teaching credential. I had studied African American history with the legendary ethnic studies scholar Ronald Takaki and absolutely loved it. I student-taught African American history at Los Angeles High School.

In fact, my first real job was teaching African American history at Morningside High School in the Inglewood Unified School District, the school system from which I had graduated a mere five years earlier. Getting a social studies teaching job in 1970 was difficult. There was a surfeit of social studies candidates and few teaching jobs. Fortunately, the IUSD's chief personnel officer, Edna Bowden, was a neighbor of our family in La Dera Heights. Every day as she drove to work she waved to my mom who was standing in her kitchen window washing dishes. She scheduled a courtesy interview with me at the UCLA placement center. None of the other social studies teaching credential candidates with whom I had trained were interviewed by IUSD. And the rest is history. Morningside High School had an opening for a social studies teacher who could teach Black History and civics (government).

This job was another in the series of fortuitous events or accidents that launched my professional career as a sociologist of education. I studied Black History and MHS needed a Black History teacher; Edna Bowden was my neighbor. I was hired and began my career in education in the fall of 1970. I taught at MHS until 1979, when my lived experiences as a teacher raised so many questions about education, race, class, and society—I required answers.

## WHAT SENT ME TO GRADUATE SCHOOL

By 1972 I had returned to UCLA and earned an MA in education. My concentration was sociology of education because I was mesmerized by the topic. I had a myriad of questions about education and society and the specialization certainly promised the best answers. Four years later, with my MA in hand, I reached another turning point in my life. Assessing my future—no longer constrained by the roles of wife and mother—I began to consider what my professional life could become. Plan A, being a teacher until I was a mother, hadn't panned out. By then I was divorced and had no prospects for remarriage. The vision of getting up every day for the next forty years and teaching social studies at MHS seemed unappealing. I was young; I needed a Plan B for my future. World travel? Nope. I settled upon either going to law school or getting a PhD.

Here is how I chose a PhD over a JD. In 1976 I was at a house party with my erstwhile sociology of education cohort from the MA program. C. Wayne Gordon, a professor with whom I studied during my MA experience was the Dean of UCLA's Graduate School of Education. He took my hand, looked me in the eye, and encouraged me to pursue my doctorate. Flattered, I became smitten by the idea. One interesting footnote: C. Wayne Gordon was the father of musician Kim Gordon, who rose to prominence as the bassist, guitarist, and vocalist of Sonic Youth, the renowned alternative band. In the early 1980s I attended a conference in New York City and Dean Gordon hosted a reception for UCLA students, faculty, alumni and their friends. He invited his daughter, Kim, to the reception. Dressed all in black, she appeared very hip and quite bored. She was with a tall man who also looked equally bored. I chatted with them and inquired about her life in New York. "I'm a musician with a rock group called Sonic Youth," she replied. "Oh, that's nice… good luck," I replied politely, and quickly exited the conversation, while thinking to myself she was wasting her time. Her dad and mom are probably quite disappointed with her for squandering her future on a rock and roll band fantasy. In retrospect, I see that this judgment of Ms. Gordon's pursuit of her dream was a projection of my own parent/child conflict. At the time, my parents were not thrilled with my choice to earn my doctorate instead of finding another husband.

Actually, my experiences as a high school social studies teacher in the Inglewood Unified School District (IUSD) from 1970 to 1979 catalyzed my graduate studies. In the late 1960s middle-class African American families began to purchase homes in its then-affordable residential neighborhoods east of Los Angeles International Airport. At the instigation of unscrupulous real estate actors, White families soon fled the community as African Americans moved into it. The small district rapidly became predominantly African American. Soon, the district once again underwent a demographic transformation. Low-income African Americans and Latinos, many of whom were refugees from Central American war zones, replaced the middle-class African Americans who had arrived in the city a mere decade earlier. These demographic shifts transformed the schools and launched me on a search to understand not only what was going on in the Inglewood community, but how these forces affected the teachers, students, educational processes and student outcomes.

## THE ATTITUDE-ACHIEVEMENT PARADOX AMONG BLACK ADOLESCENTS

The key question arising from my teaching experiences concerned the reasons so many of my African American students held attitudes that conveyed their belief in the importance of education for their future, while their day-to-day behavior in the classroom appeared to contradict their stated attitudes. An incident involving one of my high school seniors is emblematic of this paradox. EG was failing the required civics class I was teaching. One day in October 1975, he returned from being absent from school, explaining that he had slept in the day before because the previous evening he and his father had watched the Frazier-Ali "Thrilla in Manilla" boxing match. He was just too tired to come to school. Yes, he knew my class was crucial for graduation but the fight was really important and catching up on his sleep was important, too.

Like his peers, EG had frequently expressed his respect for the importance of education. But his performance in class and spotty attendance reflected another reality. His professed reverence for education went unmatched by daily actions in and out of school. I wanted to square that circle. I hypothesized that all adolescents hold two sets of attitudes toward education. Abstract attitudes, reflect the dominant ideology's account of a robust connection between education and opportunity for everyone. Because abstract attitudes do not vary they cannot predict variations in student achievement. In contrast, I found concrete attitudes vary with students' assessment of the role of education in the actual lives of their family members and larger community. If education brings family members opportunities, adolescents' concrete attitudes embrace education. People whose concrete attitudes reflect the belief that education brings opportunities commensurate with academic accomplishments do well in school. Conversely, if someone's concrete attitudes are skeptical of the education-opportunity link for people like themselves, they are unlikely to do well in school irrespective of their positive abstract attitudes.

My solution to the paradox of EG and other students' embrace of education combined with lackluster performance argued that their abstract attitudes espoused high regard for education but their actual performance was tied to concrete attitudes that captured their perceptions of the future opportunity structure that awaits people like themselves. For example, as a working class Black male, EG's lived experiences suggested to him schooling was unlikely to bring the returns promised by the dominant ideology's account of education and mobility. This research was published as "The Attitude/Achievement Paradox Among Black Adolescents" (*Sociology of Education*, 63: 44–61). Today the article is widely recognized as a foundational contribution to understanding ethnic, racial, and social class differences in adolescent academic achievement.

I replicated my initial research into the attitude-achievement paradox in 1997 when I collected survey data from secondary school students in Charlotte, North Carolina. Using a new survey instrument and a completely different samples of students, I again found evidence of the dual attitude framework and that concrete, not abstract attitudes, predict achievement. This replication was published in 2001 as "Subverting Swann: First- and Second- Generation Segregation in Charlotte, North Carolina" in the *American Educational Research Journal*. Since my initial research on dual attitudes, sociologists of education across the US (for example, Carter, 2005; Harris, 2011; Herman, 2009) and Europe (see D'Hondt et al., 2015) have replicated or refined the essence of these findings.

Four scholars shaped my thinking about the attitude-achievement paradox. Paul Willis' *Learning to Labor* (1977) analyzed British adolescents' resistance to schooling as grounded in their material realities; Jean Anyon's work "Social Class and the Hidden Curricula of Work" (1980, 1981); and John Uzo Ogbu's masterful descriptions of the job ceiling's effects on involuntary minority youth in *Minority Education and Caste* (1978). The missing link came from Frank Parkin's discussion of industrial societies' dominant and subordinate value systems in *Class, Inequality, and Political Order* (1976). He argued people hold dual sets of values, one reflecting society's abstract norms and the other situationally specific to their lives. He noted that most social science surveys mismeasure attitudes because they tap primarily abstract norms rather than the situationally specific ones that actually frame people's behaviors.

Paul Willis visited UCLA's Graduate School of Education while I finalized my dissertation. I spent a day giving him a sociologist's tour of Los Angeles. I never heard from him again. I never met Frank Parkin. Fortunately, I met Jean Anyon. Once we met, Jean and I became friends and colleagues and remained close until her death in 2012. I describe her influence on my thinking and our relationship in an essay commemorating her life and work (Mickelson, 2014). The most powerful intellectual influence on my early work was John Uzo Ogbu. He became my mentor and close friend. After his death in 2003, Ada Ogbu asked me to help her complete his final book, *Collective Identity and Schooling* (Ogbu, 2008). I recount my personal and professional relationship with Ogbu in my Foreword to that volume (Mickelson, 2008).

## CHARLOTTE, NORTH CAROLINA CHANGED EVERYTHING

I spent the 1984–1985 academic year as a postdoctoral fellow in the University of Michigan, Ann Arbor's Bush Program in Child Development and Social Policy. While living there I met and fell in love with a man raising his two small children. In 1985 I accepted a position on the UNC Charlotte sociology faculty to teach research methods and sociology of education in their new graduate program, and my new family and I moved to Charlotte. My journey to becoming a sociologist of education with an expertise in desegregation is another accidental intersection of my biography with the flow of educational history. Unbeknownst to me, taking the UNCC job positioned me to investigate school desegregation for the next thirty years. We enrolled our two elementary school-aged children in the Charlotte-Mecklenburg Schools (CMS), a district that at the time was well into its second decade of successfully implementing court-mandated desegregation (*Swann v. Charlotte-Mecklenburg,* 1971). Both children graduated from CMS after attending racially and socioeconomically diverse K-12 schools.

I became a professor, a parent, and a partner in the summer of 1985. My first year at UNCC was a blur. All I remember about that period was driving to campus and back home. The amount of teaching I did—four courses per semester—was breathtaking given that I also had pressure to publish. I submitted the first version of what would become "The Attitude/Achievement Paradox Among Black Adolescents," to the *American Sociological Review*. The reviewers were swift and brutal in their rejection of the manuscript as not ready for primetime. I was not prepared for the rejection. It figuratively knocked the wind out of me and left me intellectually paralyzed for almost two years. Eventually, I garnered the capacity to return to the piece. I sent the revised manuscript to *Sociology of Education*, which published it in 1990 after multiple revisions.

While the rejection, resubmission, revisions and ultimate publication drama of the "Attitude-Achievement Paradox Among Black Adolescents" was unfolding during the first five years of my career as an academic, I needed to continue to analyze my dissertation data so that I could publish. To that end, I sought with little success to have the IBM tape with my dissertation data mounted on UNCC's mainframe computer. This was before desktop computers became widespread. The UNCC mainframe was not compatible with my IBM data tape; eventually I had to send it back to UCLA to be reformatted so I could use it.

While I awaited the reformatting of my data tape, my research agenda advanced on two other fronts. First, I began a collaboration with two UCLA graduate students in psychology who contacted me after noticing a footnote in my dissertation mentioning that my data set included a small Asian subsample. They contacted me and requested permission to use the subsample for a MA thesis. I agreed. Psychology grad student Sumie Okazaki obtained my archived data from UCLA. Once unarchived, the data became the basis of Dunchen Zheng's MA thesis in psychology, and the basis of our jointly authored chapter, "Reading Reality More Closely Than Books: The Opportunity Structure and Adolescent Achievement" (Mickelson, Okazaki, & Zheng, 1995). We found that like Blacks and Whites, Asian students' abstract attitudes were uniformly high and only their concrete attitudes predicted their achievement. My dissertation's footnote led to a collaboration and a usable version of my dissertation dataset that I subsequently used on my desktop. By the time UCLA returned my data tape in a usable format, I no longer needed it.

## BUSINESS LEADERS AND SCHOOL REFORM

The second front in my research agenda was a qualitative study of business leaders and school reform. In 1987 UNCC hired Carol Ray, a sociologist interested in the labor process, corporate power, and social class. At about that time, the Charlotte Chamber of Commerce announced the formation of a task force ostensibly to examine school-to-workforce reform efforts implemented in CMS high schools. I was interested in school reform, especially given Charlotte's unique status as a district that successfully desegregated, and I wondered if the Chamber's committee would revisit business leaders' support for desegregation. Carol was interested in the labor process and education's role in preparing youth for work. We both were interested in how powerful local elites framed debates about school quality and solutions to the dilemmas they saw. The former Chancellor of UNCC, Dean Colvard, chaired the committee and his support ensured our access. So began the Business Leaders and School Reform Project, which initiated my thirty-year strategic case study of school reform in Charlotte. This case study was much more than a study of school reform—it became a longitudinal investigation of the relationship between school and classroom racial and socioeconomic composition and the short- and long-term outcomes of education across the life course. Once again, I stumbled into a research opportunity and my social network facilitated it.

Back in 1987, framing our investigation as a case study of the school-to-work pipeline connected us to a larger national debate, which in turn opened the doors to external funding for the project. The 1983 Nation at Risk Report critiqued public education for failing to prepare the next generation of workers. We connected the Charlotte Chamber's task force to the issues raised in *A Nation at Risk*. In 1989 Ray and I received NSF funding to support our study and since then, I have never been without external support for my research. I learned from this experience that framing one's research in terms of the topics that are fundable permits a scholar to study whatever she likes so long as the research is refracted through the lens of topics valued by the funders.

Our 1987 Business Leaders and School Reform project allowed me to follow how the school system's desegregation policies responded to the political demands of the local corporate community, the federal court's mandates, and the imperatives of changing county demographics. Researching this topic introduced me to key school board members and administrative leaders with whom I began to work formally and informally. School board members appointed me to a citizen's review panel and sought my advice on key policy issues.

Five years later many of the same CMS gatekeepers would permit me to conduct survey research in all middle and high schools in the district. Initially, I presented a desire to survey CMS students as exploring two issues: (a) the efficacy of business leadership in the direction and implementation of school reform, and (b) students' perceptions of the school-to-work preparation process. In fact, I also wanted to assess their attitudes toward education and opportunity. More precisely, I wanted to replicate my dissertation study with another population of students, this time outside of southern California. I consciously developed a survey instrument that assessed much more than students' perceived work readiness. I replicated my 1983 California study. At the time I planned the CMS survey examining school desegregation effects was not on my radar. I stumbled across that opportunity as I worked with CMS colleagues on the logistics of the data collection for the school-to-work survey.

## STUDYING SCHOOL-TO-WORK READINESS, EDUCATIONAL ATTITUDES, AND DESEGREGATION IN CHARLOTTE

I was able to obtain individual students' administrative data from CMS once gatekeepers gave me the green light. The green light followed the December 1996 resignation of the superintendent and his two top aids that did not trust or like me because of my work on a citizen watchdog committee. But CMS staff liked and trusted me. During the previous seven years I had worked formally and formally with these individuals in the district's central office. Once I pulled my random stratified sample of English classrooms from a sampling frame of all the English classes taught in Spring 1997 at every middle and high school, CMS's head of institutional research arranged to preprint all the blank survey forms with students' names and ID numbers. She also offered complete access to all student data from CMS's electronic data base for each child. Together we developed a plan whereby once students completed the survey, CMS would scan survey responses from the answer sheets, and create an electronic data file that included both the survey responses and relevant electronic data from each person's electronic file, matched by student ID and date of birth. The anonymized file would then be delivered to me.

To identify the data I needed from students' electronic files, I met with the head of institutional research. I explained to her that I needed electronic data that would be matched with students' survey responses to school-to-work and more general items about attitudes toward education and opportunity. I explained that I was interested in the individual, family, and school correlates of students' responses, and I wanted to use student test scores and GPAs as my dependent variables. She handed me a multi-page list of the various indicators the district collected on each student and said "Let me know what you'd like to have." I scanned the list. My eyes zeroed in on the entry and exit dates for every school a child attended. It took me a nanosecond to realize entry and exit dates, in combination with widely available historical data on the annual racial composition of each school, would allow me to create a profile of exposure to desegregation and/or racial isolation for each child during her or his tenure in CMS. I knew that with these indicators I could empirically investigate the effects of desegregation on CMS students' attitudes and achievement. With my heart racing, I forced myself to control my breathing. I steadied my voice and nonchalantly said, "I'll take them all." "No problem," she replied. And she gave me all the data. Once again, I stumbled into a research opportunity; this time, desegregation effects.

Using a complete list of every grade eight and grade twelve English class identified by academic track level offered in every school during the spring 1997 semester, I drew a fifty percent random selection of English classes stratified by track in every middle and high school in the district. The grade eight academic tracks were regular, academically gifted, and pre-International Baccalaureate. The grade twelve academic tracks were regular, advanced, academically gifted, Advanced Placement or International Baccalaureate. My research team and I fielded the twin surveys among the students enrolled in the randomly selected English classes and CMS anonymized the responses and matched students' survey responses with the individual, family, and school-level indicators in their electronic files.

The data on individual students' longitudinal exposure to desegregated schooling were unique for several reasons. At that point in the history of desegregation effects research, no study had examined effects of desegregation with complete longitudinal data for each student, let alone with a sample that did not suffer from serious selection bias. Because all schools and students in CMS were part of the mandatory desegregation plan for the past fourteen years, there was minimum selection bias in students and schools. Moreover, the dataset I created had exquisitely detailed information on individual background characteristics and school experiences from the time students entered the school system until either grade eight (middle school youth) or grade twelve (high school seniors).

The 1997 CMS survey data permitted me to examine the effects of school and classroom racial composition on student achievement. The results of that investigation for high school youth were published in "Subverting Swann: First- and Second-generation Segregation in the Charlotte-Mecklenburg Schools" (Mickelson, 2001). In this article I show that as CMS desegregated at the school level, it intensified segregation via racially-correlated tracking within schools. Importantly, I demonstrated that both segregated schools and racially isolated classrooms had negative effects on academic achievement for black and white students.

## *SWANN* REDUX

In the fall of 1998, having preliminarily analyzed the 1997 CMS survey and disseminated early findings through my CMS professional network, I headed off to be a Visiting Scholar at Stanford University School of Education (SUSE) for my sabbatical. My plan was to finish my book, *Children on the Streets of the Americas: Globalization, Homelessness, and Education in the United States, Brazil, and Cuba* (Mickelson, 2000). Soon after I arrived in Palo Alto, I was contacted by the law firm of Ferguson Stein Chambers & Grishom asking if I would be interested in serving as an expert witness in a then-forthcoming trial that essentially would be *Swann* redux. A White parent, William Capacchione, sought the end of race-conscious magnet school policies in CMS. If the Capacchione lawsuit were successful it could trigger the end of mandatory desegregation in Charlotte. The original legal team that represented the 1969 *Swann* plaintiffs became involved. But the Swann family no longer had legal standing, so two young Black families with children in CMS became plaintiff-interveners. The renamed *Swann* case became *Belk v. CMS*.

There were three parties to the lawsuit. The Capacchione family departed for southern CA six weeks after filing the suit. A group of white plaintiff interveners carried on in their stead. The Capacchione white plaintiff-interveners argued that CMS had done all that was practicable to end segregation in the district and asked that the original *Swann* decision be vacated and CMS declared unitary. The *Belk* plaintiff-interveners' own lawsuit argued that CMS had not done everything that was practicable to end segregation in the district. CMS was the respondent in both lawsuits. The district's position was closest to the *Belk* plaintiff-interveners, essentially arguing that it should remain under court order to desegregate because there remained work to be done to comply with *Swann*. The two cases were consolidated and adjudicated simultaneously in the spring of 1999.

The *Belk* plaintiff-interveners' attorneys, James Ferguson and Luke Largess, apparently knew of my CMS survey findings showing tracking and segregation disadvantaged Black students' academic performance vis-à-vis Whites even after controlling for student and family background, and that CMS board's policies and decisions about implementation of pupil assignment, teacher allocation practices, and tracking policies contributed to resegregation and thus harmed Black students' educational opportunities. They asked me to testify about the findings at trial, and I agreed to do so. But within days of my agreement to serve as the *Belk* plaintiffs' expert witness, CMS contacted me, too. CMS also wanted me to be their expert witness. I had strong personal and professional relationships with several CMS board members who also knew the preliminary findings of the 1997 survey. Importantly, the district provided enormous support for me in obtaining the data. In fact, the positions of the *Belk* plaintiff-interveners and CMS were largely identical: both parties believed the district had not done all that was practicable to end segregation, much needed to be done before CMS became unitary, and both parties wanted to remain under the *Swann* mandate to desegregate. But I had to choose.

I faced practical and ethical dilemmas. If I served as anyone's expert witness, my time at SUSE would be devoted to the trial preparation not my book manuscript. But I relished the opportunity to put my scholarship into 'action' and to move my research into the policy arena. I also wanted to work with lawyers who had a history of fighting for racial and educational justice. But if I said no to CMS I would be slapping the face of the people and the organization that assisted me in obtaining the data I now was preparing to use for expert testimony. But if I worked with CMS I would have to renege on my agreement to serve as the expert witness for the *Belk* plaintiffs.

I was torn. I conferred with my own attorney Edward Connette who persuaded me that if I testified for CMS I would have the best of all possible options because my CMS testimony would also advance the argument of the *Belk* plaintiff-interveners. I also conferred with UNC Charlotte Chancellor James Woodward because I perceived the situation as more than just my involvement; rather, it had the potential to be a collaboration or clash among organizational units of North Carolina public education. Moreover, there was also a potential for the university's role (through my testimony) to be seen as undermining the efforts of a locally and nationally renowned law firm's efforts to advance the educational interests of Black children. The former partner at Ferguson Stein who initially argued the *Swann* case before the U.S. Supreme Court, Julius Chambers, had served as the Director of the NAACP Legal Defense Fund and was at the time the Chancellor of North Carolina Central University. Meeting in Woodward's office, I laid out the issues as I saw them: my career as a researcher in the community; other UNCC faculty who might wish to research CMS; interorganizational cooperation; the possible visuals of race and class conflict over the schools. His solution was to call the CMS superintendent and propose a meeting between the CMS superintendent and the school board's attorney, UNC Charlotte and its attorney, and me and my attorney.

We met on a fall 1998 Saturday morning at the home of CMS's board attorney, Leslie Winner, a former member of the state legislature. Superintendent Eric Smith, Chancellor Woodward, Bill Steiner (UNCC's attorney), and Woody Connette and I discussed the situation. We were all White. Neither the *Belk* plaintiffs nor the attorneys from Ferguson Stein attended the meeting. When I pointed this out, Winner replied that she represented the school board and its Black members. I didn't argue with her rather nonsensical response. Eventually, I decided that my goals of disseminating my research at the trial and preserving interorganizational research cooperation between UNCC scholars and CMS would be best served by my testifying as an expert witness for CMS, not the *Belk* plaintiffs. I expressed additional concerns, "I want a career as an educational researcher in Charlotte after I testify." Superintendent Eric Smith assured me that even devastatingly negative testimony about CMS would not preclude future research in the district. Ultimately, I agreed to be CMS's expert witness.

Smith sealed his assurance of my future research access to CMS by bussing my check as he exited Winner's front door. He broke his promise to me. For the next eight years after my testimony as their expert witness CMS declined to cooperate with me on any research. At one point two Ford Foundation Program Officers, Janice Petrovich and Cyrus Driver, flew to Charlotte for the day to discuss with Smith my pending foundation grant that required CMS's approval to fund. Assured of CMS cooperation by Smith, they returned to New York, but Smith subsequently continued to block my access to CMS. After two additional meetings with Smith, his leadership team, and the deans of UNC Charlotte's Colleges of Education and Arts and Sciences, a working agreement between UNCC and CMS emerged and I was permitted access to Ford Foundation funds. But in general, my access to CMS data, students, and staff was curtailed until all individuals at the senior administrative level left the district in subsequent years.

Following the Saturday morning meeting amongst CMS and UNCC personnel, I had to withdraw my agreement to serve as the *Belk* plaintiff-interveners' expert witness. It was one of the most difficult conversations of my professional career. I buffered the toxicity of the conversation by suggesting that my colleague (and husband) Stephen Samuel Smith, a political scientist with extensive scholarly and activist expertise in CMS, could be available to serve as an expert witness for their legal team. He served brilliantly. Smith's expert testimony, in fact, was crucial in the 3rd Circuit Court of Appeals' initial decision to overturn the trial Judge's unitary decision. Ultimately a full panel of the 3rd Circuit Court of Appeals upheld the unitary decision and when the US Supreme Court declined to review that decision in 2002, CMS became unitary.

In April 1999 I spent a half day testifying as one of CMS's expert witnesses and three and a half days being cross-examined by the White plaintiff-interveners' attorney. I vowed never to serve as an expert witness again. The testosterone in the courtroom's atmosphere was thick enough to cut with a knife. It was a mortifying, debilitating, and demoralizing experience. When asked if I would be an expert witness again I often reply, "I'd prefer to have rectal surgery without anesthesia."

The trial judge disallowed my testimony because he declared me to be a biased witness. Why? From 1992 to 1994 I had served on a citizen's committee appointed by the school board to monitor and report on CMS' switch from mandatory busing to controlled choice among magnets as a strategy for desegregation. I had authored one of the two Committee of 25 Reports (really, it is the name of the group). The judge also disallowed the testimony of other CMS experts William Trent and Robert Peterkin, claiming their testimony was incompetent. At least I was not incompetent, just biased.

The experience of testifying as CMS's expert witness left me emotionally and physically depleted. I had been too heavily invested in the case. I naïvely believed once the social science record was out 'there' it would influence the judge's opinion despite his long history of antipathy toward desegregation. Robert Potter, as a lay citizen, was an activist against mandatory busing prior to his appointment to the bench by President Reagan. Even so, he declined to recuse himself. How ironic that he disallowed my testimony claiming I was a biased expert witness.

In the end, the *Swann* Redux experience was invaluable. I learned to: (a) avoid getting emotionally wrapped up in the outcome of my work; (b) avoid taking my own research so seriously that I believe it can change the world or the outcome of a legal or policy dispute; (c) remember ideology often trumps science in public policy; (d) take care of my body and mind; (e) be ethical in all that I do; (g) be doggedly persistent—don't take 'no' for an answer until I must; and (f) to develop a long game—the topic to which I will shortly turn.

THE SECRET DATA

By 2003, the eighth graders whom I surveyed in 1997 had either graduated or dropped out of high school. I approached a CMS staffer and asked if I could meet her for lunch. "Great," she said, "I'm retiring from CMS in a month." Over sandwiches I explained that *if* I were to obtain follow-up data from CMS records on the folks I had surveyed in 1997, I would have an incredible data resource with achievement indicators for each individual from third, eighth, and twelfth grade. Combined with my earlier attitude and achievement measures, and the school-level indicators—including all the measures of desegregation I had collected—I would have a unique dataset that would permit me to investigate the dynamic effects of student, family, and school factors moderated by gender, race, class, desegregation exposure over time on various school outcomes. Neither of us mentioned the elephant in the room: I needed to circumvent the CMS bureaucracy to get the data because the chances of its approval of a formal request were zero given the post-trial animus toward me among CMS top administrators.

The staff person understood the value of this kind of longitudinal data and the enormous value of such data from CMS. She was witnessing the resegregation of the district following the reopened *Swann* trial and the growing race and class gaps in student outcomes. She was disturbed by the administration's post-trial treatment of me as a researcher. I had been one of CMS's own expert witnesses yet the district was now placing road blocks in my ongoing research efforts. As a departing gesture to CMS and a gift to me, she asked the head of institutional research to create a dataset that included all the indicators available for the entire CMS graduating class of 2001. I soon received the next four years of electronic data for the 1997 eighth graders who completed their CMS educations in 2001. As an added bonus, she gave me a host of student- and family-level information that allowed me to geocode the neighborhoods in which students lived. Seventeen years later I still have these secret data disks and the padded envelop in which they were mailed to me. And I continue to use these data today.

YESTERDAY TODAY AND TOMORROW: SCHOOL DESEGREGATION AND RESEGREGATION IN CHARLOTTE

One aspect of my long game is telling CMS's story from my perspective as a sociologist of education. CMS returned to a neighborhood school-based assignment plan after it became a unitary school system in 2002. Because most residential neighborhoods in Mecklenburg County are racially and socioeconomically homogeneous, CMS schools also became racially and socioeconomically segregated. Although the district is almost three times larger in population and incredibly more diverse than it was in the 1970s when desegregation began (for example, the Latino population has increased 1,600% in the last twenty years), there are policy choices that can staunch or reverse the resegregation of the district. That is the story my colleagues Stephen Samuel Smith (also husband) and Amy Hawn Nelson (also my former doctoral student) and I convey in *Yesterday, Today and Tomorrow: School Desegregation and Resegregation in Charlotte* (2015, Harvard Education Press). The book recounts the last forty years of Charlotte's desegregation and resegregation, putting education reform in its political, sociological, and economic contexts. At the core of Charlotte's story is the relationship between social structure and human agency, with an emphasis on how yesterday's decisions and actions define today's choices. The book provides an interdisciplinary analysis of the forces and choices that have shaped the trend toward the resegregation of CMS. We assembled a wide range of contributors—historians, sociologists, economists, and education scholars—who provide a comprehensive view of a community's experience with desegregation and economic development. The book paints a vivid portrait of the changing realities and daunting challenges facing the school district forty-five years after the *Swann* decision and 60 years after *Brown v. Board of Education.* The book's analysis point toward larger structural forces that must be confronted if we are to fulfill *Brown's* promise of equality.

## DEVELOPING MY LONG GAME

The year 2004 marked the 50th anniversary of the *Brown v. Board of Education* decision that declared school segregation unconstitutional. Celebrations abounded, and the annual meeting of the American Sociological Association that summer included a session in which famed civil rights attorney Julius Chambers spoke. Chambers implored his audience of sociologists to do more than merely hold celebrations of *Brown*. He reminded us that the legal battles over school desegregation continued and that civil and educational rights attorneys needed the assistance of social scientists whose work supported their legal arguments. At the time Chambers spoke, he knew education rights attorneys would welcome social scientists' assistance in the Seattle, WA and Louisville KY, voluntary desegregation cases that ultimately became the 2007 US Supreme Court decision in *Parents Involved in Community Schools.*

I responded to Chambers' call to action by proposing that ASA support efforts to identify what we currently know about the relationship between school racial and SES composition and educational outcomes. Kathryn Borman and I received a small grant from the ASA's Sydney S. Spivack Program in Applied Social Research and Social Policy to convene a conference of experts in 2005. Products of that conference include a forthcoming book I am completing, three special issues of *Teachers College Record* (Vol. 110, Numbers 3, 4, and 5) devoted to the topic, and an interactive searchable database into which detailed summaries of social, educational, and behavioral science research on the topic of school racial and SES composition are entered (http://spivack.org). The Spivack Archive has 550 entries to date. Journalists, scholars, public policy actors, lay citizens, and students interested in this topic have used the database.

The Spivack Archive is a tool in my long game. I use it for my own scholarship and policy work about the relationships of school desegregation and resegregation to both the academic and nonacademic outcomes in students' lives across the life course. It allowed me to assist the authors of several *PICS* amicus briefs in their syntheses of the social science research showing the benefits of diversity and the harms of segregation. I continue to assist authors of amicus briefs by providing them with syntheses of the relevant social science research on diverse schooling. The preponderance of research in the field, and summarized in the Spivack Archive's entries, clearly shows that desegregated or diverse schools and classrooms are positively related to academic and nonacademic outcomes for all students across the life course. These outcomes are particularly true for the youth most disadvantaged by their family's class background and their membership in underserved minority groups.

I disseminate findings from the Spivack Archive in a variety of venues. Journalists interview me about educational diversity and I work with attorneys who file amicus briefs in state and federal court cases involving school desegregation or segregation. I have written policy briefs for the Poverty and Race Research Action Council, given invited presentations to Secretary of Education Arne Duncan and his cabinet, to Assistant Secretary for Civil Rights Tom Perez, and I have testified about the benefits of diversity in a hearing in Kentucky, and to a joint gubernatorial and legislative committee in Minnesota. I also continue to author scholarly chapters and articles that synthesize the social, educational, and behavioral science research on the effects of school racial and socioeconomic composition on both academic and nonacademic outcomes across the life course (e.g., Mickelson, Bottia, & Lambert, 2013; Mickelson & Nkomo, 2012). Putting accessible versions of my scholarship into the public arena is part of my long game and at least in the area of desegregation research, the Spivack Archive has my back, so to speak.

As the last paragraphs suggest, about ten years ago I stopped being an accidental sociologist of education. I became purposeful and developed a long game: I began to lay groundwork for the kinds of research and policy work I wanted to do in the future. I became much more strategic. After the *Swann* Redux expert witness experience, I vowed to develop my skill set and stock of knowledge so that I am always prepared. The scholar who influenced me the most in this regard is Gary Orfield, whose corpus of scholarship and policy work on school desegregation, the politics of education, and social justice research inspired my work on these issues.[2] Many years ago over breakfast in a New York hotel I asked him how, in the face of the reversals in school desegregation, he garnered the strength to continue his work. He recalled the advice of his own teacher, the renowned historian of the African American experience, John Hope Franklin, who encouraged graduate students to create a historical record so that skeptics could argue interpretations but not the facts. For Orfield, continuing to generate a scholarly record of desegregation's benefits and segregation's costs had value if not for today, for tomorrow.

## AWARD SEASON

I've entered the award and honors season of my career. There is a subtle downside to this phase. People in their award season tend to be near the end of their careers unless, of course, they are among the precocious few who receive Early Career Awards. I'm not ready to retire; I feel I just hit my stride. My peers have acknowledged my contributions by appointing me a Fellow of the American Educational Research Association in 2010, and in April I became the 2015 recipient of the Elizabeth G. Cohen Distinguished Career in Applied Sociology of Education Award given by the AERA Sociology of Education Special Interest Group. Cohen held a joint appointment in Sociology and Education at Stanford University. In 1979, she became the founding director of the Program for Complex Instruction, a groundbreaking pedagogy that applies sociological theory to promote racial, ethnic, and gender equity in the classroom. Cohen was one of my mentors and receiving this award is deeply gratifying.

My own institution, UNC Charlotte has honored me three times. In 2004, UNC Charlotte recognized my contributions as a teacher and mentor by awarding me the Harshini V. de Silva Graduate Mentor Award, the highest award for graduate level teaching and mentoring given by the university. The second award recognized my research contributions. In 2011 UNC Charlotte awarded me its highest honor for distinguished scholarship, the First Citizens Bank Scholar Award, for consistently contributing to major theoretical and policy debates in the sociology of education. The highest distinction I have received was being designated in 2014 as the second UNC Charlotte Chancellor's Professor in recognition of my sustained scholarly achievement in my professional field. The title is awarded to UNC Charlotte faculty who have demonstrated ability in interdisciplinary research, teaching, and service. As I write this paragraph I'm still getting used to the title and what it means for my career at UNCC and my life beyond.

## TIKKUN OLAM

My life beyond UNC Charlotte is the central force that undergirds my career as a sociologist of education. When I received the First Citizen Bank Scholars Award in 2011, I was asked to reflect on what motivates me as a scholar. The words I wrote then ring true four years later as I write this chapter. I believe that as a human being privileged with health, safety, material comfort, and as a public intellectual with a platform to disseminate my scientifically informed views, I have a responsibility to advance social, racial, and gender justice. My sense of responsibility is shaped by the Hebrew phrase *tikkun olam,* which roughly translates as "repair the world." *Tikkun olam* calls upon Jews, to be responsible for creating a just and harmonious society. I have no illusions that there is a direct line between my research and social justice. It would be sheer lunacy mixed with hubris to think there is such a connection. Rather, I envision—and hope—that my work is part of a larger collective effort toward *tikkun olam*. I believe that the moral imperative of public schooling is to contribute to the creation of a fair, socially cohesive, and humane society by expanding educational opportunity, especially to those from historically underserved populations. I strive for my research, teaching, and public service to advance these broader purposes. I remain cautiously optimistic that my life in schools contributes to this vision.

I am no longer an accidental sociologist of education. The trajectory of my story has moved from the relatively unconscious stumbling along of the 1970s to the present where I choose more organic directions for my teaching, research, and the public spaces I inhabit. These choices are connections between my immediate life choices and what is s happening in the world around me. This is my long game.

## NOTES

[1] In fact, one of the two, Sidney Altman, received the Nobel Prize in Chemistry in 1989.
[2] Orfield cofounded and codirects the Civil Rights Project/Proyecto Derechos Civiles. The website offers a glimpse of Orfield's contributions. https://www.facebook.com/pages/Civil-Rights-ProjectProyecto-Derechos-Civiles-at-UCLA/124921007573577

## MY FAVORITE TEXTS BY OTHERS

Anyon, Jean (1980). "Social Class and the Hidden Curriculum of Work" *Journal of Education* 162, 67-92. And (1981). "Social Class and School Knowledge" *Curriculum Inquiry* 11, 3-42.
Bernard, Jessie (1981). *The Female World.* New York: The Free Press.
Bourdieu, Pierre (1984). *Distinction, A Social Critique of the Judgment of Taste.* New York: Routledge.
Braverman, Harry (1974). *Labor and Monopology Capital.* New York: Monthly Review Press.
Gould, Stephen Jay (1981). *The Mismeasure of Man.* New York: W.W. Norton.
Kluger, Richard (1975). *Simple Justice.* New York: Random House.
Lareau, Annette (2003). *Unequal Childhoods.* Berkeley: University of California Press.
Ogbu, John U. (1978). *Minority Education and Caste.* New York: Academic Press.
Portes, Alejandro & Rumbaut, Rubén (2006). *Immigrant America.* Berkeley: University of California Press.
Takaki, Ronald (1993). *A Different Mirror.* New York: Little, Brown, and Company.
Wilson, William J. (1978). *The Declining Significance of Race.* Chicago: University of Chicago Press.
Wright, Eric Olin, *Classes* (1985). London: Verso.

## MY FAVORITE PERSONAL TEXTS

Mickelson, R. A.; Smith, S. S., & A. H. Nelson (2015) *Yesterday, Today, and Tomorrow. School Desegregation and Resegregation in Charlotte.* Cambridge,MA: Harvard Education Press.

Bottia, M., Stearns, E., Mickelson, R., Moller, S., & Valentino, L (2015). "Growing the Roots of STEM Majors: Female Math and Science High School Faculty and the Participation of Students in STEM." *Economics of Education Review*, 45, 14-27.

Mickelson, R. A., Bottia, M., & Lambert, R. (2013). "Effects of School Racial Composition on K-12 Mathematics Outcomes: A Metaregression Analysis," *Review of Educational Research*, 83, 121-158.

Mickelson, R. A., & Nkomo, M. (2012). "Integrated Schooling, Life-course Outcomes, and Social Cohesion in Multiethnic Democratic Societies" *Review of Research in Education*, 36, 197-238.

Mickelson, R. A. (2006). "Segregation and the SAT" *Ohio State Law Journal* 67, 157-199.

Mickelson, R. A. (2001). "Subverting Swann: First- and Second- Generation Segregation in Charlotte, North Carolina" *American Educational Research Journal*, 38, 215-252.

Mickelson, R. A., Nkomo, M., & Smith, S. (2001). "Education, Ethnicity, Gender and Social Transformation: A Comparison of Israel and South Africa" *Comparative Education Review*, 45: 1-29.

Mickelson, R. A. (2000) *Children on the Streets in the Americas: Globalization, Homelessness, and Education in the US, Brazil, and Cuba.* New York: Routledge.

Mickelson, R. A. (1990). "The Attitude-Achievement Paradox Among Black Adolescents" *Sociology of Education*, 63, 44-61.

Mickelson, R. A. (1989). "Why Does Jane Read and Write So Well?:The Anomaly of Women's Achievement" *Sociology of Education*, 62, 43-67.

## REFERENCES

Anyon, J. (1981). Social class and school knowledge. *Curriculum Inquiry*, 11, 3–42.

Anyon, J. (1980). Social class and the hidden curriculum of work. *Journal of Education*, 162, 67–92.

Carter, P. (2005). *Keepin' It real. School success beyond Black and White.* New York, NY: Oxford University Press.

Cohen, E. G., & Lotan, R. (2014). *Designing group work. Strategies for heterogeneous classrooms* (3rd ed.). New York, NY: Teachers College Press.

D'Hondt, F., Van Praag, L., Stevens, P., & Van Houtte, M. (2014). Do school attitudes influence underachievement of Turkish and Moroccan minority students in Flanders? The attitude-achievement paradox revisited. *Comparative Education Review*, 59, 332–354.

Harris, A. L. (2011). *Kids don't want to fail: Oppositional culture and the Black-White achievement gap.* Cambridge, MA: Harvard University Press.

Herman, M. (2009). The Black-White-other test score gap: Testing theories of academic performance among multiracial and monoracial adolescents. *Sociology of Education*, 82, 20–46.

Mickelson, R. A. (1990). The attitude-achievement paradox among Black adolescents. *Sociology of Education*, 63, 44–61.

Mickelson, R. A. (2000). *Children on the streets of the Americas: Globalization, homelessness, and education in the United States, Brazil, and Cuba.* New York, NY: Routledge.

Mickelson, R. A. (2001). Subverting swann: First- and second- generation segregation in Charlotte, North Carolina. *American Educational Research Journal*, 38, 215–252.

Mickelson, R. A. (2008). Foreword. In J. U. Ogbu (Ed.), *Collective identity and schooling* (pp. i–ivx). New York, NY: Lawrence Erlbaum.

Mickelson, R. A. (2014). The metaphor. *Perspectives on Urban Education*, 11(1). Retrieved from https://www.urbanedjournal.org/archive/volume-11-issue-1-winter-2014/metaphor

Mickelson, R. A., & Nkomo, M. (2012). Integrated schooling, life-course outcomes, and social cohesion in multiethnic democratic societies. *Review of Research in Education*, 36, 197–238.

Mickelson, R. A., Okazaki, S., & Zheng, D. (1995). Reading reality more closely than books: The opportunity structure and Asian adolescent achievement. In P. Cookson, Jr & B. Schneider (Eds.), *Transforming schools* (pp. 81–105). New York, NY: Garland. Publishing Co.

Mickelson, R. A., Bottia, M., & Lambert, R. (2013). A meta-regression analysis of the effects of school and classroom composition on mathematics outcomes. *Review of Educational Research*, 83, 121–158.

Mickelson, R. A., Smith, S. S., & Nelson, A. H. (2015). *Yesterday, today, and tomorrow. School desegregation and resegregation in Charlotte.* Cambridge, MA: Harvard Education Press.

Ogbu, J. U. (1978). *Minority education and caste*. New York, NY: Academic Press.
Ogbu, J. U. (2008). *Collective identity and schooling*. New York, NY: Lawrence Erlbaum.
Parkin, F. (1976). *Class, inequality, and political order*. New York, NY: Praeger.
Willis, P. (1977). *Learning to labor*. New York, NY: Columbia University Press.

*Roslyn Arlin Mickelson*
*University of North Carolina*
*Charlotte*

GERARD A. POSTIGLIONE

# 11. POWER, PURPOSE AND THE RISE OF THE REST

I

1979 was as good a time as any to be a student in the sociological study of education. *Power and Ideology in Education* had been in print for three years. *Schooling in Capitalist America* was published two years earlier. *The Credential Society* was in press. While writing my doctoral dissertation, I took time out to read the Sunday *New York Times*. There it was—an ad for a lectureship in the sociology of education at the University of Hong Kong. The ad roused my interest. I had taken a course on world systems theory. I was curious about the consequences of the War in Vietnam for Asia. And a young sociology professor named Nan Lin had given a talk at our university about his China visit. I was a twenty-eight year-old doctoral student and interest in Asia trumped my sense of career practicality. China was a world away. Cell phones were science fiction and making a call from Beijing to New York could take hours. These were the Cold War days. In 1979, the Soviet Union invaded Afghanistan, Americans were being held hostage in Iran, Vietnamese forces captured Phnom Penh from the Khmer Rouge, China withdrew its troops from Vietnam, refugees streamed into Hong Kong, and the US and China began diplomatic relations. I wrote my letter of application to the University of Hong Kong, knowing it was a long shot.

With no reply from the University of Hong Kong, I completed my dissertation and taught introduction to sociology in Europe, where I could visit Paris, Heidelberg, and Trier—cities associated with the giants of the field—Durkheim, Weber and Marx. My curiosity led me to cross into what were known then as the Iron Curtain countries of Eastern Europe. I was making my way through the Middle East when a telegram from Hong Kong caught up with me in southeast Turkey. It confirmed an interview for the University of Hong Kong, but in New York—which I left three months earlier. A follow-up telegram directed me to the University of Hamburg in Germany where I was interviewed by Neville Postlethwaite, an early designer of the International Evaluation of Educational Achievement. My dissertation had been about social theory and his research was highly quantitative—based on an international data set of school achievement. Fortunately, I had also co-authored a quantitative paper on race and sex differences in achievement oriented behaviour. It must have helped me through the interview because a contract arrived two weeks later. I hesitated for about a year, but eventually signed on to what I thought would be another brief sojourn of international teaching and research experience. It would lead to spending half of my life in Asia, including a chance to engage with the reestablishment of the sociology of education in China.

II

Hong Kong might as well have been on the moon in 1979 for a Brooklyn-born kid from an Italian-American family. My father worked an eighty-hour week and died young from a mugging in the gun-heyday of 1970s New York. I was in the Columbia University Library when I learned he was in a Brooklyn hospital with a head wound. He left me with a work ethic, a love for baseball, and the oft echoed phrase— "make sure you get a good education." His education had been curtailed due to his own father's early death, after which he was drafted to serve in WWII. My parents decided to enroll me in parochial schools of Brooklyn and Queens where nuns and brothers spent their lives teaching the city's unruly youth. The school curriculum, except for the world map that was tacked to the classroom blackboard, ignored China. In high school, I learned a great deal about Greek mythology, and the Latin courses did little for my subsequent study of Mandarin.

I began college in 1968 and majored in computer science, but the social tumult of the era led me to broaden my academic interests toward the health sciences. In graduate school, I veered more toward the social sciences, which helped me make sense in a world where I had worked part-time jobs since age thirteen to supplement what my family could afford for my education. I had delivered newspapers, handled a jack-hammer, drove a ten-ton truck, fork-lift, taxi and school bus. There were also multiple restaurant jobs in three cities. I had delivered bread in Brooklyn, served hot dogs in Coney Island, and cared for parklands on Long Island. As a musician I worked the club circuit, including Times Square and nearby the Empire State Building. I hauled cement across scaffolding on the New York Telephone Company building as I watched the Twin Towers of the World Trade Center rising floor by floor in the distance (and watched in horror at an OECD meeting in Paris as they toppled on 9–11). At college I worked in the cafeteria preparing meals for my classmates, took part in campus anti-war protests, including occupation of campus administration. Even as a doctoral student, I worked the morning shift at the Hyatt Hotel across from campus. On breaks I read paperbacks: Turkel's *Working,* Reich's *Greening of America,* Mills' *Sociological Imagination,* Berger and Luckman's Social Construction of Reality, Illich's *Deschooling Society,* and Freiere's *Pedagogy of the Oppressed* and a number of others.

III

Becoming a teacher seemed a promising path to promote change. My idealism was tempered by a Jonathan Kozol lecture after his *Death at an Early Age.* Postman and Weingartner's *Teaching as a Subversive Activity* spurred my curiosity in alternative methods of teaching. I undertook practice-teaching at an inner-city high school in Rochester. This was followed by substitute teaching in upstate New York communities before I finally landed a regular teaching post in a small but diverse school. My salary was less than what was offered at other schools, but I gladly took the post because the school permitted me to push the boundaries of alternative teaching methods. I did away with desks, brought in tables, integrated the curriculum and reframed how science was taught.

After some local media attention to my experimental format, a visit to my classroom by a professor from the nearby State University of New York at Albany campus led me toward graduate school where a group of philosophers, historians, and sociologists were challenging the status quo in education.[1] Doctoral students in educational foundations were required to take most of their coursework in one of the three disciplines, plus three advanced seminar courses in the philosophy, history and sociology of education.[2] The discipline-based format was attractive and relevant for critiques of educational issues. Unfortunately, the ground beneath the academy was shifting. Policy study was on the rise and my department was considered too theory-oriented. As the student representative of the department, I watched as it became subsumed under a larger entity known as policies, programs and institutions. Though I managed not to take any policy courses, I would later do policy research for most of the world's major multinational development agencies. I still think that the discipline-based study of education was more valuable in my policy research work than a few policy courses would have been. Meanwhile, my coursework in sociology led me to write a journal article on the poverty of paradigmaticism, and I decided to write my dissertation about the implications of conflict theory for ethnicity. Though I was probably ill-equipped at the time, I taught courses at SUNY Albany and at nearby Russell Sage University. Before leaving the United States, I won a summer scholarship to the Inter-University Consortium for Social and Political Research at the University of Michigan and spent two years in Europe.

IV

When I arrived in Hong Kong, the discussion about its retrocession was already underway. Chinese leader Deng Xiaoping hatched the idea of "one-country and two-system" as a means to unify the Chinese mainland and Taiwan, and it would be used first to reincorporate Hong Kong. China had just begun to embark on its path of economic reform and opening to the outside world following the Cultural Revolution. Many Hong Kong Chinese had migrated from the Chinese mainland. Some became semi-Anglicized with benefit to their careers, while others remained staunchly loyal to Beijing. Some managed to do both. Until 1997, graduates of so-called "patriotic schools" could not enter government service or teacher training colleges. Nevertheless, Chinese cultural heritage was a unifier. Regardless of political orientation, the vast majority had high hopes for China's future and welcomed the economic reform and opening to the outside world. The sociologist Lau Siu-kai referred to Hong Kong's colonial era as having a secluded bureaucratic polity with an atomistic Chinese society.

Much changed during the negotiations over how Hong Kong would be governed when a million people took to the streets after the Tiananmen tragedy of June 4, 1989. In the weeks before, I was in northeast China on a delegation led by the Vice-President of the University of Hong Kong. We learned about the unfolding of events in Beijing only after we returned to Hong Kong, where the media was riveted on what would cut deeply into the psyche of Hong Kong people. A few days later, I spoke to a few thousand of our university students and academic staff at a memorial to the students who had died. To this day our students at the University of Hong Kong have a towering sculpture on campus in remembrance of June 4th 1989, the only such symbol on any university campus in China.

To sort out my thoughts on Hong Kong's reunion with the Chinese mainland, I co-edited a series of books (with Ming Chan at Stanford University) that focused on politics and law, then a second book series on culture and society (with Tai-lok Lui at the University of Hong Kong). There was no better place for a sociologist to be. Both Hong Kong and the Chinese mainland were in transition, the former, a hotbed of market capitalism, would be incorporated into a socialist system; the latter a communist party-led state, would become the world's largest market economy. In 1997, we published a co-edited volume on Hong Kong's transition to Chinese rule with a Foreword by Ezra Vogel, one of America's leading Sinologists.

The University of Hong Kong was a popular venue for considering the implications of sovereignty retrocession because it welcomed contrasting voices. In one event, Governor Christopher Patten, a vociferous proponent of further democratization, chaired the lecture of Singapore Prime Minister Lee Kwan Yew, who openly expressed his dissatisfaction with Patten's view on popular democracy. In producing the volume *Hong Kong's Reunion with China* that would be released in 1997, the Centre of Asian Studies of the University of Hong Kong brought together a number of Asianists including the University President Wang Gung Wu, American Consulate General Bert Levin, Director of Asian Studies Wong Siu-lun, and other Hong Kong scholars who contributed to the book or reviewed chapters. Other community venues provided me with useful perspectives, including the National Day and Lunar New Year banquets of the Hong Kong government or Xinhua News Agency (at the time the de facto representative of Beijing in Hong Kong), at which Beijing's representative (Xu Jiatun, Zhou Nan) and the governor of Hong Kong (Sir David Wilson, Christopher Patten) would deliver a long toast containing grist for political and sociological analysis.

My central task was to understand education in Hong Kong. Since I was not familiar with its development I read up on its history and development. I taught sociology of education to practicing teachers who had already a bachelor degree and were studying for a postgraduate teaching credential. To get a better understanding of the challenges faced by teachers, I spent one afternoon a week teaching classes in a local school. As my interest and research on the education in the Chinese mainland grew faster, I began to spend more and more time visiting schools and universities there. I could not help but wonder how and if the education systems of the two Chinese systems would become integrated, a work that is still in progress.³

Early on, I believed that China would gradually become internationally influential, a belief held by few at that time. In historical terms, China has been a leading civilization for most of its history, and the neo-Confucian communities in Hong Kong, Taiwan, Korea, Japan and Singapore were moving ahead rapidly under an open, though highly unequal, economy. It seemed only a matter of time that the Chinese mainland would join them. I decided to spend every minute outside of my teaching responsibilities to continue my study of Chinese language. I was driven by the idea that the study of language and history is a necessary means of understanding a people. It turned out to be a colossal investment of time, but I have no regrets.

I worked countless hours, always carrying large piles of index cards on which I had written Chinese characters. It was a challenge to study Mandarin in Hong Kong. Until the turn of the Century, almost everyone spoke only Cantonese or English. And if not Cantonese, it was likely to be Shanghainese or Minnan dialects, but not Mandarin. For two or three months each year I would study Mandarin (Putonghua) in Beijing where I gained a deeper appreciation of China's civilization, including its viewpoint about historical humiliations endured at the hands of other nations. Eventually, by the early 1990s, my language ability became good enough for me to do fieldwork, lecture, attend meetings, and read the news and professional publications. Though I could read Chinese characters, my hand writing (even in English) was poor until I began to use software that enabled the input of Chinese characters, something I learned from a book by Singapore Prime Minister Lee Kwan Yew who, though ethnically Chinese, had not studied Chinese until after graduating from university.

V

Rather than return to New York during the summer months, I spent those months in Beijing and other cities to learn as much as I could about China, which was just opening. I started with China's educational history, first with figures of the classical era such as Confucius and Mencius, Sunzi and Mozi, and later Wang Yangming and Zhu Xi. For the modern era, it was important to try and understand Hu Shi as well as Cai Yuanpei, Liang Shuming, Ye Yangchu, Mei Yiqi, Jiang Bailing, Yan Fu, Tao Xingzhi, and Pan Guangdan, all of whom were influential in China's educational development. I tried my best to gain a handle on how these Chinese thinkers from past eras reflected the changing ethos of Chinese society and its interaction with Western culture. I also read as much of the contemporary work of noted Sinologists, including Fairbanks, Hsu, Spence, Nathan, Barnett, Eckstein, Schurman, Vogel, White, White III, So, Zweig, and others, including Madsen who had done an interesting comparison of Chinese and American societies.

I was fortunate to be in Hong Kong where many Chinese and overseas scholars would visit the universities, including the Universities Service Center for China Studies. I scoured Hong Kong's Chinese bookshops, sometimes with Stanley Rosen, one of the highly knowledgeable scholars of contemporary China society. Together we would co-edit the forty-year journal, *Chinese Education and Society*. Issues of the journal would be dedicated to China's budding field of sociology of education.

My China studies training involved several sabbaticals including the Asian studies divisions of Yale, Columbia, Stanford, Johns Hopkins, and the China studies division of the latter's School of Advanced International Studies (SAIS). At SAIS, I was hosted by Professor Doak Barnett who understood China better than most Americans, and whose encouragement helped reignite the U.S. recognition of China. While at SAIS, I was invited to the Rose Garden of the White House for an event at which I met a representative of the Chinese Embassy who would join me weeks later at a welcome dinner sponsored by the National American Italian Foundation for Luciano Pavoratti. Pavoratti had recently performed at China's Great Hall of the People, one of the first foreigners to be so permitted. SAIS had a campus in Nanjing which I visited in 1987 and again in 2000 as a senior consult to the Ford Foundation, which had made grants to SAIS Nanjing. I visited classes taught by both Chinese and American professors, met students and SAIS trustees and attended talks by speakers at opposite ends of the political spectrum. Bill Clinton was still president and Joseph Pruher, his Ambassador to China who I met in Beijing, was also at SAIS that evening. Unbeknownst to us, Paul Wolfowitz who also spoke that day at SAIS Nanjing, would soon join the new administration and irresponsibly push it into Iraq. Tom Friedman of the New York Times also spoke and gave hints about his upcoming book on the flat world. I met Tom Friedman later in Hong Kong and suggested he write more on education. Little did I know that he had already been doing so in sections of his soon to be released *That Used to be Us*.

VI

In the early 1980s, there was little available in English on the sociological study of Chinese education. Some of the best work done at that time was by political sociologists, including John Unger, Stan Rosen, Suzanne Pepper, and Susan Shirk, all of whom conducted interviews in Hong Kong of ex-Red Guards at the end of the Cultural Revolution. Since then, the field has grown with scholars like Ruth Hayhoe, Heidi Ross, Emily Hannum, Zhou Xueguang, Yang Rui, Mun Tsang, Kai-ming Cheng, Andrew Kipnis, Lin Jing, Vilma Seeberg, Julia Kwong, Gregory Fairbrother, Xiao Jin and others. A great many younger scholars have now joined the ranks, and increased the focus on education, inequality and social stratification. I supervised over twenty doctoral students from the Chinese mainland at the University of Hong Kong. About half of them wrote case studies of education in ethnic minority regions of the country. Some had completed master degrees in the North America and Europe, and most joined universities in Hong Kong, the Chinese mainland, and Australia.

After the turn of the Century, Chinese scholars became increasingly involved in the debate about what kind of education system is best for China's future society. Some continue to question the race to excel on international indicators of school achievement like PISA, or the global university rankings, like AWRU. Ever present is the longstanding issue of how to strengthen the nation in the face of historical humiliations and foreign exploitations. Some called for a commitment to be more reflective about how to bring a Western academic model into the service of the nation. A Hong Kong Chinese scholar who later became president of the Hong Kong Institute of Education raised a common question: "Will Asia be just producing more of the same of the Western-originated contemporary higher education model, or will it be able to unleash a more critical understanding and practice in higher education, a cultural and epistemological reflection on the role of universities as venues of higher learning?" (Cheung, 2013). Even Western scholars like Ruth Hayhoe contend that higher education can be much more guided by China's indigenous ideas and principles, with the Chinese academies of the Song and Tang period cited as an example.

I had approached the study of China armed with as much sociological theory as could be expected of a young Western trained scholar. I soon realized that a common viewpoint among Sinologists was that such an approach should be jettisoned. This perspective is most recently represented in David Shambaugh's *China Goes Global* (2013): "…scholars increasing obsession with social science theories and methodologies have created further impediments to understanding [China] – more often blurring than clarifying the objects of study. Unfortunately, testing of theories and application of methodologies is becoming an end rather than a means to furthering knowledge and understanding. As a result, scholars in the China field are becoming more and more divorced from their professional mission and responsibility: to illuminate and educate." This statement is not to deny the significant interest in Western sociological theories and methodologies among Chinese social scientists. Chinese social science has benefitted from study of systematically empirical approaches to research.

VII

When I visited China in 1981, it was plain to see that the Cultural Revolution had stultified sociology. It took much effort by Chinese scholars to reestablish the sociology of education. The focus on inequality and educational stratification was, and to a degree remains, sensitive. Beginning in the 1950s, China's sociology of education was heavily influenced by Russian scholars, even after the diplomatic break with the Soviet Union in the late 1950s. By 1980, many senior professors had either studied in Russia or were influenced by the Soviet studies of education. When Chinese scholars were sent to Western countries in the early 1980s, most studied science and engineering. By the 1990s, more began to study the social sciences and education. This happened much earlier in Taiwan, where scholars like Lin Ching-Chiang and Chen Po-Chang helped build the field there.

When the sociology of education received an amber colored light to proceed, it was not uncommon for a party leader to write the lead article in an education journal that set out the parameters for proceeding, and other scholars could follow in the articles that followed. Some scholar-officials, like Fei Xiaotong who studied with Bradislaw Malinowski in the 1930s and later became vice-premier, were highly influential in the reestablishment of both sociology and anthropology.

While at Beijing Normal University in the mid-1980s, I asked vice-president Gu Mingyuan who I had met in 1982, to arrange for me to study Chinese educational history. I studied the history of Chinese education with Guo Qijia who brought me to meet retired historians Mao Lirui and Chen Jingpan, the latter who told me he likened the Cultural Revolution to the Reign of Terror in France. I also met Li Yixian who played a central role in the reestablishment of sociology of education. Together with Li Jinxu from Taiwan Normal University, we three co-edited the first book in Chinese of Western readings in the sociology of education. We included forty-four chapters, including classics and contemporary readings of Durkheim, Weber, Marx, Collins, Bowles and Gintis, Boudon, Coleman, Waller, Bourdieu, Carnoy, Bernstein, Meyer, Dreeben, Rist, Young, Apple and others.

I accepted invitations to lecture about Western sociology of education at universities in several cities, and was asked to deliver a special lecture to the Beijing Sociological Association. That talk was chaired by Lei Jieqiong, who was soon to become vice-chair of the National People Congress. Madame Lei was incredibly interesting; a highly able woman who lived to over one-hundred years of age, and had studied at the University of Southern California in the 1920s when it was a Christian College. Originally from Guangdong province near Hong Kong, she bantered with me before my talk began, reminding me of the exploitation of Chinese who built the railroads in America. My talk that day discussed the main features of Western sociology of education, its development as a field in the United States, functionalist and conflict theories, macroscopic and microscopic perspectives, and research exemplars such as James Coleman's study on educational inequality.

The content of my talk was not as important as Madame Lei's adding legitimacy to the reestablishment of the sociology of education in China, with back-up support of the translator, Min Weifang. Min had recently returned to China with a doctorate from the School of Education at Stanford University. I had learned of Min while I was on sabbatical at Stanford but had not met him until I returned to Beijing. In retrospect, it was humbling to have Min, the future leader of Peking University, as translator. However, in the 1980s, being a translator for a foreign scholar was a key role for a young scholar. The translator not only had to possess an excellent command of English—a very rare commodity in the early 1980s—but he also had to know how to interpret Western ideas for Chinese leaders and the wider audience, especially after China's seclusion from the West over several decades. While at Stanford under doctoral supervision of the economist Henry Levin, Min also became familiar with the sociology of education. After returning to China he introduced the economics of education as a field.

A year or so later I was invited to speak at the first meeting of the new association for the study of sociology of education in Dagang, near the city of Tianjin. The association was established by Li Yixian under the Academy of Social Science. I was surprised when hundreds attended. However, many came from all fields of study with an interest in hearing something new. I also visited East China Normal University where I met Zhang Renjie, who studied sociology of education in Paris, and led sociology of education in southern China by setting up a sociology of education association under the China Education Research Association. Zhang later moved to Guangzhou and published a collection of readings of Western sociologists of education. I kept in contact with the development of the field, and other early proponents such as Wu Kangning and Lu Jie, who wrote textbooks in sociology of education which are still used in China.

Also at that time, a university colleague in Hong Kong presented me with a copy of the first book in China on the sociology of education. Published in July of 1931 by Qun Tonglei, the book relied on early American textbooks, including work by Ward, Small, Giddings, Smith, Sneeden, Cooley, Davenport, Dealey, Betts, Elliot, Hayes, Bagley, Ross, Ellwood, Spencer, O'Shea, Gilette, Morehouse, and Brim. It quoted sections of Peters' *Foundations of Educational Sociology*, Sneeden's *Educational Sociology*, Smith's *Introduction to Educational Sociology*, Betts' *Social Principles of Education*, and Alvin Good's *Sociology and Education*. Dewey's *Democracy and Education* was also prominent. Qun's book was republished in Taiwan in March of 1978 but unavailable on the Chinese mainland. Few of the works cited by Qun (except for Dewey) in educational sociology would become popularly known in China during the reestablishment of the sociology of education.

The aim for most Chinese scholars at the time was to construct the field with Chinese distinctiveness while keeping abreast of the international mainstream of the field. The field had to be established under "Marxism and Chinese realities." There were also critiques of Durkheim, which were interesting to me since Durkheim resonated in some ways with Confucian discourse and contemporary party dictum on social harmony. I guest edited the first of several issues of the US based journal *Chinese Education and Society* on the reestablishment of the field of sociology of education in China. It included translations of articles from Chinese academic journals. One article discussed the difference between educational sociology and sociology of education. In Chinese, these terms are usually rendered in exactly the same way in Chinese characters. The American experience was of interest because the reestablishment of the field in China began in what are called normal universities that focus on teacher education. Only later did the field make its way into comprehensive universities and the Academy of Social Science, where the emphasis of sociology was primarily on population, rural society and urbanization, among other areas.

In the 1990s, there were still only a few courses being offered in the sociology of education. Several textbooks were published but there is yet to be an academic journal dedicated to the field. The textbooks from Taiwan became increasingly available on the mainland. Hong Kong's two schools of education each offered one course in sociology of education. On the Chinese mainland, the textbooks dealt largely with conceptual matters, and how sociology of education could serve modernization. There was little empirical study at that time, partly due to a lack of research funds and training. Journal articles about the sociology of education focused heavily on higher education, where most scholars worked.

When I became associate editor of the *Chinese Education and Society* in the late 1990s, we published two special issues, guest edited by Julia Kwong and Wu Kangning—one about the indigenization and internationalization of sociology of education and the other about research methodologies in the field. Again in 2007, we published two issues based on papers from a sociology of education conference at Peking University where I was invited to be a discussant for Michael Apple's talk. It was certainly an historical event in itself to see Michael engage with Chinese Marxists. That double issue included more empirical studies by the new generation of Chinese sociologists of education, including Zhu Zhiyong and Zhao Zhenzhou, as well as scholars from Taiwan who attended the conference. Studies began to be more critical of the market economy, as well as deal more with ethnic minorities, and other underserved populations. Research methodologies also began to improve. The field had come a long way thanks to the younger generation of sociologists many of whom had studied overseas and in Hong Kong. After years of journal articles that were mere reflections, anecdotal stories, policy statements, and brief surveys, an era of systematic empirical research had begun.

VIII

China's minority population numbers over 110 million, and most live in rural, remote, and nomadic areas of western China. Unlike in urban American, China's ethnic groups were generally not migrants from other countries. Rather they were usually indigenous to their area. Coming from urban America, my thinking on ethnicity has been influenced by works such as Nathan Glazer's and Daniel Moynihan's *Ethnicity: Theory and Practice* and *Beyond the Melting Pot*, and Milton Gordon's *Assimilation in American Life*. My dissertation supervisor had been on a national panel for ethnic heritage studies in 1977 with James A. Banks, a leader in the American multicultural education movement. I came to know James Banks and contributed the China section to one of his edited volumes and was the Asia regional editor for his *Encyclopedia of Diversity in Education*. A conversation at John Ogbu's home when I was senior consultant for the Ford Foundation made me much more conscious of how most of China's ethnic groups, as involuntary minorities, were more akin to Native-Americans, Latinos of the southwest, and African-Americans.

As I learned more of the fundamental differences between ethnic relations in China and the US, I shifted to a focus on minority access to mainstream economy and society through education. My initial interest was in the nature of the processes that occur when people of different ethnic groups come together. Gaining approval for research on this topic was an uphill climb. Therefore, I modified my focus to, Why parents do or do not send their children to school? Some of my early research in China's border with Mongolia and Vietnam was supported by the Canadian International Development Research Center.

I found many opportunities to gain a more nuanced understanding of interethnic processes. As early as 1981 I travelled to Guangdong and Guangxi provinces with Hong Kong friends returning to visit relatives there. Guangxi was one of five ethnic minority autonomous areas, along with Tibet, Inner Mongolia, Xinjiang, and Ningxia. At the time, these areas were not easily accessible, but the study of ethnic minority areas provided a new angle on China's development, as well as its approach to its internationalization.

Ethnic minority education as a field of study received little scholarly attention in the 1980s. I visited several of the China's ethnic universities but only one had established an institute of the study of ethnic minority education – the Minzu University (Formerly the Institute of Nationalities) in Beijing. Since then, Southwest University and Northwest Normal University also established similar centers. Beijing Normal University also established a Center for the study of multicultural education.

A handful of dedicated and remarkable overseas scholars from Australia, Canada and the US were doing outstanding field research in minority areas from anthropological and sociological perspectives. I managed to corral that group of distinguished overseas scholars for a volume published in 1999 entitled *China's National Minority Education: Culture, Schooling, and Development*. As the field studies of ethnic minority education by scholars based at overseas universities began to grow, I brought a group together to examine the growing gap in educational access and attainment, especially for underserved communities, including girls, ethnic minorities, and the rural migrants for the 2006 volume entitled *Education and Society in China: Inequality in a Market Economy*. It noted that China had brought more people out of poverty in a short time than any country in history, and in the process implemented nine-year basic education in most of the country. But the book pointed out the highly uneven result. One of my doctoral students edited a follow-up to the 1999 volume in 2014 that lead with my chapter about what I referred to as China's critical pluralism—a phenomenon triggered by rapid changes linked to market reforms and rural migration that could turn toward plural monoculturalisms or harmonious multiculturalism. This 2014 volume differed from the last in that it contained chapters written by both Chinese mainland based and overseas based scholars. Shortly after, I co-edited a volume on language policy for ethnic minorities, which took a more critical view.

IX

A major challenge in doing research on ethnic minority education was gaining access to do fieldwork. This began to slowly improve in the mid-1990s. Even today it can take a year to gain approval to do research in some parts of the country. As ethnic minority areas opened for research by foreign scholars, I managed to reach many remote communities where I was often met by incredulous locals who had never met a foreigner. On one occasion in 1988, I arrived at the small airport in Ili, a Kazak autonomous prefecture of the Xinjiang Uyghur Autonomous Region, near China's border with the then Soviet Union. Those who were assigned to meet me at the airport held up a sign with my name in Chinese, but waved me away when they saw my non-Chinese looking face. On another occasion, when I conducted fieldwork in a remote community of the Guanxi Zhuang Autonomous Region, where students swam across a river to reach their one room school house, a couple of children took one look at me and ran away yelling out that the Japanese had returned. Much has changed since then. School facilities have greatly improved throughout the country and foreign researchers can be found almost everywhere.

By the mid-1990s, I also began to study educational access in Tibetan areas of China. The United Nations Development Programme invited me to examine the teaching of high school science to Tibetan girls in Qinghai province. In 1995, I was invited by the National Committee on US-China Relations, (the group that brought together Chinese and Americans for the first time with a groundbreaking ping-pong tournament in 1972 after Henry Kissinger's secret trips to Beijing in 1972) on a fact-finding mission to study cultural preservation in Tibet. The other members of my delegation included leaders from indigenous American ethnic groups, including a Native-American, Latino, Puerto Rican, Hawaiian, as well as two American scholars who specialized in the study of Tibetans (Melvin C. Goldstein) and Chinese Muslims (Dru Gladney). Mel Goldstein was a fluent Tibetan speaker and the most knowledgeable scholar on Tibet I had ever met.

Before long I was studying Tibetan language for hours on end with texts and tapes made for me by my Tibetan colleagues. It was a daunting task especially after years of studying both Cantonese and Mandarin. The fieldwork was even more daunting. My first research trip took place in late December and the lack of oxygen at high altitudes in winter made breathing difficult. Over severa; years, I conducted fieldwork in two prefectures and four counties of Tibet, including both semi-rural and nomadic communities, some as high as five thousand meters. When I visited in 1995, it was near impossible to make a phone call from Tibet. Five years later I was sending e-mail from an internet café located about 4,500 metres above sea level.

Quite understandably locals were inquisitive as to why I would want to venture so far from home to visit their remote ethnic minority community. It was not easy to explain academic research to farmers and nomads. On some field trips I was accommodated in a one-room school or with a household in a village. It always amazed me how families in rural and remote communities would open their homes to me and share what they had that day. My team carried our own food and if we ran short we would improvise, which could mean my having to slaughter a couple of chickens bartered from a local household because my Tibetan colleagues did not believe in killing animals.

There were ethical decisions in collecting data for academic journals from communities that were still struggling with water, electricity, roads and crumbling school buildings. I was able to get articles published in mainstream Chinese journals to alert scholars and officials to conditions in particular counties. On the practical side, I arranged for the purchase of a metal cover to be placed over a well that was level with the ground so children who hauled water would not risk falling into it, especially at night. I alerted NGOs like Save the Children Foundation who followed my visits by providing gas driven electric generators and light bulbs for reading at night in school dormitories. We also helped to provide dictionaries, notebooks, library books, and basketballs. No matter how poor a school, it had a basketball court.

The missing piece of my research was about those Tibetan students who were sent in the thousands to boarding schools. These schools located in Chinese cities were said by some to be similar to schools set up for indigenous native groups in Australia, Canada, and the US. I presented the results of my research at the Fairbanks Center of Harvard University and argued that the Tibetan boarding schools were unlike the Anglo-country experiences in key respects, research which was published in *Asian Survey* and *Comparative Education Review*.

X

By 2000, I had travelled to every province of China except one or two. I was appointed to lead the University of Hong Kong's newly established Centre for Research on Education in China, and was a member of the University's China Affairs Committee. The Hong Kong Research Grants Council was also funding my research in western China.

Seeing the realities confronting China I began to take more of an interest in practical policy issues and conducted research about policy implementation. I was invited to join policy projects by international development agencies, including the Asian Development Bank, International Development Research Center (Canadian), the Department of International Development (UK), and the United Nations Development Agency. In some of these projects I worked in tandem with Chinese government agencies where I could speak directly with those who had some influence on policy and management of ethnic minority education. Since government officials could not possibly get around to all the minority communities, my field research was of some interest to them. A one-year project of the Asian Development Bank aimed at strengthening policy research and management of education by the Division of Ethnic Minority Education of China's State Education Commission. It gave me a close-up view of how policy was made and implemented and the role of research, especially qualitative research, although we also set up a management information system.

I also began to gain an understanding of the crucial role of NGOs when I was hired as a senior consultant to the Beijing office of the Ford Foundation. My year-long task beginning in April 2000 was to write a strategic framework for funding of education reform projects. My work came to include not only educational reform, but also cultural vitality, as well as the new initiative for developing women studies programs in university. There was also interest to support research on issues affecting women, especially the production of university curriculum and teaching materials for advancing the field of women's studies, and the mainstreaming of gender studies throughout the university curriculum.

My time at Ford provided opportunities for me to work with the Ministry of Education, and the Ethnic Affairs Commission, other multinational agencies, and international NGOs. I did not start out with any specific aim to change education in China, but rather looked for individuals who had ideas, social capital, and the practical know-how for instituting innovative ways to improve educational access and equity but needed resources to make that happen.

There was a need to support study and fieldwork aimed at examining social stratification and the diversity of social and cultural factors that affect the educational access for underserved communities. This work included studies of ways to provide affordable school textbooks for poor families, while improving the textbook content by eliminating gender stereotyping. This was coupled with activities that decreased dropout rates by making schooling more relevant to local needs and by encouraging the involvement of parents, teachers, and school principals in educational planning. The education reform program also comprised innovative methods of bilingual teaching in ethnic minority communities.

In higher education and scholarship, I considered proposals to develop alternative forms of tertiary education for expanding opportunities to quality higher education, and to develop leadership skills, especially among the rural poor, women, and ethnic minorities. As success at popularizing basic education led to heightened expectations for higher levels of education, we responded to the interest in China for community college models. This empowered local communities to develop more educational opportunities that were affordable in the increasingly market oriented economy. My travels took me through most of China but especially in Yunnan where the provincial government focused on the preservation, revitalization, and transmission of traditional culture for social and economic life. Schools and community-based educational organizations transmitted indigenous knowledge within the context of the national curriculum. Policy oriented research offered strategies to improve the educational achievement levels of the less successful ethnic groups. Self-reflective cultural policies addressed the challenges of economic development and civic life.

While at Ford/Beijing I had the opportunity to meet Chinese sociologists because my host was the Chinese Academy of Social Sciences. I also met overseas sociologists who were visiting Beijing, including Ezra Vogel, who was in the early stages of what would be a major study of Chineseleader Deng Xiaoping. I decided to return to the academy in Hong Kong to head the Centre of Research on Education in China. Back in Hong Kong, I met Bill Clinton and helped facilitate a discussion session about the future of higher education for his Clinton Global Initiative that included Jack Ma of Alibaba.

XI

As China inched closer to becoming the world's largest economy, its universities increasingly expected to play a more powerful role in China's rise. It already had the largest system of higher education and more universities joining the world rankings. Yet, there is increasing debate about what kind of higher education system is best for the future. Meanwhile, more Asian countries embarked on mass higher education.

Coming from a country with a university system that was considered the best in the world, I naturally maintained an interest in the development of higher education in Asia. I was invited to join the first international survey of the academic profession at the Carnegie Foundation for the Advancement of Teaching at Princeton headed by Ernest Boyer. Carnegie had been doing surveys and working with distinguished sociologists of comparative education such as Burton Clark and Philip Altbach. The Chinese mainland decided not to participate in the first international survey of the academic profession. I was only able to arrange independent surveys of academics at universities in Beijing and Shanghai. However, I managed to get the Chinese mainland involved in the second survey – *The Changing Academic Profession*, which included 19 countries in 2007.

In 1998, I was invited to the 100th Anniversary of Peking University. The ceremony took place at the Great Hall of the People and was attended by presidents of the leading universities around the world. At that event, President Jiang Zemin announced that China would build world class universities. As the anticipation grew about the concept of World Class University, a few scholars at Shanghai Jiaotong University developed a university ranking methodology that began to rival that of the Times Higher Education and QS ranking. Since Hong Kong had most of the leading international universities of any city in Asia, I was commissioned by a number of organizations, including the World Bank, Boston College Center of Higher Education, the Organization of Economic Cooperation and Development, and later Shanghai Jiaotong University to explain the longstanding success of the University of Hong Kong and the rapid rise of the Hong Kong University of Science and Technology.

Outside of China my work began to include other Asian countries. I was invited by the United Nations Development Programme to do an evaluation of higher education in the Republic of Mongolia, by a German NGO to advise the Vietnamese Ministry of Education on privatization of higher education, by UNESCO to advise on restructuring of higher education in Myanmar, by the Asian Development Bank Institute to develop proposals for a meeting of ASEAN about the effects of the global economic crisis on vulnerable populations in Asia. This led to a two year project for the Asian Development Bank on student readiness for universities and the changing workplace.

What struck me most about the trend in Asian higher education was the contradictory effect of economic globalization. There was increased talk of harmonization of higher education in Asia and growing excitement about universities' cross-border partnerships. This also included China which was inviting overseas universities to set up campuses, as well as setting up Chinese campuses in other countriesm most notably the Tsinghua University campus in Seattle. I edited a book on the subject and became a consultant to the Xiamen University group that included Pan Maoyuan and Lin Jinhui in their Research Center on the Sino-foreign cooperation in the running of schools and universities supported by the Ministry of Education.

When New York University decided to set up a campus in Shanghai, I was invited to lecture about China's universities at their New York campus where I sensed little interest among the academic community in the Shanghai campus. It was a different story when I was invited to talk at the Harvard Center in Shanghai to university presidents and scholars from the Chinese mainland, Hong Kong and the United States. For Harvard, there was a clear sense of mission in China to deepen the discourse about liberal studies in higher education, but not to set up a campus there. Having a centre in Shanghai gave Harvard more direct access in China and facilitated many networking opportunities for their large alumni there.

## XII

Not surprisingly, I eventually came to a crossroads. When head-hunted for deanships, including one in New York, where the odyssey began, it was a chance to come full circle and bring my experience to bear more directly on American education, especially as Asia's schools and universities forge ahead in the international rankings. It was a chance to be geographically closer to my eighty-five year-old mother who still travels to China occasionally, my siblings, and extended family and old friends. However, none of the deanships worked out and I have stayed in Hong Kong. Colleagues who study ethnicity seem to have, either by choice or subject matter, a more rooted sense of place of origin than those in other fields. It is also true that globalization has shrunk our world. The phone in my pocket permits me to reach across ten thousand miles in a nanosecond. The fifteen-hour direct flight every few months is only a bit longer than the daily two-hour commute endured by many New Yorkers. And when I receive a text message from a friend in New York saying I was quoted that day in the *New York Times*, distance shrinks further, and I recall the 1979 classified ad that started it all, when China seemed so far away from the Big Apple.

In *The Rise of the Rest,* Fareed Zakaria writes of the rise of China and other developing countries. It still leaves open more questions about how and why than one lifetime could possibly answer, but there few places more dynamic and interesting to be, right now.

## NOTES

[1] Philosophy: Mark Berger, Linda Nicholson, James E. McClellan; History: Paul Vogt, Hy Kuritz; Sociology: Joseph Scimecca, Frank Femminella, Sandra Petersen.
[2] In the sociology department I had the most contact with Paul Meadows, Nan Lin, Al Higgins, and Arnold Foster, later with Maurice Richter, John Logan and Min Zhou.
[3] I currently have a research grant from the Central Policy Unit of the Hong Kong government on how the two academic systems are becoming integrated.

## MOST FAVORITE TEXTS BY OTHERS

Samuel Bowles and Herbert Gintis (1976). *Schooling in Capitalist American*, New York: Basic Books.
Émile Durkheim (1977). *The Evolution of Educational Thought*, London: Routledge Press.
Randall Collins (1979). *Credential Society: An Historical Sociology of Education*, New York: John Wiley.
John K. Fairbanks, et. al. (1973). *East Asia: Tradition and Transformation*. Houghton Mifflin.
Fei, Xiaotong (1947). *From the Soil: The Foundations of Chinese Society*, Translation by Gary Hamilton (1986).

## MY FAVORITE PERSONAL TEXTS

*Education and Social Change in China: Inequality in a Market Society*, New York: M.E. Sharpe, 2006, 207 pages.
*China's National Minority Education: Culture, Schooling and Development*, New York: Taylor and Francis, 1999, 421pages.
Dislocated Education: The Case of Tibet, *Comparative Education Review*, Vol. 53, No.4 Nov. 2009, pp. 483-512.
From Capitalism to Socialism? Hong Kong Education within A Transitional Society, *Comparative Education Review*, Vol. 35, No. 3, November 1991, pp. 627-
Global Recession and Higher Education in Eastern Asia: China, Mongolia and Vietnam, *Higher Education*, 2011, Vol.62 No.6 pp. 789-814.
Anchoring Globalization in Hong Kong's Research Universities: Network Agents, Institutional Arrangements and Brain Circulation, *Studies in Higher Education*, Vol. 38, No. 3, 2013, pp. 345-366

## REFERENCES

Berger, P., & Luckman, T. (1967). *The social construction of reality: A treatise in the sociology of knowledge*. New York, NY: Anchor.
Betts, G. H. (1912). *Social principles of education*. New York, NY: Charles Scribner and Sons.
Cheung, B. L. (2012). Higher education in Asia: Challenges from and contributions to globalization. *International Journal of Chinese Education, 1*, 177–195.
Dewey, J. (1916). *Democracy and education: An introduction to the philosophy of education*. New York, NY: Macmillan.
Freire, P. (1972). *Pedagogy of the oppressed*. New York, NY: Herder and Herder.
Good, A. (1926). *Sociology and education*. New York, NY: Harper.
Illich, I. (1970). *Deschooling society*. New York, NY: Harper and Row.
Peters, C. A. (1939). *Foundations of educational sociology*. New York, NY: Mamillan.
Postiglione, G. (1999). *China's national minority education: Culture, schooling and development*. New York, NY: Taylor and Francis.
Postiglione, G. (2006). *Education and society in China: Inequality in a market economy*. New York, NY: M.E. Sharpe.
Reich, C. (1971). *The greening of America*. New York, NY: Bantam.

Shambaugh, D. (2013). *China goes global: The partial power*. Oxford: Oxford University Press.
Smith, W. R. (1917). *An introduction to educational sociology*. Boston, MA: Houghton Mifflin.
Sneeden, D. (1922). *Educational sociology*. New York, NY: Century.
Turkel, S. (1975). *Working*. New York, NY: Avon.

*Gerard A. Postiglione*
*University of Hong Kong*

FRANCISCO O. RAMIREZ

# 12. EDUCATION, GENDER, AND DEVELOPMENT

This essay reflects on the origins and development of my core research interests in education, gender, and development. These interests emerged in my De La Salle college years in Manila, persisted through graduate studies at Stanford, and continue to characterize my ongoing scholarship. In the 1960s I gravitated toward a nationalist perspective and assumed that education was the key to national development and that amoral familism was a major stumbling block. My undergraduate thesis advisor, a Harvard trained economist, no doubt facilitated my internalizing the "education as human capital" assumption. Though I had not encountered "the moral basis of a backward society" idea, the notion that excessive loyalty to family and kinship undercut civic mindedness and other modern values was a compelling one. These were, of course, not abstract research interests but the personal concerns that lead an eighteen year old to declare (as only the young can!) that he would pursue sociology. Familial reaction was initially less than positive, but ultimately familial resources (and even blessings) facilitated this pursuit. The Prodigal Son has since morphed into the Stanford Professor. All's well that ends well.

It is not clear why I chose sociology instead of some other social science discipline. It is also not clear why I accepted an admissions offer from Stanford in lieu of one from a then much more highly regarded department. I knew little about the discipline and less about the profession. In the summer of 1967 what I knew was that I was on my way to becoming a well-educated sociologist who would subsequently launch the first Department of Behavioral Sciences in the Philippines. The declaration of martial law in the Philippines in 1972 derailed that plan. What I now know is that planning a life is mostly an illusion.

In what follows I trace the development of my research interests in graduate school and in my years in the Sociology Department at San Francisco State University. I refer to this period as the education and development and women in education projects. I then focus on my first decade in the Graduate School of Education at Stanford and the authority of science and human rights studies. Lastly, I turn to the textbook analysis project and to the emerging university organization research. The latter in good part reflects my experiences as Associate Dean for Faculty Affairs, a position I will have cheerfully vacated by the time this book is published.

All of these studies entailed explicit macro level cross-national comparisons. This innovation is today commonplace in sociology. Since most innovations fail, it is perhaps surprising that the cross-national comparative approach flourished.

Two reasons come to mind. First, this research strategy was compatible with different theoretical perspectives, not solely with the neo-institutional world society one that has informed my studies. Second, more cross-national data on multiple societal dimensions and over extended time periods has been more systematically collected and disseminated. This worldwide development invites and fosters a range of diverse cross-national investigations. None of this was predictable in the 1970s when some of the initial cross-national studies in sociology were undertaken (see the papers in Meyer and Hannan, 1979). Then, a hostile reviewer could dismiss cross-national comparisons by uttering the magic words "one cannot compare apples and oranges". Not anymore!

## EDUCATION, DEVELOPMENT, AND GENDER

Stanford sociology in the sixties was focused on formal theory building and experimental social psychology. My first research apprenticeship was with a social psychologist that reformulated Goffman's "presentation of self" ideas into testable hypotheses about situations and situated identities. The main point was that experimental subjects figured out what behaviors made them look good and acted accordingly (Alexander & Knight, 1971). Even the pristine experiment was a situation with discernable normative cues as to which actions implied favorable identities. In retrospect one can see a connection between the macro emphasis on world society standards, national identity, and legitimacy enhancing activity and the micro emphases on situations, expectations, and identities. The frames of interest shift from more local or situational to more global, but a lot of ritual enactment rather than simple goal oriented action is presupposed at both levels of analysis. All sorts of actors seek to be viewed by others as legitimate. Of course, this is reconstructive logic at work on my part. But it is worth keeping in mind when one contrasts different social science perspectives across different levels of analysis.

As a student I embraced the growing scientization of sociology, even as I became skeptical of the once dominant modernization perspective. The turning point for me came as a teaching assistant in an Introduction to Sociology course taught by John Meyer. The course focused on large-scale social change and its impact on institutional, organizational, and interpersonal dynamics. To be sure, this was a course about modernization, but not one that simply assumed that modernity was a bundle of virtues that all people everywhere should aspire to attain. There were costs and tensions and paradoxes. Education per se was not central to this course but my interest in education was revitalized. The study of education need not be limited to the study of academic achievement and educational and occupational attainment in the United States, however important these studies were (Ramirez, 2006a). Family per se was not central to this course either. But here again the comparative lens made it possible to think about how large-scale social changes impacted families and relations between women and men therein. A teaching assistant experience in a course on family and kinship did strongly emphasize gender issues. This course also offered a comparative lens. These experiences lead to my taking area exams in sociology of education and family and kinship. In both instances I had an overriding interest in development, though it was increasingly difficult to figure out exactly what development meant. An earlier innocence was eroding; societies could look progressive along some dimensions and rather backwards as regards others. More importantly, these experiences lead to my imagining myself as a comparative sociologist.

This comparative sociology identity was shared and reinforced by several other students who were also involved in the education and development project. The initial goal was to tackle the chicken and egg question—does education lead to development or is it the other way around—with panel data using educational enrollment and economic development measures. What may seem like a primitive research design in the era of randomized clinical trials and instrumental variables was fairly sophisticated in the era of cross-sectional studies and bivariate analysis. Much to our surprise we found that primary enrollments grew across the world and that economic development was not much of a trigger. Neither was political democracy nor any other societal level characteristic one could imagine. We increasingly conceptualized this phenomenon as a world educational revolution (Meyer et al., 1977), one in which many different nations seemed to be marching to the beat of the same transnational drums. Only later did we argue that the origins of mass schooling were best explained via transnational frames or models—mostly Western ones in the 19th century (Ramirez & Boli, 1987) but increasingly global ones. These frames emphasized progress and justice as goals that a legitimate nation-state would "naturally" pursue. Nation-state candidates would embrace these goals to display their legitimacy in a world of nation-states.

Early on we imagined the wider world as impinging on nation-states and other units, influencing the formation of proper structures and legitimated policies. More recently world society scholars have embraced a stronger constructivist theoretical position and argued that the very "entitivity" of nation-states and individuals is contingent on a world culture that informs and shapes them (Meyer et al., 1997). The changing nature of world culture and its organizational and professional carriers continues to be central to world society studies. But the starting point was the empirical finding that first mass schooling (Meyer et al., 1977) and now higher educational expansion (Schofer & Meyer, 2005) seem to have a life of their own, generated not by the functional needs of society or their elites but by the triumph of world educational standards.

My dissertation examined educational data cross-nationally. But it also looked at the relationship between initial ceremonies and the rise of deliberate instruction, using data from the Human Relations Cross-Cultural Files. Furthermore, I explored the rise of universities in Medieval Europe and speculated as to why universities emerged earlier therein rather than in other civilizational states. I was working on multiple loose ends when martial law was declared and a scheduled return to the Philippines was put on hold. I had enjoyed life as a graduate student in good part because I was not oriented to the American labor market. Now I was and had no publications, not even papers under review, to display. Even in that less professionalized era some evidence of promising scholarship was expected. A dissertation in progress and with multiple loose ends to boot was all I could show.

I was delighted to be offered a position in Sociology at San Francisco State (I will forever be grateful to the not to be named sociologist who turned down the initial offer). In my first encounter with the department chair, I was asked about future research directions. That seemed a tad premature, given the paucity of research produced on my part. But without blinking I outlined a research agenda that would focus on the changing status of women across the world. This was the beginning of several gender related studies, including research on women in the labor force and women in higher education (Ramirez & Weiss, 1979). A lot of the earlier work both privileged the positive impact of mobilizing incorporating states and debunked modernization imagery. The underlying point was that these states were more likely to extend citizenship and related opportunities for women to participate in the public sphere. Alternatively, one could interpret the mobilizing impact as evidence that institutions such as marriage and family did not buffer women from the imperatives of the state (Ramirez, 1981).

Further inquiries led me away from an unconditional celebration of the impact of mobilizing states on women. Perhaps what was going on was a classic instance of the double burden; women would participate more so in the labor force but they would continue to be primarily responsible for the home. Moreover, some fundamental changes in women's participation in the public sphere seemed to be taking place in all sorts of societies. Were these changes also evidence that even in this "deep gender structure" national policies and developments were increasingly attuned to transnational standards? Were the transformations driven more so by the common imperatives of a historical era than by the varying legacies of different places? Neo-institutional ideas suggest that an innovation is initially influenced by local factors but that its diffusion is not (Tolbert & Zucker, 1985). So, one might assume that the acquisition of the franchise by women, for example, is earlier influenced by specific societal factors but in a later era countries are more attuned to what other countries have done. This is precisely what my colleagues and I found in an event history analysis of women's franchise acquisition (Ramirez, Soysal, & Shanahan, 1997). This kind of analysis went beyond identifying world trends and interpreting the absence of societal effects as world influences. It revealed that historical era mattered and that world and regional influences were greater in more recent periods.

My interest in gender issues was personally motivated by a feminist worldview that was critical of the exclusion of women from the public sphere. This was a worldview grounded in the sixties and the rise of the second women's movement. My recurring research finding of positive changes in the status of women often met with skepticism. The latter is frequently couched in the "half full or half empty" metaphor. But I would argue that inclusionary logics have triumphed and paved the way for the current debates about the terms of inclusion. Though inequalities between men and women indeed persist in some domains, it is egalitarian standards reflecting a century of women's movements that has both expanded the scope of scrutinized policies and practices and the intensity of the scrutiny. These standards are at the root of nation-state ratification of the Convention to Eliminate All Forms of Discrimination Against Women (Wotipka & Ramirez, 2008). Much of the current discourse on gender goes beyond opening doors for women and focuses instead on valuing differences and changing the culture of the organizations and institutions into which women have entered. Feminists critique the gendered character of these structures. This critique resonates with multicultural critiques of dominant structures. Underlying this critique is the triumph of egalitarian standards. As earlier experimental studies in social psychology show, inequity perceptions are greater when egalitarian norms have been activated. A world characterized by egalitarian standards is one where more inequalities will be detected and experienced as inequities. Later, I made a similar argument as regards the rise and development of an international human rights regime. A more human rights oriented world was also a world full of better detected and more widely publicized human rights abuses. It is not that regimes have become more wicked than ever, but that wicked regimes are more likely to be identified, exposed, and critiqued.

## EDUCATION, SCIENCE, AND HUMAN RIGHTS

In the spring of 1987 I threw caution to the wind and accepted a non-tenured associate professorship in the Graduate School of Education at Stanford. I was engaged in both international comparative education and sociology of education. I taught courses in sociology of development and of gender. I now had a room of my own and greater access to expanded resources. To my earlier skepticism regarding modernization theory, I increasingly distanced myself from the world systems perspective. There was a lot of authority and influence going on in the world that could not be reduced to straightforward power and dependency ties. Scientists, for instance, seemed to enjoy more authority and influence than to control resources that could be effectively leveraged to attain their goals or meet their interests. To be sure, the authority of science could lead to garnering resources but the influence of scientists was based on the authority they enjoyed, not on the resources per se. The rise of economics, for example, was less about its instrumental value or the inherent power of economists as a status group but about their successful appropriation of "the scientific method." Other disciplines linked themselves to the high ground of science. Environmental concerns were increasingly framed in scientific ecological terms, not simply love of nature. Even religious fundamentalists evoked the authority of science with phrases like "creationist science." It is clearly better to have science on your side.

There were many educational implications that followed from the rise of the authority of science. The "nation at risk" narrative in the United States was largely due to the relatively low performance of American students in mathematics and science. Very strong assumptions were made about the validity of these tests and the degree to which national futures were at stake. STEM would command a lot of educational reform energy. But while earlier SPUTNIK induced reforms in this domain had emphasized nurturing exceptional talent or ability, the new international test-driven wave was more democratic and more optimistic. Everyone could and should be better STEM educated and the country would benefit from this mass learning upgrade. The evidentiary basis for these very strong assumptions has been challenged. The link between academic achievement and economic growth is questionable (Ramirez et al., 2006). Also questionable is the tie between scientific and economic development (Schofer et al., 2000). So much scientific development involves research not narrowly geared to economic production, research on the environment or genetics, for example. But overall faith has not declined, as the "Rising Above The Gathering Storm" reports illustrate. These reports further legitimate the authority and centrality of science in society.

Not surprisingly, the gender and education literature shifted from issues regarding achievement and access in general to a focus on performance in STEM and to access to STEM fields in higher education. Women had a right to better curricula and instruction in schools and to expanded access to the science and engineering fields in higher education. All sorts of inequalities were identified: it was widely believed that teachers took boys more seriously and gave them more opportunities to display their knowledge. In addition, science and engineering fields in higher education were depicted as chilly climates that unfairly excluded women. There were studies that indeed supported both of these points. But there were also changes. The gender math achievement gap in international tests is declining over time (Wiseman et al., 2009). There is a growing literature that calls attention to pedagogies that work better for girls (Boaler, 1997). However chilly, more women are enrolling in science and engineering fields than in the past. This is a worldwide cross-national trend (Ramirez & Kwak, 2014; Ramirez & Wotipka, 2001). Women may not be "destined for equality" but on many different dimensions the trends are in the direction of greater equality (Dorius & Firebaugh, 2010).

The gender domain allows us to see how scientific authority and human rights emphases can be aligned. The former is utilized to lament the underutilization of female human capital due to lack of access to education and especially to scientific and technical education. Opening the doors to women and seeing to it that they are prepared to enter and excel is a rational investment in national development. The latter is rooted in justice or equity frames and leads to the contention that it would be unfair to deprive women of their right to these fields of study, especially since these are gateways to higher paid jobs. This win/win imagery underlies a report on mainstreaming gender in science in the European Union (European Technology Assessment Network, 2010).

I reiterate that the debates today are mostly about terms of inclusion, about what are the experiences of women in institutions and organizations, rather than whether they should be allowed entry. These debates presuppose the triumph of inclusionary logics, though this triumph often goes unrecognized and under theorized in the debates themselves.

By the end of 1989 I had become a lifer, that is, a tenured professor. I waited for the post tenure crisis. It did not happen. My teaching and research interests continued along a comparative trajectory. As indicated earlier, what was changing was the growing sense that nation-states were increasingly engaged in presentations of self to exhibit or enhance legitimacy. A lot of legitimation research emphasizes what states need to do to persuade their citizens to accept their legitimacy. A lot of state initiated projects are accounted for via this internal need for legitimacy, including the "education for nation building" projects. My colleagues and I, however, emphasized external legitimacy. True, the building of schools could be justified by pointing to the people these schools served. But this dynamic made more sense in a world in which it was broadly understood that responsible national leaders expanded schooling, or at least, professed a commitment to do so. This understanding was further solidified by a worldview within which expanded schooling was emphasized as the key to national development and to greater overall equality. This worldview was transmitted through international organizations armed with scientific expertise. Education was central to this worldview, ambivalent evidence notwithstanding.

Not surprisingly, the international human rights regime increasingly bred an international human rights education regime (Ramirez & Moon, 2013; Suarez, Ramirez, & Meyer, 2006). Several developments made sense only in a world in which education was central to models of progress and justice. First, there was the rise of human rights education organizations. Some of these emerged as education-focused organizations while others evolved from a more legal lens to a more educational emphasis. Amnesty International, for example, has become more education-centric over time. There was also a corresponding increase in human rights education discourse. In addition to the highly institutionalized right to education one can see the unexpected emergence of the right to human rights education. A growing number of countries adopted UNESCO based human rights education programs. Lastly, the human rights idea surfaced in textbooks and was more pronounced in textbooks in the more recent era (Meyer, Bromley, & Ramirez, 2010).

## TEXTBOOK ANALYSES: WHO COUNTS/WHAT COUNTS

In educational policy circles history and social studies textbook battles are correctly understood as struggles to define the national soul for the next generation. So, what does it mean to discover that there has been a rise in human rights emphases as well as an increase in more references to different social groups in textbooks (Ramirez, Bromley, & Russell, 2010)? Has an increase in the valorization of humanity and diversity undercut national solidarity and common citizenship? Why are textbooks increasingly more student-centered (Bromley, Meyer, & Ramirez, 2011)? These and closely related questions add up to what is an ongoing textbook analyses project. This is a unique research undertaking in that it looks at multiple textbooks over different periods for a relatively large number of countries. Textbooks constitute a core feature of the intended curricula and these studies reveal cross-national trends for the decades after World War II (the most recent studies focus on textbooks before World War II). There is neither time nor space to summarize numerous findings. Suffice it to say that a national emphasis now co-exists with a human rights focus and that the textbooks discuss the rights of individuals but also the rights of categories of persons such as women and children. Not surprisingly, globalization emerges as a recent theme in these textbooks, but so does global citizenship (Buckner & Russell, 2013).

Taken as a whole these findings suggest that we may be veering toward a post-national era. These textbooks portray the good citizen as linked to the nation-state and national institutions but also to the wider world, sometimes depicted as a global community. These textbooks do not suggest a zero-sum game but instead imply a multilayered sense of membership and identity. Aggressive nationalism is out of fashion but the nation-state does not wither. Once excluded or ignored groups, women for example, are now added to the national portraits. However, their greater inclusion gives rise to debates about the terms of their inclusion. So, the issue becomes not simply whether women or indigenous peoples enter into national social science or history narratives but whether their struggles to have their rights recognized and identities respected are also in place.

Lastly, the more a nation-state is indeed linked to the wider world the more its textbooks reflect the post-national emphases privileged in global discourse. This is part of the more general finding that greater embeddedness in world society leads to the adoption of world legitimated policies, structures, and activities. Some of these emphases may poorly reflect local traditions and power structures, thereby creating a considerable degree of loose coupling between what is professed and what is practiced. Educational ministries may issue directives in support of progressive pedagogies and ignore long-standing rote memorization teaching practices. Or, the inconsistencies may derive from inconsistencies between pedagogical emphases on creativity and more conservative exam structures. These inconsistencies may in turn reflect the fact that some educational officials are attuned to the latest developments in pedagogy emphasizing student-centered learning and problem solving while others may be more geared to international testing and the ranking of countries by achievement. The world society is not a world state. Its influence is based on standard setting and soft power leading to varying degrees of emulation of different kinds of "winners." To wit, American schools are not celebrated; American universities are.

## IN THE ERA OF WORLD CLASS AND BEST PRACTICES

In the winter of 2011 I taught at Stanford in Oxford and was struck by how different these two institutions were. Oxford felt like a historical institution while Stanford smacked of a formal organization. Tacit knowledge seemed to fuel life at Oxford while more explicit road maps and corresponding infrastructures characterized Stanford. It would be unthinkable for a department at Stanford to forget to schedule courses, but this lapse took place during the Hilary Term at Oxford. Stanford professors seemed to be inventing and re-inventing themselves while Oxford dons seemed to know who they were. But even as I developed these early impressions the times they were a changing for the Republic of Letters. Students and professors were heading in the direction of the sciences and away from the humanities (Soares, 1999). The Oxford Centre for Management Studies (1965) would evolve and become the Said Business School in 1996. A more distinctive administrative stratum was emerging at Oxford, even as more established university organization intensified at Stanford.

I thought and wrote about the changing character of universities (cf: Ramirez & Christensen, 2013; Ramirez & Tiplic, 2014; Ramirez, 2006b). To be sure, there were persistent differences, but once again the drums beckoned the universities to march in similar directions. First, there was the overwhelming reality of expanded enrolments and more university formations. An earlier fear of the overeducated (and presumably unemployed and dangerous) population had significantly subsided. Education for all was edging to higher education for all. Next, there was the growing preoccupation with quality. Whether this preoccupation triggered the proliferation of cross-national rankings or was itself an outcome of the increasingly more visible rankings is unclear. But despite all their obvious shortcomings the world of rankings had transcended idle talk about academic reputations, a trivial game for academic insiders. Policy makers, journalists, and prospective professors and students were now more engaged in assessing universities. But, thirdly, there was the sentiment that universities and sub-units within them could be upgraded, and perhaps, even become "world-class". Moreover, being attuned to the organizational and management practices of world-class universities could rationally lead to the upgrading of universities. These practices were imagined to be portable and armies of consultants could be counted on to teach the best practices that would lead to world-class university status. The pursuit of excellence led to excellence initiatives in some European countries and to explicit state plans to create world-class universities in Asia.

This line of inquiry involved both continuities and discontinuities with my prior scholarship. The comparative lens continued as did the theoretical sense that universities were increasingly influenced by transnational standards. There are historical roots and path dependencies, but universities are under a lot of pressure to more formally organize and that in turn results in more formal organizational slots. These pressures add up to rules of the game and the game increasingly has a global character. The challenge is to try to figure out which parts of the university are most shielded from external pressures and which are more malleable. So far, I have addressed this challenge via theorizing essays without explicitly testing hypotheses using cross-national data.

I faced a different challenge when I agreed to serve as Associate Dean for Faculty Affairs in 2010. It was supposed to be a one-year gig and I was more than happy to embrace the word 'Acting' before the more formal sounding title. But, alas, the real Associate Dean retired and I continued in this capacity, no longer protected by the 'Acting' designation. This new role gave me the opportunity to further explore university organization and some of my writing clearly reflects this experience. In what follows I offer a few general and admittedly tentative thoughts about university organization.

First, as virtually all scholars examining higher education emphasize, there has been a growth of managerial roles within the university. At Stanford there are more Vice Provosts and Assistant Vice Provosts than a few decades ago. In the Graduate School of Education we have evolved from two to four Associate Deans and from one to three Assistant Deans since 1989. Throughout the university there has been an explosion of centers, and thus, the appointment of more center directors with varying academic titles. All of this can be tidily accounted for via this or that functional requirement imagery. The bottom line is that there are more people engaged in managerial activities. This is not a simple case of more bureaucracy. People are expected to grow in their jobs as well as to grow jobs, not simply to act in accordance with a fixed set of expectations. There is a strong emphasis on personnel development at all levels, from what used to be called secretaries to associate deans. There are numerous workshops and seminars with personnel development as the overriding goal. There are, of course, national workshops and seminars that also foster "getting better" or "becoming more effective." Thus, while growth in formal organization is evident, the more important point is increase in organizing activity geared toward human and organizational development. I suspect that this is true in other American universities as well. To the idea "managerial university" one should add "active university." There is an enormous amount of optimism underlying the active university.

A second observation is the expanded role of lawyers in the university. Here again one can imagine à la Weber lawyers in the service of bureaucratic control systems. If nothing else, the "rule of law" is supposed to eliminate or reduce uncertainties by creating dos and don'ts. There are indeed many processes in universities that are more rule-oriented than they were in earlier decades. Hiring, tenure, and promotion processes are by far more formalized today. Processes that directly affect students are also more regulated. One can observe these changes and contend that this is evidence of central administrative actors impinging on the discretion and authority of the faculty. But the impetus for much of the formalization lies with the rights of faculty, staff, and students, not rights as corporate groups but in the liberal tradition, as individuals. The more individual students, faculty, and staff are empowered the greater the likelihood of their perceiving that their rights have been violated. I suspect that the ombudsperson receives more visitors than in the past. I know that I have had more legally oriented workshops in the last four years than in the previous forty. I have learned that e-mail really stands for evidentiary mail! If the expanded role of lawyers simply reflects the litigious character of American society, one should not expect to see this phenomena elsewhere. However, if the trigger is the expanded rights of individuals, universities in other countries will soon be investigating the "best practices" of American universities in coping with potential conflicts.

The more active university is also the more formal one. My third and final observation though is that an extraordinary amount of informal activity flourishes. The actors in American universities are less trapped in bureaucratic iron cages and more engaged in fluid networks. Some of these are geared toward fundraising and interacting with actual or potential friends of the university or the school. These activities now permeate American universities; job descriptions for decanal positions rather routinely now emphasize fundraising activity, sometimes even indicating the percent of time that should be allocated to this endeavor. Informal networking is also evident in efforts to cope with ambiguous rules or directives. I suspect that the amount of meetings not dedicated to research or teaching issues has increased throughout American universities. Some of these meetings take place within the campus but a lot occur in the "real world." The boundaries between society and university have always been more permeable in universities in the United States. Increasingly, it is difficult to even posit boundaries, as universities become more socially engaged and non-university actors begin to look like university stakeholders. Research is clearly needed to distinguish between more buffered and less buffered university activity.

Research is also needed to see the extent to which universities around the world undergo "Americanization." "Publish or perish" imperatives have already made significant headway in Europe and Asia. But these imperatives will have to contend with the different historical roots of other universities, the more service-oriented ethos of Asian universities, for example, or the less market-induced faculty pay scales in Scandinavian ones. Here again the issue is which elements of the American university are theorized as essential to excellence and which ones are imagined as culturally idiosyncratic.

## CONCLUDING THOUGHTS

I have played a small role in developing a world society perspective and applying it to a range of issues, notably as regards education, gender, and development. I have quite frankly enjoyed both the research and the teaching. This perspective does not insist that national and local factors are irrelevant predictors of interesting outcomes. What we contend though is that these factors are not the only important ones and that focusing exclusively on these factors fundamentally misleads. Two hundred and more historicist narratives can describe changes but a more parsimonious theory is needed. This is especially the case when so many different countries undergo similar changes. Identifying some common triggers has been a task world society scholars have undertaken.

Moreover, what our studies show is that world society is more influential in more recent eras. This should not be surprising. World models are more readily available in a better integrated or more compressed world. And, there are more consultants and translators to facilitate importation. Even the constitution of North Korea looks surprisingly progressive with its positive references to human rights. So, should we assume that world society is nothing more than window dressing, given the large amount of observable loose coupling? I beg to differ. The next generation of world society studies will examine the conditions under which some enacted policies become consequential. Cole and Ramirez (2013), for example, show that human rights commissions can reduce some types of human rights violations. An earlier innocence should not be crudely replaced by unfettered cynicism.

Let me end on a very personal note. Let me thank Margie who alone supported my quixotic aspiration to become a sociologist. Let me also thank her for enabling me to give up the security of tenure to face the challenge of Stanford. Without her this journey would not have taken place. Without her this reflection would be incomplete.

## ACKNOWLEDGEMENT

For her editorial assistance I would like to thank Julia Lerch.

## MY FAVORITE TEXTS BY OTHERS

Benedict Anderson (1991). *Imagined Communities: Reflections on the Origins and Spread of Nationalism.* Verso.

Eugen Weber. *Peasants Into Frenchmen: The Modernization of Rural France, 1870-1914.* Stanford University Press.

Randal Collins (1979). *The Credential Society.* Academic Press.

Immanuel Wallerstein (1974). *The Modern World System.* Academic Press.

Michelle Rosaldo and Louise Lamphere, eds. (1973). *Woman, Culture, and Society.* Stanford University Press.

Joseph Ben-David and Abraham Zloczower (1962). "Universities and Academic Systems in Modern Societies." *European Journal of Sociology* 45-84.

Arnold Heidenheimer (1981). "Education and Social Security Entitlements in Europe and America" in Peter Flora and Arnold Heidenheimer, Eds. *The Development of Welfare States in Europe and America.* Oxford University Press.

John W. Meyer (1977). "The Effects of Education as an Institution." *American Journal of Sociology* 63: 55-77.

John W. Meyer and Brian Rowan (1977). "Institutionalized Organizations: Formal Organization as Myth and Ceremony." *American Journal of Sociology* 83: 340-63.

Paul DiMaggio and Walter Powell (1983). "The Iron Cage Revisited: Institutional Isomorphism and Collective Rationality" in "Organizational Fields" *American Sociological Review* 48: 147-60.

## MY FAVORITE PERSONAL TEXTS

Francisco O. Ramirez and John Boli (1987). "The Political Construction of Mass Schooling: European Origins and Worldwide Institutionalization." *Sociology of Education* 60:2-17.

Francisco O. Ramirez, Yasemin Soysal, and Suzzane Shanahan (1997). "The Changing Logic of Political Citizenship: Cross-National Acquisition of Women's Suffrage, 1890-1990." *American Sociological Review* 62: 735-45.

John Meyer, John Boli, George Thomas, and Francisco O. Ramirez (1997). "World Society and the Nation-State." *American Journal of Sociology* 1: 144-81.

Francisco O. Ramirez (1989). "Reconstituting Children: Extension of Personhood and Citizenship" pp. 143-165 in David Kertzer and K. Warner Schaie (eds.), *Age Structuring in Comparative Perspective*. Lawrence Erlbaum Associates, Inc. Publishers.

Francisco O. Ramirez (2012). "The World Society Perspective: Concepts, Assumptions, and Strategies." *Comparative Education* 423-39.

Francisco O. Ramirez and Tom Christensen (2013). "The Formalization of the University: Rules, Roots, and Routes." *Higher Education* 65: 695-708.

Patricia Bromley, John W. Meyer, and Francisco O. Ramirez (2011). "The Worldwide Spread of Environmental Discourse in Social Science Textbooks, 1970-2010. *Comparative Education Review* 55, 4; 517-545.

Wade Cole and Francisco O. Ramirez (2013). "Conditional Decoupling: Assessing the Impact of National Human Rights Institutions." *American Sociological Review* 702-25.

Gili Drori, John Meyer, Francisco O. Ramirez and Evan Schofer (2003). *Science in the Modern World Polity: Institutionialization and Globalization.* Stanford: Stanford University Press. 2003.

Francisco O. Ramirez and Christine Min Wotipka (2001). "Slowly But Surely? The Global Expansion of Women's Participation in Science and Engineering Fields of Study, 1972-1992" *Sociology of Education* 74: 231-251.

## REFERENCES

Alexander, C. N., & Knight, G. W. (1971). Situated identities and social psychological experimentation. *Sociometry, 34,* 65–82.

Boaler, J. (1997). Reclaiming school mathematics: The girls fight back. *Gender and Education, 9*(3), 285–305.

Bromley, P., Meyer, J. W., & Ramirez, F. O. (2011). Student-centeredness in social science textbooks, 1970–2008: A cross-national study. *Social Forces, 90,* 547–570.

Buckner, E., & Russell, S. G. (2013). Portraying the global: cross-national trends in textbooks' portrayal of globalization and global citizenship. *International Studies Quarterly, 57*(4), 738–750.

Cole, W. M., & Ramirez, F. O. (2013). Conditional decoupling: Assessing the impact of national human rights institutions, 1981 to 2004. *American Sociological Review, 78*(4), 702–725.

Dorius, S. F., & Firebaugh, G. (2010). Trends in global gender inequality. *Social Forces, 88*(5), 1941–1968.

European Technology Assessment Network. (2010). *Science policies in the European union: Promoting Excellence through mainstreaming gender equality*. Brussels: European Commission.

Meyer, J., & Hannan, M. (Eds.). (1979). *National development and the world system*. Chicago, IL: University of Chicago Press.

Meyer, J. W., Ramirez, F. O., Rubinson, R., & Boli, J. (1977). The world educational revolution, 1950–1970. *Sociology of Education, 50*(October), 242–258.

Meyer, J. W., Boli, J., Thomas, G. M., & Ramirez, F. O. (1997). World society and the nation-state. *American Journal of Sociology, 103,* 144–181.

Meyer, J. W., Bromley, P., & Ramirez, F. O. (2010). Human rights in social science textbooks, 1970–2008. *Sociology of Education, 83,* 111–134.

Ramirez, F. O. (1981). Statism, equality and housewifery: A cross national analysis. *Pacific Sociological Review, 24*(April), 179–195.

Ramirez, F. O. (2006a). Beyond achievement and attainment studies – Revitalizing a comparative sociology of education. *Comparative Education, 42*(3), 431–449.

Ramirez, F. O. (2006b). The rationalization of universities. In M. L. Djelic & K. Shalin-Andersson (Eds.), *Transnational governance: Institutional dynamics of regulation* (pp. 24–245). Cambridge: Cambridge University Press.

Ramirez, F. O., & Boli, J. (1987). The political construction of mass schooling: European origins and worldwide institutionalization. *Sociology of Education, 60,* 2–17.

Ramirez, F. O., & Christensen, T. (2013). The formalization of the university: Rules, roots, and routes. *Higher Education, 65,* 695–708.

Ramirez, F. O., & Kwak, N. (2014). Women enrollments in STEM in higher education: Cross-national trends, 1970–2010. In W. Pearson, L. M. Frehil, & C. McNeely (Eds.), *Advancing women in science: An international perspective*. New York, NY: Springer.

Ramirez, F. O., & Moon, R. (2013). From citizenship to human rights to human rights education. In M. R. Madsen & G. Verschraegen (Eds.), *Making human rights intelligible* (pp. 191–214). Oxford: Hart Publishing.

Ramirez, F. O., & Tiplic, D. (2014). In pursuit of excellence? Discursive patterns in European higher education research. *Higher Education, 67*, 439–455.

Ramirez, F. O., & Weiss, J. (1979). The political incorporation of women. In J. Meyer & M. Hannan (Eds.), *National development and the world system* (pp. 238–249). Chicago, IL: University of Chicago Press.

Ramirez, F. O., & Wotipka, C. M. (2001). Slowly but surely? The global expansion of women's participation in science and engineering fields of study, 1972–92. *Sociology of Education, 74*, 231–251.

Ramirez, F. O., Soysal, Y., & Shanahan, S. (1997). The changing logic of political citizenship: Cross-national acquisition of women's suffrage, 1890–1990. *American Sociological Review, 62*, 735–745.

Ramirez, F. O., Luo, X., Schofer, E., & Meyer, J. W. (2006). Student achievement and national economic growth. *American Journal of Education, 113*, 1–29.

Ramirez, F. O., Bromley, P., & Russell, S. G. (2009). The valorization of humanity and diversity. *Multicultural Education Review, 1*, 29–54.

Schofer, E., & Meyer, J. W. (2005). The worldwide expansion of higher education in the twentieth century. *American Sociological Review, 70*(6), 898–920.

Schofer, E., Ramirez, F. O., & Meyer, J. (2000). The effects of science on national economic development, 1970–1990. *American Sociological Review, 65*(Dec), 866–887.

Soares, J. (1999). *The decline of privilege: The modernization of oxford university*. Stanford, CA: Stanford University Press.

Suarez, D., Ramirez, F. O., & Meyer, J. W. (2006). The worldwide rise of human rights education. In A. Benavot & C. Braslavsky (Eds.), *School knowledge in comparative and historical perspective: Changing curricula in primary and secondary education* (pp. 35–54). Hong Kong: Comparative Education Research Center, University of Hong Kong/Springer.

Tolbert, P., & Zucker, L. (1985). Institutional sources of change in the formal structure of organizations: The diffusion of civil service reform, 1880–1935. *Administrative Science Quarterly, 28*, 22–39.

Wiseman, A., Baker, D., Riegle-Crumb, C., & Ramirez, F. O. (2009). Shifting gender effects: Opportunity structures, mass education, and cross-national achievement in mathematics. In D. Baker & A. Wiseman (Eds.), *Gender, equality and education from international and comparative perspectives* (pp. 395–422). Bingley: Emerald JAI Press.

Wotipka, C. M., & Ramirez, F. O. (2008). World society and human rights: An event history analysis of the ratification of the convention to eliminate all forms of discrimination against women. In B. A. Simmons, F. Dobbin, & G. Garrett (Eds.), *The global diffusion of markets and democracy* (pp. 303–343). Cambridge: Cambridge University Press.

*Francisco O. Ramirez*
*Stanford University*

JAMES E. ROSENBAUM

# 13. DISCOVERING UNSEEN SOCIAL CONTEXTS AND POTENTIAL LEVERS FOR SOCIAL CHANGE

Like many people, I entered sociology out of a concern for social justice and equity. This decision was largely inspired by my father, a pediatrician who had many low income patients, from whom he learned about the dynamics of poverty and its pervasive effects. His experiences working with low income populations led him to work in progressive causes which he considered to be preventive medicine. He started the first poison control hotline in the state of Indiana, advised the first Headstart program in Indiana, worked with Planned Parenthood, and spoke publicly about the need for increased supports for disadvantaged populations. My awareness of poverty and my commitment to social justice came out of my admiration for my father and his work.

Like fish that are not aware of the water that surrounds them, all of us take features of our society for granted, because we don't see alternatives. The study of sociology helped me see how our environment affects the people we meet, our social and career options, and even our own perceived abilities. As I now look back on it, my career was repeatedly motivated by my curiosity to see aspects of our social environment that were hard to understand without research. As my career developed, I began to see that altering our environments can lead to improved opportunities and the prevention of harmful societal influences. My curiosity, drive for social justice, and the belief that a better understanding of social forces can lead to more effective reforms have influenced my choices of studies over my career.

My pursuit of social justice professionally began when I entered Harvard's social psychology program in the Social Relations department. I was initially attracted to the multi-disciplinary approach to social issues, but my studies soon became shaped by my increasing awareness of sociology. In these early years of my career, I found that sociology provided me with a new level of understanding for social problems by identifying structured patterns that shape behaviors, and sometimes even alter the development of ability. Moreover, I realized that sociology often identified features of the social environment that could be changed by policy, ultimately identifying possible levers for social change.

## TRACKING

My sociological career has developed around a few key projects that have shaped my perception of our society and how we are influenced by our social contexts.

My first major project was my Ph.D. dissertation, a study of high school tracking. I felt that education provided the greatest leverage for improving opportunity, and that sociology provided a conceptual framework and methodology for studying ways to change schools. Although education research had studied tracking since early in the 20th century, most scholars focused on its role in shaping instruction. As I began to observe tracking in high school, however, I realized that tracking is more than pedagogy; it is a social structural microcosm, much like the social systems described by stratification theory. Moreover, like stratification in societies, tracking could come in many forms. In comparing prior studies by insightful researchers (Cicourel & Kitsuse, 1964; Coleman, 1960; Stinchcombe, 1965) with my own analyses indicated some of the key dimensions on which tracking could vary, providing alternative versions of tracking, which seemed likely to have varying student and school impacts. I discovered that, like stratification systems, tracking emerged from fundamental value conflicts around opportunity and efficiency.

My study of tracking continued into my first position as an Assistant Professor at Yale University, where I turned my dissertation into a book (Rosenbaum, 1976). I was particularly interested in exploring how tracking shapes ability, beyond its use of ability to sort. My empirical analysis found that tracking shaped both increases and decreases in ability, and was associated with differentiation and homogenization of IQ within tracks.

Tracking's influence was far from straightforward, however, and its different forms likely influenced the impact I had found. The high school I studied had a rigid track system which separated students in many subjects, allocated fewer resources to lower tracks, allowed little track mobility, and made most mobility downward, while preventing upward mobility. However, this is not the only option. I subsequently described a high school that created upward mobility, providing greater resources for lower-achieving students if they devoted extra time to studies (in the summer and after school). These students' achievement was below the requirements for the high track, but additional time and resources enabled them to achieve on a par with their high-track classmates (Rosenbaum, 1999). Similarly, Adam Gamoran, a colleague at the University of Wisconsin, who was extending the sociological understanding of tracking, showed that various dimensions of tracking have impacts on student outcomes (Gamoran & Mare, 1989). Adam also described lower-track classrooms where students learned advanced concepts, because teachers slowed the pace and devoted more time and resources to these lessons (Gamoran, 1993). Tracking studies, my first major foray into sociological research, helped me see how processes within institutions can impact its participants and how different forms of tracking might have different influences.

Although I have moved on to study other topics, tracking remains an enduring interest and tracking comes in many forms. I recently reviewed literature on another form of tracking. Early College High Schools (ECHS) select students at risk of dropping out of high school and put them together in a track where they get shared preparation starting in 7–9th grades. Although no one calls it tracking, it is a form of tracking. Like traditional tracking, ECHS programs target low-achieving students and give them a separate track where they are all taught together. However, unlike traditional tracking, ECHS programs provide more resources, more intensive instruction, and a trajectory that promises college courses by 11–12th grades, usually on a college campus. ECHS programs create distinctive tracks which have remarkable success that don't occur in traditional forms of tracking (Rosenbaum & Becker, 2011).

In retrospect, I learned a great deal from this dissertation. It raised my awareness of social structures within schools and other institutions, leading to my next study, where I examined career tracking in a corporation (Rosenbaum, 1984). My dissertation also taught me to analyze the distinctive dimensions that defined a particular form, and to consider possible variation, which enriches sociological understanding and can suggest policy reforms. That study's findings led to analyses which showed that students' misperceptions of tracking in this single school were widespread in a national sample, where students' perceived track differed from the schools' administrative records in systematic ways.

Although I began with moralistic judgments against tracking, I discovered how tracking structures often resulted from conflicts between opposing legitimate values, e.g., between efficiency and opportunity. This insight suggests that reform needs to consider conflicting values, and my findings indicate that alternate forms of tracking may resolve these conflicts more successfully and less restrictively. Finally, my dissertation helped me see how school social structures shape our discovery of ability and the development of ability, suggesting ways that alternate tracking systems might reveal more individuals having ability than we usually can see in traditional tracking.

This growth in sociological understanding came with much help from Harvard faculty members and colleagues at Yale. My faculty advisors at Harvard repeatedly pushed me beyond my tendencies to get stuck on moral judgments, making me think about the reasoning, process, and consequences of high school tracking. David Riesman, Gerald Lesser, David Cohen, and above all, my dissertation chair, Lee Rainwater helped me go beyond my first naïve efforts to more deeply understand what I was seeing. My professional training continued in my years as an assistant professor, and Albert J. Reiss, Burton Clark, John Simon, Ed Lindblom, Eric Hanushek, Mel Kohn, David Stern, and John LowBeer pushed me to think harder and better about the larger issues.

## RESIDENTIAL MOBILITY

Since junior faculty at Yale rarely got tenure, I took a tenured position at Northwestern University. Coming to Chicago at that time was fortuitous, since I learned about a new residential mobility program that seemed very important, the Gautreaux program. In an effort to improve housing and advance racial and economic integration in Chicago, this program moved low-income black families to better housing in two kinds of areas—mostly black city neighborhoods and mostly white suburbs. Assignments to the two conditions were on a first-come, first-served basis so they approximated random assignment, and indeed families moving to the two conditions were highly similar. The program stipulated that suburbs must be over 70% white, but in fact, few Chicago suburbs were that integrated, so in practice, the suburbs were mostly over 90% white. The city moves were mostly to new low-income housing units, located in predominately black, low-income neighborhoods.

My reading in sociology made me wonder how the move would impact the lives of the parents and children, and the program provided an ideal setting to study this process. Although the program expected all families to benefit from improved housing, the suburb moves could have gone either way, either helping or hurting the families. The 1980s were times of intense racial conflict, and Chicago was not immune. There were cross burnings in front of the apartments of some families, and others experienced name-calling and harassment, sometimes daily.

Moreover, there were doubts about how these African-American families would experience these moves. For the mothers, having lived all their lives in all-black urban neighborhoods, what kind of social life would they experience in white suburbs, how isolated would they feel, and how would they cope? How would they get around in suburbs that have minimal public transportation? What challenges will they face in getting access to medical care and shopping for groceries in suburbs unfamiliar with Medicaid and food stamps?

The children may face even greater difficulties. Having attended urban schools that pose lower achievement standards than suburban schools, how will these students cope with the greater academic challenges in the schools? How will they fit into nearly all white classrooms and schools? On the other hand, the middle-class suburbs had better schools and increased labor market opportunities, which could improve student outcomes.

The appeal of this study is that it radically transformed the environments for mothers and children, and it was by no means clear what outcomes might result. Sociological studies had described many of the deprivations that low income black mothers and children had faced in all-black urban neighborhoods, and how such deprivations could create problems that might prevent these families from benefiting from a move to white middle-class suburbs. Indeed, while the program might get families to move into a new neighborhood, it may not have improved the integration process. As a worst-case image, these families could become isolated, segregated, and harassed.

Sociology provided the perspective for understanding how the program was implemented to reduce potential difficulties. Encouraged by discussions with colleagues, Sandy Jencks and Margo Gordon, and with program designers, Alex Polikoff and Kale Williams, I decided this program was important to study. My co-PI, Len Rubinowitz, and I designed a study that would provide qualitative and quantitative findings about the workings of this program (Rubinowitz & Rosenbaum, 1999). We found that the program's design was well-suited to reduce some of the potential pitfalls: escalating racial tensions, avoiding segregation, and selecting good potential tenants. Although the program placed families in a wide variety of middle-class white suburbs, the program avoided two communities which were known to be racially hostile, and indeed had strong militant segregationist organizations. Gautreaux program designers were also aware of the risk of creating segregated enclaves, so they avoided placing more than four families in any single neighborhood, and they avoided communities that were rapidly changing in racial composition. Finally, the program selected families that were less likely to be evicted by ensuring they did not have large outstanding debts, serious rent delinquencies, or serious damage to their apartments, which would have caused evictions. These requirements were not highly restrictive; we estimate that they eliminated about one-third of possible families.

In a series of studies, we found that Gautreaux was in fact associated with positive outcomes for suburb-mover mothers and children. Compared to mothers who moved to black urban neighborhoods, suburb-mover mothers were more likely to be employed, although they did not have higher earnings or work hours. The children felt the true gains of the program, however. Compared to children who moved to black urban neighborhoods, suburb-mover children were more likely to graduate high school, to attend college, and to attend four-year colleges (rather than two-year colleges). Those who did not attend college were more likely to be employed and to have jobs with better earnings and benefits. They were also just as likely to have friends, to interact frequently, and to visit their friends' homes, but the suburb-movers had mostly white friends. Our qualitative analyses found that the experience of meeting and interacting with white children gave them new understandings, and that the children who moved learned middle class culture, new methods social interaction, and saw incentives for doing homework. The move helped to reduce children's misconceptions as well, and they found new points of comparison. One child reported that, before the move, the only white people she had seen were on television. For her, the move showed her that all whites were not as beautiful as television actors. Our studies revealed how the move to a new social environment, with a higher emphasis on education, a better labor market, and a different racial minority were associated with much better academic, economic, and social outcomes.

Just as I learned that tracking could shape the emergence of ability, the Gautreaux program results provide a new understanding of the concept of ability. Research often blames individuals for poor outcomes, so it blames individuals' low ability when it finds that low-income adults' employment doesn't increase from job training programs, and low-income children's achievement doesn't increase from instructional programs (Herrnstein & Murray, 1994). The Gautreaux program presents a different interpretation. Providing job training or instructional programs are not likely to help if adults remain in neighborhoods with few jobs and children remain in neighborhoods where they and their classmates face daily dangers and anxieties. Indeed, Gautreaux adults' "ability" to get a job, and the children's ability to learn in school may dramatically increase after they move to suburbs that offer dramatically better job and educational opportunities.

Sociology also provided the conceptual perspectives for understanding differences between the Gautreaux program and one of its successors. The Gautreaux program's impressive outcomes inspired the creation of a national demonstration project, Moving to Opportunity (MTO). Unfortunately, the MTO program design failed to incorporate some of the key elements that drove the success of the original program, and MTO was the polar opposite of Gautreaux in some ways. First, unlike Gautreaux, MTO did not help families locate housing, so families often chose housing in familiar nearby neighborhoods, not far from old friends (and sometimes gangs) with whom students continued to interact. Indeed, MTO families made much less dramatic moves, with 90% moving less than 10 miles compared to 90% of Gautreaux families who moved more than 10 miles. Second, unlike Gautreaux which led to few racial enclaves, MTO families tended to congregate in mostly black, low-income enclaves. Families sometimes moved to high-poverty blocks within low-poverty census tracts. Remarkably, unlike Gautreaux whose staff marched with Martin Luther King, and who advocated integration at every level, some MTO counselors encouraged racial enclaves to make families feel more comfortable. Finally, while most Gautreaux children attended schools with average achievement above the 50th percentile, MTO treatment group children attended schools where the average achievement was 22%, barely better than the schools they had attended previously (where achievement was 18%; Rosenbaum & DeLuca, 2003). MTO was a strong study of a weak program.

Despite some promising findings on health outcomes, MTO research has shown mostly disappointing outcomes in terms of employment and education. Contrasting Gautreaux with MTO placements may provide some understanding of alternate ways future residential mobility programs can be implemented if they want to improve education and employment outcomes and move children away from gang influences.

In my prior study, I learned that tracking could take many forms which could have different effects. Similarly, the MTO program showed that "residential mobility" is not a single process and its benefits are not automatic. Residential moves must consider sociological properties of neighborhoods. They must consider distant moves, much better communities, much better schools, and avoid income and racial enclaves if they want to create radically better social contexts. Residential mobility programs can differ on many sociological dimensions, which program design and analysis must consider.

## SCHOOL-WORK TRANSITION

My prior interest in education brought me back to studying education, and to studying how institutions can have a great impact, as I had seen in tracking. Everyone has to go to school, and school can be a powerful lever for change. However, American society is highly decentralized, which creates discontinuities and requires individuals to navigate multiple transitions between institutions (i.e. high school to college).

## DISCOVERING UNSEEN SOCIAL CONTEXTS AND POTENTIAL LEVERS

In my studies of high school tracking, I found it remarkable that high schools manage to affect students' access to higher education, yet I was surprised at how little impact high school tracking seems to have on jobs after high school. Other researchers found similar results from analyses of national survey data (Griffin et al., 1981). I was puzzled how this could be, given that high schools often created vocational programs that were intended to improve employment chances.

My interests in this area were greatly expanded by a Northwestern sociology graduate student. Writing me from Japan, Takehiko Kariya contacted me because he had read my book on school tracking, and he wanted to apply those ideas to understanding Japanese education. He came in 1984 on a Fulbright Fellowship, and his insights into Japanese society created a powerful lens for understanding American society. Over the next several years and continuing over the next several decades, we worked to compare Japanese and American school-to-work transitions. These comparisons allowed us to see aspects of American society that had not previously been seen. Our comparative analyses showed formal school-employer linkages in Japan which might have informal counterparts in the US.

Moreover, our analyses suggested that Japanese procedures were creating powerful incentives to motivate low achieving high school students who Americans believe cannot be motivated. In other words, comparative analyses with the Japanese school system showed clearly that the US was failing to offer possible job payoffs to work-bound students that could motivate their school efforts. Analyses of another society opened my eyes to previously unseen possibilities for US educational policy.

As our work developed, we realized that a new educational reform in Japan seemed likely to undermine the powerful incentives we had discovered. The Japanese reform was intended to relax some of the academic pressures on highly-stressed students. But it had unintended consequences, and we found that it led low SES students to reduce their school efforts, while highly-stressed, high SES students continued to work hard to gain admission to selective universities. As a result, the social class disparity in school effort increased after this reform. Our first analyses had suggested that incentivizing school effort for all students reduced social class inequalities. This new reform confirmed that lesson by showing increased social class differences in school effort. Once again, sociological research revealed how institutional procedures can alter the actions and outcomes of individuals.

Our work with Japan led us to further work to better understand the problems of American "work bound students," those who are planning to work directly after high school. These analyses, which we reported in the book *Beyond College for All*, were driven by a desire to see how disadvantaged youth fare in the labor market, which was a popular research topic at the time. Researchers had described the difficulties high school graduates experienced when trying to find employment. Dual labor market theory divided the labor market into "primary" and "secondary" markets, where the former offers opportunities for advancement. Theorists indicated that the labor market was structured in ways to prevent young people, blacks, and females from gaining access to the primary labor market, and were instead constrained to dead-end jobs in the secondary labor market (Doeringer & Piore, 1971). However, descriptions of German apprenticeships, which offer opportunities for disadvantaged youth to gain valuable skills and access to jobs with advancement opportunities, show that the US might have other options for structuring a labor market (Mortimer et al., 2002).

We examined how US students found their jobs, which students used which kinds of contacts, and how these various kinds of contacts affected students' earnings, both short-term and long-term. National longitudinal survey data allowed us to analyze these issues. Unfortunately, information about employment contacts was mostly unavailable. Indeed, only one national survey, High School and Beyond, had asked about high school-employer contacts. Using this survey data, we discovered that school contacts are relatively infrequently used method of entry into the labor market (8.5% of students), but this varies by students, with black women using school contacts the most (15.6%), Hispanic women and black men next most (10.1% & 10.3%), and white and Hispanic men the least (7.2% and 5.1%). We further discovered that these contacts had earnings payoffs, but only in the long term, which may indicate that these contacts helped students get jobs with advancement opportunities. In fact, the long-term earnings payoffs from school-employer contacts were almost double that from using relatives to secure employment. The findings are particularly remarkable because they indicate that traditionally disadvantaged groups (females and minorities) are getting more benefit from these job contacts than white males.

National survey data are good for showing outcomes from different kinds of contacts, but not for showing how it happens, so we interviewed vocational teachers to discover what they did to help students find jobs. We were particularly interested in how they were able to help the most disadvantaged groups (females, blacks and Hispanics). By once again examining social and institutional processes, we discovered how vocational teachers create trusted relationships with employers, and how they subsequently persuade employers to hire disadvantaged groups. Indeed, trusted teacher recommendations even managed to persuade employers to abandon their racial or gender biases. Many teachers report that their recommendation can convince an employer to hire students they wouldn't ordinarily consider, because of their race, gender, or disability. Employers report hiring blacks and females for certain jobs for the first time, because they were highly recommended by a teacher. Apparently, trusted social contacts can overcome biases, and trusted teachers can show employers the abilities of disadvantaged students which otherwise would be hard to see.

Despite these positive findings from school-employer linkages, we were surprised at how few students reported they were "work-bound" in our national survey data. The vast majority of students in the high school class of 1982 had plans to attend college, and many follow through on that plan at some point. Most remarkably, there was little racial disparity. While blacks and Hispanics have much lower high school graduation rates than whites, if they graduate high school, blacks and Hispanics are nearly as likely to attend college as whites in the following eight years (80%, 80%, vs 83%; Adelman, 2003).

These results told us that our focus on "work bound" students had been misdirected. We needed to look at what happens to students who think they are college-bound. We realized that the problem might lie with the students who are planning college despite poor preparation.

We turned our attention to understanding student perceptions of college and its demands. Re-analyzing national survey data, we found that most students plan to get college degrees, yet some of these students have low odds of doing so. Specifically, students who plan to get Associates degrees or higher and are in the lowest quartile of GPA (C's or lower) only have a 14% chance of attaining their degree plans over the 10 years after high school graduation. Indeed, about a third of students leave college without even a single college credit. We interviewed guidance counselors and discovered that many were aware of students' poor college prospects, but they were reluctant to "burst students' bubbles." Counselors wanted students to have a chance, and they also worried about being criticized if they gave discouraging advice. A new implicit national policy of "College for all" had emerged, and it gave students the hope and impression of opportunity, without providing any warning about realistic odds of success.

My book, *Beyond College for All*, illuminated some major societal implications. Just as I learned that different tracking mechanisms can create changes in ability, and new social contexts can improve outcomes, our work found that linkages between high schools and employers can lead to economic benefits, even for the most disadvantaged students. More importantly, however, this work highlighted a new social norm in which all students aspire to college degrees. This discovery went beyond social contexts or institutional procedures; it represented a profound shift in our thinking about the nature of and expectations around college and opportunity.

## COMMUNITY COLLEGES

Conventional wisdom holds that learning goes only in one direction: students learn from teachers. In my experience, the process is actually more dynamic. My research on community colleges began when a graduate student (Regina Deil-Amen) asked me to advise her case study of a community college. Although I was an expert on high schools, I knew practically nothing about community colleges. I held the usual misconceptions that community colleges were relatively unimportant, mostly focusing on preparing students to transfer to real colleges, and attended by few students. As I learned while advising Regina, my preconceptions were wrong on all counts.

Over the last 50 years, college attendance has radically increased, mostly thanks to community colleges. Community colleges have reduced the formal barriers of time, distance, and cost through convenient locations, flexible schedules, and low tuition. Open admissions policies eliminate the achievement barriers found in four-year colleges. Almost half of all college students attend community colleges, in which enrollments range from 5,000 to over 100,000 students. Community colleges can also provide good job opportunities, and are not restricted to BA transfer programs, offering Associate degrees as well as career certificate programs. These programs lead to mid-skill jobs in some industries, particularly health and technology, which report labor shortages, even in the current weak economy (Holzer et al., 2011; Acermoglu & Autor, 2010).

Unfortunately, community colleges have poor degree completion rates (37% of students graduate within eight years of enrolling; Stephan et al., 2009), and most reforms have been ineffective at improving completion. Sociology provides conceptual tools for better understanding student difficulties in community colleges, including the ways institutional procedures affect student success and degree completion.

As I worked more with Regina, my fascination with community colleges grew. We began doing research to learn how they serve students; we knew their unique characteristics must mean they have different procedures from four-year colleges. The traditional college model poses a smooth and continuous attainment chain: courses lead to credits, which lead to credentials, which in turn lead to job payoffs. However, in detailed studies of community colleges, we find that students face gaps at each step, causing many to drop off the chain and not reach the next stage. Traditional college procedures inadvertently inflict greater harm on disadvantaged students.

Knowing from the other projects described in this essay that procedures can make a difference in outcomes, we searched for alternatives to traditional college procedures. We focused on occupational colleges, private career schools that confer accredited degrees but they use nontraditional college procedures. They enroll similar students as community colleges, but they have higher degree completion rates (twenty percentage points). Because of the similarities in student populations, we suspected their higher completion rates were related to alternative procedures (Stephan et al., 2009). The private college sector has many problems, and even some frauds, but our aim was to describe what we learned from some exceptional occupational colleges, not to advocate the whole sector. Our findings are based on close observations and interviews with college staff and 4,000 surveys with students at community colleges and occupational colleges. In this research, we found many "sociologically smart" procedures that recognized and responded to sociological constraints their students faced. These procedures were well-adapted to disadvantaged students' needs, which community colleges might also use to improve completion rates.

Our research on community colleges discovered that we wear "BA blinders." That is, those of us who attended four-year colleges and have BA degrees assume that college is like that for everyone. As Regina and I became increasingly aware of our BA blinders, we gained a new understanding of prior research findings and of our new findings on five issues.

1. Although most community college students seek "four-year BAs" without intermediate credentials, realistically, only 4 percent get BAs in four years, 8 percent take five years, and another 16 percent take six to eight years (Stephan, 2012). Four-year BAs are almost a myth, and even after eight years few people have BAs. =Unfortunately, no one warns students about "eight-year BAs" or explains viable alternatives.
2. Our society's BA blinders tell students that a BA is the only degree of value, and we tend to ignore other valuable credentials that take much less time. In fact, despite claims about the BA's "million-dollar payoff," 24% of certificates graduates have higher earnings than the median BA graduate, and many applied associate degrees can lead to good careers (Carnevale, 2010).
3. While I was focusing on earnings outcomes, my daughter pointed out that nonmonetary payoffs from certificates and associate degrees are also substantial. Analyzing national data, Janet Rosenbaum (2011a,b; 2012a) found that certificates and associate degrees lead to significantly better jobs than high school diplomas on job status, job satisfaction, career-relevance, and autonomy (a defining attribute of middle-class jobs; according to Goldthorpe). These sub-BA credentials may confer some health benefits in addition to economic and nonmonetary job rewards.
4. Wearing BA blinders, most reformers stress remedial courses so all students can pursue traditional BA degrees. Most community college students are placed in remedial courses, in which only 33 percent of students complete the remedial sequence in math, and the rate is only 17 percent for students with low-test scores. Rates are only slightly better in reading (Bailey et al., 2010). Students are told remedial coursework is their best or only option, yet they often don't realize that these classes do not count towards degrees and failure rates are high.
5. "College-level academic skills" may be unnecessary to attain certain credentials. Students only need eighth-grade academic skills to get certificates in many occupational programs. Faculty report that these programs let students quickly become computer networking technicians, medical technicians, medical aides, and accounting staff. These are jobs in high demand industries that offer good earnings and job conditions (Rosenbaum et al., 2010). Yet no one mentions these options to entering students, who instead think that their only option is the difficult and perilous BA transfer pathway.

Sociologists often identify barriers that block opportunity for young people. The traditional procedures illustrated above, such as remedial education and BA goals, indicate some examples. BA blinders encourage one-size-fits-all cultural beliefs that are unrealistic and create barriers. These barriers include the mythical "four-year" BA degree, unnecessarily high standards of "college readiness," ineffective remediation, courses without credits, credits without credentials, credentials without job payoffs. Alternative degrees, however, can lead to quick credentials and nonmonetary job rewards that are more satisfying than earnings.

Private occupational colleges illustrate procedural alternatives to traditional procedures, such as clear course pathways, frequent mandatory advising, monitoring student progress, and degree ladders that confer certificate and associate degrees on the way to a BA. These alternatives are likely to present fewer barriers to disadvantaged students. Community colleges are attempting ambitious goals for a wide variety of students, and these alternative procedures might allow them to help more students.

## CONCLUSION

Research is often exciting because it reveals aspects of reality that have gone unnoticed. I find the discovery of my blind spots to offer the same delightful surprises as a good mystery: the evidence is all around us, but we can't see them until we apply our methods. What is truly inspiring about the projects I've worked on throughout the years is that they allowed my colleagues and me to discover options, abilities, outcomes, and rewards that we had not previously considered. Our preconceptions, like BA blinders, lead to highly constricted ideas about success. But success comes in many forms, and our findings showed us that we were looking too narrowly. In seeking to solve the puzzle of how youth gain access to careers, these findings, from tracking to housing relocation to school-work transitions and finally to community college procedures, indicate many alternatives to one-size-fits-all models.

Looking back over this set of projects, I realize that I had not noticed many of our social realities prior to beginning each study. My research career has been an intellectual journey in which I learned to see aspects of our social context, and how they shape our lives. Each study focused on powerful encompassing social forces—rigid high school tracking, residential moves to radically different neighborhoods, school-employer linkages, and colleges with structured nontraditional procedures. In all projects, I posed comparisons with alternative social contexts that used very different procedures, revealing previously unstudied alternatives that may have very different outcomes.

I had become so entrenched in the common procedures of these various projects that I could no longer see other options. Each of the social structures reflected a way of reconciling conflicting deeply-held values, and social change of these structures would inevitably reflect a different way to reconcile these conflicting values. Moreover, in each case, these different social contexts shape individuals' opportunities to develop and demonstrate their abilities. In other words, contrary to common preconceptions (including my own), our studies were not asking if tracking, residential mobility, school-work linkages, or nontraditional college procedures were good or bad. We were asking what forms each of these could take, and how they might work differently if they varied in certain ways. We were not asking whether individuals have high or low ability, but rather asking how social contexts would allow individuals to show their abilities.

High school tracking has profound effects in separating students, labeling their abilities, providing different educational experiences, and defining future opportunities, but tracking and its impacts often go unnoticed. Similarly, residential segregation creates very different social contexts, which define our standards, behaviors, and goals. Likewise school-employer linkages affect employment outcomes, and open-enrollment colleges may improve college access, but not necessarily lead to degrees or jobs. Although we take them for granted as unavoidable realities, these various institutional factors can be changed, and lead to very different outcomes many years in the future. Research is a powerful tool for seeing important societal influences that are not easily visible to the naked eye.

## MY FAVORITE TEXTS BY OTHERS

Mel Kohn's *Work and Personality* illustrates profound ideas subject to rigorous testing, and tested in multiple cultures.

Christopher Jencks' *Inequality* thoughtfully interprets status attainment research findings for policy implications.

Adam Gamoran's papers push our understanding of educational stratification into new understandings of social context, in thoughtful quantitative and qualitative studies.

David Bill's book *Sociology of education and work* provides a rich source of ideas from diverse traditions.

## MY FAVORITE PERSONAL TEXTS

Many of my studies taught me new lessons that surprised me. My first book, *Making Inequality*, taught me many lessons which shaped my later work. *Beyond College-for-all* grew out of a discovery that many of my preconceptions were mistaken, and new "college for all" policies had changed many aspects of schools and colleges. In the later book, *After Admission*, I discovered radically different forms of college than I had previously imagined, and they operated by very different social mechanisms. That insight is further extended in my newest book, which is currently in preparation.

## REFERENCES

Acemoglu, D., & Autor, D. H. (2010). Skills, tasks and technologies: Implications for employment and earnings. In O. Ashenfelter & D. Card (Eds.), *Handbook of labor economics* (Vol. 4). Amsterdam: Elsevier. Retrieved from http://economics.mit.edu/files/5571

Adelman, C. (2003). *Principal indicators of student academic histories in post secondary education, 1970–2000*. Washington, DC: US Department of Education, Institute of education sciences.

Bailey, T., Jeong, D. W., & Cho, S.-W. (2010). Referral, enrollment, and completion in developmental education sequences in community colleges. *Economics of Education Review, 29*, 255–270.

Bills, D. (2004). *The sociology of education and work*. Hoboken, NJ: Wiley.

Bound, J., Hershbein, B., & Long, B. T. (2009). Playing the admissions game: Reactions to increasing college competition. *Journal of Economic Perspectives, 23*(4), 119–146.

Carnevale, A. P., Rose, S. J., & Hanson, A. (2012, June). *Certificates: Gateway to gainful employment and college degrees*. Georgetown University Center on Education and the Workforce, Washington, DC.

Cicourel, A. V., & Kitsuse, J. I. (1963). *The educational decision-makers*. Indianapolis, IN: Bobbs Merrill.

Clark, B. (1960). The 'cooling out' function in higher education. *American Journal of Sociology, 65*, 569–576.

Coleman, J. S. (1974). *Youths: Transition to adulthood*. Chicago, IL: University of Chicago Press.

DeLuca, S., & Rosenbaum, J. (2003). If low-income Blacks are given a chance to live in White neighborhoods, will they stay? Examining mobility patterns with quasi-experimental data. *Housing Policy Debate, 2003*, 305–345.

Doeringer, P., & Piore, M. (1971). *Internal labor markets and manpower analysis*. Lexington, MA: Lexington Books.

Gamoran, A. (1993). Alternative uses of ability grouping. *American Journal of Education, 102*, 1–21.

Gamoran, A., & Mare, R. (1989). Secondary school tracking and educational inequality: Reinforcement, compensation, or neutrality? *American Journal of Sociology, 94*, 1146–1183.

Goldthorpe, J. (2000). *On sociology: Numbers, narratives, and the integration of research and theory*. Oxford: Oxford University press.

Griffin, L. J., Kalleberg, A. L., & Alexander, K. L. (1981). Determinants of early labor market entry and attainment: A study of labor market segmentation. *Sociology of Education, 54*, 206–21.

Grubb, W. N. (1996). *Working in the middle*. San Francisco, CA: Jossey-Bass.

Herrnstein, R. J., & Murray, C. (1994). *The bell curve*. New York, NY: Free Press.

Holzer, H., Lane, J., Rosenblum, D., & Andersson, F. (2011). *Where are all the good jobs going?* New York, NY: Russell Sage Foundation Press.

Mortimer, J., Zimmer, M., Holmes, M., & Shanahan, M. (2002). The process of occupational decision-making. *Journal of Vocational Behavior, 61*, 439–465.

Murnane, R. J., & Levy, F. (1996). *Teaching the new basic skills: Principles for educating children to thrive in a changing economy*. New York, NY: The Free Press.

Rosenbaum, J. (1976). *Making inequality: The hidden curriculum of high school tracking*. New York, NY: Wiley.

Rosenbaum, J. (1980). Track misperceptions and frustrated college plans: An analysis of the effects of tracks and track perceptions in the National Longitudinal Survey. *Sociology of Education, 53*, 74–88.

Rosenbaum, J. (1984). *Career mobility in a corporate hierarchy*. New York, NY: Academic Press.

Rosenbaum, J. (1992). *Youth apprenticeship in America*. Washington, DC: W.T. Grant Commission on Youth and America's Future.

Rosenbaum, J. (2001). *Beyond college-for-all: Career paths for the forgotten half*. New York, NY: ASA Rose Monograph Series, Russell Sage Foundation. Received American Sociological Association's Willard Waller Award for Distinguished Scholarship in Sociology of Education.

Rosenbaum, Janet. (2011a, October 7). *Do degrees matter? Health disparities between bachelors and associate degree holders with similar job quality*. International conference on health policy statistics, Cleveland, OH.

Rosenbaum, Janet. (2011b, November). *When do health impairments and family instability not hurt community college completion?* American public health Association, Washington, DC.

Rosenbaum, Janet. (2012). Degrees of health disparities: Health status disparities between young adults with high school diplomas, sub-baccalaureate degrees, and baccalaureate degrees. *Health Services and Outcomes Research Methodology, 12*(2–3), 156–168. doi:10.1007/s10742-012-0094-x

Rosenbaum, J., & Becker, K. (2011). Navigating the transition to college. *American Educator, 35*(3), 14–20.

Rosenbaum, J., Deil-Amen, R., & Person, A. (2006). *After admission: From college access to college success*. New York, NY: Russell Sage Foundation Press.

Rosenbaum, J., Cepa, K., & Rosenbaum, J. (2013). Beyond the one-size-fits-all college degree. *Contexts, 12*(1), 49–52.

Rosenbaum, J. E., Rosenbaum, J., Stephan, J., Foran, A. E., & Schuetz, P. (2013a). Beyond BA blinders: Cultural impediments to college success. My 4-year degree was the longest 8 years of my life. In O. Patterson (Ed.), *Bringing culture back in: Rethinking the African-American youth crisis*. Cambridge, MA: Harvard University Press.

Rubinowitz, L., & Rosenbaum, J. E. (2000). *Crossing the class and color lines*. Chicago, IL: University of Chicago Press.

Stephan, J. (2010). *Is an associates degree a dead end?* unpublished analyses, National Educational Longitudinal Survey, Northwestern University, Institute for Policy Research.
Stephan, J. L., Rosenbaum, J. E., & Person, A. E. (2009). Stratification in college entry and completion. *Social Science Research, 38*(3), 572–593.
Stinchcombe, A. L. (1965). *Rebellion in a high school.* Chicago, IL: Quadrangle.

*James E. Rosenbaum*
*Northwestern University*

ALAN R. SADOVNIK

# 14. HOLOCAUST MEMORIES

*Honoring My Mother through Applied Scholarship and
Building Academic Programs*

I was born and spent my first nine years in the Boulevard Housing Project in the East New York section of Brooklyn, a working class section of New York City. Both of my parents were Holocaust survivors and the Holocaust became a major theme of my childhood. As I grew into adulthood, I learned a sense of social justice from my parents, which would come to shape much of my work as a sociologist.

My mother, Ruth Haas Sadovnik, left Berlin at the age of eleven on the Kindertransport. She lived in Hull, England until 1945, when she was reunited with her parents and sister, who escaped Nazi Germany in 1941. Her difficult childhood left her with a sense of moral obligation, duty and social justice, which she exhibited for the rest of her life.

She was married for fifty years to her beloved husband, Morris, who with his half-brother, were the sole survivors of their family from Warsaw.

My mother's childhood was difficult to say the least. I cannot imagine what it was like at the age of eleven to leave your home and family on a train, speaking no English and to arrive in another country, never knowing if you would see your parents and sister again. My mother had to leave school at fourteen to work full time at Hammonds Department Store in Hull. She would continue to work full time until her retirement forty-eight years later at the age of sixty-two. One story in particular captures my mother's determination and spirit. At the age of thirteen, when she had been evacuated to the countryside because of the nightly bombing of Hull, a local benefactor donated pork chops to the boarding school she attended. Being kosher, my mother ate only her potatoes, but left the pork chops. Her teacher scolded her for not eating them. When my mother informed her that she could not eat them due to her religion's rules, the teacher demanded that she eat them and that she would force her to remain in the cafeteria until she did. My mother told her that the teacher would have to wait forever; as she did not escape the Nazi's to be forced to eat pork in England. Finally at midnight, when another student finally reported what was happening to the Headmistress, the Head intervened, allowed my mother to return to her room, and to her credit immediately fired the teacher.

Twice during her time in England, my mother cheated death. Once a bomb fell into the shelter and landed right next to her. Miraculously, it did not explode.

Second, upon hearing the news that her parents and sister made it safely to New York City, she begged her foster mother to allow her to make the dangerous trans-Atlantic voyage to join them. After numerous attempts to convince her, Mrs. Levine agreed and they took the train to Southampton for the journey. At the last minute, Mrs. Levine decided against allowing her to go. My mother was devastated. A U-Boat sunk the ship and fortunately for her, and especially me, she was not among its passengers, all of whom perished.

My mother was one of the fortunate ten percent of the 10,000 Kinder to see her parents again. Ninety percent perished in one of Hitler's concentration camps. Shortly after coming to New York, she met and fell in love with my father, a Polish immigrant, who came to the U.S. in 1937 and served with the Army Corp of Engineers in the Pacific. Soon after their marriage in 1948, when my mother was just twenty-one, my father began to exhibit symptoms of the severe manic-depression that would haunt him until his death in 1998. When my father was in the manic stage of his illness, he was charming, loving, and totally devoted to my mother. When he was depressed, he was angry, unable to function, and railed against a God who would allow six million Jews, including most of his family to perish. During their fifty years of marriage, my father was hospitalized numerous times, including spending his last five years in a psychiatric nursing home. Although some could not understand her staying with him, she loved him deeply and took her vows of in sickness and in health, till death do us part, seriously. For me, his mental illness became another theme of my life.

Some of my most cherished memories came when my mother and I returned to her childhood homes. In 1987, when I was lecturing at the Universities of London and Nottingham, she met me in London, where we sojourned back to Hull. We met four of the surviving Levine sisters, whom she had not seen in forty-two years, who were now all in their eighties. Nonetheless, as they entered her cousin Lotte's home, she immediately recognized each one of them. We went back to her childhood home on Beverly Road and sat together, hugging each other in tears as we sat in the bomb shelter. She took me to Hammonds, where at fourteen she exhibited the traits of diligence and perseverance that would make her an exemplary legal secretary.

For years, I asked my mother to return to Berlin with me and to show me her childhood homes. She always refused, saying that England, not Germany was her childhood home. She was forever grateful to the British for saving her life. It pleased her greatly that I have spent so much time over the past twenty years at the University of London, to the point that it is like my second home. However, in 1995, when I was giving a paper in Bielefeld in western Germany, I told my mother a little white lie: that I bought her a non-refundable ticket to go with me for a week to Berlin. Although it was non-refundable, if she had not gone, I would have received a credit. She agreed to go and I often joked with her by asking, "How do you get my Jewish mother to get on a plane? Buy her a non-refundable ticket." It was, along with our trip to Hull, among the most important trips of my life. We visited her home in Shlasenzee, where for the first time I came to understand what the Nazi's took from her family. Their house was not modest, but was large, elegant and expensive.

They went from German-Jewish bourgeoisie to working class refugees in a matter of years. We went to their apartment in Charlottenburg, the Park Avenue of Berlin, right off Kurfürstendamm, its Madison or 5th Avenue. We visited the site of her synagogue; all that was left of it was the plaque commemorating its burning on Kristalnacht. Her German, which she had not spoken since her parent's death, two decades earlier, came back immediately. And she used it to tell everyone and anyone that she had been born in Berlin, had left on the Kindertransport and that I was her son. She was saying to everyone that you did not kill us all.

As a child, I always knew that like my grandfather I would receive a Ph.D. In some way, without ever explicitly telling me this, I understood that it was my role to restore our family's level of educational attainment. Although she left school after the eighth grade, it was evident to all who knew her that if it weren't for the Holocaust, she would have continued her education and excelled.

It was these two themes, the Holocaust and mental illness that formed the basis of my childhood and continued into adulthood. Watching my father carried off in a straight-jacket when I was thirteen left a permanent imprint in my mind. Visiting him in psychiatric wards numerous times until his death at seventy-six when I was forty-five also left a permanent imprint in my mind.

## CHANGING NEIGHBORHOODS

We lived in the city housing project until I was nine. The neighborhood was integrated, but increasingly was becoming African American and poor. The junior high school I was scheduled to attend in a few years had a reputation for being dangerous. My parents' American dream was to have their own home so they bought a two family home in the Rockaways, an integrated lower middle class and middle class Atlantic Beach community in the southern point of New York City in Queens, near JFK Airport.

Growing up near the beach, about 1.5 hours from Manhattan, was like living in a small town, not New York City. When I was twelve, I learned to surf and was one of the early East coast surfers in the Rockaways. When I was in college, I decided that I would become a college professor and teach at the University of Hawaii. Shortly thereafter, I broke my wrist in a skateboarding accident, which permanently ended my surfing career, and my dream of living in Hawaii.

My parents had the misfortune of picking changing neighborhoods to live in. A few years after moving to the Rockaways, a city edict turned two middle income city projects to low income ones and an additional low income project was built. Our house was thus surrounded by three low income projects, with two others within a few miles. In a few years, the housing projects consisted of low income African Americans and Latinos. At the same time, real estate blockbusters came to the families in our community and offered to sell their houses for a fair price and told them if they did not once the block was more than fifty percent African American the values would plummet. My parents refused to sell saying they would not give in to this racism. However, within a few years they were one of three white families left on the block.

There once had been summer bungalows on the surrounding blocks, but they became abandoned and often drug dens. My mother became President of the Frank Avenue Civic Association and worked diligently to get them torn down.

My parents stayed in their house for twenty-five years and finally sold it after my father was mugged for the fourth time. It represented an end to their working class dream of owning their own home, as it had turned into an urban nightmare. Although he still did not want to leave, my mother and I made the decision and my parents bought a cooperative apartment in Little Neck, Queens, the last town in New York City before the Nassau County line. The Rockaways have yet to recover, with significant sections home to low income projects and nursing homes. Little Neck is largely middle income and upper middle income white and Asian. My parents lived in a naturally aging community within a large cooperative development and they enjoyed living there until both of their deaths.

## EDUCATION

I attended an integrated elementary, junior high school, and high school. However, although the schools were racially and socioeconomically integrated, my classes were almost all white and middle class. In elementary school I was in the IGC (Intellectually Gifted Children). This tracking system put most of the same students in class year after year. In Junior High School, we were in the SP (Special Progress) and in high school we were in Honors or AP (Advanced Placement). My own education illustrated the powerful effects of within school tracking as those in my track all went to college and for the most part went to competitive colleges.

Far Rockaway High School had over four-thousand students when I attended, so large it had to have a split session. My graduating class has 1070 students, but I probably knew about one-hundred. These were students from the SP classes in all of the peninsula's junior high schools. Of the one-hundred, the students were largely white and middle class as well. The Honors and AP classes were fairly rigorous, especially when compared to the regular classes. I decided to take regular English classes in order to devote more time to mathematics and science. The level of the English classes was very low and to this day regret not taking more advanced English classes, as my education in literature was deficient. It represented my first experience with the effects of tracking on both high and low track students.

Far Rockaway High School had no college counselor, only a few guidance counselors who could give advice on college choices, but rarely did. Even though I had a ninety-two average and graduated 43rd out of 1070, I did not have a sufficient understanding of the college application process; and my parents, neither of whom went to college, did not either. So I went to Barons and selected mostly local colleges, as going away did not enter my mind. I wanted to stay near the beach and the waves.

I was admitted to Adelphi, Brooklyn, Columbia, and New Paltz, all of those I applied to. The decision came down to Brooklyn and Columbia. My parents said they would find a way to pay for Columbia, but the free tuition at the time at City University of New York (CUNY) made Brooklyn more attractive.

I transferred to Queens College after three semesters because the student population at Brooklyn seemed too conservative. But in my first semester at Brooklyn, I took an introduction to sociology course that changed the course of my education. Up to that point I thought I wanted to be a lawyer, but the sociology course made be decide to major in it. In that first semester, I also discovered how ill-prepared I was. I received a C- on my first English Composition paper and had to work very hard to catch up. I discovered that what I thought had been a rigorous education in high school was not that rigorous. In my third semester, I took a sociological theory course and for the first time read Marx, Weber, Durkheim, Goffman and Mills. Queens's sociology department had a strong reputation so my decision to transfer seemed a solid one.

I was in the last class that received free tuition at CUNY and I always say it was the best education money did not buy. At the time, Queens enrolled more than 25,000 students on a commuter campus, so developing a community was difficult. I spent most of my out of class time working at a part time job and with my girlfriend who also went to Queens, and who I would marry upon graduation. Queens represented the mission of CUNY: it consisted of working and middle class students striving to move upward. They were smart and hardworking and my class has done exceptionally well in life. Its sociology department was world class, including Patricia Kendall, Cynthia Epstein, Samuel Heilman, Milton Mankoff, Michael Brown among others. My mentor, Sally Hillsman, went on to become the Executive Director of the American Sociological Association. Over a period of three years, Queens sent among the largest number of students to Ph.D. programs in sociology. Among those who received Ph.D.s are Beth Stevens (retired after many years at Mathematica), David Karen (now at Bryn Mawr), Martha Ecker (now at Ramapo College) and me (now at Rutgers University-Newark).

In addition to majoring in sociology, I minored in secondary education – social studies. I decided to obtain my teaching license so just in case I did not get a fellowship, I would be able to teach and go to graduate school part time. In my final semester, I student taught at the new Beach Channel High School in the Rockaways. The school took the students in the western part of the Rockaways, who used to attend Far Rockaway High School. During student teaching, I learned another lesson about tracking. During the first quarter I taught an honors course in behavioral sciences. The students were largely white and middle class. During the second quarter, I taught a regular level course in criminology. The students were largely African American and Latino and poor. When I asked my cooperating teacher why the two groups had different subjects, he replied that those taking criminology would need to know their rights and the ins and outs of the system. The lesson was that one group was being prepared to college and the other for jail.

I graduated college in 1975, during New York City's fiscal crisis. Teachers were being laid off, not hired, so I decided to go to graduate school in sociology full time. As I was getting married in July and my wife would be in her senior year at Queens, I only applied to New York City programs: Columbia, CUNY Graduate Center, the New School, and NYU. My plan was to go to the program that gave me money, and if none did, to go to CUNY, whose tuition was the lowest, assuming I was accepted. I was accepted to them all, but only NYU gave me financial aid, a full fellowship, which included full tuition and a stipend. After getting married in July, I started graduate school as a full time doctoral student in September. I had a difficult adjustment. We lived in the Rockaways, so the commute was difficult, averaging about 1.5 hours each way. This made it difficult for me to spend long hours in the library or to become part of the student community, although I tried my best to do so. The courses were far more demanding than undergraduate courses. The students came from more privileged backgrounds and graduated from Ivy League and elite liberal arts colleges and seemed more prepared than I was. The graduate school world that I was assimilating into was different than the world with my wife, which put a strain on our marriage, one that would eventually lead to its demise, although not for another eight years.

During my first semester, I was having trouble concentrating and one evening fell down the subway stairs. I went to the doctor and was diagnosed with hyperthyroidism. I was treated with medication through the end of the first year, but had to have surgery in July. Given my symptoms, I did not do well the first semester, receiving two B+s and a B. I did not tell anyone about my illness until the Director of Graduate Studies took my fellowship away. When I saw him he restored my tuition remission, but not the stipend. Instead he gave me courses to teach as an adjunct.

The Sociology Department at NYU was world class. The faculty included Eliot Freidson, Edwin Schur, Dennis Wrong, Wolf Heydebrand, Richard Sennett, and Caroline Persell, among others. But the highlight of my doctoral career was the Visiting European Scholars program, where visiting professors would teach an eight-week course. During my three years of coursework, I studied with Anthony Giddens, Basil Bernstein, Michael Mann and Jock Young. It was during my course with Bernstein that a lifelong friendship and colleagueship began, one that would blossom in the 1980s and last until his death in 2000. Bernstein taught me to connect sociological theory to empirical research and solidified my interest in the sociology of education.

In 1979, I took my oral qualifying examinations. By this time, we had moved to Flushing and I was able to spend more time in the library. Over the last four years I became a serious student and was concentrating in the sociology of education, social problems and social stratification. Caroline Persell had agreed to be on my committee, but she was on sabbatical, so Floyd Hammack from the School of Education agreed to replace her. This was fortuitous as he would become a valuable member of my dissertation committee. I passed with honors and for the first time felt I really belonged.

During the last two years of coursework and studying for exams, I adjuncted at a number of institutions to make ends meet, as my stipend had not been restored. These included New York Institute of Technology, Monmouth College, Fairleigh Dickinson University, Brooklyn College, Queens College and NYU. But in 1979, I secured a full time instructor position in the Division of Education Opportunity (DEO) at the State University of New York, College at Purchase (SUNY Purchase).

The DEO was a compensatory higher education program, consisting largely of working class and poor African American and Latino students. We were supposed to teach both content and skills. I was hired to teach two sociology courses and one English composition course per semester, which turned out to be a heavy and labor intensive load, given the need to teach underprepared students skills as well as content. During this time, I was looking for a dissertation topic. During my first year at Purchase, I discovered that the students were unhappy with the separate nature of their program (they did not mainstream for two years). The effects of what was a racialized tracking seemed an ideal dissertation topic, especially since I could get access to the site. Studying a program that I was a part of would prove to be a challenge, as I constantly had to step back from what occurred and try to be as objective as possible. There were many times I had to analyze my own behavior or position as a researcher and a member—not an easy task.

Writing a dissertation and teaching full time proved difficult and slow. It was not until 1982 that I became serious about finishing. My dissertation included the major themes of my work to come in the sociology of education, looking at issues of social class, race and the limits and possibilities of education in ameliorating inequality. My chair gave me a two afternoon teaching schedule in order to finish, so I wrote five days a week. I remember going through the dissertations in the Sociology lounge to see how short was acceptable and figured 200 pages would do. By the time I was done, I had written 651 pages, really two dissertations: a historical ethnography of the evolution and demise of DEO into an integrative, not separate program, and an empirical analysis of its outcomes compared to other SUNY programs, with an analysis of student surveys on the program.

I handed it in to my Committee (Caroline Persell, Chair, Floyd Hammack and Edward Lehman) in April, did revisions over the summer (Floyd had been reading it and giving me comments chapter by chapter) and defended in September in time for an October degree. I thought the defense was difficult, with lots of little criticisms, which Ed Lehman finally said was for the book not the defense. Patricia Kendall one of the two outside committee members disagreed strongly with my major conclusion that the evidence supported the college's decision to eliminate the program. She argued that my evidence could lead to the opposite conclusion. We had a heated debate until Juan Corradi, the other outside member, said we would have to agree to disagree. When Caroline brought me back in to tell me I passed she said it was an excellent defense. I said it would have been nice to know that during the exam. In any case, I had minor revisions and only three days to do them. Making the revisions was easy; printing the dissertation hard, as these were the early days of word processing and took eight hours to print the final version.

All of this was done under the specter of pending unemployment. In Spring 1983, I went to the Vice President's Office to read my reappointment folder. I read his glowing first few paragraphs about my teaching, service and my schedule for completing my dissertation. But I had to read the final paragraph twice to understand the implication: "The Sociology Department (where I was now appointed with the change in DEO) has eight faculty members and the Economics Department has three. Therefore, based on institutional need I am transferring Professor Sadovnik's line to the Economics Department." Thus, my appointment had been terminated and 1983–84 would be my final year at Purchase.

This final year felt like what David Sudnow called social death. My colleagues stayed away from me as they did not know what to say. The students, however, were great, writing letters to the student newspaper about changing the decision. I learned an important lesson that administrators do not give in to student pressure and when one of my colleagues got a Fulbright and there was money to hire me for another year, the Vice President hired someone else, lest it be perceived that the students won.

I looked unsuccessfully for academic positions the entire year and as late as August was prepared to teach three courses per semester as an adjunct at NYU's School of Continuing Education, where I had continued to teach one course when at Purchase. The most important thing about NYU's School of Continuing Education is this is where I first met Susan Semel, who in later years would become my collaborator on a number of books and most importantly, my wife. But in August, when in San Francisco, I received a message from a friend at NYU that I got a call from Adelphi University about an administrative job I applied for in April. I immediately called and set up an interview. I arrived for the interview and the Associate Dean was thirty minutes late. This did not bode well. He told me that his assistant failed to put me on his calendar and he offered the job to someone else, an internal candidate. He said he did not know if she would accept, so if I wanted to go through with the interview just in case. I said I had nothing to lose, so I interviewed with him and the Dean. Both went very well. In a few days, he called to offer me the position, Assistant Dean of Evening and Weekend Programs.

## THE ADELPHI YEARS (1984–2000)

The Adelphi years proved to be productive and stressful while setting the tone of a career in which I attempted to balance teaching, producing scholarship and holding administrative positions.

Although I was hired to oversee Evening and Weekend Programs, in my first year I was asked to develop a new General Studies Program for underprepared students.

Given my dissertation, it was a natural connection, and, based on my findings, I argued that it be a one-year not two-year program. We set up what we called an honors program for underprepared students, one that was rigorous and was satisfied with higher attrition rates in the first year and higher retention rates thereafter. We began in Fall 1985 with 150 students and the program proved to be very successful and still exists. This began my career in building and running academic programs.

Although I enjoyed running the General Studies Program, I missed being a faculty member. I had been teaching one course per semester in the School of Education and in Spring 1986 the Dean of the School of Education asked me to become an Assistant Professor. The transfer was approved by the Provost and in Fall 1986 I had become a tenure track faculty member. The Dean asked (told) me to become Director of Clinical Practice, an administrative position with six credits release time to oversee student field work and student teaching with the help of a graduate assistant.

Over the years, I had administrative responsibilities for most of my career at Adelphi, including Director of Secondary Education (1987–1991), Chair of the Department of Elementary and Secondary Education (1991–1996) and Dean of the School of Education (1996–1998). These years coincided with the presidency of Peter Diamandopoulos, thirteen years of tumultuous academic leadership. A protégé of John Silber at Boston University, Dimo (as he was called) had the same conflictual leadership style. He wanted Adelphi, a respectable commuter campus, to become the Wesleyan of Long Island, an elite, residential campus. He battled with faculty over curriculum, standards for tenure, shared governance, and the union (AAUP) became his chief adversary. In the mid-1990s he was among the highest paid college presidents and the union formed the Committee to Save Adelphi, which raised money, hired a private detective, and successfully lobbied the New York State Board of Regents to investigate the financial proceedings of the President and Trustees. In 1987, after public hearings, the Board removed eighteen of nineteen Trustees for financial malfeasance and appointed a new Board of Trustees, which immediately dismissed the President. One of the important pieces of data was that in 1985, when Diamandopoulos started, Adelphi had 8,500 full-time equivalent students. In 1997 it had 3,500. The dismissals represented a truly remarkable accomplishment, whereby a group of faculty managed to take down a Board and President. It also represents the necessity of tenure, as without it these faculty surely would have been fired.

My scholarly accomplishments during the Adelphi years were limited by my significant administrative responsibilities. Nonetheless, I published a number of important pieces, including *Exploring Education: An Introduction to the Foundations of Education* (1994) (with Peter Cookson and Susan Semel), the first of four editions of this textbook; *"Schools of Tomorrow," Schools of Today: What Happened to Progressive Education* (1999) (with Susan Semel), American Education Studies (AESA) Critics Choice Award; *Knowledge and Pedagogy: The Sociology of Basil Bernstein* (1995), AESA Critics Choice Award; and "Basil Bernstein's Theory of Pedagogic Practice: A Structuralist Approach," American Sociological Association Willard Waller Award. The latter two pieces established my reputation as the leading

Bernsteinian sociologist in the United States and one of the leading internationally as well. *"Schools of Tomorrow," Schools of Today* established our reputations as leading scholars of progressive education.

The Adelphi years came to define my academic career, one that tried to balance significant administrative responsibilities with the ability to publish. Given the constraints, I did little original research, but rather wrote textbooks and edited collections. The other thing that would continue to define my administrative career is that I did not and would continue not to have capacity for the programs that I ran. When I was Dean, I also served as chair of the Department of Elementary and Secondary Education, a department that went from over twenty to seven.

I knew it was time to step down as Dean in 1997, when I was in the dentist's office having a root control at 8:30 in the morning and I looked at my watch and said to myself that I hoped it would take a long time. The stress of running a below capacity school, even after Diamandopoulos left proved too much. After a semester sabbatical, I came back to just teach for the first time since coming to Adelphi. I taught my courses, wrote and became an avid fan of the women's basketball team. Two years later, Rutgers University-Newark recruited me to become the chair of its education department, to succeed Jean Anyon. I had to make a decision between the comfort of Adelphi and a new challenge. I chose to go to Rutgers.

## THE RUTGERS YEARS (2000–PRESENT)

Rutgers-Newark proved to have its own challenges. On the positive side, it was a part of a large research university, which made it easier to get grants. On the negative side, I was brought in to run two newly merged and underfunded departments, the former Department of Education, the teacher education program, and the Department of Academic Foundations, which provided mathematics and writing courses for underprepared students. Given my background in both areas, I seemed the logical choice for the position. It became clear to me that the two programs did not mesh well and I asked the Dean to separate them. I did not understand the history of Academic Foundations, which was founded after the Black Student Organization takeover of Conklin Hall in 1969 in an effort to increase black enrollment. Many on the campus saw my proposal to move Academic Foundations into the English and Mathematics Department as racist. Given my commitment to the students in these courses I believed that they would be better served in a new configuration. After heated debates, the Dean called for an external team visit. Although it took a number of years to resolve the issue, eventually my proposal was implemented and the department consisted of the teacher education program and the new joint Ph.D. program I designed. The Urban Systems Program was a joint program with New Jersey Institute of Technology (NJIT) and University Medical and Dental of New Jersey (UMDNJ) (now Rutgers Biomedical Health Sciences-RBHS), with NJIT doing the urban environment track, UMDNJ, the urban health track, and Rutgers University-Newark the urban education track. After three years of running an underfunded department the stress again got to be too much so I resigned as chair and after a semester sabbatical came back to run the Ph.D. program and to work with Paul Tractenberg as Associate Director of his Institute on Education Law and Policy (IELP).

I met Paul in my first semester at Rutgers and was greatly impressed. He was well known in New Jersey and nationally as the founder of the Education Law Center, which won the *Abbott v. Burke* school finance decisions. I worked on IELP's first major report on state takeover of local school districts, which got significant coverage. Eventually, IELP became part of the new School of Public Affairs and Administration, so I received a half time appointment there. Over the next decade we wrote over a dozen research reports. In 2007, Newark School Superintendent Clifford Janey asked our Chancellor, Steven Diner, to set up the research center modeled on the Consortium for Chicago School Research. This resulted in the Newark Schools Research Collaborative (NSRC), which I co-directed. For the next eight years, we existed on small grants and some larger grants from the Ford Foundation. We wrote a number of major reports on education in Newark and Elizabeth, but struggled to keep afloat, especially after Ford Foundation funding ended. We also became frustrated by the education reform battles in Newark between Superintendent Cami Anderson and some members of the community, which eventually led to her resignation. We could not get Cami to work with us or to give us data, which eventually led us to move our operation to Elizabeth, New Jersey. When we did this, we renamed ourselves the Rutgers University Newark Education Research Collaborative.

In 2007, my mother died at the age of seventy-nine after a quick illness. As an only child I had to handle everything myself, including cleaning out her apartment and selling it. It was again a very stressful time, combined with the difficulty of mourning.

In 2009, I received the Chancellor's Award for Applied Research for my applied research on Newark. It represented recognition of the type of research I believed in, which hopefully would have an impact on the schools and social justice. It also represented recognition of my work with the community and Chancellor Diner's commitment to applied research, particularly on Newark. The same year, I was turned down by a faculty committee for my application for Distinguished Research Professor. The rationale was I did not have sufficient refereed journal articles and that my research reports did not count for much. The Chancellor then decided to nominate me for the Board of Governors Distinguished Service Professor, which I received in 2010. This major university wide honor recognized my applied research and work with the community. In my acceptance speech I stated that the award honored my mother and the distinguished service she had done, as well as her being my role model.

Lack of capacity continued to define my work. The Ph.D. program had insufficient faculty with expertise in education to chair dissertations. At one point, I chaired 13 of 18 committees and served on them all. One year, I chaired five committees. I continually argued for hiring more faculty, but the Dean of Arts and Sciences chose, instead, to reorganize the program away from its emphasis on education. In 2015, I resigned from running the program as I did not want to be in charge of changing it. I am very proud of the mentoring I did with my students who completed their dissertations, most of whom have gone on to academic careers, either in teaching or administration, with two remaining in executive positions in non-profits. I believe I had a profound impact on their academic development and careers.

During my years at Rutgers I continued to publish a number of different types of scholarship. In addition to applied research reports, I published refereed journal articles, book chapters, and books. In 2002, *Founding Mothers and Others: Women Educational Leaders During the Progressive Era* (with Susan Semel) won a AESA Critics Choice Award. Along with *"Schools of Tomorrow," Schools of Today*, this book cemented our reputation as experts on the history and sociology of progressive education. I published three editions of *Sociology of Education: A Critical Reader* (the third with Ryan Coughlan), with its introductory chapter establishing me as a leading expert in the sociology of education. I published (with Cookson and Semel) the second, third and fourth editions of *Exploring Education: An Introduction to the Foundations of Education*, a second edition of *"Schools of Tomorrow," Schools of Today* (with Semel and Coughlan) and a major edited collection on No Child Left Behind (with Bohrnstedt, O'Day and Borman). As a whole, my publications established me as a national expert in the sociology of education, the social foundations of education, the history and sociology of progressive education and urban education.

During my Rutgers years I became involved in a number of international networks. Just before I started at Rutgers, I attended the first Basil Bernstein International Symposium, consisting of Bernstein scholars from around the world in Lisbon. Bernstein was seriously ill and could not attend, but participated electronically. This symposium continues to meet every two years at various locations all over the world. I organized the 2004 meeting at Rutgers, which was highly successful.

At the end of the Lisbon meeting, Susan and I went to London to visit Basil. Since 1987, when he came to Adelphi to give a lecutre, Basil and I had become close friends. Susan and I would visit him and his wife Marion whenever we were in London. This, we knew, we would be our last visit with him. In September, Basil died of throat cancer.

In January 2001, I was invited by Geoff Whitty, the Director of the Institute of Education at the University of London to be the second speaker, after him at Basil's Memorial. I was honored to be asked to speak with so many other distinguished professors in the audience. The Memorial was a success and I think my remarks captured both the work and the man.

Susan and I also became involved with ISCHE (International Standing Committee of the History of Education). In 2008, we hosted the annual meeting at Rutgers-Newark, with 185 attendees. According to those in attendance, the meeting was a success. We co-edited the issue of *Pedagogica Historica* with selected papers from the conference and our introduction argued for the importance of sociological history and historical sociology.

## CONCLUDING THEMES

*Tensions between Faculty and Administration and Applied and Pure Research*

From 1984–2015, I spent only two years as just a faculty member, having served in some administrative capacity. The time spent on administration has significantly cut into time for original research, but the satisfaction of building and running programs like the General Studies Program at Adelphi and the Urban Systems Program at Rutgers has made up for this.

Having spent over a decade running research centers has been an important part of my career, although writing research reports has not been recognized as much as they should be. Nonetheless, applied research on the city where your university is located is an important role for faculty in what we call an anchor institution.

*Lack of Capacity*

I often say I wish I could have run something with the capacity to make things work well. At both Adelphi and Rutgers the programs I ran were seriously under-resourced and forced me to work far more than was healthy. Five times during these years the stress resulted in depression and in some cases the need to resign from positions (Dean at Adelphi; Chair at Rutgers).

*Holocaust Memories and Memories of Depression*

My life and career have been affected greatly by my parents' lives. My mother spent her adult life doing good in the civic arena, while my father spent his adult life in and out of mental hospitals suffering from depression. The choices I made to run programs and to conduct applied civic research were always influenced by my mother's life. My father was an early proponent of a biochemical explanation of depression and he believed it was genetic. Unfortunately, he may have been right as since 1997, I have suffered five cycles of depression. These have made me better understand my father's suffering and the effects his illness has had on me. When he was alive, I was angry at him for his inability to function. Now I forgive him and understand how difficult depression is.

## LOOKING BACK: MAJOR CONTRIBUTIONS

Looking back at my career, here are what I see as my major contributions:

- *A leading Bernsteinian scholar.*
  I have been a part of an international group of Bernstein scholars and have been recognized as one of the leading Bernstein scholars in the United States. As Basil's friend, it is gratifying to be part of a group that has followed his lead in testing his theories empirically and advancing his research project.

- *Author and editor of leading textbooks in social foundations and the sociology of education.*
  I have been a leading textbook author and editor in social foundations (*Exploring Education*- four editions) and the sociology of education (*Sociology of Education: A Critical Reader*- three editions). Although these publications often don't count for much at research universities such as Rutgers, I am proud of the impact I have in classrooms nationwide.

- *With Susan Semel writing and editing important articles and books on the history and sociology of progressive education.*
  "Schools of Tomorrow" (two editions) and *Founding Mothers* established us as experts on the history and sociology of education. These books represented the first time someone had provided edited collections on numerous progressive schools and female founders.

- *Building programs such as the General Studies and Urban Systems Programs*
  Building programs has been a hallmark of my career and both the General Studies Program and Urban Systems Program have had mostly positive effects on their students. General Studies still exists at Adelphi 30 years later. Although Urban Systems has changed, it continues to exist at Rutgers thirteen years later.

- *Applied research centers: Institute for Education Law and Policy (IELP) and Newark Schools Research Collaborative (NSRC)*
  I devoted a good part of my time from 2000 onward to these research centers. Paul Tractenberg and I wrote or oversaw over a dozen reports all of which were committed to educational equity and social justice. Although my promotion committee did not believe these types of applied research reports counted for much, I believe they were important and worthy of an academic's time and effort.

## CONCLUSION

Looking back, my academic career has been greatly influenced by my parents' experiences. From my mother, I learned a sense of social justice and civic engagement. This resulted in my focus on building programs aimed in some way at increasing access or researching urban educational inequalities. It also had an effect on my working in applied research centers to help improve urban education. The title I hold, Board of Governors Distinguished Service Professor, represents my accomplishments in these types of activities, a title my mother would surely be proud of.

## MY FAVORITE TEXTST BY OTHERS

Alexander, K., Entwisle, D. and Olson, L. (2014). T*he Long Shadow of Work: Family Background, Disadvantaged Urban Youth, and the Transition to Adulthood.* Russell Sage Foundation.

Baker, D. (2014). *The schooled society: The educational transformation of global culture.* Stanford, CA: Stanford University Press.

Bernstein, B. (1977). *Class, codes, and control* (Vol. 3). London: Routledge & Kegan Paul. (Original work published 1975.)

Bernstein, B. (1990). *Class, codes and control: Vol. 4: The structuring of pedagogic discourse.* London: Routledge.

Bowles, S., & Gintis, H. (1976). *Schooling in capitalist America.* New York: Basic Books.

Collins, R. (1978). *The credential society.* New York: Academic Press.

Lareau, A. (2004). *Unequal childhoods: Class, race and family life.* Berkeley: University of California Press.

## MY FAVORITE PERSONAL TEXTS

Semel, S.F., Sadovnik, A.R., and Coughlan, R. (eds.) (2016). *"Schools of Tomorrow", "Schools of Today": Progressive Education in the 21st Century.* New York: Peter Lang Publishers.

Semel, S.F. and Sadovnik, A.R. (eds.) (1999). *"Schools of Tomorrow," Schools of Today: What Happened to Progressive Education.* New York: Peter Lang Publishers. 2000 American Educational Studies Association Critics Choice Award

Semel, S.F. and Sadovnik, A.R. (2008) The Contemporary Small School Movement: Lessons from the History of Progressive Education. *Teachers College Record* Volume 110( 9):1774-1771.

Sadovnik, A. R., Cookson, P. W., Jr., & Semel, S. F. (2013). *Exploring education: An introduction to the foundations of education.* New York: Routledge (Fourth edition).

Sadovnik, A.R. and Semel, S.F. (eds.) (2002) *Founding Mothers and Others: Women Educational Leaders During the Progressive Era.* Palgrave Macmillan. 2002 American Educational Studies Association Critics Choice Award

Sadovnik, A. R. (1991). Basil Bernstein's theory of pedagogic practice: A structuralist approach. *Sociology of Education*, 64 (1), 48–63. Willard Waller Award from the Sociology of Education Section, American Sociological Association for the best article in the Sociology of Education, 1990-1992.

Sadovnik, A.R. (2011). Waiting for School Reform: Charter Schools as the Latest Imperfect Panacea. *Teachers College Record*, Date Published: March 17, 2011 http://www.tcrecord.org, ID Number: 16370.

## REFERENCES

Sadovnik, A. R. (1991). Basil Bernstein's theory of pedagogic practice: A structuralist approach. *Sociology of Education, 64*(1), 48–63.

Sadovnik, A. R. (1995). (Ed.). *Knowledge and pedagogy: The sociology of Basil Bernstein.* Norwood, NJ: Ablex Publishing Corporation.

Sadovnik, A. R. (2007). *Sociology of education: A critical reader* (1st ed.). New York, NY: Routledge.

Sadovnik, A. R. (2011). *Sociology of education: A critical reader* (2nd ed.). New York, NY: Routledge

Sadovnik, A. R., & Coughlan, R. W. (2015). *Sociology of education: A critical reader* (3rd ed.). New York, NY: Routledge.

Sadovnik, A. R., & Semel, S. F. (Eds.). (2002). *Founding mothers and others: Women educational leaders during the progressive era.* New York, NY: Palgrave Macmillan.

Sadovnik, A. R., Cookson, Jr., P. W., & Semel, S. F. (1994). *Exploring education: An introduction to the foundations of education* (1st ed.). Needham, MA: Allyn and Bacon.

Sadovnik, A. R., Cookson, Jr., P. W., & Semel, S. F. (2002). *Exploring education: An introduction to the foundations of education* (2nd ed.). Needham, MA: Allyn and Bacon.

Sadovnik, A. R., Cookson, Jr., P. W., & Semel, S. F. (2006). *Exploring education: An introduction to the foundations of education* (3rd ed.). Needham, MA: Allyn and Bacon.

Sadovnik, A. R., Cookson, Jr., P. W., & Semel, S. F. (2013). *Exploring education: An introduction to the foundations of education* (4th ed.). New York, NY: Routledge.

A. R. SADOVNIK

Semel, S. F., & Sadovnik, A. R. (Eds.). (1999). *"Schools of tomorrow," schools of today: What happened to progressive education.* New York, NY: Peter Lang Publishers.
Semel, S. F., Sadovnik, A. R., & Coughlan, R. W. (Eds.). (2016). *"Schools of tomorrow," Schools of today: Progressive education in the 21st century.* New York, NY: Peter Lang Publishers.

*Alan R. Sadovnik*
*Rutgers University*
*Newark*

BARBARA SCHNEIDER

# 15. BEGINNING A JOURNEY AND CHOOSING A PATH

### AN AWAKENING PASSION

Why sociology? Why education? Neither of these seemed remote career interests for an aspiring artist who planned on attending art school after high school graduation; but life events can easily alter dreams, plans, and ultimately, occupational pathways. When in high school, I became critically ill and was hospitalized. At the time, there was a shortage of hospital rooms for young people, the consequence of the final years of the polio epidemic. As a result, I spent six weeks on a public assistance welfare ward, the only white child among a dozen or so African American children suffering from the untreated sickness associated with poverty and abuse. Many of the children had terrible burns from flimsy, highly combustible wooden substandard housing units that were later replaced by the concrete hornet cubicles of Chicago's infamous projects. Growing up in a middle class home on the segregated North side, it was my first real up-close experience with social and economic inequality—a rarely discussed subject in my high school history or literature classes. The lives of the children of the ward, who I lived with that cold, bleak winter in Chicago, became one of the most poignant haunting memories of my adolescent years.

Deservedly, my parents, who had concerns regarding my health and the improbability of an economically viable career as an artist, insisted that I attend a local university, and only agreed to pay my college tuition for a teaching degree. Paint brushes and watercolors discarded, three years later I received my undergraduate degree from National Lewis University, got married, had two children, and eventually found myself working as a teacher in the "worst schools in the country," the Chicago public schools. At that time, popularized books and television programs portraying the "inner city" school experience were a mere shadow of the reality of the life then (and unfortunately now some thirty years later in many urban cities) where bullets flew in playgrounds over the heads of elementary students and human and social resources were scarce and woefully inadequate. While the day-to-day experiences of teaching were rewarding, I believed that additional education would provide me with a deeper understanding of what reforms, especially in teacher education, could reduce social inequalities and how such changes should be implemented.

Idealistically committed to transforming the educational system for poor and minority children, I entered the Ph.D. program at Northwestern University becoming a graduate student in a new interdisciplinary doctoral program, where more than two-thirds of the courses had to be taken in the social sciences including political science, psychology, and sociology. I soon realized that my passion was first and foremost about learning why schools could not do a better job at educating all children, how much of the differences in educational attainment and occupational choices were the function of society, family, and personal characteristics including "luck," and how emerging analytic methods were advancing the measurement of differences and relationships between individuals and the institutional context in which they lived. I could not change the education system if I did not understand what forces were making it unequal and ineffective for particular groups of individuals—especially low income and minority students. Reading the work of James Coleman and Christopher Jencks, in addition to learning first hand at Northwestern from Robert Boruch, Donald Campbell, and Thomas Cook about how to determine which interventions were actually creating a "true" effect, my thoughts of becoming a teacher educator were soon replaced by a strong desire to learn more about how relationships, power, authority, roles, responsibilities, and moral imperatives affect human behavior and shape the institutional systems they inhabit.

Undaunted by my own inadequacies, I stepped into the academic world as an assistant professor and Director of a Deans' Network, an association of the most competitive schools and colleges of education in the U.S. which had been organized to reform doctoral training in education. Sociable when most academics were not, a woman when most were men, I found myself in my early thirties being fast-tracked into an administrative career. An associate dean for research, at thirty-five, it became apparent that this career path was leading me astray from what I truly enjoyed most. I was passionate about studying problems, especially those related to educational inequities, challenging conventional assumptions about perceived opportunities, analyzing data, and rethinking how results could and should influence education practice and policy. I regrouped, cut my losses, and took an unusual career path, beginning an eight-year collaboration with James S. Coleman, at the University of Chicago, whose gracious tutelage shaped my intellectual interests and analytic approach into a bona fide sociologist.

One of the key messages that Jim taught me, which was in many ways a "Colemanesque" variation on a theme underscored by one of his intellectual mentors, Robert Merton at Columbia University, was the value and importance of working on sociological problems at the mid-level or micro level. Post-modern societal institutions (including the family), its members, and their relationships with one another, are in a state of change both behaviorally and structurally. Studying the actions of individuals and their subjective orientations (including values, attitudes, and personal well-being) provides the basis for the development of testable assumptions verified through iterations of a continued cyclical feedback loop. At the mid-level, it is preferable to construct a set of assumptions, that when tested, provide the evidence that can lead to eventual theoretical development. This emphasis on mid-level theory, which relies on empirical evidence, spurred my research into what and how to obtain information on objective and subjective behaviors and measures. It was the possibility that high quality evidence could be used to explain social phenomena that motivated my interest and research studies in exploring new ideas for data collection and analytic methods that measured a true effect and others that approximated causal inference.

### SOCIAL CAPITAL AND THE STUDY OF RELATIONSHIPS

When I arrived at the University of Chicago, Coleman was deeply involved in refining his ideas on behavior in social systems including trust, interest, and control for his seminal book, *Foundations of Social Theory* (1990). Not an easy read, but with well-designed conceptual arguments, compelling examples, and mathematical notations, I place this book at the top of my three "must" reads for those in sociology and sociology of education in particular. Part II, "Structures of Action," has been very instrumental in my research on the formation of norms and the role of sanctions for improving education achievement—which I have continued today (Schneider, 2000; Saw, Chen, Schneider, & Frank, 2014). In Chapter 10 of the Foundation book, "The Demand for Effective Norms," Coleman articulates norms as actions, purposively generated, and imposed through overt or informal sanctions. Developed conjointly between families and their children or through other social systems including those deliberately created for the public good, Coleman argues that the study of norms is fundamentally an examination of *social actions* and the *power structures* and *sanctions* that enforce them. The creation and enforcement of norms are the exchange or currency of social capital—relational ties that facilitate actions that lead to productive outcomes. Identifying norms as the consequence of actions, control, and interests within social systems has been extremely useful for me in constructing conceptual and measurement models for isolating conditions that operate as impediments to educational opportunities for poor and minority children, gender equality in school, home, and the workplace, and school effectiveness.

One of the first projects Jim and I collaborated on was a grant from the National Science Foundation and the National Center for Education Statistics, designed to differentiate social capital in the family from social capital in the community. It was assumed that social capital in the community operated differently from social capital in the family, which affected the type, implementation, and effectiveness of various policies. Whereas policies of schools or school districts are more likely to directly affect and monitor social capital in the community, affecting norms, actions, and sanctions in the home are much more difficult. Collaborating with an impressive group of graduate students, we produced the book *Children, Their Parents and Schools* (1993), with chapters by Chandra Muller, David Kerbow, Seh-Ahn Lee, Annette Bernhardt, and Kathryn Schiller. This book examined the actions parents take with their children at home, in school, and in the community that help improve school performance, recognizing that not all parents have the same resources or opportunities to act on the educational expectations they have for their children. Our work was an analysis of different types of families, including two parent families, single parent families, mothers who worked for pay as well as "stay at home moms," families with substantial economic and social resources and families whose resources were quite limited, and finally, families that held high educational expectations for their children and some who did not. Additionally, not one to give up on examining the consequences of school choice, Coleman was concerned if children are better off purely as the result of having the free choice of school or if school choice merely affords differential advantages to those children already advantaged socially and economically by race and ethnicity.

Hardly a ripple, this book took its place quietly among the academic stacks, certainly a major change from Coleman's last book, *Public and Private High Schools: The Impact of Communities* (1987). One explanation is that for those familiar with Coleman's work, it was déjà vu from his 1966 study, *Equality of Educational Opportunity* (1966), where the biggest variation in academic performance was associated with household resources. There is a back story to this book, which is: sometimes you have the right message for the wrong times. Essentially what we found from examining literally hundreds of forms of parent involvement at home, in the school, and in the community, is that the most important relationship between children's achievement and parent involvement were the expectations and actions that parents engaged in when at home. This was consistent across all families regardless of social and economic resources and other characteristics such as race and ethnicity (see chapter by Muller). The National Education Longitudinal Study of 1988 base year data surveyed students, their parents, teachers, and school administrators. The sampled students also took an achievement test. Results consistently showed that parent involvement programs, and parent interactions with the schools, were having little impact on students' performance. Despite a very careful and systematic analysis of parent involvement in schools, the federal government took this report and for all practical purposes filed it among the "Cold Cases." At the time, there were several federal initiatives to encourage parent involvement in the schools and these findings emphasized the value of involvement at home.

One feature of parent involvement is choice of school for their children. NELS:88 and its subsequent follow-up study gave us an unprecedented opportunity to examine where parents *planned* for their children to attend and the type of high school they eventually enrolled in , including private independent schools, religious schools, public magnets, and other open or admission schools. In the last chapter of *Children, Their Parents and Schools,* we undertook an analysis to examine the difference in potential responses to school choice. We found that African American and Hispanic parents, though quite disadvantaged economically, showed a strong positive response to public schools of choice, and in the instance of Hispanics, their preferred choice was private schools. Asian American parents showed a special affinity for private schools and in educational investments outside of school. In households where parents held the lowest educational attainment, they were least likely to respond to choice either in the private or public sector.

A year later we received a data file that showed where students actually went to high school and we conducted a new analysis to confirm our initial findings. One of the major findings of that analysis was the school choice pattern of a student's eighth grade classmates was a significant predictor of high school choice. If the majority of one's classmates were planning on attending a public school of choice, then a student was more likely to report expecting to and subsequently attended a public school of choice. The compositional contextual pattern of the classroom—or said another way, if the behavioral norm was choice, then the student was more likely to replicate the behavior of his or her classmates. Douglas Lauen, in studying school choice, reported a similar finding in Chicago (Lauen, 2007).

The overriding importance of the peer classroom effect, regardless of social and economic resources, became a key part of my work today. If one could get a greater proportion of a graduating senior class to attend college, especially a four-year institution, one could expect that there would be externalities that would accrue to the other students, perhaps changing their behaviors. The strength of the contextual position of the student is a concept that two of the then graduate students on our project, Kenneth Frank and Chandra Muller, have built upon by developing a more elegant and nuanced conceptual and methodological analysis of the compositional effects of classmates on student educational outcomes. They have used the classroom context to predict behaviors—in their case achievement and postsecondary attendance (Frank et al., 2008; Frank et al., 2014). One point, which sometimes gets ignored in understanding the influence of classmates, is how instrumental parents are in this process, as my colleague Shira Offer and I (2007) showed by examining middle-class families and their reasons for selecting particular places to live and their explanations for interacting with their children's friends and their parents. Strategic in their choices, middle-class parents maximize their housing choices to facilitate the composition of their children's social networks and work to maintain them by interacting with the parents of their children's friends.

A few more observations and opportunities that resulted from my time with Jim are important to mention. Unfortunately, Jim became very ill at the time we received the follow-up to the NELS:88 study while we were in the middle of advancing some of the ideas from the first book. The second book, *Redesigning American Education* (1997) had a graduate team that included Steven Plank, Kathryn Schiller, Roger Shouse, Huayin Wang, and Seh-Ahn Lee. In the second chapter of this book, Jim articulated several principles for improving the educational system. I have often thought there were many ideas in this book that reflect on today's emphasis on increasing student achievement by establishing external standards evaluating schools, teachers, and student academic performance over time, but rewarding not sanctioning students, teachers, and schools for achievement gains. Where Coleman's ideas and today's reform goals differed widely were around practices for teacher evaluation. Instead of viewing the teacher as the evaluator of performance and blaming her for the lack of acceptable performance of her students, Coleman envisioned the role of the teacher as a coach whose focus is on instructional quality to help her students succeed. Tracing back to the discussion of norms, we argue in the book that by building strong social ties among teacher and students that work toward a set of common performance goals, rather than negotiating from one's self interests, student performance would improve. The emphasis was on establishing a collective social system where students, their parents, and teachers, all worked toward a common goal: student performance. Most recently I took up these issues again, and called upon sociologists to become more involved in the debates on teacher value-added evaluations, by stressing the importance of context for creating norms and moving toward a more holistic form of measuring school accountability (Schneider, 2011).

In writing an essay such as this, one rummages through old memos and letters, and I came upon several that Jim wrote to me. There were several methodological points he continually made and I suspect that is how I came to blend my graduate training in randomized control trials with measuring causal inference with observational data. One key point stressed the importance of triangulation, approaching a problem from a number of different vantage points with different methods. Second, in conducting policy work, one needs to be more certain about results than in discipline research, more methodologically sound, and more careful. Third, if policy research is to be effective, it must aim to answer causal questions—even though they are hard to answer but sit at the center of policy disputes. And perhaps the last, which I hear over and over again: be certain of your results, and state them unequivocally without hiding behind caveats; what you need to say to one's critics is "prove me wrong." The parent involvement and redesign book fundamentally changed how I thought about policy questions and how I investigated them, and thus began the struggle of being willing to stick one's neck out—a lesson I followed, but the scars are quite deep—research, if it is to be meaningful, will not please everyone.

The reflections on collaborators are always colored by memory and I am as guilty of that as the next person. Coleman remains somewhat a controversial figure but my recollections of working with him are that he was an intellectual giant, who was so far ahead of others on ideas; ideas that have remarkable staying power. He also read just about everything from fiction to the latest work in economics. He thoroughly enjoyed the recognition and accomplishments of his students and colleagues. I will never forget the morning he called me, exuding overwhelming joy that Gary Becker had just won the Nobel Prize in economics. Finally, he never compromised his work or ran ahead of his data—mounds of runs, re-drafts, and runs again—they came in paper then—enough to cover the long Midway that runs for a mile down the University of Chicago hundreds of times. Yes, he taught me to be confident, and a bit arrogant, but only if there was uncontestable evidence to the best of my ability to report.

## THE STUDY OF RELATIONAL TRUST AND THE SOCIAL ORGANIZATION OF SCHOOLING

Continuing my interest in social relationships, one of most enjoyable intellectual experiences was with Tony Bryk on the study of relational trust, which resulted in the book *Trust in Schools: A Core Resource for Improvement* (2002), written with Julie

Kochanek and Sharon Greenberg, two gifted University of Chicago graduate students whose knowledge of schools made our arguments come alive. With a grant from the Spencer Foundation, Tony Bryk and I, along with a team of graduate students, began to examine how local control of schools was affecting school governance and its consequences on student performance. Similar to my dissertation and subsequent research at Northwestern University, "Newcomers: Blacks in Private Schools" with the brilliant and feisty human development psychologist, Diana Slaughter, I found myself back into the throes of spending lots of time observing in elementary and middle schools. While the original trust study was about democratic control and its consequences on school organization, I quickly found myself rereading Coleman and thinking hard about social relationships, maintaining that the social actions individuals have with one another are what can change the norms in a school.

The *Trust* book was a ten-year odyssey into learning about the nature of relationships, including trust, caring, love, respect, and a number of other ideas, all of which are part of characterizing how individuals relate to one another. Coleman's interest was in identifying the properties of social capital—shared expectations, density of relational ties, family intergenerational closure, and trustworthiness. But the question of how trust is formed remained elusive. Working on the nature of what trust is, how it is formed, and what effect it can have, I went back to some seminal work in sociology, primarily Weber (1947) and others; which is how we came upon the idea of differentiating forms of trust from organic, contractual and finally relational trust, what each of these forms of trust entailed, and how they affected behaviors. Our conception of relational trust has the intellectual footprints of Blau (1986) and others in organizational behavior (Kramer & Tyler, 1996) as we tried to dig deeper into the quality of relationships, including the vulnerabilities and discernments individuals make when meeting and judging the intentionality of others. One of the major lessons of the *Trust* book was that if social relations are the glue for norms that change actions and interests, the quality of those relationships needs to be examined but with an understanding of the potential mechanisms that could alter behaviors and self-interests in a specific social system, which in our case, was the school.

One of Tony's interests that are apparent in his book, *Catholic Schools and the Common Good* (1993), is his belief in the moral imperative of behavior to change individual actions. Tony's notion of the moral imperative is one that I have crafted in my research on families and schools when arguing for taking actions in the interests of the public good. I have underscored this theme on numerous occasions especially when arguing for the need for workplace flexibility, which if we continue to ignore, places undue hardships on families, their interactions with their children, and their relationship with co-workers (Christensen & Schneider, 2010; Schneider & Waite, 2005). Acting on behalf of the public interest is a good we need more of in education. In defining our conception of the properties of relational trust which include respect, integrity, competence, and finally putting the interests of children first—it was this last property that seemed to me the most critical and relevant aspect of trust. To act on behalf of our children suggests something of a "calling" that once was used to characterize physicians, clergy, and teachers (Lortie, 1975). If our education system is to make a difference, we need to put the students' well-being at the center, and with every new policy or reform that comes along, the question must be asked and answered affirmatively, "Is this really in the interests of the students and their lives today and in their futures?"

## FORMING EDUCATION EXPECTATIONS AND CAREERS

The third major study I worked on at the University of Chicago was the Alfred. P. Sloan Study on Youth and Social Development (SSYSD), funded by the Alfred P. Sloan Foundation. The team for this work included Charles Bidwell, Mihaly Csikszentmihalyi, Larry Hedges, and myself. In applying for this initial grant, none of us expected to win. While we were experts in sociology, methodology, human development, and statistics, we were not experts in the field of vocational education—had not developed a career interest inventory and were economists interested in labor market issues. But as luck, and of course we believed creativity would have it, we won a very competitive grant process and endured the hard oral exam by the Foundation, to undertake from my perspective one of the most unique studies of young people and how they form ideas about their future lives including their education goals, career aspirations, and romantic relationships. Coleman opened my mind to a flood of ideas on social relationships. Csikszentmihalyi directed my interests to the quality of life experiences by measuring not only the social actions among individuals, but the social and emotional learning individuals experience on a daily basis. Csikszentmihalyi is another one of those once-in-a-lifetime mentors whose perspectives on research and understanding of human behavior is unparalleled. Creator of flow, that universal experience we all feel when so involved in something, it feels as if time has flown by, which is described in *Flow: The Psychology of Optimal Experience* (1990), which is my second top book choice. Thinking about flow, which is one of those universal emotions experienced by people all over the world, one comes to appreciate the creative genius of Csikszentmihalyi that has brought us this idea through careful systematic measurement on people engaged in multiple experiences throughout the world.

One of the key instruments of the Sloan study was the Experience Sampling Method (ESM) developed by Mihaly and colleagues, a form of time diary that measures what individuals are doing and feeling throughout the course of their daily lives (Csikszentimihalyi & Csikszentimihalyi, 1988; Csikszentimihalyi & Larson, 1984). Csikszentmihalyi's influence on my research interests and productivity were and continue to be profoundly generative. When involved in conducting original fieldwork, I continue to use the ESM, as I did in the 500 Family Study, in my newest work on engagement with a set of international colleagues in Finland, and in new work with the 1992 Sloan study respondents.

Why the ESM? How people spend their time, who they spend it with, and how they feel about it provides a window into human behavior that cannot easily be reconstructed with one-time surveys or videography. While researchers and the media loved the idea of "flow," acceptance of the ESM has been a much rockier path, at least for me. Having to justify burden, missing data, and precision of estimates has been one of those Colemansque intellectual battles—some of which I lost quite resoundingly. But like most stories, there are sometimes good endings. At a science meeting a few years ago, I asked if anyone in the audience was a developer, as I was trying to move the ESM into a smartphone platform. And this man, Robert Evans, came up to me, said he works at Google, and proceeded to show me "Paco" on his smartphone. Paco is his application with all the ESM categories on it where the item stems can be answered right on the phone and immediately uploaded to a web-based platform. This initial conversation has led to a wonderful collaboration with Bob, who is an engineer (probably a latent social psychologist with a sociological mother) who values the social emotional creative side of human behavior and how to measure it. Today, I have smartphone studies where we can download data in weeks instead of the good part of a year, use the web-based platform to give teachers data on their instruction, and send text messages as nudges or boosters to measure the validity of our treatments in other quasi experiment studies.

What Coleman and Csikszentmihalyi both have in common is the idea that social capital is the accumulation of capital for productive ends; similar to the idea that being "in flow" is mastering a positive purposive activity. For me, the idea of the ESM allows for the development and measurement of optimal learning moments without laboratory and MRI examinations. It can be measured when individuals are in their normal daily environments and extracted multiple times throughout the day over the course of a week. This type of data is perhaps one of the most robust indicators for operationalizing and measuring moments when students, or for that matter, adults at work, are reporting feeling engaged and primed to learn and their average feelings of interest, skill, and challenge are above their daily average.

We used the ESM in our study of how young people form ideas about work and in our study of working families. In both instances we learned new things and reaffirmed others. We found for the most part, students often felt bored at school, especially when teachers lectured—which was most of the time. They felt challenged when taking tests, and found working collaboratively with others as interesting and enjoyable. Students who had aspirations in line with their goals tended to pay closer attention in classes that led to college attendance, whereas students who were unable to differentiate their activities as either work, play or neither, had ill-defined ambitions and rarely reported feeling engaged in or out of school. For the most part their life experiences were relatively passive and they were primed to participate in activities that were high risk and undesirable.

One of the major spin offs from the SSYSD work was *The Ambitious Generation: America's Teenagers Motivated but Directionless* (1999) with my colleague David Stevenson. Using longitudinal data from the SSYSD original field work, and reanalyses of several national longitudinal data sets, we found that young people, irrespective of their social and economic circumstances, race, and ethnicity all expected to attend college. However, it was clear that while they had high ambitions, their actions were not aligned with their expectations. They expected to become physicians, but disliked their science classes intensely and assumed enrolling in the local community college would lead them to medical school – sometimes skipping college altogether. *The Ambitious Generation* underscored several important theoretical and methodological aspects of my work. It was a study of students in their context, the context of their communities, their schools, their peer groups, and their families. Young people's expectations and career formation was not the consequence of a predominant socioeconomic profile, but the convergence of a variety of social and economic resources, social capital and individual predilections that were reinforced through contacts young people had with their familial relations and significant others.

Second, the family and school community social and economic resources were so varied among rural, urban, and suburban areas. In the case of rural communities, the interest in college was predominately in the local community college and students viewed this choice of college as real college. In the urban areas, especially those that were severely disadvantaged, the students who were able to survive in school looked more closely to students in more advantaged schools; however, their numbers were a fraction of those in suburban schools and their first college choice was often the local community college. In the classrooms, high school teachers in suburban schools with above average college enrollment rates gave helpful hints throughout the year about what to learn and what was likely to be on college entrance exams; they discussed college essays and timelines; and they encouraged getting tutorial help if students were having problems learning something very important in class. College talk was everywhere: from peer group discussions at the lunchroom tables, to the athletic recruiters for both girls and boys whose comings and goings were carefully monitored by the students, their coaches, and parents.

David and I saw the ravages of inequality around college enrollment nearly fifteen years before it became the watch word and focus of the higher education and economic research community. It was at one point a bit discouraging to find the ideas that one thought were original become reinvented, reconstructed, and presented as new—but that was simply naïve and immature on my part. The better news was that the college enrollment story was and continues to be a major issue that needs further attention.

## THE COLLEGE AMBITION PROGRAM AND TRYING TO MAKE A DIFFERENCE

After finishing *The Ambitious Generation*, changing institutions, and arriving at Michigan State University (MSU), I set my mind on trying to change college enrollment patterns, building on the normative social action theories of Coleman. As I have indicated in several other places, this proved to be difficult, but with support from the National Science Foundation, we were eventually able to put in place the College Ambition Program (CAP), a quasi-intervention designed to increase the college enrollment rates in schools with lower than average college enrollment rates. CAP is now in thirteen high schools, five of which are in Detroit, and we are working with a number of partners and using a variety of resources to help young people make better college selections given their interests, skills, and economic constraints. Our success has been positive but relatively small compared to others. However, after spending a bit more time looking closely at the effect sizes of other interventions, we have learned several things that need to be underscored.

As David and I found in *The Ambitious Generation*, and tracing back to the choice work Katy and I conducted with Coleman, individuals do not make college choices within a vacuum. Where one decides to attend college depends in part on the decisions and actions of those around you. If you are a high performing student in a high performing high school, follow up letters and information to parents becomes another piece of information, but not independent of messages that have already been circulating in the school and peer groups. If all your friends are planning on attending the local community college, trying to get a student to consider alternatives can be difficult. Social and demographic cultural factors are also at work: immigrants and females are more likely to enroll in college irrespective of their high school—the nationwide data on this suggests that such young women are merely acting as their demographic profiles indicate for the nation as a whole.

Finally, the most problematic are the students, who when measured with Csikszentmihalyi items, report their daily lives as a relatively uneventful nondescript excursion into a state of "nothingness" where their choices of where to go and how to mobilize their resources and those of others is pretty much an unlikely event. For young people to be committed to and follow through on their ambitions, they need to have sustained interest, skills, and be confronted with intellectual challenges. This is the work that has now captured my intellectual passion: Can we change the motivation of individuals who are numb to their education classroom experiences into believing and exercising choice and dedication to their learning?

## STAYING THE RESEARCH COURSE

There are many people who have made significant contributions to my research career. I have had the opportunity to collaborate with Marta Tienda, who had an office next to mine at NORC at the University of Chicago, and we worked on several different projects together from adolescent work to the education experiences of Hispanics in the U.S. Marta is another researcher whose dedication to her ideas is all consuming, engaging in numerous analyses, committed to the never ending revision process, and a moral imperative to make a difference in the lives of all people and Hispanics in particular. Her passion and focus is and has been on the public good, which is evident in her work and those of her outstanding graduate students.

Another major collaborator and true friend of mine is Larry Hedges, that consummate statistician, who I also can count on to tell me, "that is or isn't very good." It is hard to find someone who is a friend and who is also willing to say something is "not so good." And the reality is, if Larry thinks it is "not so good," it most likely is pretty terrible. Larry is always willing to help and is my collaborator on multiple projects—advising me on new methods to improve my designs, analyses, and interpretations. I never stop learning from him, and even took classes from him when a full professor to refresh my knowledge on randomized control trials. I am in awe of his amazing statistical skills, standards for quality research, and the open positive way of telling you when you are right or dead wrong. Whether visiting him on a Sunday or catching him after a meeting in a quiet conference room, you can find him sitting with his pencil, writing out a set of equations to a new problem, or solution to an existing one.

Jacquline Eccles is a new collaborator, as is Richard Settersten, both social psychologists interested in human development. They have kept my interest in understanding the lives of young people as they develop through the challenging years of their twenties and thirties. At MSU, I have had the joyous opportunity to work with Kenneth Frank, learning more about what I don't know statistically every time we meet. The American Educational Research Association brought me into close contact with Mark Berends, and he has become another of my rich collaborators as we undertake one new project after another.

And finally, there are the students, whose accomplishments as researchers enrich every day of my life. Chandra Muller was a brilliant graduate student, and not surprisingly, has embarked on a career that has brought new ideas and methods to the study of social contexts. Jennifer Schmidt, Julie Kochanek, Venessa Kessler, and Nathan Jones are all pursuing work that makes a difference, and they are willing to stand up for what they believe the evidence supports. And a special thank you to all the people who supported me in my work: Kathleen Christensen and Hirsch Cohen from the Alfred P. Sloan Foundation, and Janice Earle, Edith Gummer, Barry Sloan, and Larry Suter at the National Science Foundation. Yes it takes a village, and especially today a wide network of scholars from multiple disciplines to accelerate and sustain a researchers' career—thank you all and the many others I somehow have failed to acknowledge.

## MY FAVORITE TEXTS BY OTHERS

In the text, I recommended my two favorite books by others. The third book that I highly recommend is, *Time, Love, Memory: A Great Biologist and His Quest for the Origins of Behavior* by Jonathan Wiener, which chronicles how Seymour Benzer transformed the field of behavioral genetics. It is a masterful illustration of creative elegant scientific experiments with groups of fruit flies that tied DNA with human behavior. Swarms of flies being observed in multiple situations reminds us of how the challenges and tenacity of scientific discovery can often be found in small incidences of behavior repeatedly studied over time.

## REFERENCES

Bryk, A. S., & Schneider, B. L. (2002). *Trust in schools: A core resource for improvement.* New York, NY: Russell Sage Foundation.

Bryk, A. S., Lee, V. E., & Holland, P. B. (1993). *Catholic schools and the common good.* Cambridge, MA: Harvard University Press.

Christensen, K., & Schneider, B. L. (2010). *Workplace flexibility: Realigning 20th-century jobs for a 21st-century workforce.* Ithaca, NY: ILR Press.

Coleman, J. S. (1990). *Foundations of social theory.* Cambridge, MA: Belknap Press of Harvard University Press.

Coleman, J. S., & Hoffer, T. (1987). *Public and private high schools: The impact of communities.* New York, NY: Basic Books.

Coleman, J. S., United States. Office of Education., & National Center for Education Statistics. (1966). *Equality of educational opportunity.* Washington, DC: U.S. Dept. of Health, Education, and Welfare, Office of Education; for sale by the Superintendent of Documents, U.S. Government Printing Office.

Coleman, J. S., Schneider, B. L., Plank, S., Schiller, K. S., Shouse, R. C., Wang, H., & Lee, S.-A. (1997). *Redesigning American education.* Boulder, CO: Westview Press.

Csikszentmihalyi, M. (1990). *Flow: The psychology of optimal experience* (1st ed.). New York, NY: Harper & Row.

Csikszentmihalyi, M., & Csikszentmihalyi, I. S. (1988). *Optimal experience: Psychological studies of flow in consciousness.* Cambridge: Cambridge University Press.

Frank, K. A., Muller, C., Schiller, K., Riegle-Crumb, C., Strassmann Mueller, A., Crosnoe, R., & Peason, J. (2008). The social dynamics of mathematics coursetaking in high school. *American Journal of Sociology, 113*(6), 1645–1696.

Frank, K. A., Muller, C., & Mueller, A. S. (2014). The embeddedness of adolescent friendship nominations: The formation of social capital in emergent network structures. *American Journal of Sociology, 119*(1), 215–253.

Kramer, R. M., & Tyler, T. R. (1996). *Trust in organizations: Frontiers of theory and research.* Thousand Oaks, CA: Sage Publications.

Lauen, D. (2007). Contextual explanations of school choice. *Sociology of Education, 80*(3), 179–209.

Lortie, D. C. (1975). *Schoolteacher: A sociological study.* Chicago, IL: University of Chicago Press.

Schneider, B. L. (2000). Social systems and norms: A coleman approach. In M. Hallinan (Ed.), *Handbook of educational sociology.* New York, NY: Kluwer Academic/Plenum Publishers Corporation.

Schneider, B. L., & Coleman, J. S. (1993). *Parents, their children, and schools.* Boulder, CO: Westview Press.

Schneider, B. L., & Stevenson, D. (1999). *The ambitious generation: America's teenagers, motivated but directionless.* New Haven, CT: Yale University Press.

Schneider, B. L., & Waite, L. J. (2005). *Being together, working apart: Dual-career families and the work-life balance.* Cambridge, UK: Cambridge University Press.

Weber, M., Henderson, A. M., & Parsons, T. (1947). *The theory of social and economic organization* (1st American ed.). New York, NY: Oxford University Press.

*Barbara Schneider*
*Michigan State University*

CARLOS ALBERTO TORRES

# 16. THE MAKING OF A POLITICAL SOCIOLOGIST OF EDUCATION

LIMINAR

If you scratch a theory you find a biography. (Torres, 1998b)

The primary contribution of my scholarly work in the field of sociology has been the development of a political sociology of education trying to understand how education—including schooling, universities, non-formal education, adult learning education, and popular education—contributes to social change, national and global development, and the betterment of nations, communities, families and individuals.[1]

In my research and professional practice I have tried to reconcile three fields that usually do not easily intersect, the scholarship of discovery, the scholarship of integration, and the scholarship of intervention (Boyer, 1991). I have always pursued a research agenda which studies at meta-theoretical, theoretical and empirical levels, issues and questions in the scholarship of race, class, gender, and the state in education (Torres, 2009a; Apple, in Torres, 2009a, ix).

A political sociology of education cannot be fully accomplished in the cozy environment of our offices, laboratories or libraries. It needs to be connected with action research in classrooms and with political and pedagogical struggle in the streets, and through mass media and institutions. It should relate to the work of public intellectuals, social movements, communities and unions. It must understand the desires, successes and failures of marginalized communities and people. This is, in a nutshell, the goals and responsibilities of an organic public sociology (Burawoy, cited in Torres, 2009a: xvi–xvii).

What follows is an analysis of six formative phases of my life that have significantly shaped my epistemological trajectory and research agenda in building a political sociology of education.

## THE FORMATIVE PHASE: INTELLECTUAL WORK IN THE MIDDLE OF CLASS STRUGGLE IN ARGENTINA

Numerous women arrested while pregnant have given birth in Argentine prisons, yet nobody knows the whereabouts and identity of their children who were furtively adopted or sent to an orphanage by order of the military authorities. Because they tried to change this state of things, nearly two hundred thousand men and women have died throughout the continent, and over one hundred thousand have lost their lives in three small and ill-fated countries of Central America: Nicaragua, El Salvador and Guatemala. If this had happened in the United States, the corresponding figure would be that of one million six hundred thousand violent deaths in four years. (Gabriel García Marquez)[2]

My early studies of sociology took place in Argentina during the transitional context of a dictatorship and the return to democracy in 1966–1973. This democratic experience lasted only three years (1973–76) and collapsed because of a furious class struggle with the organization of the Triple AAA (Alliance Anti-Communist Argentine), the right wing of the Peronist Movement under the government of Isabel Martinez de Perón in 1975. Political violence reached its paroxysm in another *coup d' etat* and the installation of a brutal dictatorship, known as *El Proceso de Reorganización Nacional,* on March 24, 1976. While the National Commission on the Disappearance of Persons (CONADEP, 1984) identified 8,961 persons disappeared during the dictatorship period of 1976–1983, human rights organizations estimated that more than 30,000 people were disappeared and killed, and hundreds of thousands had to exile. As I have narrated elsewhere, I was part of this exiled group when I escaped to Mexico (Torres, 2014).

The chaotic intellectual life of the early seventies in Argentina is evident it the following vignette. In 1972 a dictatorship was ruling the country. As a student of sociology in the Jesuit University of El Salvador, then one of the best schools of sociology in the country, I took a semester-long core course in the discipline, entitled Sociological Theory. The two professors in charge of the course along with their adjunct professors and teaching assistants—what is known as *la cátedra*—gave us a very elaborated and long syllabus based on Critical Theory, particularly the works of Jürgen Habermas, Max Horkheimer, Theodor W. Adorno, and Herbert Marcuse. Because I had a fellowship that paid my tuition, I was living with my parents, and teaching in a catholic school, I scrambled to pull together resources and buy all the required books.

After a month or so into the course, *la cátedra* came back and told us that given the social and political conditions of Argentina, and the shifting political-ideological debates, they had changed their theoretical position. Logically they had changed the syllabus, now focusing on Marxism and some of the key authors of the time. With my meager remaining resources, I bought two or three of the books that I thought were most important and began to read them in earnest.

Two months before the semester ended, *la cátedra* informed the students that they had changed their political and theoretical position again. They felt they were now part of the *Cátedras Nacionales*, an amalgam of the Peronist Left, national-popular movements of national liberation, and a critical reading of neo-Marxism (Argumedo, 2011). I could not buy the third set of books. My budget was exhausted.

Despite this chaotic episode and the violent environment of a civil society and state in crisis, my work as a teaching assistant for the brilliant Jesuit sociologist and political philosopher, Dr. César Sánchez Airzcorbe, allowed me to be well educated in social theory and political philosophy. My learning of Hegel, Weber, Marx, Habermas, and Marcuse served me well to understand the work of Paulo Freire which I was studying at the same time that I tried to build a commune and later a rural school linked to Theology of Liberation. In the social and political context of the country, this communitarian project drastically failed and three friends who were going to join our commune were disappeared and assassinated on October 1975 for practicing literacy training in the slums.

Speaking epistemologically, I learned that science and ideology intersect constantly, and there is no neutrality or objectivity per se. Nonetheless, conducting rigorous scholarship implies the struggle and anguish for objectivity and truthfulness, which requires making normative and analytical distinctions in our scholarship. In understanding the connections between education and power, I learned the importance of the classics of political science, philosophy and sociology, which have guided a great deal of my studies in the political sociology of education. While I am aware that the "classics" of political philosophy reflect primarily male, European, and heterosexual views, thus making it impossible to uncritically accept them as a cultural canon, I do contend that properly deconstructed and analyzed with a nuanced historical sense they continue to be an invaluable source for thinking and praxis.

In Argentina at the time there were ebullient post-colonialist traditions, including a fascinating debate about the true nature of science and authentic thinking, and against what many scientists criticizing the role of positivism as a dominant paradigm called scientificism. This is a debate far from over, and certainly crucial in the field of education. This culture of science or scientificism, separates culture from knowledge, dissociating also power from human interest. In education, science seems then narrowly defined as a mixture of positivism and instrumentalism and defended on the grounds of statistical rigor and objectivity.

Yet there is a need for a method, for a particular epistemological approach to science that endorses the postcolonial ethics in education. I learned the indispensable need to have, in addition to empirical studies, a historical and structural meta-theoretical and theoretical analysis of educational policy and practice. This is one of the few antidotes to the growing technocratization of educational studies or the simplistic pragmatism so rampant in educational environments, especially in the United States (Torres, 2009a; Dale 1983).

In addition to criticizing scientificism, I learned the importance of democracy with all its limitations. I grew up participating in intellectual debates in Argentina and Latin America where democracy was dismissed out of hand while the utopias of the sixties and seventies struggled to achieve a socialist society. In the chaotic and violent context that resulted from confrontations in Argentina I learned the importance of democratic frameworks for governance. I said two decades later

"Democracy is a messy system, but it has survived because there is a sphere for debates and a set of rules that people follow even if they don't benefit from them" (Torres, 1998a, p. 259).

There cannot be a democratic society without a democratic state. I learned the importance of the state structures when I saw the complete fragmentation of state institutions, and the obliteration of legal frameworks and the Argentine Constitution by the new authoritarianism of the seventies (Collier, 1980; O'Donnell, 1988). Theories of the state constitute the backbone of any political sociology of education.

The Argentine period includes my study of the work of Paulo Freire. In my critical work on Freire's political philosophy of education, I learned about the political nature of education (Torres Novoa, 1979a, 1979b, 1980, 1981). A few years later, in my first systematic reading of Gramsci, I became convinced that Freire's intuition dovetailing the Gramscian work about the political nature of education is correct. Gramsci proposed a suggestive hypothesis: Education, as part of the state, is fundamentally a process of formation towards 'social conformism'. Educational systems and schools in particular, appear as privileged instruments for the socialization of a hegemonic culture. This is one of the key premises for my work in the political sociology of education.

Finishing my first book on Paulo Freire in 1976 led me to a surprising conversation with Freire's editor at the time, Julio Barreiro, who was also going to publish my book.

This conversation made me realize that if I remained in Argentina after the coup d'etat, my life and that of my family would be in peril. This realization prompted me to exile in Mexico in October 1976. My then wife soon followed me with our three children in December 1976 (Torres, 2014).

Because Freire discussed the intrinsic relationships between cultural diversity, citizenship, and democracy, he tried to link these three principles in the interaction between politics and education, but not always with success. I expanded on his work, incorporating insights from Freire and many other progressive political philosophers, advancing a political philosophical proposal to link education, democracy and citizenship in the construction of a radical democratic multicultural citizenship in the global era (Torres, 1998a).

A second substantive contribution of Paulo Freire was to relate popular education with popular culture in Latin America. However, considering the multiple challenges we face in the new millennium, we need a more complex model. It is imperative to relate democratic education with multiculturalism and citizenship in the digital culture era with hybrid cultures coexisting in the contexts of multiple globalizations. In terms of the politics of culture and education, there is an urgency to unpack and criticize the principles of neoliberalism's new common sense in education (Torres, 2011, 2013a). At his untimely death, Freire was trying to articulate his criticism to liberal multiculturalism with his caustic critique to neoliberalism—what he called the "new demon of the world today" (Torres, 2014: xxv)—and with the promise of eco-pedagogy (Gadotti, 2000; Torres, 2014; Misiaszek, 2011, 2012, 2014).

Freire speaks of the 'politicity of education.' A great intuitive idea of the intrinsic nature of politics and education but lacks specifications in his work requiring theoretical mediations and practical political-pedagogical applications to be implemented. Having identified these 'silences' in Freire's oeuvre, I decided to work towards a political sociology of education focusing on the dialectic of the global and the local (Arnove, Torres, & Frantz, 2013).

The rich political and intellectual traditions of Latin America and Iberoamerica allowed me to learn the foundations of the political essay, exploring theoretical and historical-structural sources and the power of narratives. Little did I know that I would eventually blend this Latin American epistemological training with my learning of social sciences in the United States and Canada, and its emphasis on empirical work, making me a scholar of two rather distinct intellectual worlds.

Finally, with Marx's analysis as an emblematic premise, I began to explore the possibilities as well as the limits of problem-posing education. I have always taken very seriously Marx's dictum in the introduction to the Grundrisse when he taught us that:

*The concrete is concrete because it is the concentration of many determinations, hence unity of the diverse. It appears in the process of thinking, therefore, as a process of concentration, as a result, not as a point of departure, even though it is the point of departure in reality and hence also the point of departure for observation [Anschauung] and conception.*[3]

## SECOND PHASE: EXILED IN MEXICO

We have not had a moment's rest… The country that could be formed of all the exiles and forced emigrants of Latin America would have a population larger than that of Norway. (Gabriel García Marquez)[4]

Mexico, a country with a distinctive tradition of hosting political exiles, was the Mecca of literature and social sciences in Latin America in the mid-seventies. Enjoying the oil boom of the time, anybody who was somebody in social sciences and education in the world was invited to give lectures, teaching or conducting research in Mexico. The centerfold of this learning was debates between diverse factions of Marxism trying to establish its analytical superiority and political guidance over the rest. The reading of Antonio Gramsci was the most profitable intellectual exercise of the time, while I concluded my first set of books on Paulo Freire, published in Portuguese in Brazil and in Spanish in Mexico and in Spain (Torres Novoa, 1979a, 1979b, 1980).

When I finished by master's degree in political science at FLACSO I could not return to Argentina still ruled by a ruthless dictatorship. I worked for the Mexican Federal Government as one of the founding professors of the Universidad Pedagógica Nacional, a state university resulting from an agreement between the Teachers Union and the Secretariat of Public Education. Then I worked at the

General Education for Adult Education in the Secretariat of Public Education and from there I went to Stanford University in California to obtain a master's degree and Ph.D. in International Development Education. This first Mexican period as a graduate student and public servant, and the next experience of working as a university professor at FLACSO in Mexico (1984–86) after returning from Stanford, marked my initial attempts to develop a political sociology of education based on theories of the state and the analysis of educational policies as compensatory legitimation.

A focus on the state is important because the nature of educational change is related to the nature of the state. The *state* can be defined as the totality of the political authority in a given society. In Latin America, political authority implies the capacity to impose a course of action by means of a decision-making process in societies that are highly heterogeneous and characterized by very contradictory interests. While the state represents the basic pact of domination that exists between social classes or factions of the dominant classes and the norms that guarantee its domination over the subordinate groups, at the same time the state is a self-regulating administrative system, an organization that produces a system of selective and self-regulating rules.

The basic tenet of my analysis is that the nature of educational change is related to the nature of the state, more so in Latin America. Years ago I argued that "defining the 'real' problems of education and the most appropriate (e.g. cost-effective, ethically acceptable, and legitimate) solutions depends greatly on the theories of the state that underpin, justify, and guide the educational diagnoses and the proposed solutions" (Torres, 1995: 255). Thus, the transformation in the nature of the state (e.g. the emergence of the neoliberal state) and its implications for comparative analysis of education is very relevant. Otherwise we may not be able to understand the relationships between the state and public policy formation and the implications of adult education for development, particularly in the "conditioned states" located in the periphery of the capitalist world system (Carnoy & Levin, 1985; Carnoy & Torres, 1990; Torres, 1989, 1991)

Studies on the state and adult education policies and practices led me to understand the nature of theories of compensatory legitimation. I have used the notion of compensatory legitimation to refer to the need of the state to cope with a deficit of legitimacy in the overall system. This crisis of legitimation has several sources. One of the most important is the disparity between growing social demands on welfare policies and diminishing fiscal revenues to meet those demands. To confront the crisis of legitimation, the state calls upon scientific and technical knowledge and expertise, increasing policies of participation, and legalization of educational policies with a growing role for the judicial system in education. Therefore, education as compensatory legitimation implies that the state may use educational policies as a substitute for political rights and for increased material consumption, while, simultaneously, creating a system of legitimacy beliefs, which will assure the loyalty of its citizens.

Understanding the relationships between education and power constitutes the Gordian knot of educational research. It was during my Mexican period that fully planted the seeds for a political sociology of education. I began to understand the complexities associated with social theory, epistemology, and public policy in its multiple dimensions. It seems paradoxical but the experience of exile is a profound experience of learning. In exile I managed to navigate the complexities of public policy and education using as a backdrop of theories of the state and theories of legitimation (Torres, 2014: 21–23). I completely concur with Freire's conclusion about his experience of exile: "One thing I also learned in exile, maybe the best thing I ever learned, is that I could not continue being sure of my certainty" (Torres, 1994: 25).

## THIRD PHASE: FROM THE LABYRINTHS OF SOLITUDE TO STANFORD UNIVERSITY.

Poets and beggars, musicians and prophets, warriors and scoundrels, all creatures of that unbridled reality, we have had to ask but little of imagination, for our crucial problem has been a lack of conventional means to render our lives believable. This, my friends, is the crux of our solitude. (Gabriel García Marquez)[5]

When I arrived to San Francisco on a warm and sunny morning in July 1980 with a full fellowship to conduct graduate studies at Stanford University, I was full of excitement. It was my first trip outside Latin America, and my first voyage to the United States. In my excitement, I was not aware of the complexities of learning a new language while conducting my doctoral studies. I spoke no English—which became painfully evident to the admitting officer who was interviewing someone with a full Stanford fellowship to do graduate studies but who could not understand a single word of English, let alone speak the language. This officer probably thought that Stanford standards had declined beyond repair!

I did not yet understand the intricacies of the new system of higher education that I was going to experience as a graduate student and later as a professor. Nor was I fully prepared to understand a new culture or engage with the dynamics of diversity in the United States, a social formation besieged by its darkest shadows of slavery, patriarchy, annihilation of native populations and ruthless capitalism past; a darkest past which is not yet sponged but on the contrary is still living in its present conditions of the richest but also one of the most unequal societies on Earth. I was further uninitiated in how diversity intersects with knowledge, learning, and instruction in U.S. universities, as well as the implications for civic engagement.

Young scholars deal with the tensions between constructing a family and developing an academic career. In my case, trying to survive on a meager student fellowship, raising three children, and at the same time trying to excel academically was a serious challenge. The migratory patterns of a nomadic scholar, moving from

Argentina to Mexico, then to the USA, back to Mexico, then to Canada and back to the United States adds new layers of complexity to the role of father.

Our work as academics calls for a most serious self-reflectivity in our choices of the use of time and our ability to connect with the needs, practices and initiatives of our children. In retrospect, looking at my children, I realized that they have blossomed as very honest, productive and social justice education oriented as well as sensible human beings. Despite my perpetual doubts, asking myself if I have done a good job as a father, I feel good.

My studies at Stanford were marked by the transition between the administrations of Jimmy Carter and Ronald Reagan. Carter was the president that created the Department of Education and the Department of Energy as new cabinet level departments, and his administration was marked by the Iran hostage crisis and the perception of the decline of the USA as a world power. Reagan presided over the installation of a neoconservative administration, on parallel to that of Thatcher in UK and Mulroney in Canada, and by de facto, inaugurated a neoliberal economic model with worldwide implications (Torres, 1986, 2009a, 2009b). As Michael Apple has explained, neoconservatism and neoliberalism are two faces of the same coin deeply affecting the politics of educational reform (Apple, 2004). Shortly after graduation, I published an article entitled in Spanish *A Nation at Risk: La Educación Neoconservadora* that pioneeered analyzing the impact of neoconesrvatism on education in Latin American. It was an article much cited and discussed in the region in the immediate aftermath of the new authoritarianism.

This period of my studies allowed me to learn English, a very important asset in any learning process in a global era. Additionally it fostered my understanding of the different epistemological foundations of educational research in the Anglo-Saxon tradition, heavily influenced by positivism. Reading a number of scholars mostly published in English such as Michael Apple, Henry Giroux, Roger Dale, Jean Anyon, Martin Carnoy, Samuel Bowles, Gloria Ladson-Billings, Herbert Gintis, Maxine Green, Henry Levin, Joel Samoff, Geoff Whitty, and others, who are pioneers in building critical studies in education linked with the tradition of the New Left or American social liberalism, opened a new intellectual horizon for my political sociology of education. In the nineties, I decided to study the germane period of this social critique in education editing a book of dialogues with some of these scholars (Torres, 1998b). The Stanford period also allowed me to study the emerging model of neoliberalism that came to radically transform educational policies worldwide for the next two decades.

While at Stanford I listened to a presentation by John Meyer and read some of the work about a new theory of globalization he was developing, what is now known as 'new institutionalist theory' (Meyer, 1977; Meyer & Rowan, 1977). This approach did not capture my imagination because I was never convinced that their political economy framework of analysis was robust enough to account for the workings of capitalism as a mode of production. Neither was clear that in the gestation of a global culture, how performance rituals of institutions become globalized, and how neoliberalism became consolidated worldwide, particularly in bilateral and multilateral organizations. Their thirst for data to be obtained through large global databases to document their claims seemed too brittle to me. Most of these databases do not fully represent the transformation of cultures worldwide or even the regional or national civic cultures and institutional practices.

I left Stanford as a freshly minted Ph.D. in November 1983 to conduct teaching and research in Mexico (1984–86) and Canada (1986–1990), returning to California in March 1990 as an Assistant Professor at UCLA. In those years I read a formidable essay review on the political sociology of education by Roger Dale (1983), which put the kind of work I wanted to do in clear international and comparative perspective.

## THE FOURTH PHASE: THE CANADIAN PERIOD. COMPARATIVE STUDIES IN ADULT EDUCATION, AND WORKING AS AN ADVISER TO FREIRE AS PUBLIC ADMINISTRATOR IN SÃO PAULO, BRAZIL

It is only natural that they insist on measuring us with the yardstick that they use for themselves, forgetting that the ravages of life are not the same for all, and that the quest of our own identity is just as arduous and bloody for us as it was for them. The interpretation of our reality through patterns not our own, serves only to make us ever more unknown, ever less free, ever more solitary. Venerable Europe would perhaps be more perceptive if it tried to see us in its own past. (Gabriel García Marquez)[6]

In 1986, a decade after I arrived as a graduate student exiled from Argentina, I left Mexico having accepted a Fulbright Fellowship to work at a now-defunct World College West in Petaluma, California, of one of the few liberal arts utopias of learning and conviviality I have ever experienced. After World College West, I move to Canada to work as a Killam Post-Doctoral Fellow at the University of Alberta, Edmonton Alberta.

As a postdoctoral scholar, I wrote a proposal to study adult education through a comparative perspective that was generously funded by the International Development Research Centre (IDRC), a Canadian Crown corporation. This study conducted empirical research in adult learning education in Canada, Mexico and Tanzania. The University of Alberta was a place that allowed me to get to know and work with two of my students who developed into the best and the brightest that the Freirean tradition has to offer, Dr. Daniel Schugurensky, from Argentina but exiled in Mexico when I met him, and Dr. Peter Mayo, from the University of Malta. The University of Alberta was also the place I met one of my dear friends and co-author, Ray Morrow, with whom I undertook a thorough review of educational sociology resulting in several articles and two books. One book revisited the traditions of social theory and educational reproduction theories (Morrow & Torres, 1995) and another book produced a comparative study of reading Freire and Habermas (Morrow & Torres, 2002). Critical Theorist Raymond Morrow has been an extraordinary intellectual partner, friend, collaborator, and teacher to me.

In this period I finished the first version of a political sociology of nonformal education (Torres, 1990). I revisited this study two decades later producing a new book on a political sociology of adult education (Torres, 2013b). Through my studies in this field, I became disenchanted with adult learning education and the possibilities of social change given the conditions of the established structures both in the developed world and the industrially advanced societies. The main book that resulted from this period (Torres, 1990), showed the importance of adult education as a means to franchise large populations and bring them closer to the networks of the state while virtually providing no support whatsoever to their fundamental needs. When adult education is conceived as compensatory legitimation, the only alternative is to pursue a new model in the context of revolutionary societies. Our empirical research with Daniel Schugurensky on adult education policy development in countries as diverse as Canada, Nicaragua, Mexico, and Tanzania shows the different and alternative rationales-in-use embedded in adult education policy formation. Looking beyond compensatory legitimation I conducted research looking at the Grenadian experience and Nicaraguan experience, but also remembering Cuba's educational campaign (Schugurensky & Torres, 1994; Torres, 1996).

A second key finding emerging from my studies showed that bureaucratic rationality would always predominate unless there is a revolutionary transformation altering behavior, routines, rules, regulations, and laws. We identified six rationales for policy making. These rationales may take the form of constitutional prescriptions, investment in human capital, political socialization, compensatory legitimation, international pressures, and social movements. We concluded that despite the rhetoric, the dominant logic among policy makers in adult education is instrumental rationality, and the dominant *weltanschauung* in adult education policy planning is technocratic thinking. Discussing the notion of instrumental rationality as developed by Weber—that is, the rule of impersonal economic forces and bureaucratic administration—we have documented how the ideology of the welfare state has resulted in a de-politicization of policy makers' views regarding the social world.

Through a comparison of state-sponsored programs, and an analysis of opinions, aspirations, and expectations of policy makers, teachers, and adult learners, we identified with Daniel Schugurensky three different models of adult education policy: a "therapeutical model" in Canada, a "recruitment model" in Mexico, and a "forced modernization" model in Tanzania.

The three models show common traits that are surprising considering the diversity of living conditions, state structures, and political philosophies in each society. First, all three models are non-participative, where social and political issues and questions that may bring conflict into the operation of adult education services are ignored or perceived exclusively as problems that may be fixed through technical measures. Second, in all three societies, adult education is a clear instrument of the state contributing to capital accumulation and political legitimation practices, neglecting any emancipatory practices that may empower learners or communities.

Third, in all three models, literacy training is irrelevant and marginal, isolated from productive work and skill upgrading programs. Fourth, in the absence of participatory organizational structures and practices, a top- down decision-making system prevails. Despite the operation of three different models of adult education oriented by fairly different political and philosophical values, in all of them there are few opportunities for the learners or community to participate in policy making. Fifth, teachers generally have no training in adult education. In Canada, highly professional teachers trained to work with children and youth have a patronizing and paternalistic attitude regarding adult learners. In Mexico and Tanzania, paraprofessional and poorly trained teachers present high rates of job turnover and absenteeism, which in turn lead to high student dropout rates. Last, there is evidence that in Canada, Mexico, and Tanzania, adult education programs are organized in a two-track system: a more prestigious one that focuses on programs for upgrading skills, and a marginal one that emphasizes basic education and literacy training for adults (Torres, 1989b, 1991c, 1996 1998c; Torres & Schugurensky, 1993). A third and very important learning that I began to explore was the implications of this bureaucratic rationality at the global level, considering the presence of international and bilateral organizations, such as the World Bank.

The critique to neoliberalism began to intensify in Latin America in the eighties, a period particularly engaging in Brazil with the creation of the Workers Party. Paulo Freire as one of his founders jointly with the charismatic union leader and later president of Brazil, Luiz Inácio (Lula) da Silva, were part of the new dynamism that emerged in the re-democratization of the country culminating in the experience of the last 25 years of Latin American education, culture, politics and economics that have seen the implementation and failure of neoliberalism, challenged by new models of governance with the democratic election of social-democratic governments in the region.

It was my participation as adviser to Paulo Freire during his tenure as Secretary of Education in the City of São Paulo (1989–1991) that created a bias for hope. The way in which some of the premises of radical education, linked to other approaches, particularly Lev Vigotstky's human development psychology changed the way São Paulo's municipal system of education worked was quite encouraging. Freire's experience as public administrator in São Paulo linked schooling and participatory democracy in the midst of learning and teaching in bureaucratic institutions with the presence of social movements in a partnership with popular and democratic administrations (Gadotti & Torres, 1994; Freire, Gadotti, & Torres, 2005; Torres & Gadotti, 2003; Jones, 2009).

The design of a new social compact, a partnership between state and social movements, new models of school governance, teachers training and a new interdisciplinary curriculum based on generative themes offered new perspectives impacting the lives of the people, particularly those who have been marginalized (O'Cadiz, Torres, & Wong, 1998).

## THE FIFTH PHASE: UCLA

> Solidarity with our dreams will not make us feel less alone, as long as it is not translated into concrete acts of legitimate support for all the peoples that assume the illusion of having a life of their own in the distribution of the world. (Gabriel García Marquez)[7]

When I arrived to UCLA in 1990, the Graduate School of Education was a highly technocratic school, dominated by American pragmatist tradition, rational choice theories, with the neo-positivist paradigm and the empiricism underscoring a great deal of the research and policy making in the Anglo-Saxon academy. It was not a very interesting place beyond the dominance of educational psychology as the 'ruling class' in schools of education throughout the United States, or beyond GSE's research methods division. It was not a multicultural school either.

A vignette will document my perplexity inserting myself in such a scenario. Less than a year after arriving, I thought I should apply for tenure. I had sufficient material for tenure and I was actually hired below my level. I went to speak with the Chair of the Department who hired me and had been extremely supportive. I will never forget the reply of the Chair when I announced that I was planning to apply for tenure to Associate Professor. The Chair said something like this: "Carlos, we hired you because you bring the big picture to our school, but the big picture will not give you tenure. What will give you tenure at UCLA is to work on a well-defined evidence-based empirical research with a sophisticated methodology. When you feel that you are ready, come back to talk to me."

When I left the Chair's office I concluded that this was either the wrong advice or the wrong institution. I filed my papers for promotion and I got promoted immediately. The faculty thought that I should not only be promoted to Associate Professor with tenure, but I should be accelerated to Professor II, leaving me within range of my next promotion with acceleration to Full Professor which took place in 1994.

In 1995 I received an Endowed Chair and Deanship offer in another university. UCLA vigorously counter-offered, and I became Director of the Latin American Center, a very prestigious Organized Research Unit of the University of California. The next 10 years (1995–2005) working as Director of the Latin American Center intensified my studies in Latin American Education and comparative education. I also became President of the Comparative International Education Society (CIES) in 1997.

These professional commitments did not slow down my work in the political sociology of education. I finished the book with Morrow (Morrow & Torres, 1995), and my book *Education, Democracy and Multiculturalism, Dilemmas of Citizenship in a Global World* (1998a), which was translated into several languages. This text discusses the intricate relationships among theories of citizenship, theories of democracy and theories of multiculturalism in the context of the growing presence of globalization.

Among the key findings of this decade was that there is a natural interlocking of the political sociology of education with comparative and international education, more so with the globalization processes that affect our lives. In this period, I edited with Robert Arnove a book, now in its fourth edition, that became a standard text in comparative education throughout the world (Arnove, Torres, & Frantz, 2013). Additionally, I edited a book with Rob Rhoads (2006) that has been quite influential in the debates about higher education and neoliberalism in the Americas.

In my CIES presidential address (Torres, 1998c: 421–447; 1998a) I argued that we are confronting a serious theoretical and political problem. The questions of citizenship, democracy, and multiculturalism are at the heart of the discussion worldwide on educational reform, deeply affecting the academic discourse and the practice of comparative and international education. Cloaked in different robes, questions about citizenship, the connections between education and democracy, or the problem of multiculturalism affect most of the decisions that we face in dealing with the challenges of contemporary education.

The dilemmas of citizenship in a democratic diverse multicultural society can be outlined, at the beginning of my analysis, as follows: Theories of citizenship had been advanced in the tradition of Western political theory by white, heterosexual males who identified a homogeneous citizenship through a process of systematic exclusion rather than inclusion in the polity. That is, women, identifiable social groups (e.g., Jews, Gypsies), working-class people, and members of specific ethnic and racial groups—in short, people of color—and individuals lacking certain attributes or skills (i.e., literacy or numeracy abilities) were in principle excluded from the definition of citizens in numerous societies.

Theories of democracy, while effective in identifying the sources of democratic power, participation, and representation in legitimate political democratic systems, had been unable to prevent the systemic exclusion of large segments of the citizenry. Thus, formal democracy drastically differs from substantive democracy.

Theories of multiculturalism, while effective in discussing the politics of culture and identity and the differential sources of solidarity across and within specific forms of identity, had been unable or unwilling to embrace a theory of citizenship and a theory of democracy that could be workable, in practical, procedural terms; ethically viable, in moral terms; and politically feasible in the context of capitalist civil societies.

We need a theory of multicultural democratic citizenship that will take seriously the need to develop a theory of democracy that will help to ameliorate, if not eliminate altogether, the social differences, inequality, and inequity pervasive in capitalist societies. We also need a theory of democracy able to address the draconian tensions between democracy and capitalism, on the one hand, and among social, political, and economic democratic forms, on the other.

## THE SIXTH PHASE: FOUNDING THE PFI INSTITUTE AT UCLA AND THE STUDIES ON GLOBALIZATION AND NEOLIBERALISM

On a day like today, my master William Faulkner said, "I decline to accept the end of man". I would fall unworthy of standing in this place that was his, if I were not fully aware that the colossal tragedy he refused to recognize thirty-two years ago is now, for the first time since the beginning of humanity, nothing more than a simple scientific possibility. (Gabriel García Marquez)[8]

With Paulo Freire, Moacir Gadotti, myself and other colleagues, we created the first Paulo Freire Institute in São Paulo in 1991. Since then, as one of its Founding Directors, I have also assisted in the establishment of more than ten Paulo Freire Institutes around the world. These Institutes have emerged as part of a social movement. After years of conversations with many of my graduate students we decided to create the Paulo Freire Institute in Los Angeles. In this process I talked with the Dean of the school who in his business-like style told me that to create a 'named' institute at UCLA requires a large donation. Thus we decided to create the institute outside UCLA as a non-profit organization. Once we did so, I requested authorization from UCLA to be its director. By that time, there was a new Dean and a new Chair in the now renamed Graduate School of Education and Information Studies. In a very pleasant conversation, the new Dean and the Chair of the Department convinced me to bring the Paulo Freire Institute to the GSEIS at UCLA. I agreed based on the principle of mutual respect and autonomy for our work. Still registered as a private non-profit, the Institute has been working at UCLA for 12 years, conducting comparative research on global citizenship education, organizing an annual Conference of the California Association of Freirean Educators (CAFE Conference), and offering an international institute during the summer.

The focus of the last decade of my work has been on understanding multiple globalizations, the impact of neoliberalism's new common sense in culture and education, the tensions, conundrums and contradictions within the traditions of multiculturalism, and the emerging world narrative of global citizenship education. There are multiple learnings in this period, particularly the changing nature of globalization, its different faces and the possibilities of social movements (local and global) to affect social change. My work on multiculturalism and globalism is important in distinguishing the positive and negative impacts of policies in education—from affirmative action to resource distribution.

A natural outcome of this analysis is the need to move the conversation from national to global citizenship, and new models of citizenship education, currently explored by diverse institutions in the global system, particularly UNESCO. My work on Freire also seeks to provide a critique of simplistic and technocratic models of policy and practice, which tend to be blind to an understanding of history and the nuances of cultures and personalities.

Neoliberalism has been largely delegitimized given the extraordinary financial and economic crisis of 2008, but yet is still pursued by governments across the world. My work on teachers unions and social movements provides a window into a systematic critique of neoliberal policies, offering examples and new alternatives of how to reimagine education as an empowering vehicle for individuals, families and communities (Torres et al., 2013; Torres, 1998a, 1999).

I have argued that despite having utterly failed as a viable model of economic policy, neoliberalism has become the new "common sense" in shaping contemporary concepts of government and education (Torres, 2011, 2013b). I have noted the ways that neoliberalism has reorganized the modern university around the logic of economic rationalism and academic capitalism, pushing it toward market-driven policies of efficiency and accountability, accreditation and universalization, international competitiveness, and privatization. As these neoliberal reforms are being implemented and adopted, however, there are also growing resistance movements that point out the degree to which this economic rationalism limits access and opportunity along class and racial lines, as well as the degree to which it hems in the university as a viable space of critique, debate, and contestation, thus in many ways undermining the broader purpose and goals of education.

Another line of research is exploring the tensions between different models of multiculturalism. There is a fundamental distinction between a *normative* and *a constructive multiculturalism*. *Normative multiculturalism* is rooted in a rigid conception of cultures as objective, immutable, and reified. Conservatives that highlight a civilization clash have used this multiculturalism to emphasize the need to protect national cultures from the dangerous hybridization caused by incoming migrant cultures. In the public sphere, this multiculturalism entails concessions, grants, and privileges to safeguard minority cultures in various sectors (health, religion, welfare, political representation etc.), and to protect traditional languages, confessional schools, or religious habits and customs. *Constructive multiculturalism* is rooted in a mobile conception of cultures, which are never conclusively defined, but which is traceable in the private sphere and across interpersonal relationships. This multiculturalism does not aim to reorganize society on the basis of the recognition of cultural groups' rights, but seeks to establish fair rules for living together, based on cultural exchange that requires a rethinking of the notion of citizenship (Tarozzi & Torres, 2016).

## POLITICAL SOCIOLOGY OF EDUCATION TODAY

> Faced with this awesome reality that must have seemed a mere utopia through all of human time, we, the inventors of tales, who will believe anything, feel entitled to believe that it is not yet too late to engage in the creation of the opposite utopia. A new and sweeping utopia of life, where no one will be able to decide for others how they die, where love will prove true and happiness be possible, and where the races condemned to one hundred years of solitude will have, at last and forever, a second opportunity on earth. (Gabriel García Marquez)[9]

Though a political sociology of education has intimate connections with a sociology of education in the conventional sense (with questions of equity, efficiency, equality, mobility, and so on), its center of attention is an emphasis on questions of power, influence, and authority, and its goal is to explain the process of decision making and educational planning at several levels.

Using a political sociology of education with a focus on the relationships among education, power, and the state, my research agenda offers a conceptual and synthetic review of the notion of social and cultural reproduction in education and advances new directions for theoretical and empirical research in the sociology of education. Theories of social and cultural reproduction rest on the argument that schools primarily reproduce the functions required by the economic system. Thus, rather than providing a tool for changing society by reducing inequalities, schools reproduce and legitimate the social order. After a careful synthesis, analysis, and criticism of several sociological theories, including functionalism, structuralism, system theories, and Marxism, my colleagues and I have advanced an agenda for research and policy, including discussions of the interactions among class, gender, race, and social reproduction in the context of the postmodernist critique.

Raymond Morrow and I have attempted a reconstruction of theories of social and cultural reproduction in education from closed structuralist models based on economic and class determination to relatively open ones based on parallel determinations stemming from class, gender, and race. It is argued that this shift in reproduction theories took place largely within the context of critical modernist theory, even though more recently in response to postmodernist critiques. Our argument builds on a systematic criticism of social theory resting on a meta-theoretical framework, and is built on three related claims with respect to these theoretical transformations (Morrow & Torres, 1995). First, though the actual term "reproduction" has often tended to slip out of sight, we suggest that the basic problem of social and cultural reproduction remains a central preoccupation of critical theories of the relationships between schooling and society. Second, a new model, the *parallelist strategies*—social action as the product of parallel determinations of social action stemming from class, gender, and race—while highly sensitive to history, agency, and social practices, still employs structuralist methodological strategies, thus remaining within the realm of theories of social and cultural reproduction. However, the parallelist models have effectively encouraged the exploration of the independent effects of class, gender, and race, and other forms of domination in the context of schooling. Third, despite their analytical progress, the parallelist models have failed to address adequately three fundamental issues: (a) Each of these forms of domination has a significantly different systemic character with crucial consequences for their conceptualization as forms of domination; (b) the analysis of the interplay of these "variables" has been obscured by the language of "relative autonomy" left over from structuralist Marxism; and (c) even though the explanatory objectives of parallelist reproduction theory are necessarily more modest and historically contingent than envisioned by classic structuralist reproduction theories, this still involves avoidance of the postmodernist tendency to endlessly fragment and pluralize conflicts and differences as if there were no systematic links among them.

There are new and emerging perspectives in sociology. First is the emergence of the new epistemological approaches, which sharply differs from positivism and empiricism. Second, the new sociology of education is pressed to confront the dilemmas posed by the dichotomy of modernism and postmodernism, or poststructuralist forms of theoretical representation, and its implications for the scholarship of class, race, and gender. Finally, these new theoretical developments pose new risks and challenges for educational research, well-argued by the critical realism perspectives (Bhaskar, 1978; Young, 2007).

The notion of critical political sociology necessitates the study of power and relations of authority as structured in the various levels of social organization. It suggests an analytical approach concerned with the connections among religion, kinship relations, social classes, interest groups (of the most diverse type), and the political culture (ideology, value system, weltanschauung) of actors and social groups in the determination of political decisions, and in the constitution of social consensus—or, failing that, a confrontation or distancing—of actors and social classes with respect to the legitimation of public policy.

I am convinced that any study in political sociology has to consider questions of bureaucracy and rationalization, power, influence, authority, and the constitutive aspects of such social interactions (clients and political and social actors, their perceptions of the fundamental questions of political conflict, and the alternative programs that derive from these). Similarly, at the heart of any critical political sociology are the connections between civil and political society, as well as the complex interactions among individual subjects, collective subjects, and social practices.

It is useful to note that a political sociology of education is a sub-discipline, an interdisciplinary hybrid in the social sciences. Its connections with political science, anthropology (and ethnographic studies), political economy, and history are evident and require no further justification. Perhaps it is appropriate to emphasize that a political sociology of education that seeks to overcome the weaknesses of the Anglo-Saxon tradition—reflected, for example, in the classic political sociology of electoral behavior in the United States—and offer significant responses for our understanding of the formation of educational policy must be distinctly interdisciplinary, historical-structural, comparative, and macroscopic (Dale, 1983)

The research agenda of a political sociology of education includes studying the relationship between education, the state, and power; the role of schooling in social and cultural reproduction and education as a contested terrain with multiple dynamics, contradictions and controversies; the role of social theory in comprehending the nature and conflicts in contemporary education; the multiple faces of globalization and its diverse impact in the lives of teachers, schools, and educational policies; the interconnections between citizenship building, multiculturalism, and democracy both at the level of the regions and nation-states and at the global level as intended in global citizenship education, and particularly considering the new reality of our lives, growing immigration; the ways that a democratic restructuring of schooling involves engaging the dialectics of the dynamics and spheres of gender, race and ethnicity, and class in constructing cultural sensitive pedagogies that promote agency, solidarity, respect for difference, and ultimately create a more just and democratic society; and the contributions of critical studies in education to transforming education and democratizing society.

Like any research agenda, it is by definition inconclusive and unfinished because a political sociology of education will continue to confront the changing nature of the social context of schooling, and the rationalities and practices of educational policy making considering the globalization of capitalism worldwide as well as counter-hegemonic experiences.

A political sociology of education is not an easy interdisciplinary hybrid to master. It requires becoming conversant in theoretical and empirical perspectives encompassing philosophical analysis, empirical and historical research, and political and practical recommendations for reconstructing education. It requires knowledge and integration of political philosophy, social and political theory, and cultural theory with historical inquiry and empirical sociological analysis. It demands forms of representation and genres not very common or accepted in the empiricist-prone academia of the Anglo-Saxon universities.

There is a new world demanding analysis and practical actions. It seems that public education has been called upon to develop a new labor force to meet the rapidly changing economic demands, presenting policy dilemmas on issues concerning the privatization and decentralization of schools. This movement includes raising educational standards and placing stronger emphasis on testing and school accountability. Decisions based on economic changes have espoused new visions for school reform in universities as well. These reforms, associated with international competitiveness, are also known as 'competition-based reforms' (Carnoy, 1999; Torres, 2009a, 2009b).

This new normal requires keeping a serious and rigorous stocktaking on the multiple metamorphoses and reincarnations of neoliberalism, privatization, deregulation, and tax cuts for corporations and the wealthy and how that affects public educational systems. Any political sociology of education should assume that neoliberalism is an ideological obstacle to democratic educational reform, requiring a systematic criticism of the new common sense in education based on an ethos and an ethics of privatization in K-12 and institutions of higher education.

The last line of any literary or scientific work is most difficult to write. More so when I have narrated my own struggles for life, love, liberty and the pursuit of happiness. Yet I have learned with Habermas that "The thinker as lifestyle, as vision, as expressive self-portrait is no longer possible. I am not a producer of a Weltanschauung; I would really like to produce a few small truths, not the one big one" (Torres, 1992: 128).

## NOTES

1. My thanks to my colleagues Jason Dorio, Lauren I. Jones Misiaszek, Greg Misiaszek, and Guillermo Ruiz for their comments to a previous version.
2. http://www.nobelprize.org/nobel_prizes/literature/laureates/1982/marquez-lecture.html
3. http://www.marxists.org/archive/marx/works/1857/grundrisse/ch01.htm#3
4. http://www.nobelprize.org/nobel_prizes/literature/laureates/1982/marquez-lecture.html
5. http://www.nobelprize.org/nobel_prizes/literature/laureates/1982/marquez-lecture.html
6. http://www.nobelprize.org/nobel_prizes/literature/laureates/1982/marquez-lecture.html
7. http://www.nobelprize.org/nobel_prizes/literature/laureates/1982/marquez-lecture.html
8. http://www.nobelprize.org/nobel_prizes/literature/laureates/1982/marquez-lecture.html
9. http://www.nobelprize.org/nobel_prizes/literature/laureates/1982/marquez-lecture.html

## MY FAVORITE TEXTS BY OTHERS

Karl Marx, *Grundisse.*
Karl Marx, *A Contribution to the Critique of Political Economy.*
Antonio Gramsci, *Quaderni del carcere.*
Max Weber, *Economy and Society.*
Émile Durkheim, *The Elementary Forms of the ReligiousLife.*
Ernesto Cardenal, *In Cuba.*
Paulo Freire, *Pedagogy of the Oppressed.*

## MY FAVORITE PERSONAL TEXTS

Torres, Carlos Alberto. *First Freire. Early Writings in Social Justice Education.* New York, Teachers College Press, 2014. This book is 2015 recipient of the American Association for Adult and Continuing Education (AAACE) Cyril O. Houle Award for Outstanding Literature in Adult Education.

Torres, Carlos Alberto. *Globalizations and Education. Collected Essays on Class, Race, Gender, and the State.* Introduction by Michael W. Apple, Afterword by Pedro Demo. New York, and London: Teachers College Press-Columbia University, 2009. Italian translation, L' Scola, Brescia, Italy, 2014. Spanish traslation by Tirant le Blanch, Valencia, Spain.

Robert Rhoads and Carlos Alberto Torres, eds. *The University, State and Markets. The Political Economy of Globalization in the Americas.* Stanford: Stanford University Press, 2006.

Torres, C. A., and R. Morrow. *Reading Freire and Habermas.* New York: Teachers College Press-Columbia University, 2002 (translations to Valencian, 2003 and Portuguese, 2004).

Torres, C. A. *Democracy, Education, and Multiculturalism: Dilemmas of Citizenship in a Global World.* Lanham, Maryland: Rowman and Littlefield, 1998. Translated into Spanish, Portuguese, Valencian, Chinese, Armenian and Georgean; Korean and Italian translations in progress.

Torres, C. A., and R. Morrow. *Social Theory and Education: A Critique of Theories of Social and Cultural Reproduction.* Albany, New York: State University of New York Press, 1995.Portuguese translation 1999; Spanish translation, 2003; Chinese translation, 2012.

## REFERENCES

Apple, M. (2004, January–March). Creating difference: Neo-Liberalism, neo-conservatism and the politics of educational reform. *Educational Policy, 18*(1), 12–44.

Argumedo, A. (2011). *Los silencios y las voces en América Latina. Notas sobre el pensamiento nacional y popular.* Buenos Aires: Ediciones del Pensamiento Nacional. Ediciones Colihue.

Arnove, R. F., Torres, C. A., & Franz, S. (Eds.). (2013). *Comparative education: The dialectic of the global and the local.* Lanham, MD: Rowman & Littlefield Publishers.

Bhaskar, R. (1978). *A realist theory of science*. Brighton: Harvester Press.
Boyer, E. (1991). *Scholarship reconsidered: Principles of the professoriate*. Lawrenceville, NJ: Princeton University Press.
Carnoy, M. (1999). *Globalization and educational reform: What planners need to know*. Paris: UNESCO/IIEP.
Carnoy, M., & Levin, H. (1985). *Schooling and work in the democratic state*. Stanford, CA: Stanford University Press.
Carnoy, M., & Torres, C. A. (1990). Education and social transformation in Nicaragua (1979–1989). In M. Carnoy, J. Samoff, A. M. Burris, A. Jonhston, & C. A. Torres (Eds.), *Education and the social transition in the third world: China, Cuba, Tanzania, Mozambique and Nicaragua*. Princeton, NJ: Princeton University Press.
Collier, D. (1980). *The new authoritarianism in Latin America*. Princeton, NJ: Princeton University Press.
CONADEP. (1984). *Nunca Más*. Retrieved from http://www.desaparecidos.org/nuncamas/web/english/library/nevagain/nevagain_001.Htm
Dale, R. (1983). The political sociology of education. *British Journal of Sociology of Education, 4*(2), 185–202.
Freire, P., Gadotti, M., & Torres, C. A. (2005). *A educação na cidade*. São Paulo, SP: Cortez.
Gadotti, M. (2000). *Pedagogia da terra*. São Paulo, SP: Editora Fundação Peirópolis.
Gadotti, M., & Torres, C. A. (1992). *Estado y educação popular na América Latina*. Campinas, São Paulo, Brazil: Papirus.
Gadotti, M., & Torres, C. A. (Eds.). (1994). *Educação popular: Utopia latinoamericana (ensaios)*. São Paulo, Brazil: Cortez Editores and Editora da Universidade de São Paulo.
Jones, L. I. (2009). *Women's theologies, women's pedagogies: Liberating praxes of Latin American women educators in El Salvador, Nicaragua, Bolivia, and Argentina* (PhD Dissertation). University of California, Los Angeles, CA. (ProQuest # 3401751)
Meyer, J. (1977). The effects of education as an institution. *American Journal of Sociology, 83*, 55–77.
Meyer, J., & Rowan, B. (1977). Institutionalized organizations: Formal structure as myth and ceremony (with Brian Rowan). *American Journal of Sociology, 83*, 340–363.
Misiaszek, G. W. (2011). *Ecopedagogy in the age of globalization: Educators' perspectives of environmental education programs in the Americas which incorporate social justice models* (Ph.D. Dissertation). University of California, Los Angeles, CA. (Publication No. AAT 3483199)
Misiaszek, G. W. (2012). Transformative environmental education within social justice models: Lessons from comparing adult ecopedagogy within North and South America. In D. N. Aspin, J. Chapman, K. Evans, & R. Bagnall (Eds.), *Second international handbook of lifelong learning* (Vol. 26, pp. 423–440). London: Springer.
Misiaszek, G. W. (2014). Environmental education through global and local lenses: Ecopedagogy and globalizations in Appalachia, Argentina, and Brazil. In D. A. Turner & H. Yolcu (Eds.), *Neoliberal educational reforms: A critical analysis* (pp. 184–203). New York, NY: Taylor & Francis/Routledge.
Morrow, R. A., & Torres, C. A. (1995). *Social theory and education: A critique of theories of social and cultural reproduction*. Albany, NY: State University of New York Press.
Morrow, R. A., & Torres, C. A. (2002). *Reading Freire and Habermas: Critical pedagogy and transformative social change*. New York, NY: Teachers College.
O'Cadiz, P., Wong, P. L., & Torres, C. A. (1998). *Democracy and education. Paulo Freire, educational reform and social movements in Brazil*. Boulder, CO: Westview Press.
O'Donnell, G. (1987). *Bureaucratic authoritarianism: Argentina, 1966–1973, in comparative perspective*. Berkeley, CA: University of California Press.
Rhoads, R., & Torres, C. A. (Eds.). (2006). *The university, state and markets: The political economy of globalization in the Americas*. Stanford, CA: Stanford University Press.
Schugurensky, D., & Torres, C. A. (1994). Adult education and political education: Lessons from comparative, cross-national research in Cuba, Mexico, Nicaragua, and Tanzania. In B. Claussen (Ed.), *Aspects of globalization and internationalization of political education*. Hamburg, Germany: Krämer.
Tarozzi, M., & Torres, C. A. (2016). *Global citizenship education and the crises of multiculutralism: Comparative perspectives*. London: Bloomsbury.

Torres, C. A. (1984). *Educational policy formation and the Mexican corporatist state: A study of adult education policy and planning in Mexico (1970–1982)* (Ph.D. Dissertation). Stanford University, Stanford, CA.

Torres, C. A. (1986). *A nation at risk: La Educación neoconservadora* [A nation at risk: Neo-conservative education]. Caracas, Venezuela: Nueva Sociedad.

Torres, C. A. (1989). The capitalist state and public policy formation: Framework for a political sociology of educational policy making. The *British Journal of Sociology of Education, 10*(1), 81–102.

Torres, C. A. (1989a). The Mexican state and democracy: The ambiguities of corporatism. *International Journal of Politics, Culture and Society, 2*(4), 563–586.

Torres, C. A. (1989b). Political culture and state bureaucracy in Mexico: The case of adult education. *International Journal of Educational Development, 9*(1), 53–68.

Torres, C. A. (1989c). The capitalist state and public policy formation: A framework for a political sociology of educational policy-making. *The British Journal of Sociology of Education, 10*(1), 81–102.

Torres, C. A. (1990). *The politics of nonformal education in Latin America.* New York, NY: Praeger.

Torres, C. A. (1991). A political sociology of adult education: A research agenda. *Education, 4*(1), 29–34.

Torres, C. A. (1991b). State corporatism, education policies, and students' and teachers' movements in Mexico. In M. Ginsburg (Ed.), *Understanding reform in global context: Economy, ideology, and the state.* New York, NY: Garland Publishing, Inc.

Torres, C. A. (1991c). The state, nonformal education, and socialism in Cuba, Nicaragua, and Grenada. *Comparative Education Review, 35*(1), 110–130.

Torres, C. A. (1992). The state, nonformal education, and socialism in Cuba, Nicaragua, and Grenada. *Comparative Education Review, 35*(1). [Translated and published in Spanish by *Desarrollo Económico. Revista de Ciencias Sociales* 31, 31, no. 124, January-March, 1992.]

Torres, C. A. (1994). Introduction. In M. Escobar, A. Fernández, & G. Guevara Niebla (Eds.), *Paulo Freire on higher education. A dialogue at the National University of Mexico.* New York, NY: SUNY Press.

Torres, C. A. (1995). The state and education revisited: Or why educational researchers should think politically about education. *AERA, Review of Research in Education, 21,* 255–331.

Torres, C. A. (1996). *Las secretas aventuras del orden. Estado y educación.* Buenos Aires, Argentina: Miño y Dávila Editores.

Torres, C. A. (1998a). *Democracy, education, and multiculturalism: Dilemmas of citizenship in a global world.* Lanham, MD: Rowman and Littlefield.

Torres, C. A. (1998b). Democracy, education, and multiculturalism: Dilemmas of citizenship in a global world. *Comparative Education Review, 42*(4), 421–447.

Torres, C. A. (1999). Critical theory and political sociology of education: Arguments. In T. J. Popekwitz & L. Fendler (Eds.), *Critical theory in educational discourse.* New York, NY: Routledge.

Torres, C. A. (2006). *Educación y Neoliberalismo. Ensayos de Oposición.* Madrid: Ediciones Popular.

Torres, C. A. (2009a). *Globalizations and education. Collected essays on class, race, gender, and the state* (Introduction by Michael W. Apple, Afterword by Pedro Demo). New York, NY & London: Teachers College Press-Columbia University.

Torres, C. A. (2009b). *Education and neoliberal globalization* (Introduction by Pedro Noguera). New York, NY & London: Routledge.

Torres, C. A. (2011). Public universities and the neoliberal common sense: Seven iconoclastic theses. *International Studies in Sociology of Education, 21*(3), 177–197.

Torres, C. A. (2013a). Neoliberalism as a new historical bloc: A Gramscian analysis of neoliberalism's common sense in education. *International Studies in Sociology of Education, 23*(2), 80–106.

Torres, C. A. (2013b). *Political sociology of adult education.* Rotterdam, The Netherlands: Sense Publishers.

Torres, C. A. (2014). *First Freire: Early writings in social justice education.* New York, NY: Teachers College Press.

Torres, C. A., & Gadotti, M. (2003). Paulo Freire, administrador públic. In P. Freire (Ed.), *L'educació a la Ciutat. Estudi preliminar de Marina Subirats* (pp. 19–25). Valencia: Denes Editorial-Ediciones del Crec.

Torres, C. A., & Jones, G. (Eds.). (2013). New educational common sense and neoliberalism. Special Issue of the *International Studies in Sociology of Education*. (Two volumes, first volume published June 2013, volume 23, number 2; Volume 23, number 3.)

Torres, C. A., & Morrow, R. (1995). *Social theory and education: A critique of theories of social and cultural reproduction*. Albany, NY: State University of New York Press.

Torres, C. A., & Schugurensky, D. (1993). A political economy of adult education in comparative perspective: A critique of mainstream adult education models in Canada, Mexico and Tanzania. *Canadian Journal for the Study of Adult Education, 7*(1), 61–80.

Torres, C. A., Schugurensky, D., Cho, S., Kachur, J., Loyo, A., Mollis, M., Nagao, A. & Thompson, J. (2013, January). Teachers' unions, the capitalist state and the contradictions of educational reform. Special issue on education et Mondialisation, Coordination: Régis Malet et Eric Mangez, Spirale. *Revuew de Recherches en Education, 51*, 133–140.

Torres Novoa, C. A. (1979a). *Consciéncia e história: A práxis educativa de Paulo Freire*. São Paulo, Brazil: Loyola Ediçoes.

Torres Novoa, C. A. (1979b). *Diálogo com Paulo Freire*. São Paulo, Brazil: Loyola Ediçoes,

Torres Novoa, C. A. (1980). *Paulo Freire: Educación y concientización*. Salamanca, Spain: Sigueme Publishers.

Torres Novoa, C. A. (1981). *Leitura crítica de Paulo Freire*. São Paulo, Brazil: Loyola Ediçoes.

Young, M. (2007). *Bringing knowledge back in: From social constructivism to social realism in the sociology of education*. Abingdon: Routledge.

*Carlos Alberto Torres*
*University of California*
*Los Angeles*

LOIS WEIS

# 17. READING AND PRODUCING RESEARCH ACROSS BOUNDARIES THAT SO OFTEN DIVIDE

CLAIMING WHO I AM …MY STORY

My grandparents were Jewish immigrants amidst vacillating borders and boundaries that comprised Russia/Poland. Moving separately to the United States with nothing but the metaphoric clothes on their back, they met and married in the Midwest.[1] Being defined as "White" in the context of U.S. racial binaries (Brodkin-Sachs, 1998) enabled my paternal grandparents to live in neighborhoods that offered a particular kind of public education to their children. They came speaking no English and had no monetary resources. Yet both my father and his elder brother were able to attend and graduate from reputable private and public colleges respectively, and my father joined a well-known Jewish real estate firm in Milwaukee, Wisconsin.[2] The firm and his position grew with his children. By the time I attended an affluent suburban public high school, my father was General Manager of a large Commercial Division that owned and managed notable amounts of downtown commercial real estate.

The oldest of three daughters, my mother grew up in Algoma, Wisconsin, where her parents—the only Jews in a community of approximately 3,000—ran a small corner grocery and dry goods store. Moving to Milwaukee at the age of eighteen to attend secretarial school, she met and married my father. Possessing good skills and a quick mind, she was a valued employee, giving up this position only upon marriage. After raising three children, all of whom are highly educated, she pursued her own dream of furthering her education by attending the University of Wisconsin-Milwaukee.[3] Always feeling like an outsider to the well-established Milwaukee Jewish community, she made certain that I had exposure to the kinds of educational, social and cultural capitals that ultimately enabled me to move through communities with confidence.

The Civil Rights Movement, resurgence of the women's movement, and America's involvement in Vietnam changed the spirit and face of the nation, creating possibilities for some, while offering me the opportunity to build upon my past and simultaneously recreate myself. The first woman in my extended family to attend graduate school, I conducted well-funded dissertation research in Ghana, where I lived for two and a half years.[4] It is this experience—living overseas as a young woman in West Africa, at a time when graduate studies were well supported by the federal government—that, more than anything, layered on top of past biographically rooted advantages and produced who I am today. For I came to more clearly understand my structurally embedded options as a privileged U.S. citizen in global context, and the extent to which my extraordinary experiences overseas enabled me to cultivate a particular kind of understanding of the world—what I would later call "global sensibilities." I quickly learned to move deftly across a range of borders that relatively few, at the time, were crossing, a set of sensibilities and skills that fueled so much of my passion and work over the next decades, and, in large part, explain my sustained ability to "work across" methodological and theoretical borders while conducting empirical research in a range of sites, attentive always to power, privilege and fault lines of oppression.

While overseas, I met and intimately interacted with men and women of varying biography and lived experience, honing an increasingly sophisticated understanding of self in relation to "other;" produced and lived out poverty and privilege; and divergent patterns of migration and immigration, all of which would come to characterize my personal and academic trajectory. As I moved, on a daily basis, among Lebanese and other migrants who inhabited working-class, middle- and upper-level posts in the Ghanaian economy; Ghanaian and other adults across the continent who had attended elite boarding schools like Mfantsipim, Opoku Ware, and Achimota; individuals who remained connected to intellectual and political struggles for social, economic and cultural independence across the continent; members of privileged diplomatic communities from all over the world; and women and men who embodied a particular kind of poverty and privilege that laced then "third world" nations, I grew to become a very different person—one markedly de-moored from my narrowly-circumscribed roots.

Long before these particular kinds of global experiences worked to publically mark swelling numbers of "traveling" college students with a particular kind of class privilege, and even longer before the worldwide web, digital technology, and FaceTime would enable one to live simultaneously "here and there," I felt, and objectively was, at times, profoundly alone. Only the occasional blue aerogram letter punctuated my daily life, reminding me, in contradictory fashion, of my natal "home" and associated ways of understanding the world. As such sense of "home" was rapidly receding, letters simultaneously marked connection and disconnection—and it was in this liminal space that I was able to build upon all that I brought with me to the continent. Traversing a range of borders, I was pressed towards a personal and scholarly trajectory that would come to mark my life and work. Connecting over enacted and embodied difference as well as similarity, I honed a deeply felt and lived out understanding of the effects of social and economic structures, possession and dispossession, history, struggle, cultural pride, and human agency. Moving both within and across nations then known as Dahomey, Togo, Senegal, Zaire, Sierra Leone, Mauritania, Chad, Upper Volta, Nigeria, Guinea, and others, I simultaneously felt and embodied connection and disconnection. It would be years before I returned to the United States, only to return as a deeply felt stranger.

READING AND PRODUCING RESEARCH ACROSS BOUNDARIES THAT SO OFTEN DIVIDE

As I struggled to thrive in this liminal space across historically constructed and lived out difference of race, religion, ethnicity, culture, language, nation, and lived condition, I was, over time, able to intellectually and spiritually soar. Sitting alone in my tiny room in Accra, I read and re-read novels that swirled around notions of stranger, gender, race, politics, struggle, connection/disconnection and memory. I devoured Doris Lessing's *The Golden Notebook*, strongly resonating with her attempt to break certain forms of consciousness and go beyond them, while seeking refuge in and from the consequences of breakage in her written work. Despite painful periods of isolation and loneliness, I was able to grow in unimagined and unanticipated ways, setting the stage for the "self" that would ultimately stand in marked contrast to the felt young "self" that embarked upon this extraordinary journey.

Building upon and fundamentally re-imagining and re-articulating my past, present and future, it would be many years before I fully understood the relationship between this critical space of *de-mooring* and the accompanying foray into the intellectual and personal depths associated with the breaking of form. Within this space, I grew to understand the world markedly differently while gaining cultural and social capitals that enabled me to experience felt connection across deep difference. Such connection across class, race/ethnicity, lived out constraints, and nation of origin, enabled me to *hear, and more importantly perhaps, to understand,* the perspectives and choices of those very different from myself, always reflecting upon who I was and who I might be if I had comparable contextual constraints and/ or privileges. Unknown to me at the time of course, this enabled me to imagine, conceptualize and produce a particular kind of scholarly work as I moved forward in my career. Coupled with a fundamentally re-worked, or perhaps re-directed intellectual and personal self, I lived far from—and yet, in some ways so very close to—the imagination of my grandparents. Significantly, both my then departed grandmothers visited me as I slept during the week I defended my dissertation. They let me know that their suffering had been worth it. They told me how very proud they were of me—their granddaughter—who accomplished far more than they ever could have imagined possible.[5]

## AMIDST THE STARK ACADEMIC CONTEXT...

Jump-starting a genre of important future research and policy, James Coleman published *Equality of Educational Opportunity* in 1966. Commonly known as the Coleman Report (Marjoribanks, 1985), faculty and graduate students continued to pore over and assess this report by the time I entered graduate school. In this highly influential study, Coleman and his colleagues investigate the linkages between and among family background, school-related variables and academic achievement, while simultaneously offering a new definition of equality of opportunity as linked to the outputs of school (achievement, in this case) rather than the inputs *to* school.

Marking a key difference that is broadly sustained in much later research and analysis, Coleman differentiates between equality of inputs as resources put into the school, and equality of outputs as results of schooling. He asserts that the then existing notion of equality of opportunity is a "mistaken and misleading concept" as it situates equality within school structures rather than within opportunities that education holds for adult attainment. This constituted an important shift in our conception of equality of opportunity, opening the door for investment in those school-based factors that can be empirically shown to increase school outcomes. As a direct result of the Coleman Report, equality of opportunity is widely measured by how students look when they leave school (achievement, attainment and so forth) rather than by what goes into the school as disconnected from outcome variables such as measured achievement, attainment, occupational status and income. More concretely, equalizing school resources is no longer a measure of equality of opportunity unless such investment can be linked empirically to a commensurate rise in educational outcomes.[6]

Stretching further, Blau and Duncan analyzed equality of opportunity with an eye toward understanding the nature of occupational stratification. In *The American Occupational Structure*, Blau and Duncan (1967) find that although discrimination has a cumulative, prohibitive affect on the occupational attainment of Blacks, for example, once a variety of control measures are introduced into the equation, background variables, such as father's education, exert little independent effect on occupational attainment (Hopper, 1968, p. 458). The authors pry open a "life chance" research genre, which probes empirically the connection between schooling and occupational outcomes. Following this shift in focus (from the inputs to school to the outcomes of school as a measure of equality of opportunity), important quantitative research related to the production of academic achievement, academic attainment, occupational status and income dominated the field through the mid 1970s (Jencks, 1972; Sewell, 1971; Sewell & Hauser, 1975; Sewell & Shah, 1967).

When I entered a PhD program, functionalist theoretical frameworks and accompanying high-level quantitative research reigned supreme. Not long after the functionalist theoretical framework (and the accompanying empirically based political-arithmetic approach as evidenced in the work of Coleman, Jencks, Blau & Duncan, and others) became instantiated as the popular lens for analysis, social scientists widely challenged its theoretical boundaries, arguing for increased attention to the ways in which power allows some groups to exert and maintain control over others, thereby enabling those with privilege to maintain advantage in the educationally based race for ostensibly meritocratically obtained positions. This challenge, influenced by Neo-Weberian and Marxist conflict theory, attacked the functionalist paradigm as misguided (Collins, 1971, 1974; Flacks, 1970, 1971; Gintis, 1970; Touraine, 1971). Following Weber, scholars focus on educational settings and inequality as best explained through notions of power and conflicting interests among social groups, as opposed to functionalist notions surrounding the needs of the society and economy (Karabel & Halsey, 1977).

Given this challenge, what took hold most quickly in the education research community during my early graduate school days, was a focus on the ways in which school sanctioned knowledge (later called the "official curriculum") serves the interests of those in power, thereby enabling certain groups to excel in school and maintain control over others (Anyon, 1981; Apple, 1979; Wexler, 1976; Young, 1971). In the UK, for instance, the publication of Young's *Knowledge and Control* (1971) forcefully signaled increased attention to the relationship between the organization and selection of curricular knowledge and those who succeed in school. Bourdieu and Passeron (1977), Bernstein (1973, 1975), Wexler (1976), Apple (1979), Popkewitz (1987), Whitty (1985) and others subsequently argue that the organization of knowledge, the form of its transmission, and the assessment of its acquisition are crucial factors in the cultural reproduction of class relationships in industrial societies like the U.S., France, and the U.K.

As Karabel and Halsey note in their well-known 1977 review of the field, "By the early 1970s, a school of thought stressing the content of education had formed, and one of its members was describing it as 'the new sociology of education'—an emergent 'alternative paradigm'. Previous work was dismissed as a 'positivistic' version of structural functionalism using 'input-output models' and a 'normative paradigm'" (Karabel, 1977, p. 5). The challenge represented by the "new" sociology of education, popularly conceived as original thought born out of England,[7] led sociology of education scholars down an alternative theoretical/methodological path, although far more has been made of the seemingly naturalized linkage between theoretical perspective and appropriate methodology than is ultimately helpful, a point that I take up in much of my recent scholarly work.[8]

Significantly, around this same time period, economists Bowles and Gintis (1976) departed from the new sociology of education's focus on knowledge, arguing, in contrast, that there is a "correspondence" between the structural relations of production and those of the school. Putting forth their well-known "correspondence principle," Bowles and Gintis argue that schools directly reproduce social and economic inequalities embedded in the capitalist economy. As they note:

> The structure of social relations in education not only inures the student to the discipline of the work place, but also develops the types of personal demeanor, modes of self-presentation, self-image, and social-class identifications, which are the crucial ingredients of job adequacy. Specifically the social relationships of education—the relationships between administrators and teachers, teachers and students, students and students, and students and their work—replicate the hierarchical division of labor. (1976, p. 131)

Such neo-Marxist sensibilities critique the capitalist economy as the driving force behind the "need" for profit and domination as in conflict with the political economy that promotes democracy and equality. This conflict plays out in classrooms where students are marked by a larger and highly stratified economic structure (Bowles & Gintis, 1976), and this notion of stratified social structures and the relationship between such structures and educational institutions became the centerpiece of my own thinking on this subject for many years hence.

Without great interruption in the intellectual flow of theoretical debate, varying theories of reproduction begin to emerge in the late 1970s as variations on forms of conflict theory.[9] It is noteworthy that all such iterations take as their focal point the relationship between education and social and economic outcomes—outcomes more generally established as important to research on schools and schooling by earlier theoretical breakthroughs in the equality of educational opportunity and "life chance" genres, where, as I suggest earlier, "outcomes" were deemed critically important. Debate related to schooling and social and economic outcomes quickly becomes more intense, and theories of economic reproduction are soon critiqued as incapable of "provid(ing) adequate explanations of the complex and often contradictory roles that schools have in mediating and reproducing existing social orders" (Marjoribanks, 1985, p. 4691). As Sadovnik (2007) notes, "Unlike most Marxists, who tend to emphasize the economic structure of society, social and cultural reproduction theorists argued that school processes reflect the interests of cultural and social elites" (p. 7).

Initiated in Europe, and expanding upon earlier calls for a focus on the nature of school knowledge, early theories of social and cultural reproduction find form, most notably, in the writings of Pierre Bourdieu in France and Basil Bernstein in the UK. Bourdieu writes extensively on the process of cultural reproduction, powerfully highlighting the notion of "cultural capital" as knowledge that is transferred from one generation to the next through both families and schools (Bourdieu, 1973; Bourdieu & Passeron, 1977). Though noted that all groups marked within a class structure acquire and exhibit their own distinct form of cultural capital, Bourdieu's careful empirical work and subsequent theorizing suggests that it is the social and cultural capital of the elite that enables them, as a group, to maintain privilege, power and advantage in a highly stratified educational system. In turn, knowledge of elite cultural capital (fine arts, literature, and so on) enables/encourages this group to ensure a place at the most valued and prestigious educational institutions, attendance at which transfers into the most valued and prestigious placements within the occupational structure. As I moved at this time with and against these theoretical and empirical currents, I was perhaps most influenced by the empirically driven research and accompanying theorization of Bourdieu, wherein his work with Passeron (1977), and later Wacquant (1992), substantially influenced my own scholarly thinking over the next three decades.

Basil Bernstein (1971, 1973, 1975) hones in on a particular kind of cultural capital, linguistic codes, a topic that is "concerned with how the macro-level (social, political, and economic structures of institutions) is dialectically related to the ways in which people understand systems of meaning (codes)" (Sadovnik, 2007, p. 9). Like those of Bourdieu, Bernstein's important theoretical contributions rest upon careful empirical work, and it is this deeply honed connection between empirical research and deep theorizing about education and the production of economic and social inequalities that impacted my own thinking and subsequent writing. Bernstein, for example, argued that members of the working class (specifically in the UK, where his empirical work was undertaken) are at a distinct disadvantage in schools, as schools employ and promote middle class language patterns, thereby privileging those who already posses relevant linguistic codes, specifically those students from middle class backgrounds.

Working with and against an array of important empirical studies of the time, and particularly Paul Willis' *Learning to Labour* (1977), Michael Apple (1982) extends his earlier theoretical work (1979), arguing, "schools need to be seen in a more complex manner than simple reproduction" (p. 13). Apple states that what is missing from theories of reproduction, whether economically, socially or culturally driven, are the... "conflicts, contradictions, meditations, and in particular, resistances" (1982, p. 13). This argument similarly came to be deeply etched in my thinking as I moved forward in my own career, leading me to be strongly influenced by the early work of Paul Willis.

Though laced with heavy critique for its masculinist ethos (McRobbie, 1980),[10] Willis' work provides a highly regarded empirical example of the complexities associated with resistance and contestation, and the volume remains seminal to the study of class position, structure, and individual agency, and, perhaps more importantly with regard to the purpose of this essay, to me personally. Intentionally pushing back on more structurally based/deterministic models such as those of Althusser (1971) and Bowles and Gintis (1976), Willis states, "In its desire for workers of a certain type, the reach of the production process must pass through the semi-autonomous cultural level which is determined by production only partially and in its own specific terms" (1977, p. 171). As such macro determinations need to "pass through the cultural milieu to reproduce themselves at all" (p. 171). Willis argues that processes of reproduction can never be assumed—that they are always shot through with fits, starts and contradictions, all of which play out on the semi-autonomous level of culture.

Offering this major theoretical breakthrough, Willis introduces human agency to broader processes of economic and social reproduction, suggesting that in advanced capitalist societies, individuals must be understood as agents who collude in systems of domination, thereby helping to produce their own continued marginality. Offering a complex analysis of the ways in which resistance is ironically linked to reproduction, Willis notes: "It is their own culture which most effectively prepares some working-class lads for the manual giving of their labour power and there is an element of self-damnation in the taking of subordinate roles in Western capitalism. However this damnation is experienced paradoxically as true learning, affirmation, appropriation and as a form of resistance" (p. 3). Following Willis, a multitude of contemporary scholars have produced important work that uses this framework as its starting point.[11] Most importantly for me personally, Willis, like Bourdieu and Bernstein, used empirical ethnographic data as he theorized the production, reproduction and contestation of social structure. In the case of *Learning to Labour,*

Willis clearly focused on class, as this was his primary project. However, Willis opened the door for far more serious investigation of the relationship between and among race, class and gender, and, in particular, the extent to which class production processes fundamentally rest upon and can be understood only in relation to other fundamental nodes of difference.

As I moved forward in my own career, I twinned the focus on produced and lived out cultural productions and linkages to social structure with critical work on class, race and gender intersectionality (Crenshaw, 1991), wherein I began to argue that class can *never* be understood without consideration of other key nodes of difference, both between and within nations. In the case of the United States, this meant that the production, maintenance and challenges linked to social class could never be understood without serious and sustained consideration of race/ethnicity and gender (Weis, 2004, 2008). As the global context massively shifted around us (Brown et al., 2011), I began to take much more seriously the movement of capital, cultures and peoples as similarly important in the production of inequalities both within and between nations (Weis & Dolby, 2012).

After the publication of the Willis volume, in *Schooling and Work in the Democratic State* (1985), economists Martin Carnoy and Hank Levin turned their attention to contradictions embedded within the capitalist State itself. Carnoy and Levin argue that although schools play key roles in the reproduction of race, gender and class relations as per earlier theoretical advances, both the educational system as well as its internal policies and practices emerge through conflict and contestation, thereby representing a partial win for the historically disenfranchised. Focusing on contestation as a fundamental part of any State sector institution in a democratic society, including schools, they note:

> Educational institutions are not just producers of dominant class conceptions of what and how much schooling should be provided; public schools also reflect social demands. Attempts by the capitalist State to reproduce the relations of production and the class division of labor confront social movements that demand more public resources for their needs and more say in how these resources are to be used. The capitalist State and its educational system are therefore more than just a means for co-opting social demands or for simply manipulating them to satisfy dominant class needs. Social demands shape the State and education (p. 47).

Under this formulation, Carnoy and Levin (1985) argue that the educational system cannot be understood simply as,

> an instrument of the capitalist class. It is the product of conflict between the dominant and the dominated... Education is at once the result of contradictions and the source of new contradictions. It is an arena of conflict over the production of knowledge, ideology, and employment, a place where social

movements try to meet their needs and business attempts to reproduce its hegemony. (p. 50)

By focusing specifically on struggles within the State sector, Carnoy and Levin challenge and extend prior work on reproduction and contestation, and this too began to factor, in important ways, into my growing thinking on this set of subjects. My later work on the production of what I call the "new upper middle class" of the twenty-first century (with Kristin Cipollone and Heather Jenkins) takes very seriously the insights of Carnoy and Levin around demands aimed at the state sector, in particular, and the ways in which such demands and struggles over college access are linked to the intensified struggle for entrance to a range of secondary and postsecondary institutions. Such struggle was initially lodged by African Americans in the United States, expanding and growing increasingly complex in decades following early demands for access by people of color (Weis, Cipollone, & Jenkins, 2014).

In this regard and from this point forward, scholarship that probes the production of inequalities tends to run on what I call "parallel courses of difference" rather than engage knowledge/theory produced across such difference (Weis, Jenkins, & Stich, 2009). Additionally, since the 1970s, alignment with a particular research methodology/method in the sociology of education tends to imply alignment with a particular theoretical framework, wherein research inside reproduction or "new" sociology of education frameworks, for example, tends to be qualitative, whereas that linked to educational opportunity research programs is almost entirely quantitative. Given these intensifying "parallel courses of difference," scholars rarely read or take account of theory, data and method across theoretical and/or methodological divides. Such wholesale dismissal of a range of theory, data and method both limits imaginative possibilities and is, quite frankly, counterproductive to scientific progress.[12] This perspective has fundamentally fueled my own "working across" theory and method (Weis, 2008a; Weis, 2008b; Weis & Dolby, 2012; Weis, Cipollone, & Jenkins, 2014), where I work to simultaneously mine important quantitative and qualitative research on the production of social and economic inequalities both within and between nations.

The 1960s, 1970s and into the 1980s constituted a particularly heady time in the sociology of education, a period that represents significant scholarly struggle in the field as well as in the broader context within which such scholarly work was conceived and produced. From my perspective, it is arguably the case that the level of theoretical debate and associated scholarly movement is both less vibrant and *increasingly less informed by a range of theory and evidence* than was the case during my graduate student days and early in my career. Unlike the situation chronicled earlier in this chapter as formative to my own scholarly youth, wherein the very definitions of equality of educational opportunity emerge out of struggles over scholarly difference, and where conflict theory re-emerges in relation to functionalism, and variations of reproduction theory emerge in relation to one another, current day scholars in sociology of education seem less compelled by the norms of the field to *read* across and engage varying lines of research on education and social and economic inequalities. Rather than representing any kind of "normal scientific practice," this actually suggests and reveals substantial ignorance around a range of work that *could and should inform* any given project.

Seeking to retain this sense of struggle, I continue to work across the kind of methodological and theoretical difference that characterized intellectual struggles in my academic youth. For example, *The Way Class Works* (2009) and *Social Class and Education: Global Perspectives* (Weis & Dolby, 2012) embody difference at the outset, as do my projects that intellectually work across what have increasingly become constricting borders and boundaries. In these two edited collections, for example, we offer a template for *ways* of studying education and social class inside the shifting global and intentionally showcase important research produced by a diverse group of authors whose empirical work is situated in varying national contexts. The goal here is to highlight a range of perspectives, research methods, and associated designs through which such work can be accomplished, and I hold firm to the value of this perspective and associated scholarly work.

Although much has been made, for example, of the qualitative/quantitative distinction in social research, it is important that we move beyond such staunchly defended methodological distinction and borders so as to answer critical research questions. This is *not* a call for a "mixed methods" approach in any simplistic sense. Rather, it is a stark statement that we need sophisticated quantitative, qualitative *and* mixed methods studies that address education and class in global context, for example, in order to unearth the extent to which and mechanisms through which class and social structure are being produced and realigned all over the world. No one method can answer all relevant questions, and we must increasingly read and build upon stellar research that employs a range of research methods in varying national contexts and with groups differentially positioned within such contexts.

This similarly applies to *narrowly* conceived perspectives, as we can respectfully *disagree* as to the definition of social class, for example, as well as the drivers of class production, and at the same time use our collective energies to amass research on the production of social and economic inequalities as related to education. It is, in fact, only by understanding the extent of such inequalities and the mechanisms through which inequalities are now produced in global context that we can engage meaningful ameliorative actions. *No single orthodoxy will suffice here.* We need broad based collective engagement and respect across both method and perspective if we are to make meaningful headway in this globally fuelled research arena. One only needs to carefully read the voracious team-based and sophisticated corpus of quantitative research produced by Thomas Piketty (2014), Piketty and Saez (2003, 2006, 2012), Chauvel (2010) and others, to understand the profoundly intensifying economic inequalities that characterize our national and global context. This profoundly intensifying set of inequalities and their linkages to educational institutions, should sit at the *center* of our analyses, wherein ignoring a range of research produced outside narrowly conceived methodological and/or theoretical orthodoxies is, at best, unproductive.

## AND TO METHOD...

In line with early dominant frameworks I was highly trained quantitatively. Through the use of national databases collected by large organizations and research centers, quantitative research methods were the most widely used techniques for sociological investigation of education at the onset of the 1960s (Sadovnik, 2007) and remained dominant throughout my graduate student career. Quantitative research generally involves the use of sociologically relevant theory in the area of inquiry; development of a research question and corresponding hypotheses grounded in theory; formation of an explicit research design/framework; empirical testing of hypotheses and counterfactuals; evaluation and analysis of results; and subsequent generation of informed conclusions. Such studies have enabled us to look at differences and changes over time in achievement based on race, class, gender and other socially significant variables (Reardon, 2011; Bailey & Dynarski, 2011; Duncan & Murnane, 2011), as well as assess the effects of school-based practices while holding background characteristics constant in the analysis. Important work has been conducted on the independent effects of tracking and ability grouping (Gamoran, 1987; Gamoran & Mare, 1989; Haller, 1985; Haller & Davis, 1980; Kelly, 2004, 2008; Rosenbaum, 1976), and Martin Carnoy (1994) offers an empirically-based analysis of the politics and economics of race in America, contributing to our understanding of educational/occupational opportunities among the historically disenfranchised. Quantitative methodology has been largely employed by those who work within the equality of educational opportunity and life chance/status attainment traditions, although some crossover is evidenced in the work of scholars such as Carnoy and Levin, among others.

While quantitative research studies within and outside of the sub-field have been highly valuable to sociologists of education in understanding school effects, interactionist theorists ardently note that these studies do not fully address the "reasons for these effects, as they [do] not examine school processes" (Sadovnik, 2007, p. 16). Based on this critique, researchers utilizing ethnographic methods have examined, among other areas, issues of social background and schooling (Cookson & Persell, 1985), nature of knowledge (McNeil, 1986), ability grouping (Rist, 1970), and achievement and tracking (Oakes, 1985). The researcher, as an integral part of the research process and design (often serving as the research instrument) must understand his or her own biography, power as researcher, ethical and political stance, and relationship to the research site and that of other participants (Denzin & Lincoln, 2005).[13] While there are certainly important ways in which qualitative and quantitative research methodologies differ, these differences can both enhance methodological strengths and serve to reduce or offset methodological weaknesses.

Additionally, it should be noted that while considerable effort has been made to highlight the differences between major research frameworks, important similarities have not been articulated and/or emphasized to the same degree. Both methodologies, for example, engage in empirical work to address a particular research question, and both explain data strategically (Johnson & Onwuegbuzie, 2004).[14] Likewise, both qualitative and quantitative researchers use data to create a sound argument pertaining to the research question at hand, speculate about and/or test for causality, and include provisions to protect their participants while minimizing potential biases in the research process (Johnson & Onwuegbuzie, 2004). It is also worth noting that neither major methodology necessarily nullifies important political and power issues embedded in the research process itself. In point of fact, researchers who engage either methodology can abuse their subjects, authorize highly questionable and even destructive accounts of particular communities that result in grave consequences with regard to subsequent policies and practice, and engage in research solely for reasons of one's own career enhancement.[15]

Michelle Fine and I (2012, 2013) recently put forward what we call "critical bifocality" as a way to think about epistemology, design and the politics of educational research; a theory of method in which researchers make visible the linkages or circuits through which structural conditions are enacted in policy and re-form institutions, as well as the ways in which such conditions come to be woven into community relationships and metabolized by individuals. Detailing macro-level structural dynamics associated with globalization and neo-liberalism, we focus on the ways in which broad based economic and social contexts set the stage for day-to-day actions and decisions among privileged and non-privileged parents and students in relation to schooling. We suggest that *critical bifocality* enables us to consider how researchers might account empirically for global, national and local transformations as insinuated, embodied, and resisted by youth and adults trying to make sense of current educational and economic possibilities in massively shifting contexts. We seek to trace *how* circuits of dispossession and privilege travel across micro and macro geographic spaces and institutions, re-routing resources, opportunities and human rights upward as if deserved, and depositing despair in low-income communities, particularly those of color in the United States. While *critical bifocality* is today a lens on neo-liberal policies and practices, our commitment to *bifocals*—dedicated theoretical and empirical attention to structures *and* lives—can be adjusted to varied contexts, historic moments, and accompanying institutional arrangements in a wide range of nations across the globe.

*Critical bifocality* as a framework, encapsulates so much of what I came to understand in that liminal space of the years I lived overseas. Through my day to day experiences with a wide range of individuals differentially positioned in relation to power and privilege, I came to understand, at a highly visceral level, that social theory and analyses can *never* afford to separate lives from social and economic structures, and that stratified social and economic positionalities are dialectically produced. As researchers, we cannot reproduce the conceptual firewalls separating present from past; resilience from oppression; achievement from opportunity; progress from decline. Decades after I lived in Ghana, Michelle and I collectively affirm that we have a responsibility to "connect the dots" across these presumed binaries, refusing to reproduce representations of individuals as if autonomous, self-contained units, dangling freely, and able to pursue their life choices unencumbered by constraint. Our dedicated theoretical and methodological commitment to a bifocal design, that documents at once the linkages and capillaries of structural arrangements and the discursive and lived out practices by which privileged and marginalized youth and adults make sense of their circumstances, builds upon and encapsulates so many of my early understandings forged and concretized in a key space of liminality.[16]

## AND MY MOST RECENT STUDY...

Having conducted five full-scale ethnographic investigations that centered on poor and working class youth and/or young adults (1985; 1990; 1996; 1998; 2000a; 2000b; 2001; 2002; 2004, among others) and produced edited volumes on class, race and gender that centered largely on the lives and experiences of the poor and working class (2012; 2008; 2004; 2000; 1997a; 1997b; 1993; 1988), I recently turned my attention to the production of privilege. Following in the footsteps of Angela Valuenzela (1999), Douglas Foley (2010), Stacey Lee (2005), Michelle Fine (1991), Paul Willis (1981), and others who track and theorize the production of class, race/ethnicity and gender in relation to intense ethnographic investigation, our recent volume theoretically and empirically *drills down* into the production of a distinctly located upper-middle class—one that is increasingly working, we argue, to differentiate itself from the broader middle class within which it is embedded (Weis, Cipollone, & Jenkins, 2014). Employing "critical bifocality," *Class Warfare: Class, Race and College Admissions in Top-Tier Secondary Schools (2014)* connects the story of students, parents, and school personnel to broad social and economic arrangements through specific focus on the secondary to postsecondary "linking process" (Perna et al., 2008; Hill, 2008). In so doing, we engage a triplet of theoretical and analytic moves—deep ethnographic work within schools and families in three purposively selected secondary school sites, serious relational analyses between and among relevant race/ethnic and class groups in markedly altered global context, and broad structural connections to social and economic arrangements.

*Class Warfare* takes up this theoretically located "class" project via multi-year ethnographic research with three distinct groups of students in three upper-middle class secondary schools—defined here as schools serving a largely professional and managerial parental population (Apple, 2010; Kivel, 2004). This purposively selected tri-school student sample enables deep focus on actions and activities engaged by differentially located parents, students, counselors, teachers, and other school personnel across class and race/ethnicity in both iconic private and public privileged secondary institutions While each group independently reveals a great deal about schooling, family practices, and the college process, putting these groups in sharp relief, as we do here, starkly portrays the ways in which "class works" and is put to work by varying groups in schools.

A major finding is the intense and targeted "class work" of a now highly insecure broad-based middle class that engages in a very specific form of "class warfare," one in which a segment of the middle class individually and collectively mobilizes and enacts its own located and embodied cultural, social, and economic capital both to preserve itself in uncertain economic times while simultaneously attempting to instantiate a distinctly professional and managerial upper-middle class through access to particular kinds of postsecondary destinations. Employing *critical bifocality*, we unravel and reveal the mechanisms through which observed, macro-level, globally-induced phenomenon are produced at the lived level on a daily basis, whether by explicit design/work, or by virtue of what Bourdieu refers to as "'habitus'—a system of lasting and transposable dispositions which, integrating past experiences, functions at every moment as a matrix of perceptions, appreciations and actions and makes possible the achievement of infinitely diversified tasks" (Bourdieu & Wacquant, as cited in Bourdieu, 1982, p. 18). As such, we acknowledge the explicit "class work" on the part of a segment of the broad-based middle class involved in maintaining advantage under massively shifting global conditions, and as particularly linked to a now national and increasingly segmented U.S. marketplace (Hoxby, 1997) for postsecondary education.

In contrast to the recent media construction of "helicopter parents," we do not presume that relatively "rich" people have a "culture of anxiety," but rather interrogate the underlying structural conditions that help to produce these expressed panics, paying close attention to the explicit linkages between collected ethnographic action and narratives and what is happening in broad context. Our data and ensuing on-the-ground analysis must be understood as linked to larger social structural arrangements as they simultaneously refract back on such arrangements, thereby *creating*, in part, *future* class structure and relative position of individuals and groups.

## A GRANDDAUGHTER OF IMMIGRANTS COMES "HOME": KEY EXPERIENCES AND LESSONS LEARNED ALONG THE WAY

*Class Warfare* spotlights and encapsulates much of what I articulate at the beginning of this essay. I am, partially by personality perhaps, in combination with the re-articulation of self inside heady academic debates of the 1970s and 1980s and particular kinds of international opportunities made available to me by virtue of my own class/race background and linked educational opportunities, able to span a range of borders that so often divide.[17] These lived out intersections enabled and encouraged me to hone an ability to understand, theorize, and write about constructed and lived-out "difference" across a range of populations and sites in massively altered global context. Coupled with a perhaps inborn interest in the lives and experiences of others, the accumulation of these experiences enabled me, over time, to interact with a wide range of peoples with great alacrity—from the very rich to the very poor, across social and geographic location and condition.[18]

More than feeling simply at home in the midst of broad based humanity, however, lie well schooled and well honed practices that encouraged me to intellectually work across lived experience and knowledge in relation to a wealth of theoretical, methodological and empirical material. This has enabled me to consistently theorize the production of social and economic structures and the linkages of such structures to the lives and experiences of differentially located individuals and collectivities. Standing on the shoulders of those who came before me, I was privileged to engage a life-altering period of disconnection and liminality that I associate with living in West Africa by myself as a young woman for two and a half years. This particular space of liminality must be understood as linked to a specific historic moment—a time when connection to "home" meant only the occasional blue aerogram that took weeks to travel from the US to Accra.[19] Layering on top of bequeathed advantages coupled with training in my PhD program at the University of Wisconsin-Madison, this space, perhaps more than any other, fueled a research trajectory that spans three decades.

I am the granddaughter of Jewish peasants who immigrated to the United States amidst vacillating borders and boundaries between Russia and Poland… I am the granddaughter of then designated "Hebrews" who became "White" in the US… I am the daughter of a White father who reaped the benefits of the GI Bill in the form of college tuition and expenses and low-interest mortgage rates that enabled home ownership linked to attendance at particular kinds of elementary, middle and secondary schools… I am the daughter of parents who accumulated economic capital linked to home ownership in particular parts of the city… I experienced the Civil Rights struggle, resurgence of the women's movement and massive protests against the War in Vietnam… I left the country for years… I came back a stranger… I embody and intellectually traverse boundaries that so often divide…

## NOTES

[1] This essay benefited from ongoing discussion with Michelle Fine, and earlier comments from Joyce King, a past Editor of RER. Portions of this essay, specifically those related to my interpretation of the sub-field, are drawn from Lois Weis, Amy Stich and Heather Jenkins (2009) "Diminishing the Divisions Among us: Reading and Writing Across Difference in Theory and Method in the Sociology of Education," *Review of Educational Research* 79(2): 912–945. Thanks, in particular, to Amy Stich and Heather Jenkins with regard to their work on the RER paper. Thanks also to Kristin Cipollone and Heather Jenkins, co-authors of *Class Warfare*, both of who influenced my thinking about class construction as we authored this volume.

[2] Significantly perhaps, with regard to the tone of this essay, my father attended a Catholic, Jesuit college, Marquette University in Milwaukee, and played tennis for the school. His elder brother attended the University of Wisconsin. Both my father and uncle were able to attend and complete university by virtue of the Servicemen's Readjustment Act of 1944, otherwise known as the G. I. Bill. This particular version of the G.I. Bill made low-income mortgages available to returning veterans and granted stipends that covered tuition and expenses to those who attended college or trade school.

Brodkin-Sachs (1998) and Oliver and Shapiro (1995) discuss the ways in which the G. I. Bill overwhelmingly benefited Whites.

[3] Like all such stories, these snippets cannot do justice to the complexity of the situation, as they both rely on memories that were themselves shaped and re-articulated by context and by what was willingly passed on to the next generation. When my mother later took classes at the University of Wisconsin-Milwaukee, she wrote an essay entitled "The Ethnic Background of Gertrude Levin Weis," in which she articulates the felt complexity of being both an "insider" and "outsider" in Algoma, Wisconsin, an entirely non-Jewish community. Many years later, my aunt returned to this community and was effusively embraced by remaining elders, as one of the "Levin daughters."

[4] The fact that I was able to spend two and a half years living in West Africa is linked both to the very low cost of living at that time and available federal monies for dissertation research. As I was alone, I also did not have expenses other than those involving my own routine maintenance. My dissertation was highly quantitative, involving the collection of primary data from a stratified sample of secondary schools and students all over the nation. Given that planes flew only to a few cities within the country, and roads were far less than optimal, data collection involved a great deal of arduous travel by often broken down buses. This was particularly the case when I traveled to the North of Ghana, a far poorer region than the South, where, at times, I was on buses without windscreens (wind shields) for seven or more hours. Petrol (gas) was in short supply and we were often stranded as drivers attempted to locate more petrol. School officials were very understanding when I arrived later than a given negotiated appointment. A car that I bought for five hundred US dollars enabled me to drive to schools in the South rather than travel by bus, but poor roads often introduced unanticipated delays.

[5] The first "visit" was in Columbia, Missouri, where I was working for a federally funded desegregation center associated with the University of Missouri-Columbia. The second "visit" was the night before my defense in Madison, Wisconsin. Although obviously their experiences were very different than mine, I strongly felt that they affirmed my "travels" and resonated with the "self" I had become. This set of experiences continues to give me great strength.

[6] While the Coleman report exhibits long-term effects on the field, it is important to note that it has been subject to much important scholarly debate and critique. See, for example, Mosteller and Moynihan (1972) and particularly Bowles and Levin (1968) for important critical consideration of Coleman's study. Despite trenchant critique, however, a long-term effect of the report is the shift in definition of equality of opportunity to one of school outputs rather than inputs. Working from within the life-chance and equality of opportunity genres, Christopher Jencks et al. (1972) offer an important challenge to this line of research, suggesting that equalizing educational opportunity, no matter how defined, cannot in itself result in equality of social or economic outcomes. Jenck's work was similarly subject to important debate and critique. See Levine and Bane (1975).

[7] The conception of the "new sociology of education" is commonly perceived as having originated in the minds of British scholars, but as Joyce E. King (2007) reminds us, Black scholars like George Washington Ellis, W.E.B DuBois, and Carter G. Woodson were thinking, theorizing, actively pursuing change, and producing scholarship about issues related to power, ideology, and the development of school knowledge prior to White scholars within and outside of the United States and Britain.

[8] Although beyond the scope of this essay, it is important to point out that only certain scholarly literature was taken into account as these shifts and challenges took place. Important work by Woodson and others on what King (2005) calls "alienating school knowledge or what is (and is not) taught—about African history, culture, and the significance of the contributions of African people on world development, community building, and economic development" (p. 11) as well as the ways in which such knowledge serves to disenfranchise Black students, is never seriously taken up in this set of challenges. As noted in note 7, this is in spite of the fact that numerous Black scholars were writing on this subject long before White sociologists of education took up the ways in which school knowledge serves to advantage or disadvantage students from particular backgrounds.

[9] Paul Willis (1981) and Michael Apple (1978) author important pieces regarding the similarities and differences among these sub-theories, carefully pointing out the ways in variations of reproduction theory emerge in relation to prior empirical and theoretical work.

10. Rather than pursuing strains of heavy gender-based critique, Arnot (2004) suggests, in contrast, that Willis pries open a sociology of masculinity, thereby establishing its intellectual terrain for the next twenty-five years. Important work on masculinities by Connell (1995, 1995, 2000), Kenway and Fitzclarence (1997), Jackson (2002), Kimmel (1996) and others follows.
11. Notable examples here include but are not limited to Jean Anyon, 1981; Amira Proweller, 1998; Philip Wexler, 1987; Stacey Lee, 1996; Jay McLeod, 1987; Patrick Solomon, 1992; Michelle Fine, 1991; Signithia Fordham, 1996; Angela Valenzuela, 1999; Doug Foley, 1990, 2010; Lois Weis, 1990, 2004; Wendy Lutrell, 1997; and L. Jannelle Dance, 2002.
12. In so arguing, I am suggesting something very specific. Here I mean that those who do work on gender, race or class, for example, should read across work in these areas (both across race, class and gender as well as across method and perspective within each category) rather than take account of literature that uses only a specific method (quantitative versus qualitative) or reflects a specific theoretically driven sub-orientation. To be clear, I am not suggesting that we take account of work conducted from a wildly divergent political perspective—I am simply suggesting that we read across a broader range of work.
13. It is worth pointing out that all researchers must reflect upon their own power as a researcher in authorizing knowledge about others. While qualitative researchers take on this task directly, quantitative researchers ought not be exempt from this form of reflexivity.
14. We take up this methods point in the RER paper (Weis, Stich, & Jenkins, 2009). Some of the material presented in this chapter is drawn from that paper. For too long now quantitative research has been considered empirical research while qualitative research is rarely accorded this status. The fact is that both major methodologies rely on empirical data. The "AERA Standards for Reporting on Empirical Social Science Research in AERA Publications" are exceptionally helpful in this regard as they make clear that qualitative research is empirical. These standards insist that both qualitative and quantitative researchers offer sources of empirical evidence that are warranted and transparent.
15. While the argument has been made that participatory research strategies aim to be more empowering and inclusive, as well as being more located within and for community, consideration of this point is beyond the scope of this essay (Fine, 1994; Fine et al., 2004; Tuhiwai Smith, 1999). Michelle Fine et al. (2004), for example, argue that their participatory action research conducted within a prison (referring to themselves as university-based researchers and the insiders as inmate-researchers) to understand the impact of college on the inmates' lives, requires a democratic approach to research, an approach that seeks to affect social change.
16. I cannot, of course, speak for Michelle, as she has her own biography as well as her own version of this "story." The story of "how we came together" is another story entirely, to be told at another time. The key point however, is that theorizing builds upon the debates in the discipline as historically and structurally located and as coupled with lived out experiences that collectively encourage and enable us to produce and actualize particular kinds of understandings about the world. Some of the discussion of critical bifocality included in this chapter appears in our HER article (Weis & Fine, 2012).
17. I benefited enormously from the tutelage, brilliance and unwavering support of the extraordinary faculty in Educational Policy Studies at the University of Wisconsin-Madison. Faculty members collectively had a huge effect on my thinking during the course of my graduate studies and beyond. I attribute much of my own academic success to their guidance and involvement. Michael Apple and Michael Olneck, in particular, were instrumental to my developing ways of thinking.
18. I am fortunate to share my life with my husband, whose own lived-out biography as an Ethiopian who attended Emperor Haile Selassie's school, followed by NYU, Columbia and the University of Wisconsin-Madison, informs my ever shifting understanding of global circumstances and sensibilities; migration and immigration; and the movement of capital, cultures, and peoples in massively shifting times. His eyes on the global economy, structurally produced possession and dispossession, and lived out linkages between new forms of capitalism and class productions as inextricably tied to re-articulating forms of race/ethnicity in varying global context and circumstances, continues to inform my scholarly imagination. Intimately living in international spaces, as additionally embodied in my larger extended family, continues to enrich my understanding of the ways in which the shaping powers of education, in all forms and at all levels, embody and retain both possibility and centrality.

[19] It is worth noting that I had no phone service while living in Accra. The only phone service available to me was at the post office, and involved a trip to the central post office, long wait times, and uncertain connection outcomes. I only made one phone call to the US in the years I was overseas. This stands in sharp contrast with current technological possibilities that enable physically de-moored international graduate students, for example, to Skype and/or FaceTime their families every day.

## MY FAVORITE TEXTS BY OTHERS

Apple, M. (1982). *Education and power*. Boston: Routledge & Kegan Paul.
Bourdieu, P. (1984). *Distinction: A Social Critique of the Judgment of Taste*. Cambridge: Harvard University Press
Bourdieu, P., & Passeron, J.C. (1977). *Reproduction in education, society and culture*. Beverly Hills, CA: Sage Publications.
Carnoy, M., & Levin, H. (1985). *Schooling and work in the democratic state*. Stanford: Stanford University Press.
Crenshaw, K. (1991). "Mapping the margins: Intersectionality, identity politics, and violence against women of color". *Stanford Law Review*, 43, 1241-1299.
Kerckhoff, A. (1995). Institutional arrangements and stratification processes in industrial countries. *Annual Review of Sociology*, 21, 323–47.
Oliver, M. L., & Shapiro, T. M. (2006). B*lack wealth/white wealth: A new perspective on racial inequality*. New York: Routledge.
Shavit, Y., Arum, R., & Gamoran A. (2007). *Stratification in higher education: A comparative study*. Stanford, California: Stanford University Press.
Willis, P. (1977). *Learning to labour: How working class kids get working class jobs*. Farnborough, England: Saxon House.

## MY FAVORITE PERSONAL TEXTS

Weis, L., M. Eisenhart, K. Cipollone, A. Stich, A. Nikischer, J. Hanson. S, Ohle, C. Allen, and R. Dominguez (2015). "In the Guise of STEM Education Reform: Opportunity Structures and Outcomes in Inclusive STEM-Focused High Schools". *American Educational Research Journal*. Vol. 52 No. 6. 1024-1059
Weis, L., K. Cipollone & H. Jenkins. (2012). *Class Warfare: Class, Race and College Admissions in Top Tier Secondary Schools*. Chicago. The University of Chicago Press
Weis, L., & N. Dolby (eds.) (2012). *Social Class and Education: Global Perspectives*. New York. Routledge
Weis, L., & Fine, M. (2012). "Critical bifocality and circuits of privilege: Expanding critical theory and design". *Harvard Educational Review*, 82(2), 173-201.
Weis, L. (2004). *Class Reunion: The Remaking of the American White Working Class*. New York: Routledge
Weis, L. (2001). "Race, Gender and Critique: African American and White Women in 1980s and 1990s" *Signs* Vol 27 No 1. 139-169
Michelle Fine and Lois Weis. (1998). *The Unknown City: The Lives of Poor and Working Class Young Adults*. Boston: Beacon Press
Weis, L. (1990). *Working Class Without Work: High School Students in a Deindustrializing Economy*. New York: Routledge

## REFERENCES

Althusser, L. (1977). *Lenin and philosophy and other essays*. London: New Left Books.
American Educational Research Association. (2006). Standards for reporting on empirical social science research in AERA publications. *Educational Researcher*, 35, 33–40.

Anyon, J. (1981). Social class and school knowledge. *Curriculum Inquiry, 11*, 3–42.
Apple, M. (1978). The new sociology of education: Analyzing cultural and economic reproduction. *Harvard Educational Review, 48*, 495–503.
Apple, M. (1979). *Ideology and curriculum*. Boston, MA: Routledge & Kegan Paul.
Apple, M. (1982). *Education and power*. Boston, MA: Routledge & Kegan Paul.
Apple, M. (2010). Global crisis, social justice and education: An introduction. In M. Apple (Ed.), *Global crises, social justice and education* (pp. 1–24). New York, NY: Routledge.
Arnot, M. (2004). Male working-class identities and social justice: A reconsideration of Paul Willis's learning to labor in light of contemporary research. In N. Dolby & G. Dimitriadis (Eds.), *Learning to labor in new times*. New York, NY: Routledge Falmer.
Bailey, M. J., Dynarski, S. M., & National Bureau of Economic Research. (2011). *Gains and gaps: Changing inequality in U.S. college entry and completion*. Cambridge, MA: National Bureau of Economic Research.
Bernstein, B. (1971). *Class, codes, and control (Vol. 1): Theoretical studies towards a sociology of language*. London: Routledge.
Bernstein, B. (Ed.). (1973). *Class, codes and control (Vol. 2): Applied studies towards a sociology of language*. London: Routledge.
Bernstein, B. (1975). *Class, codes and control (Vol. 3): Towards a theory of educational transmissions*. London: Routledge.
Blau, P., & Duncan, O. (1967). *The American occupational structure*. New York, NY: Wiley and Sons.
Bourdieu, P. (1973). Cultural reproduction and social reproduction. In R. Brown (Ed.), *Knowledge, education, and cultural change* (pp. 71–112). London: Travistock.
Bourdieu, P., & Passeron, J. C. (1977). *Reproduction in education, society and culture*. Beverly Hills, CA: Sage Publications.
Bourdieu, P., & Wacquant, L. (1992). *An invitation to reflexive sociology*. Chicago, IL: The University of Chicago Press.
Blau, P., & Duncan, O. (1967). *The American occupational structure*. New York, NY: Wiley and Sons.
Bowles, S., & Gintis, H. (1976). *Schooling in capitalist America: Educational reform and the contradictions of economic life*. New York, NY: Basic Books.
Bowles, S., & Levin, H. M. (1968). The determinants of scholastic achievement: An appraisal of some recent evidence. *The Journal of Human Resources, 3*, 3–24.
Brown, P., Lauder, H., & Ashton, D. (2011). *The global auction: The promise of education, jobs, and income*. New York, NY: Oxford University Press USA.
Carnoy, M. (1994). *Faded dreams: The politics and economics of race in America*. New York, NY: Cambridge University Press.
Carnoy, M., & Levin, H. M. (1985). *Schooling and work in the democratic state*. Stanford, CA: Stanford University Press.
Chauvel, L. (2010). The increasingly dominated fraction of the dominant class: French sociologists facing the challenges of precarity and middle class destabilization. In *Facing an unequal world: Challenges for a global sociology* (Vol. 3). Taipei, Taiwan: Institute of Sociology at Academia Sinica, Council of National.
Collins, R. (1971). Functional and conflict theories of educational stratification. *American Sociological Review, 36*(6), 1002–1019.
Collins, R. (1974). Where are educational requirements for employment highest? *Sociology of Education, 47*, 419–442.
Cookson, P., & Persell, C. (1985). *Preparing for power: America's elite boarding schools*. New York, NY: Basic Books.
Connell, R. W. (1995). *Masculinities*. Cambridge, UK: Polity Press.
Connell, R. W. (2000). *The men and the boys*. Berkeley, CA: University of California Press.
Crenshaw, K. (1991). Mapping the margins: Intersectionality, identity politics, and violence against women of color. *Stanford Law Review, 43*, 1241–1299.
Dance, L. J. (2002). *Tough fronts: The impact of street culture on schooling*. New York, NY: RoutledgeFalmer.

Denzin, N., & Lincoln, Y. (2000). *Handbook of qualitative research*. Thousand Oaks, CA: Sage Publications.

Fine, M. (1991). *Framing dropouts: Notes on the politics of an urban public high school*. Albany, NY: State University of New York Press.

Fine, M. (1994). Working the hyphens: Reinventing self and other in qualitative research. In N. Denzin & Y. Lincoln (Eds.), *Handbook of qualitative research* (pp. 70–82). Thousand Oaks, CA: Sage Publishers.

Fine, M., & Weis, L. (1998). *The unknown city: The lives of poor and working class young adults*. Boston, MA: Beacon.

Fine, M., Torre, M. E., Boudin, K., Bowen, I., Clark, J., Hylton, D., Martinez, M., Rivera, M., Roberts, R. A., Smart, P., & Upegui, D. (2004). Participatory action research: From within and beyond bars. In L. Weis & M. Fine (Eds.), *Working method: Research and social justice* (pp. 95–119). New York, NY: Routledge.

Fine, M., Weis, L., Powell Pruitt, L., & Burns, A. (2004). *Off White: Readings on power, privilege, and resistance* (2nd ed.). New York, NY: Routledge.

Flacks, R. (1970). Young intelligentsia in revolt. *Transaction, 7*, 47–55.

Flacks, R. (1971). *Youth and social change*. Chicago, IL: Markham.

Foley, D. (1990). *Learning capitalist culture: Deep in the heart of Tejas*. Philadelphia, PA: University of Pennsylvania Press.

Foley, D. (2010). *Learning capitalist culture: deep in the heart of texas* (2nd ed.). Philadelphia, PA: University of Pennsylvania press.

Fordham, S. (1996). *Blacked out: Dilemmas of race, identity, and success at capital high*. Chicago, IL: University of Chicago press.

Gamoran, A. (1987). The stratification of high school learning opportunities. *Sociology of Education, 60*, 135–155.

Gamoran, A., & Mare, R. (1989). Secondary school tracking and educational equality: Compensation, reinforcement, or neutrality? *American Journal of Sociology, 94*, 1146–1183.

Gintis, H. (1970). The new working class and revolutionary youth. *Socialist Revolution, 1*, 13–33.

Haller, E. (1985). Pupil race and elementary school ability grouping: Are teachers biased against Black children? *American Educational Research Journal, 22*, 465–483.

Haller, E., & Davis, S. (1980). Does socioeconomic status bias the assignment of elementary school students to reading groups? *American Educational Research Journal, 17*, 409–418.

Hill, L. (2008). School strategies and the college-linking process: Reconsidering the effects of high schools on college enrollment. *Sociology of Education, 81*, 53–76

Hoxby, C. M. (1997, December). *How the changing market structure of U.S. higher education explains college tuition* (Working Paper 6323). Cambridge, MA: National Bureau of Economic Research.

Jencks, C., Smith, M., Acland, H., Bane, M. J., Cohen, D., Gintis, H., Heyns, B., & Michelson, S. (1972). *Inequality: A reassessment of the effect of family and schooling in America*. New York, NY: Harper Colophon Books.

Johnson, R. B., & Onwuegbuzie, A. J. (2004). Mixed methods research: A research paradigm whose time has come. *Educational Researcher, 33*, 14–26.

Karabel, J., & Halsey, A. (1977). Educational research: A review and an interpretation. In *Power and ideology in education* (pp. 1–85). New York, NY: Oxford University Press.

Kelly, S. P. (2008). Social class and tracking within schools. In L. Weis (Ed.), *The way class works: Readings on school, family, and the economy* (pp. 210–24). New York, NY: Routledge.

Kivel, P. (2004). *You call this a democracy?* New York, NY: Apex Press.

Lee, S. (2005). *Up against whiteness: Race, school, and immigrant youth* (pp. 51–86). New York, NY: Teachers College Press.

MacLeod, J. (1995). *Ain't no makin' it: Aspirations and attainment in a low-income neighborhood* (2nd ed.). Boulder, CO: Westview Press.

Marjoribanks, K. (1985). Sociology of education. In T. Husen & T. Postlethwaite (Eds.), *The International encyclopedia of education* (pp. 4680–4700). New York, NY: Oxford, University Press.

McRobbie, A. (1980). Settling accounts with subcultures: A feminist critique. *Screen Education, 34*, 37–49.
Oakes, J. (2005). *Keeping track: How schools structure inequality* (2nd ed.). New Haven, CT: Yale University Press.
Oliver, M. L., & Shapiro, T. M. (1997). *Black wealth/White wealth: A new perspective on racial inequality.* New York, NY: Routledge.
Piketty, T. (2014). *Capital in the 21st Century.* London: Belknap Press Harvard University.
Piketty, T., & Saez, E. (2003). Income inequality in the United States, 1913–1998. *The Quarterly Journal of Economics, 118*(1), 1–41.
Piketty, T., & Saez, E. (2006). *Income inequality in the United States, 1913–2002.* Oxford: Oxford University Press.
Piketty. P., & Saez, E. (2012, November 8–9). *Top incomes and the great recession: Recent evolutions and policy implications.* Paper presented at the 13th Jacques Polak Annual Research Conference. Hosted by the International Monetary Fund, Washington, DC.
Proweller, A. (1998). *Constructing female identities: Meaning making in an upper middle class youth culture.* Albany, NY: SUNY Press.
Reardon, S. (2011). The widening academic achievement gap between the rich and the poor: New evidence and possible explanations. In G. J. Duncan & R. J. Murnane (Eds.), *Whither opportunity? Rising inequality, schools, and children's life chances* (pp. 91–116). New York, NY: Russell Sage Foundation.
Rist, R. (1970). Student social class and teacher expectations: The self-fulfilling prophecy in ghetto education. *Harvard Educational Review, 40*, 411–451.
Saez, E. (2013). *Striking it richer: The evolution of top incomes in the United States* (Updated with 2012 Preliminary Estimates) (An updated version of "Striking it Richer: The evolution of top incomes in the United States" ). *Pathways Magazine* (Stanford Center for the Study of Poverty and Inequality, Winter 2008), 6–7.
Saez, E. (2013). Striking it richer: The evolution of top incomes in the United States (updated with 2012 preliminary estimates). Retrieved from http://elsa.berkeley.edu/~saez/TabFig2012prel.xls
Sodovnik, A. (2007). Theory and research in the sociology of education. In A. Sodovnik (Ed.), *Sociology of education: A critical reader.* New York, NY: Routledge.
Valenzuela, A. (2005). Subtractive schooling, caring relations, and social capital in the schooling of U.S.-Mexican youth. In L. Weis & M. Fine (Eds.), *Beyond silenced voices: Class, race, and gender in United States schools* (Rev. ed.). Albany, NY: State University of New York Press.
Weis, L. (1985). *Between two worlds: Black students at an urban community college.* Boston, MA: Routledge, Kegan and Paul.
Weis, L. (1990). *Working class without work: High school students in a de-industrializing economy.* New York, NY: Routledge.
Weis, L. (Ed.). (2008). *The way class works: Readings on school, family and the economy.* New York, NY: Routledge.
Weis, L., & Dolby, N. (Eds.). (2012). *Global perspectives.* New York, NY: Routledge.
Weis, L., & Fine, M. (Eds.). (2000). *Construction sites: Excavating race, class and gender among urban youth.* New York, NY. Teachers College Press.
Weis, L., & Fine, M. (2004). *Working method: Research for social justice.* New York, NY: Routledge.
Weis, L., & Fine, M. (2012). Critical bifocality and circuits of privilege: Expanding critical ethnographic theory and design. *Harvard Educational Review, 82*(2), 173–201.
Weis, L., & Fine, M. (2013). A methodological response from the field to Douglas Foley: Critical bifocality and class cultural productions. *Anthropology & Education Quarterly, 44*(3), 222–233.
Weis, L., Cipollone, K., & Jenkins, H. (2013). *Class warfare: Class and race in affluent and elite secondary schools.* Chicago, IL: University of Chicago Press.
Wexler, P. (1976). *The sociology of education: Beyond equality.* Indianapolis, IN: Bobbs-Merrill Co.
Willis, P. (1977). *Learning to labour: How working class kids get working class jobs.* Farnborough, England: Saxon House.

Willis, P. (1983). Cultural production and theories of reproduction. In L. Barton & S. Walker (Eds.), *Race, class, and education*. London: Croom Helm.

Young, M. (Ed.). (1971). *Knowledge and control: New directions for the sociology of education*. London: Collier-Macmillan.

*Lois Weis*
*University at Buffalo*
*The State University of New York*

PHILIP WEXLER

# 18. CRITICAL THEORY AND EDUCATION

### STARTING OUT FROM BROOKLYN

It doesn't take much to become a sociologist, if you grow up in New York, even more so, Brooklyn. It is in the air. The multiplicity, the contextualism and relativism, the irony, skepticism and reflexivity, the cool, analytic distance and the sporadic attention to the specifics and perpetual grabbing for big ideas with easy handles, the critical attitude sprouting from self-protective arrogance and condescension, the love of books, nature and people.

I read a lot, from an early age, and by high school, I was moving around intellectually, between Marx and Nietzsche. But, it was not just books. Rebellion, in daily life and in art, was already displacing indifference and what we learned to call "conformity." Almost before I could finish reading Kerouac's "On the Road," we seemed to be at Woodstock, near where I was a summer camp counselor, singing songs of the civil rights movement, and generic anti-war, people's socialism. Pete Seeger was our visiting weekend guest. There too, I managed some New York distance, irony and to have fun criticizing the very sober and serious social reformers who were my friends and co-workers. To have a reflexive critical stance toward whatever was going, whatever was being taken for granted as natural and better, was something I seemed to have imbibed early on, and which I brought to the intellectual work that has drawn my attention for so long.

### SOCIOLOGY

Sociology read and sounded like a sublimation of those times. It was already almost the public culture of the sixties, the antithesis of the fifties taken-for-granted, since it turned everyday life into a science, or at least, a series of concepts, that could be rethought and reordered, one step removed from the natural, and a respectable and systematic way of distancing oneself from the present, and even of being disdainful of it; rebellion through scientific systematicity. Sociology could do that and one could transmute the rebellious attitude into a respectable area of study, a "major," and eventually, by just staying that displaced course of an historical, cultural revolt against early corporate capitalism and its social character in America, learn to get paid for it, and to be able to maintain a guarded social skepticism while having a job, career, profession, within "the system."

The traffic between popular culture and academic theory, while complex, does flow. "System" may have been a slur, but not in the Sociology that I learned at Princeton. A far cry from Coney Island and Woodstock, Princeton Sociology was at once quintessentially Parsonian, and in that sense, organized around study of "The Social System" and closed, looking for balancing and integrating mechanics. At the same time, it was open, looking beneath Parsons's roots in *The Structure of Social Action*, toward European Sociology and the longer history of social theory. I had read Mannheim's *Sociology of Knowledge* in college, but at Princeton, within its theoretical straight jacket, that was soon to be removed, there was also the larger world of Pareto, Sorokin and British Anthropology. While my sociological colleagues were doing well-delimited empirical studies in the professionally dominant mid-Western, big ten universities, the Harvard spore that defined Princeton sociology, was doing the history of Sociological and Anthropological theory. Of course, despite the presence of Charles Page (*Class in American Sociology*), we were doing very little Marx and the tradition of Western Marxism and Critical Theory, was virtually unspoken. Only Chandler Davidson raised an alternative voice, when he wrote of a "dirty little war in Vietnam" in *The Nation*. At least then, Princeton was not proud of him.

Graduate school strengthened my theoretical predisposition (we did learn also to do multivariate statistical analyses, as well as to read ethnographies), while it dampened the sublimated expression of a rebelliousness hatched at the intersection of biography and history. When I went to Madison, Wisconsin, after a brief New York and political infusion at Queens College, I discovered mid-Western radicalism, and the opportunity not only to see a concentrated alternative daily life, but to read the varieties of Marxism, including the Frankfurt School, which has an episodic, but enduring influence on my attempts to translate social dissatisfaction into intellectual expression and academic work. But in Madison, even Marxism was multivariate, and Anthroplogy was somewhere else, no ethnography in sociological sight at ground zero of the positivist mainstream.

Education, however, was more inviting, and given my graduate school specialization in sociology of education—we learned to catalogue all research in any area—I had been able to teach that first, in a very orderly, empirico-analytical fashion at Queens College. I soon discovered Michael Apple, in Educational Policy Studies in Madison, in a basement office, with a picture of an apple on his door. From Apple, and, much later from Len Barton's visits to the U.S., I learned about a critical corpus of work in Education in the U.K., which was not being done in the U.S., with the exception of a small group of American historians of Education, like Michael Katz and Joel Spring. The British critics were really in Education, working especially on curriculum questions, and while they were sympathetic and interested in Sociology, generally, they did not have the general theoretical background in the history of Sociology and Anthropology. Still, in London, they were creating a "new sociology of education." Sometimes more constructivist than critical, in their willingness to see knowledge reflexively and socially, they offered an alternative to what C.Wright Mills called the 'abstracted empiricism' of sociology generally, in sociology of education. Two already emergent, later preeminent figures, Bernstein and Bourdieu, were also putting knowledge and society back into the study of Education, although neither would have wanted to have been thought of as doing that from the vantage point of Marxism or the Frankfurt School.

## CRITICAL SOCIOLOGY OF EDUCATION

With this history, it was almost a natural that I should rethink and reorder Sociology of Education contextually, historically and socially, when I needed to make sense of the field again. It was already evening, and in the Fall, also cold in Madison, when reading American history in the library (regrettably, I did not follow through on my intention to study immigration and education historically, in the U.S., as a sequel to my dissertation based on field work in a boarding school in Israel, *Children of the Immigrants*) that I began to see the parallels between the key ideas of American Progressivism and the neat categories that I had earlier set out to teach, as given, empirically—rather than as historical cultural expressions of social movements and social change. The earlier work in sociology of knowledge, the critical edge, the intellectual habit of trying to grasp whole subfields of sociology, and the paradigm shifts (Thomas Kuhn was at Princeton while I was studying Sociology, and "paradigms" were afoot) in British sociology of education were combined in my first book, *The Sociology of Education: Beyond Equality*. The emergent ideas in the field meshed with the central direction of the most salient contemporary social movements. The "field" could be seen not only as "normal" empirical research (especially sophisticated quantitative studies of academic achievement and social mobility and education, as magnets for accumulation), but as structured within paradigms; and, beyond Kuhn, these paradigms were anchored in basic ideas and assumptions that could readily be interpreted as academic recodings of broader cultural commitments, especially of the social movements which led to wider social and cultural changes.

The dynamism of Sociology of Education, in this view, came less from our cumulative knowledge and more from attunement to the wider context in which we were practicing our professional craft. Sociology belonged to society, with its movements and conflicts, more than to an academy that enabled us to have good order to our findings and concepts. In the leap from the scientized Progressivism of basic ideas in Sociology of Education to the paradigmatic playing out of socially revolutionary movements in a "new sociology of education," what equality, organization and knowledge meant in Education, was not to be an unquestioned, conceptually emergent natural fact of specialized scientific discourse; these ideas were part of something larger, a wider social and cultural history.

This meant not that one had to stop doing normal science, regular empirical work. On the contrary, when I left Madison a few years later to go to Rochester, I tried to recapitulate my Israeli study, but in a comparative, urban ethnography of high schools, which was later to be published as *Becoming Somebody*. Along with "knowledge" as social, including academic, scientific knowledge, another main focus of work that I brought from earlier interests was on questions of self and identity. These questions relating to identity had emerged in my dissertation, but they were reinforced by the way in which I continued to explore Critical or Frankfurt School social theory. I had studied Psychology as well as Anthropology in graduate school. Here too, as with Sociology of Education, I did not accept the facticity of the structuring assumptions of subfields. As I wrote about sociology of education, these fields were also grounds for the playing out of ideologies, and, to a much lesser extent, utopias. Though it was then heresy to see such a firm positivist pillar of social science as Social Psychology as ideology, I took the same historical, social and cultural approach to academic knowledge that I did for Sociology of Education. Here too, though sharpened and more explicitly theoretical, after reading Frankfurt School theory. *Critical Social Psychology* was not as mild and relatively a-theoretical as *Beyond Equality*, and I made no secret of my view that American Social Psychology, beneath its scientific finery, was a thinly veiled ideological representation of an emergent corporate capitalism. I offered a social psychological reading of Marx and a return to the Frankfurt School, as part of "the way out." There were a few people who liked the book, but very few. Nonetheless, I would come back to Sociology of Education from there with a clearer commitment to a more modest, contextual understanding of academic knowledge and a willingness to breach the norms of the "objectivity" and "neutrality" of research, in which I had been educated. Max Horkheimer's essay on "Traditional and Critical Theory" was an eye-opener for me and gave me the courage to continue asking questions about knowledge and society as well as about the social uses of social science.

As a result of these experiences, I went back to Anthropology, and to my dissertation research, to begin doing what was being called in Education, especially, both in research and teaching, "qualitative research." When I first started teaching qualitative research at Rochester, the course had been called "non-quantitative research." Both that mode of work, which itself has increasingly not been taken for granted and instead, critically interrogated (Dennzin & Lincoln, 2012), and the interest in studying "identity" later become mainstays in social analyses in Education, if not in Sociology of Education, proper (the history of the relation between sociology of education and sociological studies done under the umbrella of the Education disciplines, has yet to be fully written, particularly in light of the crisis of "Social Foundations of Education." See Wexler & Hotam, 2015, *New Social Foundations of Education*).

## TEXTUAL TURNS

I took seriously both theoretical traditions and empirical, sociocultural changes, trying not to neglect, as Marx accused the "bourgeois theorists" of doing, of seeing "what is in front of their eyes." For me, that had become a combination of the defeat of the New Left by the New Right, in Education and in society—the recognition of a cultural shift, from modernism, to a postmodern set of emphases, a corollary intellectual interest in explanatory discourses drawn from cultural studies, literature, linguistics and semiotics, and a renewed interest among sociologists in revising that turn of the century European sociological theory in which I had been educated, which had now been solidly named as "classical sociology." The Marxist tradition had been unearthed, but remained in the background, as Durkheim and Weber were rediscovered. In the return to theory, I continued to take sustenance for my work in Sociology of Education from "outside" "the field."

These social and intellectual tendencies were represented, I think, in *Social Analysis of Education*. There, I replaced the "new", "critical", "radical" sociologists and curriculum theorists of Education into social history, not exempting them, and myself, from the social and cultural contextual analyses which had been applied to earlier "carriers" of social ideas. We wanted to now not only go beyond the Progressivist foundations of sociology of education, but also beyond the neo-Marxism that had become triumphalist in claiming the full space of the social analysis of Education for itself. Criticizing the critics is not always a well-received past time. Still, in *Social Analysis* I tried also to describe shifting grounds of Educational practice, on the one hand, and on the other, to introduce discourses newer to Education, such as semiotics and poststructuralism.

In contrast to the narrower versions of the neo-Marxist new sociology, here there was an emphasis on cultural analysis, language and the importance of texts. "Structure, Text and Subject" had been a precursor paper to the book, at least on the textual side (emphasizing less the movement and identity which I saw as emergent foci), and I tried to get beyond a simple ideology analysis of curriculum, or even an uncritical appeal to what had by then already become sloganized as the "radical" alternative to Education's functionality in societal maintenance, namely, "social and cultural reproduction." Instead, I took texts as processes of action and aimed to connect product and process, taking symbolic work seriously and not as a mere reflection of class and the economics of the labor process. My hope was that the Critical, broadly Marxist, model of social analysis could be combined with post structuralism, giving the mobilization of symbolic resources a place in social dynamics. On the larger playing fields of social and cultural theory and practice, there was little of such combining. I took from this work the importance of symbolic practice, but not the purist post structuralism of textualism and ahistoricism.

Seeing Education as a social text, and taking literature and language seriously for social analysis, was one aspect of the 'textual turn.' In Sociology, and not only for me, there was the other face of textualism, a return of interest in the canonical texts, which meant especially rereading Durkheim and Weber. Again, I went outside of Sociology of Education, to more general social theory. These rereadings almost always brought me back to Education, but often only years later, which I believe led some of my colleagues to think that I had "left the field." Indeed, from a "field perspective" (on the other side, when he came to visit me in Rochester, Basil Bernstein exclaimed: "So, I see you are a 'field man'."), rethinking Sociology of Education from the perspective of different discourses is part of the necessary process of intellectual "revitalization." It would, I think, be interesting to study the history of Sociology of Education not only in terms of research and conceptual continuities, or paradigm shifts, but also as it has been influenced by "revitalization movements," which in academic discourse, I understand increasingly, as positive effects of multidisciplinarity and continuous movement across fields and modes or methods of study.

## RELIGIOUS TURN

The return to classical Sociology had unanticipated outcomes. The pattern that emerges in the changes that I have described is one of an interaction between academic discourses and wider social, cultural and personal changes, leading to new paths of academic investigation and theorizing. My readings of Durkheim and Weber coincided with observations about changing everyday life, especially the appearance of languages and practices from domains of religion and the sacred that sociologists had claimed long disappeared beneath the bulldozer of "secularization."

Even casual observation in bookstores revealed new terms, languages that I thought had been forgotten and abandoned. I recall my surprise at increasingly seeing the word "soul" in book titles—a term that I thought had gone the way of all pre-modern culture. Of course, soul would come to be replaced by "spirituality," and systematic research began to report evidence of still a different cultural shift, beyond postmodernism, to renewed interest in religion, though in an "unchurched" form. This was the beginning of what academics later called "re-sacralization" (Davie, 2010). During this time, I had long been practicing Yoga, but began to notice a change in the social acceptability of such activities, as my friends stopped looking at me askance for this, and indeed, the local health club began offering regular classes in Yoga, alongside aerobics.

Historical social and cultural change, personal change, and discursive changes coalesced, and I began to take seriously what sociologists would later call "the religious turn" (Turner, 2010). I took religion seriously for social analysis in part because Durkheim and Weber did. What I learned in those rereadings was how central religion had been for them, as being right beneath the surface of modern social practice, and indeed, its enduring, if, regrettably, continuing contemporary, though quiescent and transfigured, existence. Durkheim's last major works, indeed, his magnum opus, is not simply about the *Elementary Forms of Religious Life*, but about how these forms are the kernel of the elementary forms of social life and cultural belief. Furthermore, the source of social dynamism is in "collective effervescence," which is primordially modeled by religious ritual. Even more, this originally "religious" collective force is seen by Durkheim as now absent in a "cold" modern society, and he openly longs for its return. Weber too built his sociology on religion, where Protestantism is the palimpsest of the modern culture of capitalism. "Charisma," or religious grace, is the antithesis of the rationalization that now ossifies social life; and though it continues to exist in private life, it is gone from public life, probably not to return. Still, Webber maintains cautious hope for a cultural revolution against secularized ascetic rationalism. But, don't wait, he advises, following the prophetic discourse from the Book of Isaiah,

Taking the religious turn seriously meant to me, taking it analytically as well as practically. It was not simply that there was now more unchurched spirituality, religious seeking and resacralization in everyday life that could be studied and explained sociologically. Rather, it meant also a change in discourse, and with that, an enrichment of the stores of symbolic resources that could be used for contemporary social understanding, but had been depleted by modern life and what I have called, a bit ironically, the "positivist accumulation" of the hegemonic sociological modality. Millbank (1990) asserted that religious discourse has socially explanatory value: Hattam for Christianity, and independently Rosch for Buddhism, and most recently Giri for Hinduism. I took up Judaism, which, despite my interest in Yoga philosophy, was closer to hand for me. But, I took it up dissidently, going for the least favored aspect of Jewish wisdom, and the most anti-rationalistic, and began studying Jewish mysticism.

By the time that I was ready for an extended sabbatical from Rochester, I already had some connection to very accomplished academic scholars of Jewish mysticism who were willing to help me approach the daunting field. So, to the surprise, and consternation of many of my friends and colleagues, our family went to Israel on sabbatical, where we ended up remaining for more than a decade. I used the initial sabbatical time to get beyond my rudimentary Hebrew, eventually becoming reasonably fluent, though reading the ancient texts of Kabbalah, and even the more modern works of Hasidism, is challenging. Still, in Jerusalem, I found willing teachers, even as I accepted an appointment as Professor of Sociology of Education at the Hebrew University. I was moving along two tracks at once: social science and Jewish mysticism.

I had already begun bridging that distance, before I came to Jerusalem, by attempting to show confluences between classical sociology and religious ideas, especially mysticism, in *Holy Sparks* and in *Mystical Society*. Increasingly, I aimed to fuse analysis of the changing societal, re-sacralized context with sociological and then, mystical, thought. I carried the Education interest into both of those books, trying to expand the conceptual and methodological horizons of Sociology of Education. I began an empirical study also (unpublished), extending the identity analyses of *Becoming Somebody* from class analyses of identity, to the existential 'religious turn' made by young people who came to Jerusalem to study in religious boarding schools. My main goal, however, was to show that we could move beyond the West European canon of modern thought to ground social analysis in non-instrumental, non-rationalized traditions that included a wider range of experience and thought as legitimate, than I could find within Sociology. In fact, Sociology's founders had themselves (though Durkheim was a self-proclaimed anti-mystic) already foreshadowed this move. I wanted to do social theory from Jewish mystical concepts and to show that it works better as social explanation that what we are accustomed to re-mining and refining, within the Sociological canon. Again, to go "outside" the field, to see better, and perhaps further. After all, I am not what Weber proclaimed of himself, as author of his sociology of religion, especially the section later published separately as "The Protestant Ethic and the Spirit of Capitalism," a "product of West European civilization."

The act of "going outside" the field seems to have always led back to questions of the field of sociology of education. On the one side, practical, everyday, educational life had begun to register the cultural shift and there was increasing evidence of changes in curriculum and pedagogy amid moves toward 'spiritual' 'holistic' and various types of Buddhist education, at least in the U.S. In the work of John Miller (2005), Oren Ergas (2014), Rob Hattam (2000) and others, the changing grounds of educational practice were represented in an effort to show how mystical religious traditions, from American Transcendentalism to Yoga and Hinduism could make sense of education, differently, for theory as well as for practice. I brought the mystical scholarship to sociology of education in a recent series of papers and forthcoming book on rethinking sociology of education (Wexler & Hotam, 2014, 2015), which have been first given at conferences, mostly outside of the U.S., in Israel and in Germany, particularly. In part, this is work about analyzing education in a changed environment—the meaning of educational practice in "post secular society." At the same time, it is an effort to rethink education analytically and socially, but from the point of view of a different, wider, and, I have even written, "cosmic" horizon (Wexler, 2014: "Toward a Cosmic Sociology of Education").

This is the horizon I aimed for in trying to show how ideas from Jewish mysticism could make sense of contemporary social phenomena. *Mystical Sociology* (2013) takes up especially Hasidism, which is a relatively 'modern' expression of Jewish mystical traditions (for the definitive, early statement of the field, see Scholem, 1946), that scholars have referred to as "Kabbalah become ethos." Hasidism is the most 'socially' oriented and accessible articulation of this tradition, one could argue, and represents what in Weber's language is an "innerworldy mysticism," which is to say, everyday social life. I try to show how contemporary aporias of "excess" are foci for emergent social forms, which are themselves, increasingly, secularized or still sacred, solutions to these problems. At once, they are social practices, but also the basis of systematic social analysis. Here, my emphasis was on the microsociology of social interaction, but one not derived from the Chicago School, but from canonical Hasidic texts, which aim to capture social dynamics that take place on a larger and more "vertical" platform than the way we ordinarily think of social life. Mysticism can be a contemporary social practice and a contemporary social theory, and like other symbolic resources drawn from outside the sociological canon, also as a way to think of Education—both as social practice, and sociologically, as systematic social interpretation and understanding.

## BACK TO THE (PAST) FUTURE: CRITICAL THEORY AGAIN

The revitalization of symbolic resources in the service of social understanding can happen by reviving ancient languages and practices and showing their relevance and power in the present. Modern ideas can also be re-thought and returned to the discursive theater from which they too have been forgotten and excluded. It is fair to say, that in Europe, and to a lesser extent, in the U.S., there is now a renaissance of Critical Theory.

I discovered this quite by surprise, in Germany, where I am visiting professor now, naively thinking that I was alone in remembering the value of the Frankfurt School. What has happened, however, since the work of the original Frankfurt School, especially Horkheimer and Adorno (*Critical Theory*; *Dialectic of Enlightenment*; and *Aspects of Sociology*), is revision of that work which incorporates American social science, notably the work of Habermas, and more recently, of Axel Honneth (2014). Beyond this, there are new book series and attempts to apply Critical Theory to a variety of social questions. Interestingly, with the exception of the work of my colleague, Heinz Sunker on "bildung" (2014), I cannot easily identify any prominent presence of the tradition of Critical Theory/Frankfurt School analyses in the sociological study of Education. The 'new' sociology of education, and its successors, did include (for a review, see Wexler, 2009) class analyses of Education, and there are exemplary studies based on the fundamental ideas of Marxism.

Yet, the Frankfurt School of Critical Theory, which is a recasting of Marxism into a more cultural, psychological, and even interactionist analysis, was not in the new sociology, and is not now being deployed in a parallel rethinking of sociology of education. This is my current work, where I am ideally situated to collaborate with Sunker on going back to the earlier Frankfurt School (in which I include Fromm, as well, of course, as Horkheimer, Adorno and Benjamin) and also in critically reviewing the more contemporary work of Honneth and his colleagues. (Wexler, 2015; "The Americanization of Critical Theory"). We want to do Critical Theory in a different key, and take further the transcendental opening that is undeniable in Benjamin's messianic view of history, as well as the more indirect cultural and aesthetic transcendental opening in Marcuse and Adorno. Here is the bridge to my studies in Jewish mysticism. Benjamin was Gershom Scholem's friend and colleague, and their correspondence documenting mutual influences has been published (Scholem/Benjamin); and of course, Scholem was the undisputed founder of the modern, academic study of Jewish mysticism. Furthermore, recent biographies (Friedman, 2013) of Fromm show the influence of Jewish thought in his dissertation, and his extra-university studies in Jewish mysticism, notably Hasidism.

I want to round this circle a bit, and to show the Jewish mystical connection to German Critical Theory, which is certainly not total, but arguably, present and influential. And, what I have done in my most recent paper, is to discuss—perhaps not surprisingly—what this would mean for a Critical Sociology of Education, one which draws on the basic concepts of the Frankfurt School to again, rethink how we do Sociology of Education (Wexler, 2015; "Critical Theory and Sociology of Education"). Perhaps Bernstein was right. After all the quests for a larger screen and broader playing field, I return to Sociology of Education, a "field man," as he put it.

## MY FAVORITE TEXTS BY OTHERS

Davie, Grace (2010). "Resacralization," pp. 160-178, in Turner, Bryan S. (ed.). *The New Blackwell Companion to the Sociology of Religion*. Oxford: Blackwell.

Durkheim, Émile (1995). *The Elementary Forms of Religious Life*. Trans. Karen Fields. New York: Free Press.

Frankfurt Institute for Social Research (1973). Trans. John Viertel. *Aspects of Sociology*. Boston: Beacon.

Habermas, Jurgen (1984, 1987). *Theory of Communicative Action*. 2 vols. Trans. Thomas McCarthy. Boston: Beacon.

Honneth, Axel (2009). *Pathologies of Reason: On the Legacy of Critical Theory*. New York: Columbia University Press.

Horkheimer, Max (1972). "Traditional Theory and Critical Theory," pp. 188-244, in Max Horkheimer, *Critical Theory*. New York: Herder and Herder.

Horkheimer, Max and Theodor W. Adorno (1972). *Dialectic of Enlightenment*. New York: Herder and Herder.

Mannheim, Karl (1936). *Ideology and Utopia: An Introduction to the Sociology of Knowledge*. New York: Harcourt, Brace and World.

Parsons, Talcott (1951). *The Social System*. Glencoe, Illinois: Free Press.

Scholem, Gershom (1946). *Major Trends in Jewish Mysticism*. New York: Schocken Books.

Turner, Bryan S (2010). "Religion in Post-Secular Society," pp. 650-667 in *The New Blackwell Companion to the Sociology of Religion*. (ed) Bryan S.Turner. Oxford: Blackwell.

Weber, Max (1978). *Economy and Society: An Outline of Interpretive Sociology*. (eds) Guenther Roth and Claus Wittich. Berkeley, California: University of California Press.

## MY FAVORITE PERSONAL TEXTS

*The Sociology of Education: Beyond Equality* (1976). Indianapolis: Bobbs-Merrill.

"Ideology and Utopia in American Sociology of Education," (1978), in A. Kloskowska and G. Martinotti, eds. *Education in a Changing Society*. Beverly Hills, California: Sage.

*Critical Social Psychology* (1983). Boston and London: Routledge and Kegan Paul.

*Social Analysis of Education: After the New Sociology*. (1987). London and New York: Routledge and Kegan Paul.

*Becoming Somebody: Toward a Social Psychology of School* (1992). Washington, D.C.: Farmer

*Holy Sparks: Social Theory, Education and Religion* (1996). New York: St. Martins.

*Mystical Society: An Emerging Social Vision* (2000). Boulder, Colorado: Westview Press.

*Symbolic Movement: Critique and Spirituality in Sociology of Education* (2008). Rotterdam: Sense Publishers.

*Social Theory in Education* (2009). New York: Peter Lang.

*Mystical Sociology; Toward Cosmic Social Theory* (2013). New York: Peter Lang.

"Toward a Cosmic Sociology of Education," *Critical Studies in Education*, vol. 55, no.1. February, 2014, pp. 73-87.

*New Social Foundations of Education: Education in Post Secular Society* (2015), eds. Philip Wexler and Yotam Hotam. New York: Peter Lang.
"Critical Theory and Sociology of Education" (2015), in *New Social Foundations of Education*.
"Americanization of Critical Theory," (forthcoming). Conference and published proceedings, in honor of Axel Honneth, May, 2015, Wuppertal, Germany.

## REFERENCES

Davie, G. (2010). Resacralization. In B. S. Turner (Ed.), *The New Blackwell companion to the sociology of religion*. Chichester: John Wiley & Sons.
Denzin, N. K., & Lincoln, Y. S. (2011). *The Sage handbook of qualitative research* (4th ed.). Thousand Oaks, CA: Sage.
Durkheim, E. M., & Swain, J. W. (1915). *The elementary forms of the religious life*. London,: G. Allen & Unwin, Ltd.
Ergas, O. (2016). *Philosophy east-west: Exploring intersections between educational and contemplative practices*. Hoboken, NJ: Wiley Blackwell.
Friedman, L. J., & Schreiber, A. M. (2013). *The lives of Erich Fromm: Love's prophet*. New York, NY: Columbia University Press.
Horkheimer, M. (1972). *Critical theory: Selected essays*. New York, NY: Herder and Herder.
Horkheimer, M., & Adorno, T. W. (1972). *Dialectic of enlightenment*. New York, NY: Herder and Herder.
Kerouac, J. (1957). *On the road*. New York, NY: Viking Press.
Mannheim, K. (1952). *Essays on the sociology of knowledge*. London,: Routledge & K. Paul.
Milbank, J. (2010). A closer walk on the wild side. In M. Warner (Ed.), *Varieties of secularism in a secular age*. Cambridge, MA: Harvard University Press.
Miller, J. P. (2005). *Holistic learning and spirituality in education: Breaking new ground*. Albany, NY: State University of New York Press.
Page, C. H. (1940). *Class and American sociology*. New York, NY: The Dial press.
Parsons, T. (1968). *The structure of social action*. New York, NY: Free Press.
Scholem, G., & Lichtheim, G. (1946). *Major trends in Jewish mysticism* (Rev. ed.). New York, NY: Schocken Books.
Voigt, S., & Sünker, H. (2014). *Arbeiterbewegung – Nation – Globalisierung : Bestandsaufnahme einer alten Debatte* (Erste Auflage. ed.). Weilerswist: Velbrück Wissenschaft.
Weber, M. (1976). *The protestant ethic and the spirit of capitalism* (2nd ed.). London: Allen & Unwin.
Wexler, P. (1976). *The sociology of education: Beyond equality* (1st ed.). Indianapolis, IN: Bobbs-Merrill Co.
Wexler, P. (1983). *Critical social psychology*. Boston, MA: Routledge & Kegan Paul.
Wexler, P. (1991). *Critical theory now*. London: Falmer Press.
Wexler, P. (1992). *Becoming somebody: toward a social psychology of school*. London: Falmer Press.
Wexler, P. (1996). *Holy sparks: Social theory, education, and religion* (1st ed.). New York, NY: St. Martin's Press.
Wexler, P. (2000). *The mystical society: An emerging social vision*. Boulder, CO: Westview Press.
Wexler, P. (2009). *Social theory in education primer*. New York, NY: Peter Lang.
Wexler, P. (2013). *Mystical sociology: Toward cosmic social theory*. New York, NY: Peter Lang.
Wexler, P., & Hotam, Y. (2015). *New social foundations for education: Education in 'post secular' society*. New York, NY: Peter Lang.

*Philip Wexler (Emeritus)*
*Hebrew University of Jerusalem*

GEOFF WHITTY

# 19. MY LIFE WITH THE SOCIOLOGY OF EDUCATION[1]

INTRODUCTION

Soon after I was appointed as Director of the Institute of Education, University of London in 2000, someone referred to me as 'Geoff Whitty, who used to be a sociologist of education'. As the post of Director at IOE is roughly equivalent to President and Provost combined in a US higher education institution such as Teachers College Columbia, I have to admit that there were times during my ten-year tenure as Director when I was distracted from sociology of education by administrative and financial preoccupations. However, I have always seen my primary academic and professional identity as a sociologist and continue to do so, although strictly speaking I only studied sociology officially as a postgraduate student, having studied history and political theory as an undergraduate at Cambridge in the 1960s. Yet it was a course at Cambridge on 'Theories of the Modern State' that introduced me in some depth to the works of the 'founding fathers' of sociology and from then on I never looked back. Formally, I had the words sociology in my job title only when I succeeded Basil Bernstein – of whom more later – in the role of Karl Mannheim Professor of Sociology of Education at the Institute of Education in 1992. My earlier posts were in Education more broadly or urban education in particular, but even in that context that I found sociological perspectives invaluable, indeed indispensable, as indeed I personally found them in school teaching (see preface to Whitty, 1985).

For about nine months before I went up to Cambridge in 1965 at the age of 18, I was a temporary teacher at an inner city primary (elementary) school in west London at a time when the area was experiencing significant immigration of families from the British Commonwealth, mainly from the Caribbean, the Indian sub-continent and parts of Africa. The area also had a longstanding white working class population with low educational attainment. Interestingly the area has now long since been gentrified and is nowadays among the most expensive areas of London to live in. But at the time it exposed me to lots of experiences that had been unknown to me growing up in the outer suburbs of London. In particular, it forced me to confront and question a lot of my taken for granted assumptions, especially those that informed my own schooling at a selective grammar school.

It also turned me against the elitist educational environment I was about to enter at Cambridge and I spent, as was not uncommon in the 1960s, most of my time as a student activist protesting against everything from the Vietnam war to my college's

*A. R. Sadovnik & R. W. Coughlan (Eds.), Leaders in the Sociology of Education, 287–300.*
*© 2016 Sense Publishers. All rights reserved.*

ban on overnight guests of the opposite sex (see Linehan, 2011). I did not spend anything like as much time studying history and political theory, apart from that which was directly relevant to my political activities. Much of that was Marxist literature but, early on in my time at Cambridge, I was also involved in a Fabian Society study group that exposed me to the sociology of education for the first time, in particular work that is usually called the 'political arithmetic tradition' in Britain (equivalent to the 'status attainment' studies in the USA), an approach that studies the relationship between social background and educational achievement, largely in quantitative terms (e.g. Floud et al., 1956). As I indicate later, such work dominated our field in Britain in the early 1960s. Even though it was very different from much of the Marxist literature I was also reading, political arithmetic's identification of school drop-out both an economic and a social justice issue convinced me that sociological studies of education – including the mapping of inequalities by class in particular but also race and gender – could be an important educational and political resource.[2]

When I left Cambridge in 1968, I trained as a history and social studies teacher at the Institute of Education in London and then became a secondary school teacher not far from where I had been an unqualified temporary teacher a few years earlier. Although I was one of a generation whose student activism was thus superseded in employment by a 'long march through the institutions', I increasingly felt the need to understand why the change that was so obviously needed in overcoming embedded inequalities was so difficult to achieve. I discussed this experience some years later in the preface to *Sociology and School Knowledge* (Whitty, 1985). I was reminded of this very recently when a statement I made there about the grammar school curriculum being 'meaningless' to the working class students I was teaching was attacked by Christodoulou (2013), a neo-conservative member of the academy (charter) school movement, as feeding a dangerous progressive myth that teaching knowledge is (middle class) indoctrination and therefore to be avoided.[3]

Ironically, I had turned to a serious study of the sociology of education to avoid such simplistic analyses, even though I was soon to find they often thrived within the discipline itself. I wanted sociology not only to help me understand why change was so difficult but also what strategies of change might be feasible – whether at an individual, institutional or societal level. So in the early 1970s I returned to the Institute of Education to undertake postgraduate studies in the sociology of education, being taught by some of the leading figures in the field in England at that time such as Basil Bernstein and Michael F. D. Young, both of whom I had already encountered and been inspired by when I had trained as a teacher there a few years earlier.

## THE 'OLD' AND 'NEW' SOCIOLOGIES OF EDUCATION

When I started studying sociology of education in earnest, I discovered that I had been born days before the untimely death in January 1947 of Karl Mannheim, who some would consider the founding father of sociology of education in Britain. Even though we could not be said to be members of the same 'generation unit', to use one of his more enduring concepts, there are some aspects of his approach to the subject that have always appealed to me more than that of some of my closer contemporaries. His dual commitment to theory and policy prefigured my own and I could identify with his struggles with relativism within the sociology of knowledge and with his difficulties in demonstrating the connections between his theoretical work and his policy prescriptions. It was therefore fitting that Karl Mannheim himself would subsequently be the subject of a commemorative professorial lecture I delivered as Karl Mannheim Professor at the Institute in 1997 (Whitty, 1997).

Educational sociology had already been developing in the UK before the second world war, but it was arguably the appointment in 1946 of Mannheim, a leading European social theorist who had left Germany in the 1930s, to a Chair of Education at what was then called the University of London Institute of Education that established the sub-discipline of sociology of education within English academia. Although Mannheim himself did not publish much specifically on the subject in his lifetime, his lectures and notes in this field were published posthumously in 1962 by his student, W. A. Campbell Stewart, as *An Introduction to the Sociology of Education* (Mannheim & Stewart, 1962). This was staple reading on the subject when I first became familiar with it in the mid-1960s, but it did not define the field for long and I never found its substantive, often social psychological, content particularly compelling.

But even in the 1950s, the sociology of education had begun to take a rather different path in Britain. Among its leading exponents was Jean Floud, Reader in the Sociology of Education at the Institute of Education, who had known Mannheim at the London School of Economics. Floud's own work lacked the theoretical sweep that characterised Mannheim's, and she explicitly rejected what she saw as his heavy-handed approach to post-war social and educational planning (Floud, 1959).

Instead, Floud herself was linked to the so-called 'political arithmetic tradition' of studies on social class and educational achievement (Floud et al., 1956; Halsey et al., 1961) that I mentioned earlier. This was the work that first led me into the sociology of education as a member of that Fabian Society study group in Cambridge. Political arithmetic's identification of 'early leaving' and 'wastage of talent' as both an economic and a social justice issue influenced the Labour Party in its espousal of comprehensive secondary education and this apparent link between academic work and political action excited me. As Olive Banks – whose textbook on the subject (Banks, 1968) soon superseded Mannheim and Stewart's – said of the political arithmetic tradition there were 'some grounds for thinking that the sociology of education has changed to some extent the policy makers' way of thinking about educational issues' (Banks, 1974, p. 6). Much later I came to understand and appreciate the tentativeness of that claim (see Whitty, 2016).

One of Floud's successors as Reader in the Sociology of Education at the Institute of Education was Basil Bernstein. Described by Banks (1974) as 'perhaps the most eminent of the sociologists to work in this field' (p. 5), he took its study at the Institute back into the realm of social theory via his socio-linguistic studies of class differences in children's language (Bernstein, 1971). While his own work was firmly located in the Durkheimian tradition, the Chair to which he was subsequently appointed was called the Karl Mannheim Chair of the Sociology of Education and this was the Chair that I later held and which was until recently held by Stephen Ball, another contributor to this volume.

As it happens, I studied at the Institute just at the time when its sociologists, led by Michael F. D. Young, who Bernstein recruited to the Institute in 1967 and whose student I became, were producing the ground breaking edited collection called *Knowledge and Control* (Young, 1971). This heralded 'new directions for the sociology of education', which self-consciously distinguished themselves from the 'old' sociology of education of Floud, Halsey et al. This work was becoming dominant at the Institute when I studied the subject there in the late 1960s and early 1970s and, to some extent, my own contribution was identified with this 'new' sociology of education when I was teaching at the University of Bath in the 1970s.

Yet I would contend that both the 'old' and the 'new' sociology of education, along with studies from the Manchester School like Hargreaves (1967) and Lacey (1970), which also influenced me as a student and as a teacher, had a common theme that brought me into the subject then and continues to motivate me today. Despite its various turns and brief forays into other issues, the sociology of education in England has always been centrally (but by no means exclusively, of course) concerned with the differential performance of affluent and disadvantaged students in the education system.

As I have described elsewhere (Whitty, 1985), I saw the 'old' sociology of education of the 1950s and 1960s as largely concerned with mapping social inequalities in education or exploring how the cultural features of working class homes and communities militated against children from such backgrounds succeeding in school (Craft, 1970). Its policy focus was therefore on how those 'deficits' might be compensated for in order that children from such backgrounds could succeed. While the school system, and particularly its selective nature, was seen to be implicated in this wastage of talent, relatively little attention was paid to the content of schooling itself. In many of the studies at that time, there was a confident assumption that what we took for granted as education was a worthwhile 'good' in itself and that it was in the interests of both individuals and the national economy that they should receive more of it. In other words, the key issue was access to schooling.

The 'new' sociology of education rather reversed the argument. It suggested that the crucial determinant of who succeeded and who failed was the nature of what they encountered in school and that it was therefore hardly surprising that affluent middle class children succeeded because they understood the culture of the school, which was essentially consonant with their own. This seemed to justify various forms of 'progressive' or 'child-centred' pedagogy or alternative curricula closer to the experience of working class children in the terms of which they could succeed.

I characterised this approach at the time as 'naïve possibilitarianism' (Whitty, 1974). For me, it failed to recognise that, although the curriculum as it existed was but one of a number of possibilities, each of which might interact differently with the culture of the home, its dominant form served particular social functions that might not be so easily overturned.

Similar arguments were made by Sharp and Green (1975) and by the late 1970s the second phase of the so-called 'new' sociology of education in England came to be dominated by neo-Marxist approaches influenced by the American writers Bowles and Gintis (1976). In complete contrast to the possibilitarianism of the earlier phase, much of this neo-Marxist work seemed to deny any real possibility of change from within the education system, whose nature was seen as structurally determined by the needs of the capitalist economy.

It seemed that everyday professional practices, even if carried out by well-meaning professionals, merely sustained broader structures of oppression whose origins lay elsewhere. Ethnographic studies of everyday practices in schools and classrooms at this time were sometimes rather less pessimistic, but even pupil agency was often seen to contribute to social and cultural reproduction, as writers like Willis (1977) and Corrigan (1979) demonstrated how working class pupils actively participated in their own positioning in the class structure.

Both phases of the 'new' sociology of education were seen as dangerous by rightist critics, particularly in terms of their potential impact on teachers. An Open University course on *Schooling and Society* came in for particular criticism in this respect (Gould, 1977) and my own association with it was raised as an issue in the interview for my lectureship at King's College London in 1980. My defence in terms of academic freedom seemed to do the trick! Yet, at about the same time, Dawson (1981) argued that sociology of education, initially 'ineffectual' but no longer 'harmless', should 'be cut out of courses for student teachers...to improve the intellectual and moral environment in which would-be teachers are taught' (p. 60). However, in reality, the sociology of education's influence on policy and practice at that time was probably much less significant than either its advocates hoped or its critics feared.

## THE SOCIOLOGY OF EDUCATION POLICY

Michael Young has rightly pointed out to me that our own joint work at that time (Whitty & Young, 1976; Young & Whitty, 1977) does not fit neatly into either the possibilitarian or the deterministic approaches characterised above. This is perhaps one of the reasons why my own substantive interest shifted somewhat in the 1980s towards education policy and into empirical studies of education policy making. One particular interest was the role of private schooling in English education, which I pursued with my old school history teacher, Tony Edwards (Edwards et al., 1989), who had himself by then become a leading scholar in the sociology of education (Edwards, 1976).

During this period, English education became increasingly overtly politicised. Elected in 1979, Margaret Thatcher's Conservative government introduced neo-conservative policies of state control and prescription in relation to the National Curriculum and national assessment, whilst also encouraging neo-liberal market forces through parental choice and school autonomy. Another aspect of our work during these years was trying to make sense of these apparently contradictory developments in sociological terms (Whitty, 1989; Whitty et al., 1998).

The sociology of education in Britain became increasingly dominated by the sociology of education policy at this time and I was by no means the only sociologist of education who took this route. Although it had already been a feature of the work I myself had undertaken at King's College London in the early 1980s, the sociology of education policy soon came to be identified with a group that grew up around my successor there, Stephen Ball. This group pursued an extensive empirical research agenda developed out of Ball's pioneering work on policy making in education (Ball, 1990). Another group joined me at Bristol Polytechnic where I headed up the Education Faculty in the second part of that decade.

Within this work the longstanding focus in British sociology of education on what is usually regarded as working class 'failure' remained evident, although the way of approaching it was often via an attempt to understand how education policy, whatever its claims, has in practice consistently favoured affluent middle class children (for example, Power et al., 2003; Ball, 2003; Reay, 2008). In some ways, this was rather less novel than we sometimes claimed (Power and Whitty, 2006), as this phenomenon was central to what had been demonstrated by the political arithmetic tradition (Halsey et al., 1980). Ball (2011) has similarly pointed out that *Education and the Working Class* (Jackson & Marsden, 1962) 'anticipated Bourdieu's point that we need a theory of advantage as well as disadvantage' (p. 960). What was perhaps more novel at this time was the emphasis, particularly by Ball himself and his colleagues, on the class strategies employed by affluent parents to maintain their advantage.

Even so, as Young has pointed out, the debate between the 'old' and the 'new' sociologies, 'which seemed all-important to many of us at the time', was in large part 'an example of generational conflict within the academic community' (Young, 2008, p. 220). I guess the same might be said of the lack of enthusiasm on some of our parts for the post-modernist perspectives that gained currency within the sociology of education in the 1990s, although it also created different generation units among scholars of the same generation (Hill et al., 2002). It may also be, as Young hints, that the 'extreme relativism' of those perspectives reminded some of us of the shortcomings of the first phase of the 'new' sociology of education.

## RETURN TO THE KNOWLEDGE QUESTION

Tony Blair's New Labour government, first elected in 1997, emphasised neo-liberal policies of parental choice and school diversity as the key to educational improvement and closing the social class attainment gap (Whitty, 2008, 2009). The Conservative-Liberal Democrat Coalition government elected in 2010 continued this trend with its policies on Academies and Free Schools. However, neo-conservative policies, reminiscent of the Thatcher era, also experienced a revival at that time and the nature of school knowledge was put firmly back on the policy agenda. Michael Gove, who served as the Conservative Secretary of State for Education in the Coalition government from 2010 to 2014, took the view that what working class children needed to succeed was exposure to the traditional curriculum. His so-called English Baccalaureate reinforced the role of traditional subjects in the curriculum and reflected his belief that it was an indictment of recent educational history 'that just around 16 per cent manage to succeed in getting to secure a C pass or better at GCSE in English, Maths, the sciences, a language and history or geography' (Gove, 2011). A whole series of other reforms to school examinations sought to roll back any tendency towards a skills-based curriculum and 'progressive' approaches to teaching and assessment.[4]

In a lecture while in Opposition, Gove had cited the Italian Marxist Antonio Gramsci to support his view that educational methods which called themselves 'progressive' were actually regressive in social terms. He argued that 'with the abandonment of subject disciplines, the poorer lose out...Richer parents who can afford it access specific subject teaching earlier rather than later with the most successful prep schools introducing discrete subjects taught by subject specialists before pupils go on to secondary education' (Gove, 2008). Not surprisingly, Gove was also an admirer of E D Hirsch (1999).

Meanwhile, the sociology of education itself went back to the 'knowledge question', but in very different terms from those it employed in the 1970s. In particular, my colleague Michael F. D. Young, whose earlier work had been seen as supportive of progressive approaches to education, now distanced himself from such an interpretation of his position. He questioned whether subject-based curricula only favoured affuent middle class children and suggested that project or theme-based curricula, which had been thought to better suit working class children, were even more socially regressive. Thus, Young's *Bringing Knowledge Back In* (Young, 2008) was a critique of progressivism and constructivism, and indeed of the 'new' sociology of education itself, at least as powerful as any offered by Conservative politicians, although his more recent work also identifies the limitations of the their own position on the curriculum (Young, 2011). Even so, Young's apparent volte face has been warmly welcomed by neo-conservative critics of progressive education such as Christoloudou (2013).

Young now considers that the distinctive role of schools is to transmit knowledge. While his earlier work critiqued what counted as knowledge and who had access to it, he now stresses the necessity of what he calls 'powerful knowledge', as this is the knowledge needed to progress in the world (Young, 2009). He argues that 'the everyday local knowledge that pupils bring to school...can never be the basis for the curriculum [because] it cannot provide the basis for any generalisable principles

(Young, 2009, p. 16). He further suggests that 'powerful' knowledge is especially important for working class pupils who do not have access to it at home, arguing that 'the knowledge issue is both an epistemological issue and a social justice issue' (quoted in RSA Journal, 2008, para. 6). He is therefore concerned that some apparently progressive curricular offers open to such pupils, including too many vocational courses, lack both substance and currency.

I have sometimes teased Young by pointing out that his current position is not only rather close to that of some neo-conservatives but also (and this is perhaps more palatable to him) reminiscent of the arguments put by two of the groups who were his major antagonists when I was a student of his in the 1970s. At one level it appears similar to the position of philosophers like Paul Hirst (1969), who then argued for a curriculum based on 'forms of knowledge', either for epistemological reasons or because in a stratified society there are principled and expedient reasons for giving all pupils access to high status knowledge. Young also now seems much closer to the materialist critics of the 'relativism' associated with the phenomenological version of the new sociology of education that emerged from his early work (Young, 1971). The Marxist historian Brian Simon (1976), for example, feared that its relativist ideological position would deny the working class access to knowledge, culture and science, a criticism that troubled me at the time, if not too many of my contemporaries in Young's classes at the Institute. My own relations with Young have occasionally been strained over the years because I have not been prepared to go as far as him in either direction, though thankfully this has not seriously impaired an enduring friendship.

## THE CONTINUING RELEVANCE OF BASIL BERNSTEIN

The sociologist whose work, in my view, remains most helpful in thinking through the relationship between social class and school knowledge is Bernstein, who remained the dominant presence within the sociology of education in the UK until his death in 2000 and indeed beyond. He died just three weeks into my Directorship of the Institute and both the Institute and the field knew they had lost their greatest contemporary scholar (Power et al., 2001).

Significantly, Young himself now resorts to Bernstein – with whom he had 'differences' in later years (Young, 2008, p. 220) – in support of his own current approach to the curriculum. I too have returned to Bernstein's work in recent years. As I have argued at greater length elsewhere (Whitty, 2010a), some of his key concepts help explain why it has proved so difficult for working class children to succeed in English schools and also to clarify enduring issues about the role of curriculum and pedagogy in educational success and failure (Bernstein, 1977). In my view, it is thus highly relevant to contemporary policy and curricular issues.

In his comments on 'compensatory education', Bernstein (1971) certainly suggested that schools needed to take into account children's experience in the family and community. However, he recognised that the idea that simply weakening boundaries between home and school would of itself make a significant difference was both empirically and theoretically difficult to sustain. His later work on knowledge structures questioned both the possibility and the desirability of collapsing such boundaries (Bernstein, 1996). Even in an early article, he argued that education must involve the introduction of children to the universalistic meanings of public forms of thought (Bernstein, 1970). So, while Bernstein sometimes urged teachers to forge greater connections between school knowledge and everyday knowledge, I suspect that, despite some ambiguity in one of his papers, this was more a pedagogic than an epistemological point.

In the present debates about the school curriculum, I would imagine that Bernstein would have argued that all children should have access to high status knowledge but might get there by different means. He would probably have supported the kind of approach recommended by Fantini and Weinstein (1968) in the 1960s, who argued that 'a curriculum for the disadvantaged must begin as closely as possible to the pupils' direct experience' because 'without such an approach, the abstract cannot be attained' (p. 347). This is very different from the position of writers like Nell Keddie, who rejected the idea that home culture might be used as a 'bridge' into mainstream culture and 'bodies of knowledge', as this would be unnecessary if, as some relativists claimed, 'all cultures – class and ethnic – [had] their own logics which [were] capable of grappling with …abstract thought' (Keddie, 1973, p. 18).

Unfortunately, it is the latter position that politicians still use to deny the value of sociological perspectives on education, a stance that may also be encouraged by some postmodernist writings in our field (see Apple, 1993). More generally, as Beck (2012) has pointed out, Michael Gove's passion when Secretary of State for the teaching of the '"traditional" disciplines' in schools was not matched by any enthusiasm for the inclusion of 'education disciplines' like the sociology of education in teacher training. Our work was once again regarded as 'ideologically suspect' and part of a conspiracy on the part of the 'educational establishment' (which he called 'the blob') to excuse failure and deny the working classes a proper education (Whitty, 2014).

Although it is often disregarded on the grounds of the difficulty of its language, Bernstein's work would nevertheless bear careful study by Michael Gove and his likes, not least because Gove himself argues that 'the greatest pleasures are those which need to be worked at' (Gove, 2011). He would find that Bernstein's work demonstrates the intractability of the relationship between knowledge, schooling and inequality, but also provides a way of thinking about what would need to be put in place if that relationship were to be interrupted. Of course education cannot, as Bernstein (1970) himself noted, compensate for society in any simple way, but that does not mean that educators should accept the continuing failure of the disadvantaged as inevitable. Some of the key challenges in giving disadvantaged pupils access to powerful knowledge – and giving them meaningful and critical purchase on their everyday lives – are pedagogic rather than curricular. And, even though it may not offer politicians simplistic policy prescriptions, Bernstein's work identifies key issues and gives us resources for thinking through what needs to be done.

## SOCIOLOGY AND EDUCATION POLICY TODAY

Social class inequalities in education have been an enduring policy theme in English education since the early part of the twentieth century and, as I have argued here, they have also been the predominant theme of the sociology of education. So, if there is both theoretical and empirical work relevant to the key policy issues of today, why is sociology of education not in greater evidence in current debates about social class attainment and participation gaps in English education? After all, one of my predecessors as Director of the Institute, Sir Fred Clarke, justified the creation of a post for a sociologist[5] on the grounds that 'educational theory and educational policy that take no account of [sociological insights] will be not only blind but positively harmful' (quoted in Whitty, 1997, p. 4).

Banks (1974) has claimed that sociology 'has a particularly close and complicated relationship with social policy and political decision-making' (p. 21). Although we sometimes tend to look back to the 1950s and 1960s as a 'golden age' in that relationship, Banks herself was sceptical about the extent to which even the political arithmetic tradition had influenced policy makers and indeed about the desirability of sociology doing so. However, Halsey (1972) has argued that 'the task of the sociologist is, literally, to inform the political debate' (p. 4) and his own earlier work certainly did that more successfully than sociologists of education have done recently.

Sociology of education is not, of course, exempt from the more general problems in the contemporary relationship between educational research and education policy, which I discussed in my Presidential address to the British Educational Research Association (Whitty, 2006). Furthermore, some of the concerns of sociologists are now taken for granted in the wider policy debate and do not therefore tend to be identified as specifically sociological insights. In addition, a number of sociologists have become identified with the more politically respectable tradition of school effectiveness and school improvement, although ironically one of the persistent criticisms of that work is its downplaying of the significance of social class (Hatcher, 1976; Coffield, 2011).

Some people would no doubt argue that, by focusing on work on education and social class, I am understating the influence of the discipline. Particularly during the 1980s and 1990s, the sociology of education broadened its concerns to other social differences and social inequalities, notably gender, sexuality, 'race' and disability. And, especially in relation to gender, it could certainly claim some significant influence over policy. Now that the policy emphasis is again very much on social mobility and social class differences in education, although policy makers do not always use those terms, we need to make sure the voice of sociology is once again heard in that context too. Even if not directly influencing policy or the political debate narrowly conceived, it should surely be contributing to wider public debate, even perhaps 'inoculating' the public mind against inappropriate policies (Levin, 1998).

Thus, in my view, work in the sociology of education should currently be doing more to inform public debate and, where possible, encouraging the development of policies that help enhance levels of achievement and participation amongst working class children. Although our work may suggest that most of the causes of the attainment gap are not within the remit of the school system, some of them undoubtedly are. For instance, in addition to the example given earlier concerning the curriculum, we can demonstrate that good teaching is especially important for disadvantaged pupils and that those students who do not have the sort of cultural capital that more affluent middle class families provide at home need better access in school to information, advice and guidance on careers and university entrance (Curtis et al., 2008).

In some ways, then, the view that I reached about the importance of sociology of education in that Fabian Society Study Group at Cambridge 50 years ago remains my position today. That is why, in my valedictory interview at the Institute, I argued that the foundation disciplines, including sociology of education, were 'mission critical' to an Institute of Education pursuing educational excellence for all and that they should therefore continue to have an important place in its portfolio of activities (Whitty, 2010b). But I have no doubt that, particularly in these days when research impact and public engagement are considered so important, the sociology of education will need to do a great deal more to justify that place in the public mind.

## NOTES

[1] This chapter is developed from an article previously published in the *British Journal of Educational Studies*. It is printed by permission of Taylor & Francis Ltd, www.tandfonline.com on behalf of Society for Educational Studies. Geoff Whitty (2012) "A Life with the Sociology of Education" *British Journal of Educational Studies*, 60:1, 65–75, doi:10.1080/00071005.2011.650945

[2] I continued to take this view about the importance of quantitative research in the sociology of education even when it was unfashionable among the 'critical' sociologists of education with whose work my own was usually associated. See my interview with Carlos Torres in Torres (1998). It also influenced my determination as Director of the Institute of Education to encourage growth in quantitative research alongside the qualitative research that was already well established there.

[3] I hope the present chapter will indicate that my position is rather more sophisticated than that – as indeed I believe it was when I wrote that book thirty years ago.

[4] Gove's allies accused Ofsted, the English school's inspectorate, of favouring progressive teaching methods (see, for example, Christodoulou, 2013), something which Ofsted was forced to deny.

[5] This was the post to which Mannheim was eventually appointed.

## INFLUENTIAL TEXTS BY OTHERS

Ball, S. J. (1990) *Politics and policy making in education: explorations in policy sociology*. London: Routledge.

Bernstein, B. (1977) *Class, Codes and Control* (Vol. 3) London: Routledge and Kegan Paul.

Floud, J., Halsey, A. H., & Martin, F. (1956) *Social class and educational opportunity*. London: Heinemann.

Hargreaves, D. (1967) *Social Relations in a Secondary School*. London: Routledge and Kegan Paul.

Jackson, B. and Marsden, D. (1962) *Education and the Working Class*. Harmondsworth: Penguin.

Young, M. (Ed) (1971) *Knowledge and control: new directions for the sociology of education*. London: Collier-Macmillan.

## MY FAVORITE PERSONAL TEXTS

Power, S., Edwards, T., Whitty, G., & Wigfall, V. (2003) *Education and the Middle Class*. Buckingham: Open University Press.

Whitty, G. (1974) "Sociology and the problem of radical educational change," in: Michael Flude & John Ahier (Eds.) *Educability, Schools and Ideology*. London: Croom Helm.

Whitty, G. (1985) *Sociology and School Knowledge: Curriculum, Theory, Research and Politics*. London: Methuen.

Whitty, G. (2002) *Making Sense of Education Policy*. London: Paul Chapman Publishing.

Whitty, G., Power, S., & Halpin, D. (1998) *Devolution and Choice in Education: The School, the State and the Market*. Buckingham: Open University Press.

Whitty, G. (2016) *Research and Policy in Education: Evidence, ideology and impact*. UCL IOE Press.

## REFERENCES

Apple, M. (1993). What post-modernists forget: Cultural capital and official knowledge. *Curriculum Studies, 1*, 301–316.

Ball, S. J. (1990). *Politics and policy making in education: Explorations in policy sociology*. London: Routledge.

Ball, S. J. (2003). *Class strategies and the education market: The middle class and social advantage*. London: Routledge Falmer.

Ball, S. J. (2011) Social class, families and the politics of educational advantage: The work of Denis Marsden. *British Journal of Sociology of Education, 32*(6), 957–965.

Banks, O. (1968). *The sociology of education*. London: Batsford.

Banks, O. (1974). *Sociology and education: An inaugural lecture*. Leicester: Leicester University Press.

Beck, J. (2012). Reinstating knowledge: Diagnoses and prescriptions for England's curriculum ills. *International Studies in Sociology of Education, 22*(1), 1–18.

Bernstein, B. (1970, February 26). Education cannot compensate for society. *New Society*, 344–347.

Bernstein, B. (1971). *Class, codes and control* (Vol. 1). London: Routledge and Kegan Paul.

Bernstein, B. (1977). *Class, codes and control* (Vol. 3, 2nd ed.). London: Routledge and Kegan Paul.

Bernstein, B. (1996). *Pedagogy, symbolic control and identity*. London: Taylor and Francis.

Bowles, S., & Gintis, H. (1976). *Schooling in capitalist America*. London: Routledge and Kegan Paul.

Christodoulou, D. (2013). *Seven myths about education*. London: The Curriculum Centre.

Coffield, F. (2011). Why the McKinsey reports will not improve school systems. *Journal of Education Policy, X*(Y), 1–19.

Corrigan, P. (1979). *Schooling the smash street kids*. London: Macmillan.

Craft, M. (1970). *Family, class and education: A reader*. London: Longman.

Curtis, A., Power, S., Whitty, G., Exley, S., & Sasia, A. (2008). *Primed for success?* London: Sutton Trust.

Dawson, G. (1981). Unfitting teachers to teach. In A. Flew, D. Anderson, & others (Eds.), *The Pied Pipers of education*. London: Social Affairs Unit.

Edwards, A. D. (1976). *Language in culture and class: The sociology of language and education*. London: Heinemann.

Edwards, A. D., Fitz, J., & Whitty, G. (1989). *The state and private education: An evaluation of the assisted places scheme*. London: Falmer Press.

Fantini, M., & Weinstein, G. (1968). *The disadvantaged: Challenge to education.* New York, NY: Harper and Row.
Floud, J. (1959). Karl Mannheim. In A. V. Judges (Ed.), *The function of teaching.* London: Faber and Faber.
Floud, J., Halsey, A. H., & Martin, F. (1956). *Social class and educational opportunity.* London: Heinemann.
Gould, J. (1977). *The attack on higher education: Marxist and radical penetration.* London: Institute for the Study of Conflict.
Gove, M. (2008, November 18). *Higher standards, freer minds.* Haberdashers' Aske's Education Lecture, Haberdashers Hall, London.
Gove, M. (2011, November 24). *A liberal education.* Speech to Cambridge University, Cambridge.
Halsey, A. H. (1972). *Educational priority* (Vol 1). London: HMSO.
Halsey, A. H., Floud, J. E., & Anderson, C. A. (Eds.). (1961). *Education, economy, and society.* New York, NY: Free Press.
Halsey, A. H., Heath, A., & Ridge, J. (1980). *Origins and destinations.* Oxford: Clarendon Press.
Hargreaves, D. (1967). *Social relations in a secondary school.* London: Routledge and Kegan Paul.
Hatcher, R. (1976). The limitations of the new social democratic agenda. In R. Hatcher & K. Jones (Eds.), *Education after the conservatives.* Stoke-on-Trent: Trentham Books.
Hill, D., Mclaren, P., Cole, M., & Rikowski, G. (2002). *Marxism Against postmodernism in educational theory.* Lanham, MD: Lexington Books.
Hirst, P. H. (1969). The logic of the curriculum. *Journal of Curriculum Studies, 1,* 142–158.
Hirsch, E. D. (1999). *The schools we need and why we don't have them* (2nd ed.). New York, NY: Anchor Books.
Jackson, B., & Mardsen, D. (1962). *Education and the working class.* Harmondsworth: Penguin.
Keddie, N. (1973). *Tinker, tailor... the myth of compensatory education.* Harmondsworth: Penguin.
Lacey, C. (1970). *Hightown grammar.* Manchester: Manchester University Press.
Levin, B. (1998). An epidemic of education policy: (What) can we learn from each other? *Comparative Education, 34*(2), 131–141.
Linehan, P. (Ed.). (2011). *St John's College Cambridge: A history.* Woodbridge: Boydell Press.
Mannheim, K., & Stewart, W. A. C. (1962). *An introduction to the sociology of education.* London: Routledge and Kegan Paul.
Power, S., & Whitty, G. (2006). Education and the middle class: A complex but crucial case for the sociology of education. In H. Lauder, P. Brown, J. Dillabough, & A. H. Halsey (Eds.), *Education, globalization and social change.* Oxford: Oxford University Press.
Power, S., Brannen, J., Brown, A., & Chisholm, L. (2001). *A tribute to Basil Bernstein, 1924–2000.* London: Institute of Education.
Power, S., Edwards, T., Whitty, G., & Wigfall, V. (2003). *Education and the middle class.* Buckingham: Open University Press.
Reay, D. (2008). Tony Blair, the promotion of the 'active' educational citizen, and middle-class hegemony. *Oxford Review of Education, 34,* 639–650.
RSA Journal. (2008). *Shopping for skills.* Retrieved May 19, 2009, from http://www.thersa.org/fellowship/journal/archive/spring-2008/may-2008/shopping-for-skills
Sharp, R., & Green, A. (1975). *Education and social control: A study in progressive primary education.* London: Routledge and Kegan Paul.
Simon, B. (1976). Contemporary problems in educational theory. *Marxism Today, 20,* 169–177.
Torres, C. A. (Ed.). (1998). *Education, power and personal biography: Dialogues with critical educators.* London: Routledge.
Whitty, G. (1974). Sociology and the problem of radical educational change. In M. Flude & J. Ahier (Eds.), *Educability, schools and ideology.* London: Croom Helm.
Whitty, G. (1985). *Sociology and school knowledge: Curriculum, theory, research and politics.* London: Methuen.
Whitty, G. (1989). The new right and the national curriculum: State control or market forces? *Journal of Education Policy, 4*(4), 329–341.

Whitty, G. (1997). *Social theory and education policy: The legacy of Karl Mannheim*. London: Institute of Education.

Whitty, G. (2002). *Making sense of education policy*. London: Paul Chapman Publishing.

Whitty, G. (2006). Education(al) research and education policy making: Is conflict inevitable? *British Educational Research Journal, 32*(2), 159–176.

Whitty, G. (2008). Twenty years of progress? English education policy 1988 to the present. *Educational Management Administration and Leadership, 36*, 165–184.

Whitty, G. (2009). Evaluating "Blair's Educational Legacy?": Some comments on the special issue of Oxford Review of Education. *Oxford Review of Education, 35*, 267–280.

Whitty, G. (2010a). Revisiting school knowledge: Some sociological perspectives on new school curricula. *European Journal of Education, 45*, 28–45.

Whitty, G. (2010b, Winter). A decade of achievement: Interview with Diane Hofkins, *Alumni Life* (IOE), 9–10

Whitty, G. (2014). Recent developments in teacher training and their consequences for the 'University Project' in education. *Oxford Review of Education, 40*(4), 466–481.

Whitty, G. (2016). *Research and policy in education: Evidence, ideology and impact*. London: UCL IOE Press.

Whitty, G., & Young, M. (Eds.). (1976). *Explorations in the politics of school knowledge*. Driffield: Studies in Education Ltd.

Whitty, G., Power, S., & Halpin, D. (1998). *Devolution and choice in education: The school, the state and the market*. Buckingham: Open University Press.

Willis, P. (1977). *Learning to labour: How working class kids get working class jobs*. Farnborough: Saxon House.

Young, M. (Ed.). (1971). *Knowledge and control: New directions for the sociology of education*. London: Collier-Macmillan.

Young, M. (2008). *Bringing knowledge back in: From social constructivism to social realism in the sociology of education*. London: Routledge.

Young, M. (2009). What are schools for? In H. Daniels, H. Lauder, & J. Porter (Eds.), *Knowledge, values and educational policy: A critical perspective*. London: Routledge.

Young, M. (2011). The return to subjects: A sociological perspective on the UK coalition government's approach to the 14–19 curriculum. *Curriculum Journal, 22*(2), 265–278.

Young, M., & Whitty, G. (Eds.). (1977). *Society, state and schooling: Readings on the possibilities for radical education*. Lewes: Falmer Press.

*Geoff Whitty*
*UCL Institute of Education*

CPSIA information can be obtained
at www.ICGtesting.com
Printed in the USA
BVHW01s2255221217
503485BV00009B/113/P